The General Assembly in World Politics

The General Assembly in World Politics

M. J. PETERSON
University of Massachusetts at Amherst

Boston
ALLEN & UNWIN
London   Sydney

Allen & Unwin, Inc.,
8 Winchester Place, Winchester, Mass. 01890, USA

Allen & Unwin (Publishers) Ltd,
40 Museum Street, London WC1A 1LU, UK

Allen & Unwin (Publishers) Ltd,
Park Lane, Hemel Hempstead, Herts HP2 4TE, UK

Allen & Unwin (Australia) Ltd,
8 Napier Street, North Sydney, NSW 2060, Australia

First published in 1986

Library of Congress Cataloging-in-Publication Data

Peterson, M. J, 1949–
  The General Assembly in world politics.
Bibliography: p.
Includes index.
1. United Nations. General Assembly. 2. International relations.
3. World politics – 1945–
I. Title
JX1977.A495P48   1986   341.23'22   85-32066
ISBN 0–04–327079–4 (alk. paper)

British Library Cataloguing in Publication Data

Peterson, M. J.
  The General Assembly in world politics.
1. United Nations *General Assembly*
I. Title
341.23'22   JX1977.A495
ISBN 0–04–327079–4

Set in 10 on 11 point Bembo by Computape (Pickering) Limited
and printed in Great Britain by Billings and Son Ltd, London and
Worcester

To
Oliver J. Lissitzyn

Contents

Preface

This book is the product of one American's effort to understand the United Nations General Assembly. This effort began in 1980 as an attempt to look dispassionately at the subject, without falling into the exaggerations being offered by neo-conservatives or liberal internationalists. Though more nuanced accounts of the Assembly's work are being offered today, there remains room for a study that looks systematically at the whole of the Assembly's forty-year history.

Much current writing on the General Assembly assumes considerable familiarity with its internal workings. I have tried to make this study accessible to all educated readers by describing the basic facets of Assembly proceedings in the Appendix. I hope this will aid the uninitiated while permitting the knowledgeable to begin at once with the main argument.

The late C. Clyde Ferguson, Fen O. Hampson, Joseph S. Nye, Jr, Michael G. Schechter, Louis Sohn, Raymond Vernon and the publisher's anonymous reader had the patience to criticize earlier drafts. Lisa Anderson, Stephan Haggard, Ethel Klein, and Sidney Verba offered comments on particular chapters or a short summary of the broad argument. Lisa Anderson, Nat. B. Frazer, Fen O. Hampson, Terry Karl, Ethel Klein and Maynard Silva also offered general encouragement during all the times when the rewriting became particularly frustrating. All of these friends and colleagues helped improve the manuscript, but none can be held responsible for its conclusions or its remaining infelicities.

Most of the research and early drafts were completed while I was an Assistant Professor of Government at Harvard. I am grateful to the Government Department for a term of paid leave, for small grants that paid for several trips to New York and for facilities that permitted entering an early draft on to a word processor. I am also grateful to the Harvard Center for International Affairs for additional support and for opportunities to meet diplomats from all parts of the world able to add to my understanding of the Assembly. The staffs of the Harvard Law School's International Legal Studies Library, the Harvard

Government Documents Collection and the United Nations Association of the USA in New York City helped guide me through their collections or secure particular UN documents. I am particularly grateful to Paul C. Szasz of the Legal Department of the UN Secretariat for granting access to his office's unpublished notes on General Assembly procedure, and to him and the other members of his office for their assistance.

Later drafts were written at the Woods Hole Oceanographic Institution while I enjoyed a research fellowship at its Marine Policy Center. Both the Center and the Pew Memorial Trust, which provided the bulk of my fellowship, tolerated my taking time from other work to complete this study.

At Harvard, Geraldine Bolter entered the manuscript on the university's word processor. Beverly Peterson at Harvard and Chris Lynch at the Oceanographic arranged transfer of the accumulated computer files to Woods Hole. Judy Fenwick, Ann Goodwin, Ellen Gateley, Ethel LeFave and Jane Zentz provided help whenever imminent deadlines caused a crisis. Rosamund Ladner arranged transfer of the Woods Hole computer files to a format usable when I moved to Brandeis University.

This book is dedicated to Oliver J. Lissitzyn, Hamilton Fish Professor of International Law emeritus at Columbia University. Though ill health prevented his reading any of the drafts, the finished product reflects the many lessons in scholarship and international cooperation that he imparted while guiding my doctoral dissertation.

Note on Citations

General Assembly records are cited by session, body and meeting. Until 1977 plenary and main committee meetings were numbered consecutively without regard to session. Since then they have been numbered consecutively within sessions, each session starting anew with a first meeting. Thus, the first plenary meeting in the 2nd session is normally cited as A/PV.189, while the first in the 35th session is cited as A/35/PV.1. Main committee meetings add a notation for the committee (C.1 through C.6 and SPC for the Special Political Committee) between the first and second element of the code. For consistency, I indicate the session number even with the pre-1977 meetings.

Chapter One

Introduction

In recent years a growing number of observers have argued that states are ignoring the United Nations. Even Secretary–General Javier Perez de Cuellar pointed out in his first annual report that "[T]ime and time again, we have seen the Organization set aside or rebuffed, for this reason or for that, in situations in which it should, and could, have played an important and constructive role" (UN Doc. A/37/1, 7 Sept. 1982, p. 4). At the same time, however, statesmen and scholars continue their arguments about the functions and nature of the UN with a vehemence that suggests they do not ignore it.

Most of these arguments center on one part of the organization, the General Assembly. There are a number of reasons why this body attracts the most attention. Though only one of the six "principal organs" of the organization, it is clearly first among them. The Secretariat, the Trusteeship Council and the Economic and Social Council are named as principal organs by the Charter and have their tasks and composition defined there, but report to and receive direct guidance from the General Assembly. The other two principal organs, the Security Council and the International Court of Justice, are not subject to Assembly guidance, but their significance is limited by the specificity of their mandates. The Security Council deals only with disputes or situations that threaten to lead or have led to an outbreak of war, while the International Court of Justice rules on legal questions brought before it voluntarily by states and gives legal advice to other UN bodies at their request. The General Assembly, however, may discuss and make decisions on any matter mentioned or implied in the Charter.

The General Assembly's organizational predominance is also assured by the fact that most subsidiary UN bodies and organs report to it, either directly or through the Economic and Social

Council. These are a diverse group, including the specialized agencies dealing with international cooperation in defined technical areas, other bodies created to deal with particular global issues (such as the UN Conference on Trade and Development or the UN Environmental Program), temporary committees studying a particular question (such as the *ad hoc* Committee on International Terrorism), or continuing committees charged with monitoring activity and framing proposals about matters of continuing concern (such as the Committee on Peaceful Uses of Outer Space or the Disarmament Commission).

Politically, the Assembly's predominance is assured by the fact it is the only principal organ in which all member states participate on an equal basis. Each has one vote, and most decisions can be made by a simple majority. It has also proved hospitable to member concerns by imposing no real barriers to putting a question on the agenda. This encourages members unsure of where to take a question to use the Assembly. The egalitarian nature of the Assembly also makes it the favorite principal organ of weak states, which have always constituted a majority of the UN's membership, because it gives them an influence over decisions that they lack anywhere else in the international system.

Many Western observers view the General Assembly as a place where unfriendly majorities use their numbers to pursue conflict and where dictatorships of various stripes impose double standards at the West's expense (e.g., Buckley, 1974; Yeselson and Gaglione, 1974). This opinion is held most strongly by United States neo-conservatives, who regard the UN as the weapon of a radical Third World–Soviet bloc alliance out to discredit the West, destroy free enterprise and abolish democracy so that it can impose totalitarian forms of socialism around the world (e.g., Moynihan, 1980; Pilon, 1982; Kirkpatrick, 1983). However, distrust of the UN is sufficiently widespread that when journalists want to criticize something inspiring outbursts of extreme nationalism, they are apt to compare it to the Assembly. For example, the London-based *Economist* commented that

> Any resemblance between the World Cup football tournament and sport is purely coincidental. Those Spanish commentators who discuss it in terms of the fashionable "north–south conflict" are only just offside. As a threat to international harmony, it is in the same league as the United Nations General Assembly.
>
> (3 July 1982, p. 36)

At the same time, Third World statesmen and observers view the Assembly with greater confidence. They see it as a place where the weak and the developing can protect their interests, restrain the strong and promote a more equitable world order. Rather than questioning the value of the Assembly, they focus much of their attention on how best to use the opportunities it offers (such as discussion of whether the Nonaligned and the Group of 77 should establish permanent Secretariats in Nyerere, 1979 and Ramphal, 1979).

As in most debates, each side is aware of the other's views. Each also then uses those feelings as evidence, if not of the correctness of its own views, then as confirmation that others, too, see the subject of debate as important. If the West, particularly the United States, is fearful of the General Assembly, then Assembly decisions must somehow hurt it. If the Third World is enthusiastic about the Assembly, then the Assembly must serve its interests in ways that Western statesmen had better not ignore. The emotions of each side help reinforce those of the other. In the heat and dust of the argument, neither side seems particularly interested in exploring the extent to which control of the General Assembly really does affect the general conduct of international relations or the fortunes of individual states. Yet it is impossible to evaluate the assertions made by either side or to form an accurate assessment of the body itself without a clear conception of the effects that control of the General Assembly has in international politics.

International politics, like domestic politics, occurs within a definite political system where the various actors know what others also form part of the system, possess various material and moral resources for political activity and interact according to certain generally understood and largely shared sets of guidelines. For the system to work well, a number of functions must be performed. New actors need to be socialized. Some actors must be recruited and trained for leadership roles. All actors need to articulate their material and moral interests or desires. Since no one actor can expect to control the whole system by itself, groups of actors need to aggregate their similar interests so that they can form coalitions able to have a greater impact on outcomes. Decisions determining how resources will be used or distributed and what rules will be enforced must be made. Decisions have to be implemented and rules applied to the behavior of particular actors in specific situations.

As the only permanent political body in which all states are represented, the General Assembly helps assure the performance of all these functions in the international system. Its existence and practices have different effects and different degrees of influence on the performance of each function. As a deliberative body, it is concerned mainly with aggregating interests and making decisions. It also provides one, but by no means the only or the most powerful, set of leadership roles. It also serves as an important socializer of new governments (whether of new or old states) by providing for intensive interactions with virtually all others under a well-developed set of formal and informal rules for transacting business. It has some effect on the articulation of interests, though more on the choice of place for expressing them than on their content, except in so far as it helps governments pick up ideas from one another more quickly. Though the application of rules and implementation of decisions are outside its direct purview, it seeks to influence how these are carried out.

Any assessment of the General Assembly must start from the realization that it does not determine either the structure of the international system or the choices of goals and means made by individual states or other actors. This relatively modest role stems from the basic nature of the international system, which remains essentially anarchical. There are no central institutions enjoying the predominance of material power and the moral authority over individual states that mark relations between governments and peoples in domestic politics, particularly in the industrial states. Lack of agreement on the need for and proper nature of a centralized world government and a dispersion of power preventing its imposition by force combine to keep the international system one where each state must rely essentially on self-help.

Today there is no great demand for a world government. Not only do national governments seek to preserve their autonomy, but populations remain uninterested in world government or unpersuaded that it would be useful. Discussion of world government in the West, where it is most active, is confined to relatively small groups. Popular discussion elsewhere, even when free of government control, features even fewer calls for world government. Most people are concerned with local and national problems, and worry about foreign affairs only when they impinge on personal life or well-being. Most people, not only in states where governments actively encourage the feeling, remain solidly nationalistic. They tend to assume that there are strong differences between "us" inside the national borders and "them" outside.

Even if governments and populations felt that a world government would be useful, the strong moral disagreements among them would make its peaceful (or relatively peaceful) establishment and operation very difficult. Though certain common moral terms are used around the world, there remain enough differences in interpretation to make many moral appeals unpersuasive. Americans, Soviets, Chinese, Indians, Ghanaians, Libyans, Colombians and Argentinians all talk about "freedom", "democracy", and "justice" but have different understandings of those terms. These differences plus a nationalism-fostered suspicion of the outsider make it difficult to create the mutual trust and forbearance needed for the peaceful exercise of central authority.

It is possible to establish government by force. The history of domestic politics provides many examples of this. Until fairly recently it was technically impossible to govern the whole world, but advances in transportation, communication and means of coercion probably make it feasible today. Yet today power is divided among mutually suspicious states in such a way that no single state can conquer the world and no coalition able to do so is likely to form. The power of different ideas and national loyalties remains strong enough that attempts to impose a global government would probably founder on the fierce resistance of those outside the coalition of would-be world conquerors.

This abiding anarchy means that institutions are not among the independent variables determining either the structure of the international system or the goals and policies of actors within it. The system's structure is determined by the distribution of material power among individual states and other actors. The goals and means selected by states and other actors depend more on their individual calculations than on guidance provided by institutions.

Rather, the General Assembly, like all other international organizations, is one of the elements that affect the process of world politics by providing the norms and institutions within which states and other actors interact in pursuit of their various goals. These norms and institutions act sometimes like a filter and sometimes like a levee, encouraging some forms of interaction while discouraging others or channeling interactions along particular lines. The Assembly, like the rest of the UN, usually attempts to encourage peaceful resolutions of conflict rather than war. This does not always prevent war, but does force states to explain why they are using force and sometimes leads to actions, such as the creation of the first UN Emergency Force in the Sinai, that makes it easier for states to disengage from hostilities. The

Assembly has also been used not only to speed the end of colonialism but to ensure that this end takes the form of independent statehood for the colony rather than amalgamation with the metropolitan power.

This filtering and channeling cannot prevent a highly likely event, such as conflict between the superpowers, or ensure the occurrence of a highly unlikely one, such as voluntary South African withdrawal from Namibia. Yet in cases where the probabilities are more evenly balanced in favor of and against a particular outcome, the filtering and channeling are important. The admission of Belize to the United Nations constitutes world endorsement of the proposition that Belize is an independent state with a distinct people having the right of self-determination. This makes it more difficult for Guatemala to persist in claiming that Belize is Guatemalan territory wrongly taken by Great Britain in the nineteenth century.

A more extended example should make the point clearer. In the current world recession, and particularly since the second oil price shock of 1979, important domestic interest groups in all the industrialized market economy states have sought a greater restriction of trade. These groups believe that foreign competition is costing them jobs, sales, income and profits, and that they would be able to maintain all four if the foreign competition were restricted. Demands for restriction are particularly intense when foreigners suddenly take over a large share of the local market, as happened in the United States with automobiles after 1973 or in France with consumer electronics after 1980. They also rise when a foreign government appears to be aiding its country's industries with subsidies or measures to restrict foreign competition in their own home markets.

In the early 1930s such feelings, spurred to greater heights by a more severe economic crisis, quickly led to vast restrictions on trade in the form of very high tariffs. Today restrictions take a variety of confusing forms – "orderly marketing arrangements," "voluntary export restraints," special technical or safety requirements, or rules drastically slowing the delivery of goods to foreign customers. They have not taken the form of tariffs because the major states involved are all parties to the General Agreement on Tariffs and Trade, by which they renounced the use of high tariffs and promised to uphold a free trade regime. The GATT has also slowed the adoption of other forms of restriction by forcing the proponents of restriction to justify their measures against the standard of a free trade regime and by imposing certain institutional checks on parties' actions. If the recession continues, protectionist pressures may overwhelm the GATT norms and institutions; so far, however, that outcome has been avoided despite widespread creeping restrictions. It is safe to say that without the GATT, protectionism would have spread faster and been adopted more openly than has been true so far.

Of course, once a rule or organization proves capable of affecting outcomes in any way, states and other actors will try to take advantage of that rule or organization, converting it into a power-related resource if they can. This does not convert rules and organizations into independent variables, however, because they can be used as a power resource only when all or most actors – particularly the strongest ones – agree that interaction should be governed by or undertaken through them. It is possible for states to destroy rules or institutions, as Nazi Germany did with the Treaty of Versailles. However, such cases remain rare, particularly in matters not related to military security. Most of the time, the rules and organizations are left in place.

This means there are outcomes in world politics that cannot be understood without reference to intervening institutions like the General Assembly. Structuralist theories of international relations, whether viewing military potential (e.g., Morgenthau, 1951; Waltz, 1979) or economic systems (e.g., Mandel, 1970; Wallerstein, 1974; Gilpin, 1975) as the main determinant of outcomes, tend to relegate other things to the category of epiphenomena that may safely be ignored. Yet it is impossible to understand many aspects of contemporary relations, such as the amount of attention devoted to economic development or the elimination of racial discrimination, by relying on structural analysis alone.

Like all intervening institutions, the General Assembly has a different effect on outcomes in different situations. Its impact depends greatly on the phase of the political process and the goals and nature of the coalition controlling the Assembly. To a lesser extent, it depends on the type of issue being considered.

Because the Assembly is a deliberative body in a decentralized political system, its influence depends greatly on the stage of the political process at which interaction occurs. All politics, international no less than domestic, is a process of distributing desired symbolic and material values among members of society. Particularly in modern political systems, members of society view the political process as one way in which they can protect the values they now possess or seek a redistribution that will give them what they want but do not now possess. When filtered through political institutions differentiated from the rest of society, the seeking of effective distributions or redistributions of values (that is, of outcomes) requires overcoming four barriers, with failure at any one preventing attainment of the desired result (Van der Eijk and Kok, 1975).

These barriers are: (1) desire–demand conversion – translating amorphous wishes of individuals and groups into specific requests phrased in such a way as to be accepted as political and as properly addressed to the institution asked to handle them; (2) agenda formation – persuading the political institution addressed to include the demand on the list of issues it will formally take up; (3) decision-making – securing a decision from the political institution that directs relevant institutions and actors to make the value distribution desired; and (4) implementation – assuring that the decision is actually carried out as specified. The path from vague desire to political output which translates that desire into an effective distribution of values can be diagrammed as in Figure 1.1.

Desires	/	Demands	/	Issues	/	Decisions	/	Outputs
Desire–demand conversion		Agenda formation		Decision-making		Implementation		

Figure 1.1

Many hazards lie along this path. A desire may not be translatable into a political demand for a host of reasons, such as failure of the actor to see that it can be made political or a social convention that particular matters are handled outside the political institutions. A demand may not become an issue because the political institution decides against placing it on the agenda. This can occur if the institution decides that the demand ought to be addressed to a different institution (thus, for instance, a resident of Massachusetts would not get a demand for state tax reduction considered by the US Congress), that the demand is not political, that – for whatever reason – the demand is raised at a bad time, or that the demand has so little support that it may safely be ignored. Even if the demand becomes an issue, the decision-making process itself poses other barriers. A demand may be rejected after consideration. It may be combined with other demands in such a way as to be buried in the end. It may be so modified or qualified in the process of seeking enough support to make a decision as to be unrecognizable to the original proponents. It may be deferred on the grounds that further study is needed or that there is not enough time to consider the question now. Even the adoption of a decision fully corresponding to the demand does not guarantee that outcome will match demand. The implementation phase provides many opportunities for last-minute modification of the decision. All political actors, especially those charged with implementation, know the tactics of delay, inattention and selective enforcement that can produce a final result different from that specified in the decision. At this point, too, hazard in the form of accidents, changed conditions, or unintended consequences of action can wreak havoc with decisions.

Politics is a continual process. As long as an actor or group maintains its initial demands it will try again to get them adopted. The slippage of implementation means that groups and individuals monitor performance and raise new demands if performance does not live up to expectations. Changed circumstances or things learned in earlier attempts to use the political process may lead to a modification of initial demands. Thus, failure at any one of the barriers most often means only the end of one attempt to secure its adoption, not final disposition of the demand.

The first stage of the political process, the conversion of desires into demands, occurs outside the General Assembly in the councils of individual states or groups of states. Study of the Assembly does not greatly illuminate why states form certain desires or decide to convert some of them into demands at the international level. In its broadest sense, therefore, the study of desire–demand conversion is the study of an aspect of foreign policy making. However, the existence and character of the Assembly, the nature of issue and the coalition controlling the Assembly have some effect on choices at this stage. States are aware of the Assembly's ability or inability to handle different types of issue effectively. They can also predict the preferences and sympathies of the controlling coalition with a high degree of accuracy. This awareness influences decisions about where to raise an issue by affecting a state's estimate of whether the demand will be considered, a favorable decision made and effective implementation follow. Though certain types of states, weak ones for instance, tend to raise particular types of demand, the timing of decisions to bring demands to the Assembly and the particular formulations proposed depend on calculations understood only by studying their whole foreign-policy-making process.

The General Assembly begins to have real impact on world politics at the agenda-formation stage. When a state decides to take a demand to the Assembly, others must decide whether to give it any attention. When a state decides not to take some matter to the Assembly, it must still watch the Assembly because others may try to bring it up. Decisions to place an item on the agenda and to deal with it are important. Even if they do not lead to a later decision, the mere fact they have been made forces governments to allocate attention to some matter. At the very least, this alters the definition of what is "important" at the moment and focuses government energies on some things rather than others.

Most Assembly activity involves decision-making. Here the Assembly makes its strongest bid to affect world politics by endorsing some ideas and rejecting others or praising some policies while condemning others. Like most large deliberative bodies, the General Assembly has elaborate formal rules on decision-making which regulate the conduct of debate, the submission of formal proposals and the adoption of proposals. Like many political institutions, the Assembly has also supplemented its formal rules with a whole series of informal practices that help the formal rules operate more smoothly and permit adjustment to the needs of a particular issue or moment. Like political parties in national legislatures, the regional groups in the General Assembly provide an infrastructure that channels consultations, negotiations and coalition building.

In the General Assembly, the process of supplementing formal rules with informal ones has gone so far that it often seems to be two different bodies each with its own character. Though the rules for debate and the adoption of decisions can be viewed as internal matters of interest only to participants and students of the legislative process, the manner in which debate and decision occur influences both the outcome on a particular question and the way in which member states view the Assembly. One cannot, therefore, assess the political impact of the Assembly without understanding these matters.

In the implementation stage, the Assembly loses control of the political process. Some of its decisions, such as the election of states to other UN bodies, the creation of new UN bodies like the UN Conference on Trade and Development, or the allocation of funds from the UN budget, are carried out without difficulty since they are addressed to entities obliged to follow Assembly instructions. However, most of its decisions are recommendations addressed to member states and other actors not obliged to carry them out. Here, the Assembly cajoles rather than commands. The narrowness of its command over material resources has pushed the Assembly toward a heavy reliance on symbolic politics, the use of verbal praise or condemnation to persuade actors that they should do or refrain from various things. Though these exhortations do not carry direct material benefits or costs, they do affect the way in which actors think about issues or each other. This ability to influence perceptions keeps states highly interested in what the Assembly does. Yet the limited material resources at its command mean that coalitions controlling the Assembly must consider the likelihood of implementation when making decisions intended to have material effect.

Some of the Assembly's effects on world politics stem from the fact that its rules provide weak states with more influence in the Assembly than they enjoy outside. Others, however, depend greatly on the nature and intentions of the coalition controlling it at a particular time. Formal Assembly rules provide that each member state has one vote, and that decisions are made by a majority. In most cases, the rules specify a simple majority, but in a few significant instances a two-thirds majority is required. This means that any stable coalition of states comprising a majority of the membership can control most decisions, but that full control can be assured only when the stable coalition musters two-thirds of the members.

Creating such a coalition requires forging agreement among a sufficient number of governments. Building a two-thirds coalition is hard, but not impossible. So long as the same governments remain in power, and in most cases even when one is replaced by another, the intergovermental communities of interest and opinion that underlie the Assembly coalition are likely to remain undisturbed. So long as they do, the coalition can look forward to controlling the Assembly. This makes the General Assembly very different from a national legislature, where securing control requires either winning elections or imposing some form of one-party control over the population. This means national legislative majorities must worry about their position within the wider national political system as well as about their legislative cohesion. Assembly coalitions can devote much more of their attention to maintaining cohesion within the Assembly since their links are to governments rather than to populations.

Two controlling coalitions have existed in the Assembly's history. From late 1947 until 1955 the General Assembly was controlled by a coalition composed of Western European, Latin American and Commonwealth states led by the United States. This coalition was particularly united on any issue that involved, or could be presented as involving, Cold War competition with the Soviet Union. It also usually stayed together on issues of human rights, social concerns and internal UN administration. However, there were sharp disagreements on colonial and economic questions which could be papered over only with difficulty.

Though this coalition worked well, it was not a cohesive group. It might best be compared to a multiparty coalition in a national legislature, where power is kept by concessions ensuring that none of the parties defects to the opposition. None will get everything it wants, but each has to be given enough to be kept satisfied. In international terms, the US-led majority was a very mixed group. Led by a superpower, it included several temporarily weakened but still rather powerful states, a number of states large enough to be at least regional powers in the future and many states that would always be weak. The inclusion of the strong states meant the coalition had ample material resources for putting ideas into action, but the division between weak and strong was a source of tension as the weaker members wanted more attention paid to norms protecting weak states while the strong wanted to pursue conflicts with other strong powers.

At first the Cold War was sufficiently intense to keep the coalition together. As time passed, and even before Soviet policy became more flexible after Stalin's death in 1953, the internal tensions began rising to the fore. The colonial–anticolonial rift became too sharp to control in 1949, and differences between industrial and less developed members were growing. Internal tensions were worsened by external pressure in the 1950s. Decolonization brought to the UN a number of new African and Asian states less interested in the Cold War and more interested in decolonization and economic development. As UN membership slowly rose from 51 in 1945 to 82 in 1957, the US-led coalition began eroding. The influx of African and Asian members in the early 1960s simply overwhelmed a weakened US-led majority in two ways. First, it increased the preexisting tensions between colonial and anticolonial states and between industrial and developing states. Second, the new members were less tied to the United States and often frankly anti-Western. Close observers of the numbers realized even in the mid 1950s that the US-led coalition was having trouble raising two-thirds majorities; after 1960 it was clear to all that the US-led coalition could not even muster a simple majority.

The late 1950s and early 1960s were thus a time of exploration. Alone, the Africans and Asians almost constituted a majority. They were often put over the top by Eastern European support as the Soviet Union exploited opportunities to break out of the minority position in which it had been kept for so long. The Africans and Asians knew they could form a new stable two-thirds majority if they could secure consistent Latin American support. This development had to wait upon changes in Latin American perceptions of the world, and the soothing of Latin American feelings that the Africans were too aggressive in the Assembly (see, for example, the exchange in A/C.4/17/SR. 1369, 1 Nov. 1962, paras. 1–11). Not until 1964 was the new coalition stabilized on the full range of issues before the Assembly, though it was functioning of colonial and economic questions before then.

Since 1964 the General Assembly has been controlled by a stable coalition of African, Asian and Latin American states known collectively as the Third World. In 1964 this coalition consisted entirely of weak states. Today it is still composed mainly of weak states, but some members, because of size, success at industrializing, or possession of large quantities of oil, wield more material power than they did in the past. Some members, like Brazil or India, could become second-rank powers on the global level. Even so, the coalition still maintains itself by assuming (at least rhetorically) that all members are disadvantaged in the current international system. This coalition of weak states is interested in using the UN to create norms and rules protecting the weak from the strong and to advance group demands for changes in international regimes perceived as working to Third World disadvantage. It is particularly interested in ending colonialism, attacking all other forms of imperialism, promoting development and creating new rules for international activity ensuring the Third World as a whole a greater share of material benefits and decision-making power. Even today the Third World majority does not always have the material resources needed to translate ideas into outcomes. This lack of material resources encourages compromise on material questions, but also greater resort to symbolic politics on matters that are, or can be presented as, mainly moral issues.

With virtually all states now members of the United Nations, this coalition will not be eroded from outside as was the US-led one. Yet differences among members in level of economic development, basic structure of the economy, regional situations, individual interests and orientations in superpower conflicts are creating some strong internal tensions. These have become most apparent in the political realm, where the once-united Nonaligned Movement has split into three identifiable camps: those members siding with Moscow, those siding with Washington and those still pursuing a policy of distance from both. So far, the Third World majority has been able to manage these tensions by using two devices. First, proposals are kept at a broad level of generality and tend to consist of adding everyone's demands together. Second, the coalition devotes much attention to issues on which all can agree, such as the eradication of racist regimes in Southern Africa, the promotion of Palestinian claims to statehood, the advancement of economic development and the promotion of Third World influence in international decision-making. How long the Third World coalition will succeed in managing these internal tensions is one of the most interesting current questions in international politics, and particularly important to the future of the General Assembly.

The main contrasts between the two controlling coalitions lie in their access to material power and their goals. The US-led coalition had access to ample material power and used the Assembly as one of many fora for affirming and refining the goal of an open and universalistic international system allowing scope for individuals and other non-state actors that had been stated during the Second World War. For it, then, the Assembly was a one of many fora used to reaffirm previously settled normative stands. The Third World coalition has access to rather limited material power but wishes to challenge many of the existing international norms and regimes. For it, the Assembly is one of the major fora available for any purpose and one of the few places where those with the power to make changes can be forced to pay attention to the whole range of Third World demands. Further, it finds in the UN's modest resources a significant addition to its own. The Third World coalition thus uses the Assembly more intensely than did the US-led coalition, but its relative lack of power has exposed more clearly the limits on Assembly control over outcomes in world politics.

Finally, the Assembly's impact depends somewhat on the type of issue being discussed. The Assembly deals with five main types of issue: the definition of general norms that should apply to broad areas of world politics; the specification of the international regimes that should govern interactions in particular fields; the commitment of UN resources to various undertakings; the management of conflict; and the pursuit of conflict.

The Assembly is one of the best fora for discussing general norms of international behavior since virtually all states of the world are represented in it. The Assembly has always devoted a considerable fraction of its time to such discussions, and these discussions have greatly influenced the development of norms by showing that some enjoy wide support or that others do not. Over the years the Assembly has been important in debates on such questions as the status and ramifications of self-determination, the principle that states should not intervene in other states' affairs and the specification of acts constituting forms of impermissible pressure on other states.

The Assembly is also a good forum for discussing the rules of international regimes intended to apply in particular fields. Here, though, it faces greater competition from other fora, such as the specialized agencies or regional organizations. States wishing only to refine or amend existing international regimes tend to prefer a more technical forum. States wishing to challenge the basis of an existing regime or to create one where there has been none are more likely to use the Assembly, at least for making their initial demands. Therefore, the amount of discussion about the rules of specific regimes depends on the newness of the field as an international problem and the ambitions of states.

The Assembly is also the best place for most discussions about committing UN resources to various tasks. The Security Council has the advantage of being able to order member participation in collective measures against states threatening the peace, while the specialized agencies have their own realm of activity. However, the veto often prevents the Security Council from exercising its powers to the fullest, and specialized agency activities are often limited by the technical nature of their mandates. The Assembly can create new UN bodies and controls allocation of the UN budget, giving it the ability to commit the organization to a wide range of activities. To the extent that UN activity is viewed as important to the resolution of other issues or to the management or pursuit of conflict, states will make great efforts to have the organization's resources committed in particular ways. This is also the realm in which the Assembly has the greatest impact on outcomes since its decisions on the commitment of UN resources are binding.

The Charter specifies that states should first try to manage conflict by recourse to non-UN procedures or institutions, and assigns primary responsibility for UN conflict management efforts to the Security Council. Even so, the Assembly has tried to help manage various conflicts. Sometimes this results from the Security Council's failure to find a course of action acceptable to all five permanent members. Sometimes this results from states' decisions that they prefer to bring the conflict to the Assembly. In any event, the Assembly has not been a very effective manager of conflict. Despite some noteworthy successes, such as its response to the Suez Crisis of 1956, the Assembly is too large to play an effective role and seldom controls enough material resources to make a difference.

Frequently conflicts are brought to the Assembly in order to be pursued more effectively. If one side believes that it can improve its position by enlarging the number of states paying attention to the conflict, it will bring the matter to the Assembly. If the other cannot keep the conflict out of the Assembly, or also thinks it can improve its position by enlarging the number of states paying attention, it will also use the Assembly to raise support. In many cases, the other members decide not to devote much time to this activity, dealing with the matter only long enough to urge restraint and direct negotiations among those directly involved. In some cases, though, there are enough members committed to supporting one side that the Assembly becomes another arena for the conflict. The Assembly cannot impose a solution, but can be used to erode an opponent's position by demonstrating the thinness of its international support or the moral weakness of its position.

Though concerned with differences in the General Assembly's influence on world politics stemming from changes in all three variables, this study is organized along the lines of greatest difference, the phases of the international political process. Readers unfamiliar with the General Assembly may wish to consult the Appendix, which provides an overview of Assembly activity, before reading the following chapters. The substantive treatment begins in Chapter 2, which deals with agenda formation. Decision-making will be treated in Chapters 3 and 4. Chapter 3 examines the rules for adoption of decisions while Chapter 4 examines the rules and practices of debate and negotiation that precede adoption. Chapters 5 through 8 assess the Assembly's influence in the implementation phase. Chapter 5 explores the extent and effects of Assembly decisions accepted by member states as binding on themselves. Chapter 6 explores the extent and effect of Assembly authority over other UN bodies. Chapter 7 discusses the effect of Assembly decisions that are simply recommendations to member states at a general level, while Chapter 8 explores the ways in which Assembly decisions and proceedings affect the foreign policy process within states. Chapter 9 brings the individual elements together to present an overall assessment of the Assembly's effects on world politics.

Chapter Two

Formation of the Agenda

The international political process begins with individual actors' choices to pursue certain goals. At this point the General Assembly has little direct influence. Yet it does exercise indirect influence to the extent that governments' calculations about what types of demands are likely to receive a sympathetic hearing help determine whether, when, or where they pursue a particular goal.

The Assembly has greater, and direct, impact when actors decide which desires should be converted into demands addressed to the political system. Here the Assembly affords governments, but not other actors, one of many fora for making demands. The particular character of the Assembly's formal rules and informal practices for setting out the agenda each year means that this influence is felt in specific ways, some of which are unusual in any political system.

The formal rules of the Assembly have always provided for an open nominal agenda permitting any member to place almost any demand on the list for possible Assembly decision. Over the years the nominal agenda has become even more open because the substantive limits on Assembly activity have been narrowed by interpretation, and many formal procedures for limiting the nominal agenda have fallen into disuse. This means that the General Assembly maintains an extraordinarily high level of receptivity to demands.

Yet like all political institutions, the Assembly cannot give effective attention to every demand raised in the political system. Limited time as well as preferences of the majority work to restrict extended attention to certain issues. The nominal agenda is therefore supplemented by a shorter effective agenda. Since no one wishes to change the formal rules providing for the open nominal agenda, the effective one has to be created by informal practices. A number of these have developed since 1945, and give the Assembly control over its effective agenda comparable to that of other deliberative bodies.

The Nominal Agenda

Most of the formal rules defining the nominal Assembly appear in the United Nations Charter, which hedges a broad grant of competence by two limitations. The broad authority is bestowed in Article 10, which provides that

> The General Assembly may discuss any questions or any matters within the scope of the present Charter or relating to the powers and functions of any organs provided for in the present Charter and, except as provided for in Article 12, may make recommendations to the Members, to the Security Council or to both on such matters.

The list of questions or matters within the scope of the Charter is broad indeed, including the maintenance of international peace and security, the settlement of international disputes by peaceful means, the development of friendly relations among nations, the encouragement of cooperation in international economic, social, cultural and humanitarian matters, the promotion of respect for human rights and the development of self-government in territories where the populations do not govern themselves. All these definitions are sufficiently broad that any question arising between two states can be defined as coming within the scope of the Charter.

The Charter contains two formal limitations on Assembly competence: Articles 12(1) and 11(2) regarding Security Council authority to deal with particular crises threatening peace, and Article 2(7) prohibiting intervention in the domestic affairs of states by any UN organization. The first provides a specific, and the second a general, limit on Assembly authority to consider certain matters or to pass certain resolutions about them.

The Charter provides that the General Assembly should defer to the Security Council when it comes to settling particular disputes that have led or might lead to war. Article 12(1) provides that

> While the Security Council is exercising in respect of any dispute or situation the functions assigned to it in the present

Charter, the General Assembly shall not make any recommendations with regard to that dispute or situation unless the Security Council so requests.

Article 11(2) provides that, when states have decided to bring a dispute to the General Assembly rather than the Security Council, "Any such question on which action is necessary shall be referred to the Security Council by the General Assembly either before or after discussion."

Article 12(1) was never interpreted as preventing the General Assembly discussion of the matter. Initially the Assembly tended to avoid direct conflict by discussing the question under a different title than the Security Council. Thus when the future of West Irian became a point of particular contention between Indonesia and the Netherlands in 1954, the Assembly took up the "West Irian Question" while the Security Council discussed it under the broader "Indonesian Question", which had been on its agenda off and on since 1948 (A/BUR/9/SR.92, 22 Sept. 1954, p. 4). Later, the Assembly was more open about the fact that it was discussing the same matter. While it was impossible to avoid such a position in such long-running problems as the Arab–Israeli conflict or the Rhodesian situation, this direct approach fitted well with Third World views that the Assembly should be the predominant body.

The Assembly also found ways around the ban on passing resolutions about the particular dispute. There was never objection to resolutions embodying indirect comment by making recommendations to all states about settling a type of dispute that just happened to be raging between particular ones at the time. Similarly, resolutions commenting on a specific dispute but stopping short of recommendations were also deemed unobjectionable. There were also no difficulties if the Security Council considered a dispute but failed to pass any resolutions about it. After 1960 the Assembly became more assertive, adopting resolutions even when the Security Council had done so, addressing them directly to parties and urging particular steps upon them. This has been a favorite tactic of the Third World coalition when its members agree on identification of villains and victims, as in the Arab–Israeli conflict or the Rhodesian situation, since in this way the coalition can make its views known without fear of a veto. This has often caused problems because the fact that the General Assembly and Security Council have been controlled by different coalitions since 1964 means that Assembly decisions are not always fully consistent with those of the

Security Council. On the Middle East, Assembly Resolution 2628 (XXV) contradicts Security Council Resolution 242 in ways that have complicated all negotiations (see debate in A/25/PV.1890–6, 29 Oct. – 2 Nov. 1970). The Third World coalition has tended to regard these problems as incidental since it feels the Council should yield to Assembly desires.

The general mandate to discuss the maintenace of international peace and security, as well as the provision allowing members to take disputes to the General Assembly, helped inspire the first clear expansion of the Assembly's authority at the expense of another UN organ. In the late 1940s members of the Security Council claimed that they were still actively considering a particular crisis, even if permanent members had vetoed all proposed resolutions, by the expedient of keeping the item on the agenda. Both the US-led and the Third World majorities contributed to removing this obstacle to Assembly activity.

To protect its interests in Cold War disputes, the Soviet bloc argued that a decision to transfer a dispute from the Security Council to the General Assembly was a substantive one, requiring positive votes or abstentions by all five permanent members. This would allow the Soviet Union not only to stop Security Council action but also to prevent consideration by the US-controlled, and hence hostile, General Assembly. In 1950, the US-led coalition solved the problem to its satisfaction in the Uniting for Peace Resolution (Resolution 377 [V]). This defined the question of whether the Security Council was still dealing with a matter as procedural, allowing a simple majority of the Council membership to release it. Since the US-led majority then usually occupied 9 of the 11 seats on the Council at the time, this provided a way to bypass Soviet vetoes without undercutting its own.

However, the US-led coalition also provided the foundation for tipping the political balance betwen the General Assembly and the Security Council. The same resolution permitted a majority of the Assembly to convoke an emergency session on its own if the Security Council did not meet or failed to adopt any resolutions. The next step in eroding Security Council control over the disposition of disputes referred to it occurred in 1956. An unusual *ad hoc* coalition of the USA, the USSR and the non-permanent members of the Council voted to refer the Suez Crisis to the General Assembly before all proposals had been voted upon because it was clear Britain and France would veto them (S/PV.751, 31 Oct. 1956; A/E–1/PV.561, 1 Nov. 1956). The full implications of these two precedents were demonstrated in 1967 when the Soviet Union made a bid for Third World support by initiating Assembly convocation of an emergency session once it was clear that the United States would veto any resolution too hard on Israel (A/E–5/PV.1525, 17 June 1967). The Third World coalition completed the shift of initiative by tacitly adopting a doctrine that the Assembly could take over a dispute any time the Security Council was not "actively" considering it (doctrine described without comment in *UN Juridical Yearbook*, 1968, p. 185).

All these developments mean that the General Assembly can define the occasions when Article 12(1) limits its ability to act. This allows the Third World majority to involve the Assembly, which it controls, in virtually any international dispute. Actual deference to the Security Council's "primary role" in peace and security issues thus reflects political choices of the Assembly majority rather than any Charter norm.

Article 11(1) never limited the Assembly agenda; it simply reminds the Assembly that only the Security Council can invoke collective action under Chapter VII of the Charter. However, the Assembly has always been deemed competent to recommend that members take individual action, which would amount to the same thing if all act as requested. This let the Assembly create peacekeeping forces (UNEF), keep them operating when an initial Security Council consensus broke down (ONUC) and recommend trade embargoes against certain states (South Africa, Rhodesia, Portugal). Governments remain aware that the Assembly cannot require members to implement such measures, which is why the Third World majority has spent much time and energy on appealing to the members of the Security Council to invoke Chapter VII against colonial or racist regimes and against Israel.

The Article 2(7) prohibition against intervention in members' affairs has not been interpreted as impeding the Assembly's ability to put questions on the agenda. This has been accomplished, not by approaching the thorny question of what activities or matters lie "essentially within the domestic jurisdiction" of states, but by adopting a restrictive definition of what constitutes "intervention". Most of the Assembly's explicit discussion of this question occurred during early debates about South African discrimination against people of Indian origin, a matter India had brought up in 1946 on grounds that South Africa was violating an Indian–South African agreement covering at least some of the individuals involved. The special features of the case, many members' abhorrence of racist policies and most members confidence that they would never be subject to the same treatment because they did not maintain or were repealing laws supporting racial discrimination probably led them to more permissive interpretations than they might otherwise have adopted. Further, there was a strong feeling that no matter what South Africa claimed, the question was international since it involved respect for human rights.

Most members soon agreed that Article 2(7) does not prohibit debate, because debate is not interventionary in itself and must occur before members can decide if action on the matter would constitute intervention; and does not prohibit adding a question to the agenda, because this is a necessary preliminary to debate. Thus, Article 2(7) has been deemed irrelevant to formation of the agenda. While useful for keeping the range of Assembly activity as wide as possible, this definition was also consistent with the definition of intervention as restricted to the use of military force favored by most members of the US-led majority.

This broad view of Assembly competence to debate remains unchallenged. This has not prevented delegates from attempting to persuade their colleagues not to discuss particular matters. Unsuccessful efforts are often given public expression, as when the French delegate protested an Assembly decision to discuss "The Question of Mayotte" in 1980:

> The inscription of agenda item 25 [is] contrary to Article 2(7) of the Charter. The present debate should not be taking place, and my delegation will feel in no way bound by any decisions that may be adopted under this item.
> (A/35/PV.74, 28 Nov. 1980, pp. 24–5)

Successful efforts appear only negatively in the lack of Assembly discussion.

Saying that debate does not constitute intervention means that even if the Assembly cannot make a decision, it is always available as a forum for efforts to put pressure on governments through public discussion. Assembly majorities have always been eager to discuss other states' domestic politics or internal actions if this would yield advantages in efforts to assert new international norms or embarrass particular states. Of course, Assembly majorities usually avoid picking on their own members. The Nonaligned group has been more disciplined about this than the US-led coalition since it has been able to avoid anything like the colonial–anticolonial split that afflicted the former. This accounts for the pattern, so distressing to many observers, of the Assembly condemning the misdeeds of a few states while remaining silent about similar or worse conduct by others. A forum that could be used to increase the international or even domestic accountability of governments by exposing their activity to public comment has not reached its potential because of the one-sided way it has been used by successive Assembly majorities.

The Assembly's own Rules of Procedure provide three mechanisms that could be used to limit the nominal agenda: (1) use by the General Committee of its authority to recommend dropping particular items, (2) strict use of deadlines for submission of items and (3) formal challenges of Assembly competence to consider particular items.

As part of its work preparing the agenda, the General Committee recommends deleting particular items. This requires only agreement by a simple majority, but the final decision about whether to drop or retain the item rests with a simple majority of the plenary. In most of the Assembly's history, the distribution of places in the General Committee among the main regional groups has assured that the majority coalition in the Assembly also held a majority of the seats on the General Committee. At such times it would not be difficult to use the General Committee as a filtering device.

However, the General Committee has never asserted its authority very far, and members, even majority coalitions, have not encouraged it to do so. The General Committee quickly decided that any item proposed by a member at least thirty days before a regular session (thus in time to figure in the provisional agenda or the supplementary list) should always be included on the agenda (Spaak, 1948, p. 607). This was reinforced by adding a prohibition on deciding political questions to Rule 41 in 1947 (Resolution 173 [II]) and adding a ban on substantive discussions to Rule 40 in 1949 (Resolution 362 [IV]). The continuing vitality of these preferences can be seen in the membership's rejection of any proposals to give the General Committee real authority over the agenda (A/26/Supp. 26, Doc. A/8426, Sept. 1971, para. 44) or to create a separate Agenda Committee (A/937, 12 Aug. 1949, para. 15; A/C.6/4/SR.156, 8 Oct. 1949, paras 1–43; A/5423, 28 May 1963, para. 62).

At first glance, this self-denial by the US-led coalition appears surprising, for it was not reluctant to push its advantages in other ways. Yet a closer look at the internal politics of the coalition yields a different perception. Allowing smaller members to bring any concern to the General Assembly was part of the price for their support on Cold War and other issues of particular interest to the United States. In addition, many members did not want the General Committee to become as influential as the League Assembly's Bureau had been. Self-denial also serves the Third World coalition by assuring members that their particular concerns can be heard. In addition, the Third World coalition's emphasis on the principle of sovereign equality in other realms inhibits the development of formal devices that too obviously seem to rank the concerns of some states higher than those of others.

The General Committee has asserted its authority only in three ways, none of which affects the nominal agenda significantly. First, but only when the press of numbers forced members to accept, it recommended consolidating or grouping similar items for simultaneous debate. Second, it has occasionally recommended that the names given to items be changed so that they do not prejudge the issue (see example in A/15/BUR/SR. 127, 22 Sept. 1960, pp. 2–4, and SR.128, 23 Sept. 1960, p. 7). While a change of name does not inhibit debate, it provides an early indication of whether a majority intends using the Assembly to reduce or to pursue conflict. Third, it has sometimes recommended that items on the agenda year after year (the "hardy perennials") be considered only every second year. This experiment never extended to the political "hardy perennials", such as South Africa's apartheid policies or the Arab–Israeli conflict, lest omission would be taken to mean the Assembly had lost interest in or given up on the issue. Even with nonpolitical questions, the first attempt at large-scale staggering of perennial items lasted for only three sessions (idea proposed in A/26/Supp. 26, Doc. A/8426, Sept. 1971, para. 84; experiments noted in A/25/Annex 8, A/26/Annex 8 and A/27/Annex 8). The press of business forced the readoption of staggering for the Second Committee starting at the 40th session in 1985 (Resolution 39/217).

The rules governing the agenda provide a basis for discriminating among items by the date of submission. For regular sessions, the proposed items are grouped into three categories: (1) the provisional list of items submitted at least 60 days before the opening of the session by other UN organizations, member states, the Secretary-General, or non-member states invoking Article 35(2) of the Charter to refer a dispute to the Assembly; (2) the supplementary list of items proposed by the Secretary-General, principal UN organs, or member states between 60 and 30 days before the start of the session; and (3) additional items proposed by the Secretary-General, other principal UN organizations, or member states less than 30 days before the start of a session or even after the session has begun.

Rule 15 provides that additional items should be "of an urgent and important nature," but allows their inclusion on the agenda by the same simple majority that determines inclusion of other items. Though the 2nd and 4th sessions did set deadlines after which no additional item was supposed to be accepted (A/BUR/83, 12 Sept. 1947, p. 2, and A/2/PV.91, 23 Sept. 1947, p. 300; A/BUR/102, 19 Sept. 1949, para. 6, and A/4/PV.224, 22 Sept. 1949, p. 23), the members have been unwilling to limit the nominal agenda in this way. Additional items are often accepted as late as the second week in December. A proposal to require that a two-thirds majority be required for inclusion of additional items at regular sessions was rejected in 1949, and never heard again. Thus, the time of proposing an item does not affect its chances of being included in the nominal agenda.

Since the short notice involved places great burdens on delegations, groups and foreign ministries alike, Assembly reformers have often thought that they could limit the nominal agenda by proposing stricter deadlines for suggesting new items not stemming from sudden crises (e.g., Committee proposal in A/937, 12 Aug. 1949, para. 11, or Greek proposal in A/26/Supp. 26, Doc. A/8426, Sept. 1971, Annex IV, para. 50). However, the same dynamics of coalition politics that have hobbled the General Committee have also doomed these proposals. Further, many governments like to present what they regard as major initiatives – whether the USA's "open skies" proposal of 1955, Malta's 1967 proposal to examine uses of the ocean floor, or the USSR's 1979 proposal of a treaty on the non-use of force – in the plenary general debate. In this way, the proposal gets more immediate publicity than it would if the normal procedure of submission were used. All delegations realize that domestic or foreign policy needs might lead them to make such a public initiative themselves, so tolerate others' use of the mechanism. Thus, late items are as hard to keep off the nominal agenda as early ones.

Members can try removing an item from the nominal agenda by challenging the Assembly's competence to take it up or arguing that consideration would be inopportune. These objections may be raised in the General Committee, in the plenary, or in both successively. Challenges to competence are unlikely to be successful for two reasons. First, the Assembly has adopted very broad definitions of competence, at least regarding its authority to include items on the agenda. Second, arguments about competence are guided by political considerations rather than by any notion of general rules determining when the Assembly should or should not act.

Acceptance of this political style of argumentation is widespread, which should not be surprising in a body that considers itself a political rather than a legal institution and operates in a political system where the members (states) accept few common norms. Sydney Bailey quoted one head of delegation as telling his subordinates, "Whenever possible, use good political arguments. If there are no good political arguments, use bad political arguments. If there are no bad political arguments, use legal arguments" (Bailey, 1960, p. 90). Since both weak states, which have always formed a majority of the Assembly's membership, and enduring majority coalitions are interested in maintaining and extending Assembly authority, it is not surprising that a majority ready to accept an item for the agenda can be found on almost any occasion. Though proposers have been persuaded to withdraw items on occasion, few formal objections to including an item on the agenda by any other state have been sustained. Members usually find it easier to bury inopportune items by quietly dropping them from the effective agenda.

Only during special and emergency sessions do the formal rules place serious limits on the nominal agenda. Since these are special cases, these limits will be discussed below in the examination of the effective agenda (see pages 46–9).

Member states defend the maintenance of an open nominal agenda so stubbornly because it serves important political and organizational ends. Politically, it offers two advantages: (1) reaffirmation of the principle of sovereign equality of states, and (2) assurance that states will have the widest freedom in their decisions about whether to bring particular matters to the Assembly. Organizationally, it assists efforts to assert General Assembly authority *vis-à-vis* all other UN organs.

The open nominal agenda might be dismissed as a relatively unimportant concession, but it does give constant symbolic reinforcement to the principle of sovereign equality. Weak states defend the open agenda because they have a particular interest in strengthening the principle of sovereign equality. Being unable to resist stronger states in any contest of material power, they have to encourage the acceptance of norms promoting self-restraint by the strong. The principle of sovereign equality is one of the more prominent of such norms, so worth their protection.

The open nominal agenda also lets states decide what to bring to the Assembly without having to worry about a priori limits keeping some types of question off the agenda. This lets any state raise a global problem that seems to be getting less attention than it deserves. Thus Malta brought up regulating mining and oil drilling on the seabed in 1967, and protecting the natural environment in 1968. A problem that worries one state may seem remote to others, like Grenada's 1977 proposal to study "Coordination and dissemination of the results of research into Unidentified Flying Objects and related phenomena." In many cases, however, the majority comes to agree that the problem does deserve international attention. When that occurs, the Assembly has served the international system as a device for articulating new concerns.

The open agenda can also be used for more selfish purposes. When a state – or group of states – brings its particular conflict with another before the Assembly, it expects that widening the scope of the conflict by bringing in the rest of the UN membership will help secure its interests. It may hope to have the Assembly put pressure on the other to stop some objectionable activity, as when Greece and Cyprus got the Assembly to condemn the Turkish invasion of Cyprus and call upon Turkey to withdraw its forces (most strongly in Resolutions 3212 [XXIX] and 3395 [XXX]). It may hope to deter the other from some drastic step, as in the African campaign to have the Assembly recommend against selling nuclear equipment to South Africa and warn South Africa that the acquisition of nuclear weapons will have "grave consequences" (Resolution 35/164A). It may hope to tip the balance in negotiations by having the Assembly endorse its own positions as legitimate and condemn the other side's positions as illegitimate, as in Arab efforts to have the Assembly condemn virtually every aspect of Israeli policy in the Middle East and endorse the claims of Palestinian nationalism as led by the Palestine Liberation Organization. Or it may simply hope that Assembly attention will bring the other to negotiate. Whatever the reason or reasons for attempting to widen a conflict, the open nominal agenda permits doing so fairly easily regardless of the substantive issue involved.

The open nominal agenda has an organizational implication useful both to weak states, which see the Assembly as more sympathetic to their concerns than most other international fora, and to stable majorities in the Assembly unsure of their ability to control other UN bodies because of differences in membership or voting rules. The Charter provides the basis for influencing or controlling other UN bodies by giving the Assembly broad authority of discussion and decision, stipulating that certain UN bodies report to or are subject to direction from the Assembly, and granting the Assembly power to create its own subsidiary organs. The extent and implications of this influence or control will be examined in Chapter 6, but one aspect of the question deserves mention here. Though discussing an item in the Assembly does not guarantee that a majority will be able to impose its views on another UN body, the open agenda allows those majorities a wide field of initiative. Assembly majorities can easily put other UN bodies on the defensive, which in itself means they have forced the target body to respond. The open nominal agenda is particularly important to a majority attempting to use the General Assembly and the rest of the UN system as a lever for major changes in the rules of international conduct or the distribution of resources. The open nominal agenda permits a revisionist or revolutionary majority to raise such issues and place the burden of responding or looking reactionary by failing to respond on those content with the existing situation. The Third World has been able to use this device against the West quite effectively since it has also been able to link up with sympathetic elements of Western public opinion applying pressure on their own governments through the democratic processes of Western domestic politics. Such a strategy has less effect against Soviet bloc states because of their closed political systems.

The Effective Agenda

Placing a question on the Assembly's nominal agenda does not assure that it will receive extended attention or become the subject of a decision. Like all political institutions, the General Assembly is subject to the fact that time is limited. A regular session is supposed to last thirteen weeks, from mid-September until late December. It is possible, and almost normal practice, to add more meetings in the spring or summer by resuming a regular session or calling a special one. Though most delegates prefer avoiding this because of the heavy schedule of UN-related and other international meetings in those seasons, the Assembly usually has been unable to complete work by the end of December in recent years.

The effective Assembly agenda is created through several informal processes. First, the rule that main committees set their own work schedules has been used to create a mechanism for deciding which items will receive the earliest or the most extensive consideration. Second, the Third World majority, unlike the US-led one before it, uses group meetings for deciding which items will be pursued on a priority basis. Third, items can be removed (at least temporarily) from the Assembly agenda by transfer to another UN body. Fourth, all members participate in a negative form of agenda-setting when they choose to keep certain issues out of the Assembly.

When adopting the agenda, the Assembly allocates each item for preliminary discussion in one of seven main committees or for direct consideration in plenary. Each main committee receives a list of the items being referred to it in the order in which they appear on the agenda. Rule 99 authorizes main committees to decide when and how to proceed with the items referred to them.

Rule 99's injunction to complete consideration of all items has never been taken literally. Main committees have always brought up some items simply to decide that, since there is insufficient time, interest, or agreement to complete consideration at the current session, work should be postponed to a later one. Such postponement may be decided by a two-thirds majority before any general discussion of the item has begun, or by a simple majority once it has (interview with member of the Legal Department, 1981). Main committees seldom decide against discussing an item; they generally make formal obeisance to the principle of sovereign equality by holding some debate before deferring work. On occasion a lack of speakers has been taken as a decision to defer consideration (e.g., A/SPC/37/SR.46, 7 Dec. 1982, para. 3).

Main committees set their schedule by simple majority. This means that any coalition controlling 50 percent plus 1 of the votes controls formation of the effective agenda in that committee. The specialization among main committees means that it is possible for different coalitions to control agenda formation in different main committees. An anticolonial majority of African, Asian, Eastern European and Latin American states had effective control of the Fourth Committee's agenda by 1950, while the agendas of the First and Special Political Committees remained under the control of the US-led majority. Differences became greater in the era between stable majorities. Today the Third World majority is sufficiently large and cohesive to control the agenda in all main committees. Yet the strong influence of East–West divisions in the First Committee and the growing diversity of the Non-aligned and Group of 77 have eroded the strength of Third World control.

In the early sessions, main committees debated at length about which item would receive how much attention when, and often put rival preferences to a vote. In an Assembly of fifty-one members having a 64-item agenda, the main committees could afford to spend a certain amount of time this way. By the early 1950s, however, delegates were beginning to consult beforehand on the schedule. Today it is rare for a main committee to have a public argument over scheduling or to put rival preferences to a vote. This stems in part from better consultations among the regional groups and in part from using much the same schedule from year to year since so many of the same items keep reappearing on the agenda.

A stable majority controls the scheduling no matter how decisions are made. If disagreements are put to a vote, it can outvote the others. If matters are settled in consultations, the knowledge that the stable majority would prevail in a vote keeps others from pressing too far. If the stable majority has been in existence for some years, it even controls the decisions made by copying earlier schedules because those earlier schedules also reflect its preferences.

Arguments about scheduling have not completely disappeared because scheduling discussion close to the end of the session increases the chance that an item will be deferred. Majorities have at least two reasons for deferring issues other members wish to discuss. Sometimes deferral is used to preserve a fracturing majority. The United States, knowing that its coalition was splitting on the issue, sought to delay Third Committee discussion of self-determination between 1954 and 1957 in hopes of meanwhile negotiating a decision that would be acceptable both to the eager Latin Americans and Asians and to the wary European colonial powers. In the end this effort failed, and the eager went ahead confident that they had the votes. Deferral may also be used to avoid revealing existing divisions. Between 1965 and 1975 the Third World majority avoided serious discussion of Costa Rica's proposal to create a UN High Commissioner for Human Rights with real power to investigate charges that individual member states were violating human rights. Most members of the Third World majority preferred retaining the existing human rights commissions and committees, which have more limited powers, but did not want to say so publicly. Yet not all delay stems from partisan motives. Some issues may be deferred for real lack of time because other negotiations took longer than expected. Third Committee consideration of a draft declaration on the right of territorial asylum, which met with wide approval among the members, was delayed between 1960 and 1962 because of lengthy arguments about various provisions of the International Covenants on Human Rights. On other occasions all groups agree to postponement while they seek an acceptable compromise.

Whatever the reasons, delegations try to minimize the chances that items they propose will be deferred. While an individual delegation can do little about a majority decision, it can try to minimize the risk of accidental delay. This means trying hard either to get the matter placed a bit earlier in the schedule or to secure promises that the committee will actually get to it.

While scheduling remains important, growing efficiency in main committee work habits has made it less salient politically. Initially, main committees insisted on taking one item at a time, holding all debates and voting on all proposals before proceeding to the next. This created a situation in which minorities fearful of their position or mistrustful of the Assembly could "gum up the works" by constantly slowing debate and votes. Soviet bloc delegations frequently resorted to such tactics, often to the fury even of delegates prepared to regard their ideas with some sympathy (Spaak, 1971, p. 109). No matter how embattled individual Western delegates may feel today, the same range of opportunities for delay through obstruction is not available to them (maneuvers available in early sessions are discussed in Hovey, 1951).

By the early 1950s the press of business and of numbers was such that main committees were beginning to depart from this mechanical style of work. One device was scheduling two items for the same meeting so that if debate on one got interrupted for any reason the committee could turn its attention to the other, as the *ad hoc* Political Committee did with items on Eritrea and Palestinian refugees in 1950 (A/AHPC/5/SR.34, 6 Nov. 1950, paras. 32–5). Another involved having the whole committee go on to general discussion of some other matter while a working group attempted to negotiate a widely acceptable decision (e.g., A/C.2/9/SR.314, 17 Nov. 1954, para. 60). Today, with the grouping of items for general discussion and the replacement of formal examination of rival drafts by informal negotiations, main committees follow very flexible work plans in which the place in the order of work is less important than the amount of time needed for informal consultations. With tighter rules on scheduling, committees are better able to guess how long general discussion will take and can schedule on that basis, leaving certain intervals free so that any proposals that have been worked out informally can be introduced and voted upon (e.g., committee program of work in A/C.1/34/2, 1 Oct. 1979).

Rule 97 says, "Committees shall not introduce new items on their own initiative." If a member has a new idea it wants considered after the session has started, it is supposed to propose the matter as an additional item. The plenary is then supposed to decide whether the item should be added to the session's agenda. In practice, members often get around the ban by persuading main committees to take up new items on their own.

Most agenda items are given such broad names that it is quite easy to justify considering something as part of that main question (a tendency deplored by Secretary-General Lie in A/2206, 1 Oct. 1952, paras. 25–6). Throughout the 1950s and 1960s Special Political Committee consideration of aid to Palestinian refugees was used to debate the whole future of the Arab–Israeli conflict. The Arabs knew they lacked sufficient support to get Assembly endorsement of their view that all refugees should be allowed to return to Israel and that territory held by Israel should be transformed into a secular state. They used the debates as an annual opportunity to present their views. An item labeled "Information Questions" can be used to discuss a whole variety of things, such as the draft convention on freedom of information first drawn up in 1948, aid to developing countries for expansion of their media services, problems stemming from possibilities for direct television broadcasting from satellites, controls on journalists' activities, or implications of transnational data banks. Annual debate on "Implementation of the Declaration on the Strengthening of International Security" provides a vehicle for the trading of accusations between the superpowers, for polemics between other pairs or groups of countries at odds with one another, or for the rapid consideration of evolving situations. In the 1979 discussion, for example, Venezuela took initiatives that led to condemning the Somoza government of Nicaragua for violating human rights at home and creating tension in Central America, a move criticized as illegal by Brazil but accepted by most other members (A/C.1/33/PV.68, 8 Dec. 1979). Imagination is limited somewhat by specifying particular sub-items under the main heading, but even the sub-items have names broad enough to permit a good deal of interpretation.

This permits vocal minorities to heavily influence the tone of public debate and to advance their own proposals. It is also one of the mechanisms by which items initially raised by one group can be diverted to serving the purposes of another.

Main committees can also delay the consideration of items on the agenda by deciding that they should be referred to a special committee or some other UN body for further study or negotiation. This is often done in hopes of reaching a compromise. For instance, the draft convention of freedom of information, which had been drawn up by a special conference on the subject in 1948, was allocated to the Third Committee for consideration at the third session. Members soon realized that it would be difficult to satisfy both those states that had strong traditions of freedom of expression and those that had strong traditions of government control over expression and information. In hopes of securing a draft convention they referred it to an *ad hoc* committee and then to the Commission on Human Rights. A brief set of discussions of a revised draft in 1959–61 showed that there was still no formulation commanding wide support, at which point the Third Committee began postponing the item from session to session (Resolutions 313 [IV] and 426 [VI]; discussions in A/C.3/14/SR.970–9, 27 Nov.–7 Dec. 1959; A/C.3/15/SR.1028–45, 21 Nov.–5 Dec. 1960; and A/C.3/16/SR.1126–34, 6–14 Dec. 1961). Similarly, consideration of further steps to be taken to implement the "New International Economic Order" was postponed from the fall of 1976 to a resumption of the 31st session to be held in the spring of 1977, and then until the 32nd session when it became clear that negotiations of a compromise were not yet completed (*UN Yearbook*, 1977, p. 385). Yet referring an item for study can also be a way of burying it, particularly if given to a body that has plenty of other work. Thus, the Grenadan proposal to study UFOs was referred to the Committee on Peaceful Uses of Outer Space in 1979 and never heard of again (A/SPC/33/SR.47, 8 Dec. 1978).

While adding, delaying, or burying items gives scope for political maneuver, the overall schedule of each main committee clearly reflects the priorities and interests of the majority. Where the majority is a stable coalition, a study of committee work schedules over time reveals shifts in preferences. A comparison of work in 1955 and 1975 vividly demonstrates the differing priorities of the US-led and Third World majorities.

Though the First Committee did not formally shift to exclusive concern with disarmament until 1978, the trend toward that result was sufficiently strong in 1975 that the First and Special Political Committees should be considered together in the comparison. As can be seen in tables 2.1 and 2.2, many of the issues remained the same, but the emphasis given to them had changed.

Table 2.1   First committee

Issue   *Number of meetings*

1955

(1)	Peaceful uses of atomic energy	16
(2)	Effects of atomic radiation	10
(3)	Korea	11
(4)	Morocco	1
(5)	Disarmament and relaxation of international tensions	14
(6)	West Irian	$\frac{1}{2}$
		$52\frac{1}{2}$

1975

(1)	Cooperation in space, treaty on direct TV broadcasting from satellites	6
(2)	Implementation of the Declaration on Strengthening International Security	6
(3)	Korea	12
(4)	Disarmament questions (10 relating to nuclear weapons, 8 relating to conventional weapons or to both)	36
		60

Table 2.2   Special political committee

Issue   *Number of meetings*

1955

(1)	Race conflict in South Africa	10
(2)	Report of the UN Works and Relief Agency in Palestine	12
(3)	Admission of new members	8
(4)	Treatment of persons of Indian origin in South Africa	2
		32

1975

(1)	South African apartheid policies	22
(2)	Effects of atomic radiation	1
(3)	Report of the UNRWA	7
(4)	Cyprus	2
(5)	Peacekeeping operations	5
(6)	Report of the special committee to investigate Israeli policies in the occupied territories	7
		44

Of the particular situations discussed by the two committees in 1955, two, Morocco and West Irian, were related to decolonization. The Korean Question remained from the US-led majority's efforts to use the UN collective security mechanism in resisting North Korea's invasion of South Korea. The strong interest in South Africa was already apparent. In 1955 the committee paid some attention to persuading South Africa to give up its bad policies, a theme that had disappeared by 1975. The only new issues in 1975 related to Cyprus, where tensions between the Greek and Turkish communities had resulted first in a coup that seemed to be leading to union of the island with Greece, and then in a Turkish invasion to protect the Turk communities and prevent any such union, and outer space, which had been discussed in the UN since 1961. With the Palestine question being discussed in plenary, the Special Political Committee had to deal only with aid to refugees, which allowed it more time for denouncing South Africa.

The shift in the Second Committee's agenda reflects changes in the way most members think about economic development. Rather than lumping the whole problem together in one undifferentiated mass, the members now treat various aspects separately as different lines of UN action have developed over the years. Further, ideas of what is necessary for economic development have been refined and have become more wide-ranging. The degree of this shift is seen in the inclusion of "implementation of the NIEO" in the 1975 list. The US-led coalition approached development as a matter of helping individual countries do better within the postwar economic rules. The Group of 77 believes that major changes in the rules are required before individual countries can progress very far.

Table 2.3 Second committee

Issue	*Number of meetings*
1955	
(1) Report of the UN Korean Reconstruction Agency	2
(2) Economic development of underdeveloped countries	$34\frac{1}{2}$
(3) Economic and Social Council report	$4\frac{1}{2}$
(4) Economic assistance to Libya	1
	42
1975	
(1) General discussion of world economic questions	5

(2)	Report of the UN Institute for Training and Research	2
(3)	Food problems	4
(4)	UN Special Fund	$1\frac{1}{2}$
(5)	Economic and technical cooperation among LDCs	4
(6)	UN Environmental Program	$6\frac{1}{2}$
(7)	Operational activities for development	$10\frac{1}{2}$
(8)	UN Industrial Development Organization report	$5\frac{1}{2}$
(9)	Disaster relief	5
(10)	Economic and Social Council report	2
(11)	Implementation of the New International Economic Order	2
(12)	Midterm review of the Second UN Development Decade	1
(13)	UN Conference on Trade and Development report	4
(14)	UN university	11
(15)	Unified approach to development analysis and planning	1
		65

The change in priorities between the US-led and Third World majorities is most apparent in the Third Committee, where the older focus on individuals has been largely replaced by a focus on groups, particularly races and peoples. The Third Committee also became more of a forum for verbal attacks on particular states; the First Committee lost much of that role as it shifted to working on space and disarmament.

Table 2.4   Third committee

Issue		*Number of meetings*
	1955	
(1)	Report of the UN High Commissioner for Refugees	8
(2)	Drafting the International Covenants on Human Rights	$36\frac{1}{2}$
(3)	Advisory services in the field of human rights	$2\frac{1}{2}$
(4)	Draft convention on the nationality of married women	$5\frac{1}{2}$
(5)	Economic and Social Council report	3
(6)	Safety of commercial aircraft near or inadvertently crossing international frontiers	2
		$57\frac{1}{2}$
	1975	
(1)	Elimination of racism	$13\frac{1}{2}$
(2)	Economic and Social Council report	$7\frac{1}{2}$
(3)	Status of the International Covenants on Human Rights	$\frac{1}{2}$

(4)	Universal attainment of self-determination	8
(5)	Human rights and scientific and technological developments	5
(6)	Adverse consequences for human rights of aid to colonial and racist regimes in Southern Africa	$\frac{1}{2}$
(7)	Appeal to Chile on human rights	3
(8)	ESC report, section on situation in Chile	10
(9)	Torture	$5\frac{1}{2}$
(10)	Report of UN High Commissioner for Refugees	3
(11)	Alternative methods for enhancement of enjoyment of human rights	3
(12)	International Women's Year	10
		$69\frac{1}{2}$

The great Third World interest in decolonization and self-determination means that the Fourth Committee remains active despite the vast reduction in the number of colonies. While still urging independence for the few remaining colonies, it has become a forum for attacks on racism and "neocolonialism" as well. This change was not fully apparent in 1975 because Portugal had just accepted the idea its African colonies should become independent and many members remained skeptical about Portuguese intentions. The difference in world view between the two coalitions is obvious from the titles of certain items. In 1955 attention focused mainly on securing information and making the charter provisions or trusts and other non-self-governing territories work. By 1975 the Fourth Committee was a major sounding board for theories that capitalism both causes and feeds on colonialism and racist rule. Though the strongly anti-Western cast of this agenda gives the Soviet bloc many opportunities, the Third World coalition seldom adopts Soviet bloc proposals as written.

Table 2.5   Fourth committee

Issue	*Number of meetings*
1955	
(1) Trusteeship Council report	12
(2) Report of Committee on Information from NSGTs	18
(3) Renewal of Committee on Information from NSGTs	3
(4) Petitions from Trust Territories	1
(5) Situation in South West Africa	$19\frac{1}{2}$
(6) Elections to Trusteeship Council	$\frac{1}{2}$

(7) Cessation of transmission of information on particular
     NSGTs   8½
(8) Togoland unification problem   30½
                                                              ─────
                                                               93

1975

(1) Situation in Rhodesia   13
(2) Situation in Namibia   13½
(3) Activities of foreign economic and other interests
     impeding decolonization and elimination of racism   7
(4) Individual NSGTs   15½
(5) General discussion of situation in NSGTs   2½
(6) UN educational and training program for Southern
     Africa   1
(7) Member offers of educational opportunities for
     inhabitants of NSGTs   1
(8) Information from NSGTs   1
(9) Specialized Agency work assisting decolonization   1
(10) Territories under Portuguese administration   6½
(11) Trusteeship Council report   ½
                                                              ─────
                                                              62½

The comparatively broader interests of the Third World
majority in elaborating new rules of international law appear
relatively clearly in a comparison of Sixth Committee work.
Most of the 1955 debates referred to procedural issues; at least half
of the 1957 ones raised important substantive questions. The
1975 issues also reveal a far greater tendency to question the basic
assumptions on which international law is made and to elaborate
new sets of rules based on new conceptions.

Table 2.6   Sixth committee

Issue   *Number of meetings*

1955

(1) International Law Commission report   12½
(2) Continuation of the UN Tribunal in Libya   4
(3) Correction of votes in the General Assembly   3
(4) Registration and publication of treaties by the
     Secretariat   12
(5) Arbitral procedure   10

(6)   Third Committee request for advice about Articles 4–11
of the Convention on the Nationality of Married
Women $5\frac{1}{2}$

        47

1975

(1)	State succession to treaties	$12\frac{1}{2}$
(2)	UN Commission on International Trade Law report	6
(3)	International Law Commission report	8
(4)	Question of diplomatic asylum	$8\frac{1}{2}$
(5)	Report of Committee on Relations with the Host Country	11
(6)	Report of the *ad hoc* Committee on Review of the Charter and Strengthening of the Role of the Organization	11
(7)	Human rights in armed conflicts	2
(8)	UN program to aid the study of international law	$\frac{1}{2}$
(9)	Implementation by states of the 1961 Vienna Convention on Diplomatic Relations	1
(10)	Prevention of terrorism	1
(11)	Resolutions adopted by the UN Conference on Representation of States in their Relations with International Organizations	$\frac{1}{2}$

        62

Though polemics flow in many directions in the Assembly, the origins and targets of those polemics figuring in the effective agenda provide a good indication of who is controlling the Assembly at any moment. Both stable majorities devoted a proportion of Assembly time to attacking their particular enemies. In 1955 First Committee consideration of Korea and disarmament included a heavy dose of Cold War polemic as did the Special Political Committee discussion of admitting new members (though this was mild because 1955 was the year of the "package deal" solving the problem). Second Committee consideration of Korean reconstruction was Cold War-related. The Third Committee discussion on aircraft safety was inspired by Israeli concern about incidents of firing on airliners flying near international borders. Though less than in earlier years, the Cold War still received a fair amount of Assembly attention. Meanwhile the anticolonial majority was finding its voice in attacks on South Africa, while the Eastern European states used

Fourth Committee and Second Committee debates to attack
Western positions generally.

In 1975 discussion of Korea was one of the few remnants of the
Cold War left on the agenda. By then attacks were most often
made against the West or against specific targets. The favorite
targets, Israel and South Africa, were criticized in several committees. Marxist theories that capitalism is inherently exploita-
tive found particular favor in Fourth Committee debates, where
Western relations with South Africa, Portugal and Rhodesia
provided irresistible targets. Chile came under sustained attack in
the Third Committee for its record on human rights. This
record, though bad, was not any worse than those of several of
the attackers; Chile's real sin lay in having a military junta that
had overthrown a leftist government. The discussion of relations
with the Host Country in the Sixth Committee is an annual
excuse for speeches about the decadence of New York City and
the allegedly insufficient efforts of local authorities to protect
permanent missions from incidents.

The Third World majority has developed a second, completely
informal mechanism for controlling the effective agenda. Meetings of the Nonaligned Movement and the Group of 77 are used,
among other things, for drawing up joint proposals to submit to
the Assembly and deciding what priorities should be attached to
the groups' various desires. Meetings of Nonaligned foreign
ministers in early September and later discussions among the
Third World regional groups refine understandings or react to
new developments. These mechanisms ensure that the Nonaligned Movement in particular exerts great influence over the
effective agenda. Since the Nonaligned's anticolonial ideology
and the strong influence exerted by the more radical members of
the movement push its positions even further in an anti-Western
direction, the whole Assembly agenda takes on a similar cast.
This encourages Western states, particularly the United States, to
avoid the Assembly as much as possible.

The US-led majority never developed any comparable
mechanism, though its Latin American, Commonwealth and
Western European members often consulted among themselves.
This stemmed less from the split between industrial and developing members on colonial and economic issues than from the
fact that the pressure of time was not felt as keenly before 1955.
In that year the Assembly had a membership of 76 and an agenda
of 66 items, a far cry from the 143 members and 136 items
of 1975. This contention is supported by the slowness with
which the Assembly reformed rules on formal debate that

wasted considerable amounts of time (see below, pages 106–11).

Third, items can be moved off the agenda by reference to another UN body, whether another principal organ, a specialized agency, or a subsidiary organ of the Assembly. Such referrals can represent attempts to obstruct by imposing delay, attempts to allow time for development of wider agreement on an issue, or attempts to move it into a forum members find more congenial.

The tempo of Assembly work depends greatly on the solidity and intensity of a majority formed around an issue. Where a clear majority knows what it wants and wants it quickly, minorities have little scope for obstruction by referral to another body. This can be seen in the history of the UN Covenants on Human Rights, where many issues bounced back and forth between the Human Rights Commission and the Third Committee. Debate about whether to have one or two Covenants went back and forth between the Human Rights Commission and the Third Committee while a majority formed in favour of the latter. In contrast, an *ad hoc* coalition of weak states virtually wrote the article on self-determination in the Third Committee during the sixth (1951) session. Similarly, the whole issue of self-determination was moved from the Economic and Social Council and the Human Rights Commission, where the Western countries had buried it in the late 1950s, to the plenary in 1960 when admission of new African and Asian states created a majority insisting on more immediate attention to the issue.

Particularly with new issues, both majority and minority groupings may desire a leisurely pace while testing opinion or arriving at policy preferences. Examples of this sort of activity abound. Creation of the Special Committee on Peaceful Uses of the Seabed gave all members time to consider how they wanted to approach ocean issues. All of UNCLOS III was an exercise in negotiation among shifting coalitions as states refined their views on specific questions and arrived at what they hoped would be workable agreements.

These motives often combine. Treatment of Antarctica in the Assembly provides a very good example. Malaysia, which initiated the debate, clearly wants to replace the current Antarctic Treaty with a UN-sponsored convention and has definite ideas about what form the new Antarctic institutions should take. However, the Group of 77 as a whole had no clear position. Time was needed for exploring the depth of interest in a new regime. For their part, the sixteen Antarctic Treaty Consultative Parties, which together manage the current Antarctic regime and include India, Argentina, Brazil and Chile, wanted to delay action so other members could be persuaded to see the virtues of the existing Antarctic regime and leave it alone. At the 38th session, all agreed to have the Secretary-General prepare a study of the question. At the 39th session, decisions were deferred for at least a year. Both sides seem to be moving towards a solution leaving the Antarctic Treaty system intact but opening its operations to greater scrutiny by the rest of the international community (Puchala, ed., 1984, pp. 106–9; Eckhard, ed., 1985, pp. 103–6).

All diplomats know that the composition or traditions of a forum can affect the content of decisions. Therefore they "forum-shop" continually. For instance, information questions were mainly considered in an *ad hoc* Assembly Committee in the 1950s, which followed the then prevailing approach of attempting to write an international treaty on the subject. When the issue was reviewed in the late 1970s, the Third World coalition preferred discussing it in UNESCO and the Third Committee, two fora of the whole UN membership controlled by people highly sympathetic to Third World concerns. On certain issues, the superpowers can also determine the forum. In 1967 proposals to ban all military uses of the seabed were referred to the Special Committee on Uses of the Seabed. Though the Soviets favored wide-ranging bans, while the United States wanted simply to place limits on the uses or deployments of certain weapons, both agreed that the matter related to disarmament. They were able to secure a decision referring these proposals to the Eighteen Nation Disarmament Committee where the tripartite composition (United States and 5 allies, Soviet Union and 5 allies, 6 neutrals) allowed them to exert joint control of the negotiation (Wolfrum, 1981, pp. 221–2). Though the Law of the Sea Convention contained a provision reserving the deep seabed "exclusively to peaceful uses," the formulation is vague enough to accommodate several definitions of permissible military activity.

Finally, all states, not just those in a stable majority, share use of a negative device for controlling the Assembly's effective agenda. An item not proposed for inclusion in the nominal agenda normally will not become part of the effective agenda. Thus, if the states involved do not refer a matter to the Assembly, it probably will not be considered at any length. States may decide to keep a question out of the Assembly for a number of reasons. They may prefer to handle it in a regional organization. They may consider it a technical or administrative matter best handled in the relevant specialized agency. Parties to a dispute may prefer to deal directly, take it to a regional forum, or seek third party adjudication through the International Court of

Justice or another tribunal. A whole range of questions concerning two or a few states are handled through traditional bilateral channels. Finally, a state may initially desire to raise a question in the Assembly but back off when the initiative receives little support or it finds that persisting would lead to a decision inimical to its interests.

Most states belonging to the United Nations also belong to one or more regional organizations each of which deals with a wide range of regional issues and promotes cooperation among its members. At the behest of members of the Arab League and the Organization of American States (Ross, 1966, pp. 218–19), the UN Charter takes account of such regional organizations. It allows for regional efforts to maintain local peace and security in Article 52, and lists the use of regional organizations as one method of dispute settlement recommended to members in Article 33. This allows the members of regional organizations to remove local matters from global scrutiny by handling them in their own organization rather than the UN. Sometimes regional organizations help a strong power prevent Assembly discussion of its behavior. The United States used the regional argument to prevent much Assembly discussion of its 1965 intervention in the Dominican Republic. The Soviet Union raised the argument less successfully after its 1956 intervention in Hungary and its 1968 intervention in Czechoslovakia. At other times weak states use it to prevent too much outside interest in their conflicts. The Organization of African Unity long succeeded in isolating African conflicts from global politics because all members agreed that, except in conflict with colonial or white minority regimes, Africa would be better off if outside attention and assistance were not sought. OAS involvement in peace efforts meant that the Assembly did not discuss the 1969 war between El Salvador and Honduras.

Charter provisions on economic and social matters rested on an assumption that there is a clear separation between the "technical" or "administrative" tasks left to specialized agencies and the broader political questions deserving Assembly consideration. Though easy to formulate, the distinction was hard to maintain in practice. During the Cold War many discussions took on ideological overtones because it was impossible to separate approaches to technical tasks from broader social implications. As the specialized agencies also became service agencies providing technical assistance in the 1950s, their activities became part of the broader debate about attaining economic development. Thus, the old separation broke down, to be replaced by a different one in which the Assembly was used to raise new issues or point out general concerns while the specialized agencies (and other UN bodies) handled practical arangements or detailed negotiations. The separation also broke down because no Assembly majority could resist carrying certain political issues, particularly those about participation, into other UN bodies. This was as true of the US-led majority as of the Third World one, though the latter's campaigns tend to be more strident. As Leon Gordenker commented, "it cannot have come as a surprise to the United States that other governments can also comprehend humanitarian and technical issues as offering opportunities to make statements about who should rule, who should benefit and how" (Gordenker, 1983, p. 45). For these reasons, and others to be explored in Chapter 6, the old tactic of fencing off issues by claiming they are "technical" does not work very often today.

The Charter not only allows but encourages members to keep disputes out of the General Assembly or other UN bodies. In Article 33(1) of the Charter they promise to settle disputes peacefully, but are given a wide choice of methods:

> The parties to any dispute, the continuance of which is likely to endanger the maintenance of international peace and security, shall, first of all, seek a solution by negotiation, enquiry, mediation, conciliation, arbitration, judicial settlement, resort to regional agencies or arrangements, or other peaceful means of their own choice.

Article 33(2) states that members should try other methods of settlement before coming to the Security Council or General Assembly.

This provision permits a disputant not wishing the problem discussed to claim that Assembly consideration might prejudice the success of other efforts at settlement. A state with enough friends can keep its disputes out of the United Nations, even if those disputes have resulted in a war. Thus, the United Nations hardly discussed the "American Indochina War" of 1965–73 (Finger, 1980, pp. 124–8, 207–8). Nor has it considered the Iran–Iraq War in detail (Puchala, ed., 1982, pp. 19–21; 1983, pp. 21–3; 1984, pp. 18–22). The dispute between Libya and Tunisia over delimitation of the maritime border between them has not come to the Assembly because the states involved first attempted negotiations and then submitted the dispute to the International Court of Justice for settlement (*Continental Shelf, Tunisia/Libyan Arab Jamahiriya, Judgment, ICJ Reports*, 1982, p. 18).

These decisions to keep conflicts out of the Assembly are simply the obverse of decisions to bring them in. Here, one or both parties believes that widening participation in the matter would not serve its interests. The United States knew full well that most members would condemn its action, which would add to its difficulties maintaining consensus to home in favor of continuing involvement in Indochina. Neither Iraq nor Iran has been anxious to have the Assembly discuss their current war.

A state's success at keeping an issue out of the Assembly depends on several factors. Obviously activity started in or continuing through the last quarter of the year is more likely to gain attention because the Assembly is in session. Though emergency sessions can be convened at other times, the process is sufficiently cumbersome and expensive for governments to avoid it in most cases. A *fait accompli* inspires far less sustained comment in the Assembly than a continuing activity no matter the time of year it is undertaken.

A state's ability to keep an issue out of the Assembly often depends on the constellation of coalitions. No majority is anxious to see its members quarrel openly. This is particularly true of the Third World coalition since group unity is one of the few political resources it possesses. When discussion of a quarrel between two members would create or reveal fissures in the coalition, it is even more likely to avoid Assembly discussion. Thus it is not surprising that Assembly discussions of economic issues have not squarely faced the issue of how OPEC oil increases have hurt other developing states. This stems in part from the others viewing OPEC success against the West as an example for themselves and in part from the desire not to raise serious internal conflicts that others could exploit (on energy, see Fukai, 1982, p. 83 n. 30; Jackson, 1983, pp. 28–9; on wars between Nonaligned states, see Finlayson and Zacher, 1983, pp. 165–6). Being in minority positions, both superpowers prefer that the Assembly does not discuss either inter-bloc relations or their specific activities. While both find this hard if a particular activity cuts directly across the Third World's nationalist and anti-intervention ideologies, US commentators often feel this singles out the United States for virtually all of the criticism. Yet – despite the best efforts of the pro-Soviet group within the Nonaligned – the Soviet Union is also criticized by name when the Third World finds its conduct abhorrent. The Soviet Union comes in for less criticism not because it is morally superior but because it has been able to align its position with that of the Third World on a wide range of issues, including the three that inspire the greatest Third

World emotion: revision of the global economic system, South Africa and the Arab–Israeli conflict.

Though international organizations have become more important in the formulation and conduct of foreign policy since 1945, it is still true that most relations between states, particularly at the level of individual transactions, are carried on bilaterally or in small groups. Serious negotiations between the superpowers have always been carried on bilaterally, occasionally using the General Assembly as a forum for side comments or securing international legitimization of agreements reached. The superpowers and their respective European allies pursue intra-bloc discussions in alliance and in economic organizations, and now have a continuing forum for inter-bloc discussions in the Conferences on Security and Cooperation in Europe. Other states, too, undertake their serious negotiations on particular questions outside the Assembly, as constant travel by foreign ministers and heads of state attests.

Some initiatives wither on the vine for lack of support even before they get to the nominal agenda. Though it is difficult for an outside observer to determine how often this occurs, some examples are known. In a number of instances, states have proposed an item for the agenda only to withdraw it before the General Committee finishes its preliminary scrutiny of items. This happened more frequently in the early sessions when informal consultations were less prevalent; 6 of the 12 cases apparent from General Committee debates occurred before 1954 (see reports of the General Committee, printed as an annex to each year's Assembly records). These figures understate the actual number of incidents; India wanted to raise the question of Antarctica in 1956 but was talked out of doing so (Quigg, 1983, pp. 165–6).

The rules governing special and emergency sessions of the Assembly permit the majority to control the nominal agenda quite closely. This, in turn, strengthens its control of the effective agenda at such sessions. Rules 8 and 9 provide that for both special and emergency sessions the initial agenda consists of the item or items proposed by whoever requested the session. Once a special or emergency session begins, other items may be added to the agenda only if two-thirds of the members present and voting agree. Though intended to ensure that the agendas of such sessions do not become loaded down with too many items and distract the Assembly from its main business, this gives the majority tight control. In the case of emergency sessions, the rules impose an additional safeguard by stating that additional

items shall refer to other crisis situations, but majorities have
ignored that rule when it suited their purposes (such as starting
debate on admitting several new members before beginning
consideration of the Congo situation in A/E–4/PV.858, 17 Sept.
1960).

Emergency sessions allow Assembly majorities or *ad hoc*
coalitions to take over an issue from the Security Council. This
does not mean, however that every issue is taken over, even
when all proposals have been vetoed. As Table 2.7 shows,
emergency sessions have been convened only on a few issues.

Table 2.7 Emergency sessions

Session	Year	Source	Agenda
1st	1956	US, USSR and Afro-Asian response to British and French vetoes	Suez Crisis
2nd	1956	Western response to USSR veto	Hungarian Crisis
3rd	1958	Security Council after US–USSR agreement to change venue	Situation in Lebanon and Jordan
4th	1960	Western response to USSR veto	Congo
5th	1967	Soviet response to US veto	Arab-Israeli War
6th	1980	Nonaligned–West response to Soviet veto	Afghanistan
7th	1980	Nonaligned delayed response to US veto	Palestine
8th	1981	Nonaligned	Namibia
9th	1982	Nonaligned	Israeli annexation of Golan Heights

Special sessions have usually been used to provide more time
for discussion of particular issues that the majority feels cannot or
did not receive adequate attention in a regular session. Such
sessions can also be used to give a particular issue special
prominence. These various purposes can be seen in Table 2.8.

Table 2.8 Special sessions

Session	Year	Source	Agenda
1st	1947	UK request	Future of Palestine
2nd	1948	SC request	Palestine

3rd	1961	request by 38 Afro-Asian states	Tension stemming from Tunisian efforts to oust French forces from the Bizerte base before the agreement allowing use of the base expired
4th	1963	GA Res.	Problems of financing the Suez and Congo peacekeeping operations
5th	1967	GA Res.	Namibia (peacekeeping and postponement of an outer space conference added later)
6th	1974	Majority request by G-77	Establishment of a New International Economic Order
7th	1975	GA Res.	Same
8th	1978	GA Res.	Financing peacekeeping in Lebanon
9th	1978	GA Res.	Namibia
10th	1978	GA Res.	Disarmament
11th	1981	GA Res.	Progress on attaining the NIEO
12th	1982	GA Res.	Disarmament

Though financing peacekeeping has inspired a number of special sessions, those called since 1960 clearly reflect the priorities of the Third World majority. Since the Assembly's 1966 decision to revoke the League of Nations Mandate under which South Africa ruled Namibia (South West Africa) and to provide for direct UN administration of the territory, continued South African presence in the territory has been a sore point with the majority. Third World interest in the New International Economic Order is obvious. Interest in disarmament is more general, but the discussions in the special sessions have focused mainly on nuclear questions and disarmament as a way of freeing resources for use in economic aid programs.

The Assembly has sometimes found it necessary to continue a regular session into the spring. Initially this occurred because the session had not completed its agenda and members did not want to put off the questions involved until the following fall. In recent years, though, resumed sessions have become another way to secure extra time for discussing particular questions or symbolizing Assembly interest in some developing situation or negotiations (Jackson, 1983, pp. 134–5, overestimates the time spent in meetings but not their significance). This change is readily apparent in the agendas of the resumed sessions shown in Table 2.9.

Table 2.9   Resumed sessions

Session	Year	Items discussed
1st	1946	Fall half of a session begun in the spring
3rd	1949	Finish the agenda of a late-starting session
5th	1951	Korean War
6th	1952	Finish the agenda of a late-starting session
7th	1953	Same
11th	1957	Mainly Suez and Hungary
13th	1959	Future of the Cameroons
15th	1961	Congo, other items
16th	1962	Colonial questions
19th	1965	Cope with stalemate produced by arguments over financing the UNEF I and Congo peacekeeping operations
22nd	1968	Mainly Namibia
28th	1974	Situation in the Middle East (1 mtg)
29th	1975	Situation in the Middle East (1 mtg)
31st	1977	NIEO negotiations
33rd	1979	Finish the agenda
34th	1980	Complete elections to the Security Council
37th	1983	Finish the agenda
38th	1984	Finish the agenda (1 mtg)
39th	1985	Finish the agenda

Summary

The General Assembly pays obeisance to the decentralized nature of the international system and to most member states' concern for maintaining the principle of sovereign equality of states by having a nominal agenda open to virtually any issue any member state cares to raise. The overlapping interests of stable majority coalitions and weak states in assuring the Assembly a great influence over the rest of the UN system has encouraged the development of Charter interpretations that widen the range of issues which the Assembly can take up.

The interest of majorities in seeing their preferences adopted plus the unavoidable constraints imposed by the fact that sessions cannot extend indefinitely mean that the open nominal agenda is supplemented by a shorter effective one. The effective agenda has the usual result of making those who are already influential within the institution even more influential. Strength is thus added to strength. Effective conversion of demands into issues in the General Assembly, as in other political institutions, occurs only if a majority of the members thinks the demands merit discussion.

This does not mean that all minority demands are rejected immediately; it simply means that the majority must find something of interest in the demand or the broader questions it raises before investing a lot of time in its discussion. Thus, the 1960 Soviet proposal that colonialism be ended by the simple declaration that all colonies be declared independent by 31 December 1961 received great attention. Though the emerging Third World coalition quickly decided that the Soviets were going too far too fast and mainly attempting to score propaganda points in the Cold War, the whole question of ending colonialism was one very dear to them. Third World states thus took up the item, decided that it should receive lengthy high level attention and then reformulated the original demand to meet their own preferences. The shift was apparent from the Assembly debate, which occurred less along East–West lines than among proponents of different views about how to end colonialism among African, Asian and Latin American states (A/15/PV.925–39, 28 Nov.–7 Dec. 1960). Similarly, Western Europe initiatives on refining the definition of torture and strengthening the minimum standards for treatment of prisoners or for securing better cooperation against aircraft hijackings sparked broad interest because Third World states also felt affected by those problems.

Nor can an individual member of the majority assume that its ideas will receive effective attention. The fates of the Grenadan proposal on UFOs and the Costa Rican proposal to create a UN High Commissioner for Human Rights have been mentioned. Similarly, the Arab proposals for a UN custodian of refugee property located in Israel never received great attention.

As in other political institutions, the majority in the Assembly is sometimes in flux, with the composition changing issue by issue. In the era between the stable two-thirds majorities there was considerably shifting around. Today many issues are inspiring alignments that break out of the Third World majority/West minority pattern that has marked much Assembly activity in the past two decades. The Eastern Timor Question, where part of the Third World supports Indonesia's claim to the territory, but a slightly larger part does not, is one current example. When these ephemeral coalitions appear, demands that might not normally seem to command majority interest may well receive extensive attention.

No matter what majority coalition exists, there is a considerable amount of cooperative agenda construction. All agree that the Assembly is one of the better places to discuss certain global problems like broadcasting from satellites or environmental protection. This is particularly true when they first begin to be perceived as common and seem to lack a natural home in the existing UN structure. The General Assembly can serve as a forum for "consciousness raising", and may even become the creator of the new organizations for handling the problem if the members decide that some form of UN auspices best serves their needs. Later, as new institutions are created or existing ones expanded, Assembly attention decreases and is confined to encouraging the ongoing cooperation or settling broad questions of principle that members want discussed in a political body. This result should not be seen as detracting from the Assembly's role; rather it is a sign of the Assembly's success as a channel for securing new issues a lasting place on the international agenda.

Particularly since the formation of the Third World majority, the General Assembly creates an unusual situation: the existence of a political institution that permits the weak to formulate an alternative agenda for the political system. Few national political systems possess institutions as receptive to demands from the weak. In international relations, the Assembly has affected a major transformation. Traditionally the agenda of international politics has been set by the great powers, with other states coping as best they can and seeking to interest the great powers in their concerns. This was particularly true before the First World War when international politics consisted mainly of politico-military questions. The General Assembly gives weak states a chance to set an agenda and force the strong to pay some attention. Weak states have always been the majority of the Assembly. During the era of the US-led majority this fact was somewhat obscured by alignments of the weak around the strong. Yet its implications were felt even then. The US found it could lead the coalition only if it let the weak members have time for matters they wanted to discuss. Thus even in the early 1950s considerable time was devoted to colonial questions, economic development and rules to restrain the strong in their conduct toward the weak. Since the Third World majority has stabilized, this weak state control has become more apparent. The majority now consists almost entirely of weak states; all the strongest states are in various minorities.

Today weak and strong states are concerned with the same sorts of issues: health of the domestic and global economies, self-protection from all manner of internal and external foes,

management of natural resources, promotion of cooperation in a
wide range of technical and administrative fields and the relations
of states to other actors in the international system. Yet the way
these issues are handled differs depending on where they are
considered. In the Assembly, all issues take on colorations
reflecting the concerns of the weak. Thus, the international
economy means "how can we forge a new international
economic order?" Human right tends to mean "how can we
assure self-determination, an end to racism and decent levels of
economic well-being?" Outside, issues are colored by the concerns of the strong. Thus, civil wars in Central America or
regional attempts at conquest in Southeast Asia take on aspects of
East–West or Sino–Soviet rivalry. International economics tends
to mean "how can the industrial states maintain or improve the
present state of their own and the international economy?" These
differences have encouraged and will continue to encourage
"forum-shopping" by states.

In the agenda-formation phase, then, the Assembly serves as
an open forum where all states may attempt to convert their
demands into issues addressed by the international political
system. Yet conversion of demands into issues is only one step
towards producing outcomes that will satisfy demands. The next
step involves persuading the relevant political institutions to
make a decision directing a distribution or redistribution of
values that will satisfy demands. Decision-making in the General
Assembly is the subject of Chapters 3 and 4.

Chapter Three

Adoption of Decisions

Once a demand receives a place on the Assembly's effective agenda, the decision-making phase begins. Though the decision produced is the most politically significant element of this phase, the ways in which proposals are considered and decisions taken in a political institution have independent significance for both the content of decisions and addressees' attitudes toward them. An institution's rules affect the content of decisions in several ways. The rules specifying the support needed to make a decision set the broad outline of coalition formation by providing the goal each rival coalition must attain if it is to secure its preferences or frustrate those of others. The rules specifying the preliminary steps in consideration before the moment of adoption also influence the formation and success of coalitions by providing or not providing opportunities to impose delay, encourage compromise, or attempt splitting other coalitions by offering amendments or rival proposals. The rules also provide addressees with a standard for assessing the propriety of the decision. Decisions attained by violating the rules or taking advantage of short cuts may not be given as much moral weight as those made in full accordance with the rules. This means that coalitions must not go so far in exploiting opportunities to maximize attainment of their wishes that their maneuvers rob the decision of legitimacy.

The decision-making phase is a contest in which supporters of the demand attempt to move one step closer to creating an effective political outcome by securing a decision that commits the Assembly to the desired distribution (or redistribution) of values. Those backing a particular demand must prevail over both those who oppose any decision on the matter and those who think there should be a different decision. The decision-making phase thus contains many hazards. A proposal may be defeated outright. It may succeed only after so much compromise that the final decision bears faint resemblance to the original proposal. The ideas advanced may be combined with others and this synthesis adopted instead.

The Assembly operates within a horizontal political system marked by institutional decentralization and low moral consensus among the actors in the system. Yet many of its formal rules derive from parliamentary traditions developed in stable national polities which are vertical systems having strong central institutions and a high degree of moral consensus among the actors. This is particularly true of Assembly rules governing formal debate, specifying that each member has one vote and provided that decisions can be made by a majority. Many of the informal practices that now supplement the formal rules also give the Assembly a legislature-like appearance. The large number of loosely instructed delegates often seem more like legislators acting on behalf of their constituents than diplomats instructed by their governments. The regional groups through which so many of the informal consultations and negotiations occur often seem to operate just like parties in a national legislature. Yet the General Assembly enjoys neither the material resources nor the moral legitimacy that would allow it to govern states. This limits the number and weight of Assembly decisions and affects the formal rules and informal practices governing decision-making in many ways.

The formal and informal rules specify in advance how much influence each member has over decisions, the procedures by which proposals will be considered and the amount of support necessary to turn proposals into decisions. They provide the framework within which members compete for support. They also help legitimize whatever decision is made by assuring the members, and others in the wider system served by the political institution, that the decision was properly considered and represents a widely supported distribution of values.

The Assembly has developed two sets of rules for decision-making. The first set, the formal rules written into the UN Charter and the Assembly Rules of Procedure, is majoritarian. The second set, which has developed informally, is consensual. The choice of rule for making decisions shapes the course of debate and negotiation because it determines the amount of support needed to get particular proposals adopted as decisions. The majority rule, which requires less support than the consensus one, is used either when confrontation is sought from the outset or when efforts to reach a consensus fail but a majority has formed and then decides to press ahead anyway. The consensus rule, which requires that virtually all members support or at least acquiesce, is used when supporters believe they need to have the decision accepted as representing a generally agreed rule for relations among states, or to secure the cooperation of others possessing the material resources necessary for implementation of the decision. Though the regional and caucusing groups are always active, and informal negotiations of all sorts are always in progress, their character in specific instances depends greatly on the rule for decisions that has been selected. The origins, development and uses of the majority and consensus rules will be examined in this chapter, while the related rules governing debate and negotiation will be examined in Chapter 4.

Influence of the One-State/One-Vote Rule

All Assembly decisions, whether made by a majority or by consensus, are influenced by the formal rule that each member state has one vote. This rule, which ignores the vast differences of material capability among states, has strong roots in international practice. In the late nineteenth century, when general international conferences began to be organized regularly, prevailing notions of national sovereignty held that all states were formally equal because all were free of legal obligation to obey any external authority. Rather, obligation could stem only from rules that they had explicitly or tacitly accepted. These doctrines meant that the one-state/one-vote rule was combined with a requirement that decisions be made unanimously. In this way, each state had an equal influence over decisions, and none (at least in legal theory) had to submit to decisions it did not accept. The unanimity rule was formally maintained in the League of Nations Covenant, though weakened informally in practice (Burton, 1941, ch. 6). The International Labor Organization made the first formal shift away from unanimity in 1920 by specifying that most decisions of the General Conference could be made by a simple majority.

The United Nations Charter retained the one-state/one-vote rule for the Assembly, but dropped unanimity in favor of decision by a simple or a two-thirds majority. Member states were prepared to accept this because most of the Assembly's decisions are recommendations (Claude, 1971, p. 120). Much governmental and private commentary has criticized the combination of the one-state/one-vote and majority rules as unrealistic in the current international system. Though changing the one-state/one-vote rule has been proposed (debate in A/AC.149/SR.25, 14 June 1971; rejection noted in A/8426, Sept. 1971, Annex IV, para. 136), the fact that change would require amending the UN Charter means it will never occur. Amendments are adopted when accepted by two-thirds of all member states, including all five permanent members of the Security Council (UN Charter, Article 108). Since the losers under any proposal for weighted voting number more than one-third of the members, they could prevent the adoption of any such amendment.

Weighting votes by population appeals to many because it would make voting in the General Assembly conform more closely to the democratic notion of treating each person as equally significant. It will never be adopted, however, because more states would lose than would gain from the change. As Table 3.1 shows, a shift to allocating votes by population would make the Assembly an Asian-dominated body.

Table 3.1   1983 UN membership and population compared

Group	Number of members	% of UN membership	Population (millions)	% of world population
Africa*	51	32	491.20	11
Asia†	40	25	2662.69	58
Latin America	33	21	380.81	8
Eastern Europe	11	7	406.31	9
Western	23	14	662.42	14

*Includes South Africa.   †Includes Israel.
Source: Population estimates for 1983 from *UN Demographic Yearbook 1982*.

This is why Ali Mazrui wrote in 1964:

> and if population were the criteria, many is an African who might in 1962 have settled for eight UN votes answerable to Mr Nehru on the Katanga issue for every vote answerable to Lord Home. A few might even settle for, as it were, two Sukarnos for every De Gaulle on almost every issue discussed in the United Nations since 1962.

All the same, it remains true that in the United Nations, if nowhere else, the African prefers "sovereign equality" (as between states) to "human equality" (as between men).

(1964, p. 513)

Table 3.2 shows that allocating votes by material capability, as measured by contributions to the UN regular budget, would also win little support because losers would again outnumber gainers.

Table 3.2 1983 UN membership and budget contributions compared

Group	% of regular budget	Number of members	% of UN membership
Africa*	1.63	51	32
Asia†	14.96	40	25
Latin America	4.23	33	21
Eastern Europe	16.16	11	7
Western	63.03	23	14

*Includes South Africa.   †Includes Israel.
Source: Scale of assessments from Resolution 37/125.

Informally, however, the consensus rule – like the earlier practice of seeking more than a simple majority – weakens the impact of the one-state/one-vote rule. Both, but particularly the former, require that strong states be included among the supporters of a decision. This reduces the likelihood that weak states will ignore the strong in making decisions, so the one-state/one-vote rule is seldom taken to its logical conclusion. Thus an appreciation of power realities has limited the practical effect of the one-state/one-vote rule.

Even so, the one-state/one-vote rule affects even consensus decisions. The consensus rules can always be set aside in favor of the majoritarian ones. This permits the many weak states to retain a strong influence over decisions. During the era of the US-led coalition, they could threaten to withhold their support unless the United States modified its position or supported their initiatives on other issues. The categories of weak state and stable majority have almost merged under the Third World coalition, and any state or group pressing an initiative knows it must secure widespread support within the Third World if the idea is to win majority backing.

Before a solid majority has formed, minorities have considerable room for political maneuver. Once one has formed, the best a minority can do is express opposition, insist on a vote if the majority keenly desires consensus and promise non-cooperation in implementation. What then happens depends on how much the majority wants consensus for its symbolic value or needs cooperation in implementation. These dynamics will be examined in the discussion of consensus decisions below.

The one-state/one-vote rule is simple in its application but complicated in its implications. The Assembly is not the legislature of a central government able to impose decisions on the various units of global society when efforts at persuasion fail. Rather it is a forum where largely autonomous units of very different size and power meet to negotiate and coordinate. Much, though not all, of a particular state's attitude toward the Assembly and its decisions can be understood by comparing the relative power of the group to which it belongs in and outside the Assembly. Kurt Jacobsen (1970, pp. 241–2) proposed a 2 × 2 matrix, shown in Figure 3.1, which illuminates attitudes nicely.

		Within the Assembly	
		Majority	Minority
Outside the	Strong	a	b
Assembly	Weak	c	d

Figure 3.1   Group power

A group that forms a majority in the Assembly and commands considerable resources outside uses the Assembly mainly to legitimate its action. Whether this puts the Assembly in the position of endorsing the status quo, some reform, major reform, or replacement of current international rules and practices depends on the goals of the coalition. The US-led coalition supported the status quo its leading members had defined in 1944–5, though it also endorsed certain further reforms. The occasional Soviet bloc–Third World grouping is prone to endorse major reform on economic issues and replacement on such questions as colonialism, Palestine and South Africa. This latter coalition has been less successful carrying out decisions because of opponents' strength in some areas (e.g., Palestine) and internal division in others (e.g., economic issues, where the Soviets endorse but put few resources into action and Third World states disagree on the amount of change needed).

Yet even such a strong group may prefer to deal with intra-group issues or disagreements in other fora, such as alliances or regional organizations. In this way, it can hide the extent of disagreement or deal with issues in more congenial gatherings including only the like-minded. Thus, the United States and Western European countries dealt with global issues or some Cold War propaganda in the Assembly, but handled alliance problems and economic adjustments in such fora as NATO and the GATT.

A group with formidable power resources outside but controlling few votes inside has little interest in going to the Assembly since it can do better in bilateral relations and other multilateral fora. If such a group views the Assembly as implacably hostile, it will avoid taking issues there and adopt extremely defensive postures. Though the Soviet bloc is less isolated than it was before 1955, it (or at least the Soviet Union) is still very defensive because it regards international organizations as intruders on sovereignty. Even when such a group sees possibilities for positive results, it will tend to prefer dealing with the issues it deems most important in other fora. Thus the superpowers have been united since 1955 in a determination to deal with intra- and inter-bloc issues outside the Assembly.

A group that commands a majority in the Assembly but few resources outside tries to use the Assembly as a lever for moving the strong. Hence such groups will also seek legitimization of preferences. But this legitimization is aimed less at reducing opposition than at securing support. The success of such efforts depends heavily, therefore, on the degree of difference between the preferences of the weak majority and those of all or some of the strong minorities. If powerful minorities want the status quo or mild reform while the weak majority wants major reform or replacement, the gap will be impossible to bridge. Both sides are apt to end up more stubborn in their views and angrier at one another. If, however, differences revolve upon the amount of reform, there is room for accommodation. Today the differences between the Third World and the West appear irreconcilable on Palestine and certain economic issues, but open to mutual accommodation on most others.

A group that is weak both inside and outside the Assembly is in the worst position of all. Pariah states form one such group. Even where a pariah musters considerably local power, it finds UN diplomacy very uncomfortable and prefers dealing with all issues outside UN auspices whenever possible. It can maintain presence in the Assembly only if strong states are ready to threaten dire action if it is expelled. The United States remains ready to do so for Israel, but not for South Africa. Yet pariahs do not exhaust the category of groups weak both inside and outside the Assembly. Many clusters of states find themselves in the same position on certain issues. Sometimes they curl up defensively, as did the Western Europeans on colonialism in the early 1960s. Sometimes they use this double weakness to carve out a mediator role, as have the Scandinavians. The choice depends on how their preferences compare to those of others, the opportunities presented by fluid alignments or a lack of hardened opinions and the readiness of others to view them as acceptable mediators. Most of the time these doubly weak clusters use the Assembly simply to present their views, though occasionally their ideas attract broad support.

All of this is relevant to decision-making in the Assembly because countries' positions influence their choices of decision-making mode. Those seeking legitimization want as much backing as possible, particularly if they must rely on others to provide the resources for action. Those seeking only to defend their positions need to prevent unfavorable decisions. Failing that, they seek every possible outlet in debate and parliamentary maneuver to present their views. Any group or state having the power to obstruct action in a particular field must be taken into account in any decision about it. This, as discussion of consensus will show, greatly influences Assembly decision-making.

Majority Decisions

In the early sessions, at least two-thirds of the resolutions adopted by the Assembly were put to a formal vote (see Table 3.5), often after various members and groups of members had used some or all of the parliamentary maneuvers allowed by the rules to modify proposals, demonstrate the strength of support for competing ideas, or simply obstruct proceedings. Parliamentary maneuver was particularly sharp during the years 1948–54 because the Soviet bloc pursued obstructionist tactics not only as a defense against United States influence but because of its generally wooden and inflexible diplomatic style under Stalin. With the domestic loosening up after Stalin's death and realization that decolonization and nonalignment offered chances to spread its own influence or at least erode that of the West, Soviet diplomatic style relaxed.

The fracturing of the US-led coalition also created situations where different groups fought hard for their preferred results.

This tendency appeared in the early 1950s on issues of self-determination and decolonization. It also spread to what are now North–South issues of global economics. In the era between stable coalitions, parliamentary maneuver was also important since the fluidity of alignment let many clusters contend for support. On a number of issues, the Latin Americans provided the "swing vote" – sometimes siding with the Afro-Asians and sometimes with the West. The Afro-Asians themselves were driven by divisions between "radicals" and "moderates" that often found expression not only in debate but in rival formulations of decisions.

While the Third World coalition now controls the Assembly when it is united, this unity must often be created and then defended on particular issues. This allows scope for initiatives by other groups and for attempts to split the Third World on particular issues. Though some 60 percent of Assembly decisions are adopted without a formal vote today, the majoritarian rules remain available anytime any member insists upon using them. Since these times tend to be those when disagreement is greatest, the majoritarian rules and the forms of maneuver they permit remain significant to understanding the General Assembly.

The formal, majoritarian decision-making rules allow several forms of preliminary maneuvering aimed at increasing or decreasing the likelihood of a proposal being adopted. The formal definitions of how many votes constitute a majority, or what majority is necessary for a particular decision, permit changing the number of positive votes needed for decision. Several rules permit attempts to substitute other proposals for the one under consideration before a vote is taken. Yet others allow for the modification of proposals before the vote by changes to or deletions from the text.

Determining the Support needed for Decisions

The basic formal rule for General Assembly decisions is established in Article 18 of the UN Charter. It reads:

1. Each member of the General Assembly shall have one vote.

2. Decisions of the General Assembly on important questions shall be made by a two-thirds majority of the members present and voting. These questions shall include: recommendations with respect to the maintenance of international peace

and security, the election of non-permanent members of the Security Council, the election of members of the Trusteeship Council in accordance with paragraph 1(c) of Article 86, the admission of new members to the United Nations, the suspension of the rights and privileges of membership, the expulsion of members, questions relating to the operation of the Trusteeship System, and budgetary questions.

3.   Decisions on other questions, including the determination of additional categories of questions to be decided by a two-thirds majority, shall be made by a majority of the members present and voting.

Two aspects of this provision – definition of the phrase "present and voting" and determination of when a two-thirds majority is necessary for adoption of a decision – permit members to adjust the amount of support needed for a particular decision. The latter is particularly important because there have been many occasions in the Assembly's history when supporters could muster a simple but not a two-thirds majority for their proposal. On these occasions a determination of which majority should be required was actually the decision about whether to adopt the proposal.

Yet the phrase "present and voting" also allows members some leeway. The term "present" is defined, not surprisingly, as being at the meeting when the vote is taken. Here, the only important question is how many members must be represented in the room for the vote to be deemed valid. Before 1945 this never posed any difficulties. The small size of most international conferences together with use of the unanimity rule meant that most participating states were represented at the time of voting. When majoritarian rules were adopted for the General Assembly, however, the situation changed. Without any quorum rule, it would be possible for a vote to be taken when, say, delegates from only one-fourth of the members were present, meaning that on many questions some 13 percent of the members could adopt a decision. To prevent this, Rules 67 and 108 specify that no procedural or substantive decision (A/AC.149/SR.15, 19 May 1971, p.6) can be made unless representatives of a majority of the members are present (the quorum for debates is one-third of the members in plenary and one-fourth in main committees; A/C.6/ 4/SR.151, 4 Oct. 1949; A/26/Supp.26, Doc. A/8426, Sept. 1971, paras. 193–5; A/C.6/26/SR.1299, 3 Dec. 1971, para. 3). This still allows the possibility that a minority of the total membership decides, since 25 percent plus 2 of the members would be a simple majority of those present if a bare quorum was attained. This has seldom occurred in practice; usually delegates of a much larger portion of the membership are present for votes.

Definition of the words "and voting" offers scope for adjusting the amount of support needed for making decisions. General Assembly rules and practices permit five different expressions of opinion on proposals: voting in favor, voting against, abstaining, announcing nonparticipation in the vote and absenting oneself from the meeting (the first three by Rules 87 and 126; the third by an understanding noted in A/18/PV.1266, 6 Nov. 1963, paras, 19–20). If "present and voting" includes all members actually represented at the meeting, the number of affirmative votes needed for adoption is much higher than if abstention and nonparticipation are treated as equivalent to absence. In a 100-member Assembly where all members are represented at the meeting, counting all expressions of opinion as votes means that 51 must vote yes to constitute a simple majority. If, however, abstention and nonparticipation are not counted as "voting", fewer affirmative votes are needed. If 10 members abstain or announce nonparticipation, then 90 are deemed "present and voting", and only 46 affirmative votes are needed to carry the proposal. A similar effect occurs when a two-thirds majority is required. If all 100 are present and all opinions deemed voting, 67 affirmative votes are needed for adoption. If abstention and nonparticipation are not deemed voting, and 10 members choose these options, then two-thirds of the remaining 90, or 60 affirmative votes, are required.

In the League of Nations, abstention was not considered a form of voting, so those who abstained were not counted as "present". In the context of a unanimity rule, and great efforts to ensure that the number of abstentions never rose above three or four, this practice did not greatly affect the amount of support needed to carry a proposal (Burton, 1941, pp. 19–20). The provisional rules of the UN General Assembly permitted abstention, but did not specify its effect for calculating whether the requisite majority had been attained. Yet it soon became apparent that members intended to continue with the League rule despite the different context.

It was clear by the end of the first session that most members felt that abstention should not be counted as "voting" (A/C.1/PV.13, 5 Nov. 1946, pp. 43–6). To ensure that there would be no further misunderstandings on the point, the rules of procedure adopted in 1947 included a provision that "For the purposes of these rules, the phrase 'members present and voting' means members casting an affirmative or a negative vote. Members which abstain from voting are considered as not voting" (this now appears in Rules 86 and 126). Thus, abstention remained what it had been in the League, an expression either of mild reservation or of willingness to accept whatever the majority of those voting decided.

Politically, this definition gives advantages to supporters of any proposal. If they can persuade doubters to abstain rather than vote against, adoption is made easier. Opponents, on the hand, must persuade all doubters to vote against if they are to maximize their chances of defeating a motion.

These implications were clear immediately. In debates about adoption of the rule in 1947, Soviet bloc delegates argued against its adoption. With the Cold War worsening and their isolation in the Assembly becoming apparent, the Soviets had an interest in any rule that would make adoption more difficult. Leading the majority, the Americans were content with the rule. In fact it served their purposes well by allowing followers a way to express reservations without helping defeat a proposal. This provision for "voice" (to borrow from Hirschman, 1970) made "exit" from the coalition less necessary. It has also helped the Third World coalition maintain unity despite strong divisions on particular matters, such as the future of Eastern Timor.

The rule that abstention and nonparticipation do not count as voting also assists the building of *ad hoc* majorities. Anything that reduces the number of affirmative votes needed for a decision makes it easier to collect enough votes here and there. Thus, it also contributed to the fluidity of alignment that marked the Assembly between 1955 and 1964, and surprises those relying on a two-camp "South and East versus West" image of the Assembly today. It is less important for stable majorities dealing with issues on which all members are united; at these times sufficient affirmative votes would be available no matter how abstention and nonparticipation were defined.

Abstention is widespread. Edvard Hambro noted more than a decade ago that

> The habit has insinuated itself into the practice of the United Nations of registering disagreement with a proposal only by abstaining. The casting of a negative vote is today interpreted as such a strong demonstration that it might very nearly be considered an offense against good manners.
>
> (Hambro, 1972, p. 295)

Allowing for a Westerner's disenchantment with an Assembly even then run by the Third World, there is a core of truth in this observation. Today abstention can mean mild doubt, disinclination to go on record as supporting or opposing some idea, lack of timely instructions from home, cross-pressures resulting from the fact that friendly states are not all taking the same view, or strong opposition to some part of what would be an acceptable decision without it. The precise meaning of any abstention becomes clear only when an explanation of vote is offered afterward.

The general rule that abstentions do not count as votes has saved many proposals from defeat, particularly when a two-thirds majority has been necessary for adoption. In 1946, for instance, Resolution 44 (I) urging South Africa to negotiate with India over problems stemming from the application of South African racial laws to people of Indian origin would not have been adopted if the opposite rule had been in effect, since the vote was 32 in favor, 15 opposed and 7 abstaining (A/Jt.C.1&6/SR.6, 30 Nov. 1946, p. 51; A/1/PV.52, 8 Dec. 1946, p. 161). In 1979 it saved a proposal that needed only a simple majority when a resolution calling for a UN-supervised plebiscite to determine whether the inhabitants of Eastern Timor wished to join Indonesia or form an independent state was adopted by a vote of 61 in favor, 31 opposed and 45 abstaining (A/34/PV.75, 21 Nov. 1979, p. 31).

The problem of determining when decisions must be adopted by a two-thirds majority provides a more fertile field for political manipulation. Unlike determining how to count abstentions, which had to be settled permanently one way or the other, the breadth of definitions used to identify decisions needing a two-thirds majority allows the issue to be raised continually either to increase or to decrease the number of affirmative votes needed. This issue can be raised only in the plenary, since main committee votes are formally only decisions to recommend favorable action and always adopted by a simple majority. When a proposal has been considered in committee, plenary arguments about whether a two-thirds or a simple majority is required follow a preliminary test of strength giving cues to supporters and opponents alike.

A literal reading of Article 18(3) of the Charter suggests that the Assembly can decide to expand the range of decisions requiring a two-thirds majority only by defining whole categories of questions. However, the Assembly has always treated these choices on an *ad hoc*, case-by-case basis. Sometimes debate centers on arguments about how the particular question did or did not fall within the categories defined in Article 18(2). Sometimes it centers on whether the particular proposal is or is not intrinsically important. In many cases choices have been made without any discussion of the reasons (*UN Repertoire*, 1:573–88; *UN Repertoire*, Supp. 1, 1: 198–203; *UN Repertoire*, Supp. 2, 2: 198; and UN Repertoire, Supp. 3, 1: 391–4).

Proposals that adoption of some decision requires a two-thirds majority generally arise when opponents believe they cannot muster a majority against the idea but can raise a blocking third. Since, however, the decision about whether a simple or a two-thirds majority is required is itself made by a simple majority, opponents must persuade some supporters (probably the more lukewarm ones) that the decision is "important". Supporters of the proposal under consideration know what the opponents are trying to do, so they work hard to prevent defections on the preliminary question. Even so, there have been occasions when opponents have won over enough support to get a question defined as important and have then defeated a proposal by raising a blocking third.

In many cases, this happens because some of the supporters are tied by alliance, friendship, or sense of specific obligation to a powerful opponent. Between 1961 and 1971 the United States was able to prevent the seating of People's Republic of China delegates in this way. Each year the United States would argue that the decision about seating Chinese delegates was "important" on a variety of grounds, particularly the fact that since seating Peking's delegates would mean expelling Taipei's, the act would amount to expelling a member. A number of US allies, like Britain and (after 1964) France, reconciled their recognition of the Peking government with their alliance ties to the United States by going along with United States arguments that the decision was "important". They were then able to express their recognition policy by voting in favor of seating Peking's delegation, confident that the United States and other countries refusing to recognize the Peking government would raise a blocking third (e.g., A/25/PV.1913, 20 Nov. 1970, para. 74). In the late 1960s the excesses of the 'Great Proletarian Cultural Revolution" temporarily dampened many governments' enthusiasm for seating Peking's delegation. Some may then have supported the US government's maneuver as a way to combine outward support with avoidance of actually having to deal with the People's Republic as a UN member. Only when the United States itself shifted policy and began public contacts with the Peking government in 1971 did this maneuver fail. That year the

Assembly decided that a simple majority would suffice and then seated Peking's delegation while excluding Taipei's.

In some cases many members can be persuaded that a proposal relates to an "important" question whatever their views on the proposal itself. Such considerations may have lain behind a number of choices that doomed proposals having majority support. In 1952 a decision that resolution of the Palestine Question was "important", on grounds that it related to maintaining international peace and security, prevented adoption of any resolution because no proposal was able to attract the support of two-thirds of the members (A/7/PV.406, 18 Dec. 1952, paras. 64–73). In 1961 a proposal to enlarge the UN Conciliation Commission for Palestine and give it a strong mandate to protect the rights of Palestinian refugees failed for the same reason (A/16/PV.1068, 20 Dec. 1961, paras. 43–4).

Conversely, a majority unsure of its ability to muster two-thirds of those voting will resist attempts to require the qualified majority. Sometimes this requires defining a question that might seem to be included in the Article 18(2) list as something else that is not on the list. In 1953 Denmark proposed that any decisions relating to defining or applying the concept of self-determination required a two-thirds majority. The Danes argued that this had been the constant practice of the Assembly and that the matter was intrinsically important. Most members decided, however, that the opposing Mexican arguments were better founded. The Mexicans read Article 18(2) narrowly and concluded that since questions of self-determination did not come under those listed in any way – even as an aspect of the functioning of the Trusteeship System – a simple majority would suffice. This decision saved Resolution 742 (VIII), which affirmed that the General Assembly, not the metropole, decides when a territory has attained self-governing status for purposes of Chapter IX of the Charter, contained the first expression of preference for independence over all other forms of self-government, asserted that colonial powers had a duty to submit information to the UN about all colonies whether or not Trust Territories, and adopted a list of conditions as guidelines for determining whether a particular territory was or was not self-governing (A/8/PV.459, 27 Nov. 1953, paras. 6–30, 32–4, 36).

In 1965 the West failed to secure agreement that a two-thirds majority would be necessary to adopt a resolution calling on colonial powers to dismantle all military bases in their colonies. Western delegations argued that this was an important question because it constituted a recommendation about security matters.

Third World delegations rejected such ideas, insisting that a simple majority was competent to pass any resolution dealing with any aspect of colonialism (A/20/PV.1405, 20 Dec. 1956, paras. 1–170). Despite controlling more than two-thirds of the votes, the Third World coalition has continued to narrow the range of "important questions". In 1978 it rejected a US motion that an Iraqi proposal to recommend an embargo on sales of nuclear and military equipment to Israel constituted such a question. This meant implicit rejection of arguments that the recommendation involved the maintenance of international peace and security in a particular case (A/33/PV.84, 14 Dec. 1978, paras. 183–215).

The Assembly's *ad hoc* approach to determining when decisions require a two-thirds majority provides a field for continuing political maneuver. Arguments about the majority to be required are most likely to arise when alignments are in flux or particular issues inspire serious divisions of opinion

Obviously, such maneuvers make no difference when it is clear there is already a two-thirds majority behind some proposal. Yet even on those occasions the question might arise because supporters or opponents insist the decision requires the higher majority. Supporters might insist on the larger majority because they believe the Charter requires it, a consideration that weighs heavily with many of the Western European and Latin American states. Supporters might also want the larger majority to ensure that potentially divisive decisions have wide backing, particularly when states will be asked to contribute substantial resources to some activity.

Finally, members of a two-thirds majority might be anticipating the day when it has split on an issue and are trying to create precedents that will make the adoption of uncongenial decisions more difficult. Such a calculation no doubt lay behind Western European support of the Danish stand on self-determination questions in 1953. However, this is true only when the crumbling majority can see a particular replacement forming. In the mid 1950s leaders of the US-led majority needed little imagination to see that either an Afro-Asian coalition with Soviet bloc backing or an all Third World coalition of African, Asian and Latin American states would soon control two-thirds of the votes. Leaders of the Third World coalition and, within it, of the Nonaligned Movement see their coalition crumbling on some issues but cannot see the shape of any alternative stable alignment. They can prolong their influence in the Assembly by treating as many questions as possible under the simple majority rule, even if this means ignoring clear Charter requirements. In this way, their ability to control the Assembly's decisions would not be weakened by a defection of part of the current coalition.

More often opponents of a proposition will insist on defining it as affecting an "important question". Opponents, whether an *ad hoc* coalition or a permanent minority bloc, prefer the two-thirds rule because it gives them greater opportunities to prevent a decision.

Substituting Other Proposals

In the early sessions, main committees usually received more than one draft resolution on a particular question. With the development of informal consultations, two patterns have developed. If efforts to write a generally acceptable proposal succeed, then only one draft is presented. However, informal consultations sometimes fail to produce a single draft, leaving the main committee or the plenary to choose among rival formulations.

At first Assembly practice followed the League of Nations rule that proposals be voted upon in "logical order"; that is, the one proposing the most far-reaching change should be voted on first, then the one making the second largest change, etc. Though having the advantage of discovering quickly how far-reaching a change members were willing to accept, this rule had the disadvantage of inspiring long discussions about which proposal implied the largest change. The General Assembly soon found the rule unworkable, and by the end of the first session had adopted the far simpler rule of voting on proposals in the order in which they had been submitted. In 1947 the Assembly formally adopted the change, which has been its practice ever since.

The use of chronological order means that whoever gets a written draft to the Secretariat first (definition of "submission" in A/C.1/3/SR.149, 5 Oct. 1948, p. 75; A/SPC/18/SR.405, 12 Nov. 1963, pp. 155–7; A/C.1/33/PV.51, 27 Nov. 1978, p. 2) will have it voted upon first. This pulls delegates two ways, because further consultations with others may improve the proposal's chances by attracting more support. When it seems likely that competing proposals will be offered, delegates must decide whether an early vote is more important than an extra chance to refine the proposal.

The use of chronological order also means that later proposals consolidating features of two or more earlier ones will be voted upon after any of the initial proposals not withdrawn by their sponsors. Most of the time this makes little difference since a carefully negotiated consolidated draft is likely to have more support than any other proposal before the meeting. If, however, supporters of the consolidated draft still fear that some other draft might be adopted instead, they can seek priority for their new draft.

The Assembly's rules on order of voting leave open two areas of political maneuver. Rules 91 and 131 permit the plenary or a main committee to change the order in which they will vote on proposals. The same rules also provide that the plenary or a main committee "may, after each vote on a proposal, decide whether to vote on the next proposal." In addition, Rules 74 and 116, which permit motions to adjourn debate on a particular matter have been used to head off voting at least since 1962 (e.g., A/C.1/17/SR.1245, 5 Oct. 1962, paras. 31–41; A/C.6/23/SR.1045, 21 Oct. 1968, paras. 25–37; A/38/PV.34, 23 Oct. 1983, p. 37).

Changes of the order in which proposals are voted upon occur: (1) in certain routine cases, (2) when informal consultations show that most members prefer some order other than the strictly chronological, or (3) when a simple majority agrees to a motion changing the normal order. The routine practices enjoy general acceptance. Since 1947 the Second Committee has sorted the various proposals inspired by parts of the Economic and Social Council's report and voted on all proposals on each topic, using chronological order within topics, before moving to the next (A/C.2/2/SR.42, 11 Oct. 1947, p. 56; A/C.2/3/SR.64, 25 Oct. 1948, pp. 102, 108). In Fifth Committee consideration of the budget, priority is usually given to the proposals from the Advisory Committee on Administrative and Budgetary Questions over proposals from individual delegations (as explained in A/C.5/33/SR.70, 16 Jan. 1979, paras. 36–42). This allows for consideration of the proposals from specialists who have scrutinized the entire budget before taking those of delegations reacting only to some part of it. As other main committees have shifted toward debating groups of related items together, they have emulated the Second Committee and voted on sets of proposals by topic using chronological order within each set (e.g., A/C.1/33/PV.51, 27 Nov. 1978, p. 2). Committees dealing with large numbers of proposals sometimes decide to take up those proposals likely to be adopted by consensus first, then deal with the rest organized by topic (e.g., A/C.1/38/PV.32, 15 Nov. 1983, pp. 28–9, dealing with sixty-eight drafts on the various disarmament items on the agenda).

Individual motions to change the order of voting are geared to improving the chances that one draft is adopted rather than another. Since such motions must be proposed and voted upon before any of the drafts that would be affected are put to a vote (discussed in A/C.1/11/PV.846, 13 Feb. 1957, paras. 10–39), they also serve as a preliminary test of strength between sponsors of rival drafts. The adoption of such a motion has often inspired supporters of rival drafts to withdraw theirs (e.g., A/C.1/26/PV.1857, 17 Dec. 1971, pp. 8–9) rather than see them defeated after the first is adopted. Despite the intensity with which rival proposals are often advocated, motions to change the order of voting are not very numerous, and many reflect a general agreement to change the order on a particular set of drafts. In no session has their number exceeded 20, and most sessions feature less than 10. As Table 3.3 shows, at least half of these motions were accepted by consensus, rejected by consensus, or withdrawn in any session.

The reasons for the rarity of these motions, particularly in recent years, are quite simple. First, the growth of informal consultations has reduced the number of proposals submitted formally. On many issues, there is either a single proposal or else a set of proposals that complement rather than contradict one another. Second, a stable majority does not need to change the order of voting to secure the decisions it wants. Assuming it has a clear line and can hold together, a stable majority can reject or accept proposals no matter the order in which they are raised. Such motions are made when members are uncertain how the vote will go.

A decision not to vote on a proposal means its defeat. At the very least, such decisions allow a majority to deny a minority the chance to register its views and demonstrate its strength in a formal vote. This can be particularly frustrating to a minority hoping to show that its ideas have more support now than in the past. On occasion a decision to dispense with further voting means nonadoption of a proposal that might have secured majority support. While the Assembly is usually willing to adopt several decisions on one question, even if they are somewhat contradictory, there are occasions when a majority agrees that adopting more than one decision will create unnecessary confusion or lend support to undesirable notions.

One such occasion arose during the 1967 discussion of the problems facing Palestinian refugees. The Special Political Committee recommended three draft resolutions to the plenary. The first, adopted by a vote of 99 to 0 with 2 abstentions, focused on general administrative and financial problems of the UN's refugee relief operations. The second, adopted by a vote of 102 to 0 with 1 abstention, focused on the need for aid to people displaced by the 1967 War. The third, an Arab proposal adopted by a vote of 42 to 38 with 24 abstentions, provided for appointment of a UN custodian for refugee property in Israel, an idea Israel vehemently opposed as constituting intervention in its domestic affairs and a derogation of its sovereignty (A/SPC/22/SR.594, 16 Dec. 1967, paras. 6–7). In plenary the first two were adopted by similarly wide margins. Before the third could be brought to a vote, the Assembly accepted a Nigerian motion to dispense with further voting (A/22/PV.1640, 19 Dec. 1967, paras. 4–6). In this way, a number of Third World states, particularly the more moderate segment of the African group, were able to help prevent adoption of a resolution Israel and the West opposed without having to go on record as voting against their fellow Third World states. This result told the Arabs that if they hoped for African support for other ideas on Palestine, they would have to work harder at winning it. They appear to have succeeded in this because later resolutions affirming the right of the Palestinian people to self-determination and accepting the PLO as their authentic representative did win widespread African support (see roll call votes on Resolutions 3236 and 3237 [XXIX] in A/29/PV.2296, 22 Nov. 1974, pp. 46, 51).

Since using motions to adjourn debate as a way to head off votes rests on an informal interpretation of Rules 74 and 116, the success of such maneuvers depends heavily on others' tolerance. In 1982 the Belgian delegate attempted to head off voting on an amendment to a draft that would have toughened condemnation of Chile's human rights policy. After considerable discussion in which various delegates offered divergent interpretations of the procedural niceties involved, the plenary decided that the Belgian motion was out of order by a vote of 65 to 53 with 19 abstentions (A/37/PV.110, pp. 133–48).

One other way of challenging whole decisions should be mentioned: their subsequent cancellation or revision by other decisions. Successive sessions of the Assembly, just like successive sessions of a national legislature, are always modifying resolutions adopted earlier, usually in the direction of greater intensity but occasionally in limiting fashion. Thus, resolutions of the late 1960s endorsing armed struggle against colonial or racist regimes spoke generally of national liberation movements. In 1973 more cautious minds had gotten to work, and the endorsement was limited to groups recognized by the OAU.

The formal Assembly rules also permit a quicker challenge to decisions through reconsideration. Rules 81 and 123 provide that "When a proposal has been adopted or rejected, it may not be reconsidered at the same session unless the meeting, by a two-thirds majority of those present and voting, so decides." The rule has seldom been applied to a substantive decision since its adoption in 1947 (an earlier case appears in A/C.5/SR.75, 24 Oct. 1947, pp. 231–4, and SR.86 4 Nov. 1947, p. 336). Its existence did help other delegates persuade the Jordanians to withdraw a request that the vote on a draft proposing creation of a University of Jerusalem for Palestinian refugees be reopened on grounds that Jordan was still organizing informal consultations when the initial vote was taken (A/SPC/36/SR.46, 30 Nov. 1981, paras. 1–17). The rule has been used mostly to prevent changes in committee work schedules. Despite some examples to the contrary (A/C.3/13/SR.843, 6 Oct. 1958, paras. 35–44; A/C.1/17/SR.1245, 5 Oct. 1962, paras. 20–37), it is now agreed that decisions to change the schedule constitute reconsideration (e.g., A/C.2/15/SR.650, 19 Oct. 1960, paras. 45–50; A/SPC/20/SR.460, 18 Nov. 1965, paras. 1–18).

Modifying Proposals

Proposals can be modified significantly before they are put to a vote. The formal Assembly rules permit three types of modification: amendments to change certain parts of the proposal, motions to change the proposal by deleting certain parts and requests for separate votes on certain parts of the proposal. The last two may lead to the same result, the dropping of a particular provision, but have distinct political uses. Today these formal mechanisms tend to be last resorts. The informal negotiations that precede the submission of proposals usually lead to revisions meeting the objections of many members. Though not the case in the early sessions, when the art of informal negotiation had not developed very far, today the use of formal modification procedures indicates that consensus is not being sought or that an effort to reach consensus has broken down.

The General Assembly is no exception to the parliamentary tradition than any non-sponsoring member may suggest modifications to a proposal. Following the common tradition, Rules 90 and 130 provide that amendments are put to a vote before the proposal to which they refer. When the plenary considers proposals recommended by a main committee, all amendments must be put to a vote because the draft is considered the work of the committee rather than of particular delegations (explained in

A/9/PV.514, 17 Dec. 1954, paras. 228–40). When the plenary or a main committee considers proposals submitted directly by members, amendments need not be put to a vote when the sponsors of the proposal to which they refer agree to incorporate them. An objector may, however, request a separate vote on the part of the draft affected by the amendment (e.g., A/C.4/14/ SR.960, pp. 452–53). Many amendments are "friendly", seeking only to reword a proposal so that it translates more easily (the Assembly has six working languages: Arabic, Chinese, English, French, Russian and Spanish), does not cause offense or misunderstanding in other cultures, reads better, or attracts wider support. In the 1950s and 1960s many such amendments were offered and accepted in the course of formal meetings. Today they are handled in the informal negotiations though may still occur in formal meetings if they represent last-minute ideas or attempts either to head off or to heighten a confrontation.

If the sponsors of the proposal do not accept an amendment, then it is put to a vote. Here the formal rules raise two tactical problems for delegations. First, they provide that amendments will be taken in "logical order", starting with that one furthest removed from the main proposal. This make the chronological order of submission in writing irrelevant. A delegation seeking priority for its ideas must try to make a great change. However, it cannot take this desire for a change too far. Rules 90 and 130 define an amendment as something that "merely adds to, deletes from, or revises part of the proposal." An amendment seeking too much of a change may be defined as a competing proposal and, since it is invariably submitted later than the proposal it seeks to modify, be put to the vote later.

Use of logical order has often sparked long discussions about which amendments should be voted upon first. In general an amendment that would delete part of a proposal is treated as further removed than one that would substitute new language for a provision already in it. Amendments that would add new provisions appear to be treated as least furthest removed. Sometimes arguments are avoided by treating some amendments as subamendments to others.

The formal rules do not provide for subamendments, but by custom they are treated in the same way as amendments, being voted in logical order and taken up before the amendment to which they apply. For example, when the Third Committee was considering the draft Convention on the Non-Applicability of Statutory Limitations to War Crimes and Crimes Against Humanity, some members proposed including apartheid in the list of crimes covered. Offering a subamendment including the idea ensured it was voted upon first, and adopted (A/C.3/23/ SR.1567, 10 Oct. 1968, paras. 13–19; voting in A/C.3/23/ SR.1568, 10 Oct. 1968, para. 41). Politically, having an amendment treated as a subamendment can get a delegation the priority it seeks for consideration of its ideas. Yet it has limited consequences. Adoption of a subamendment modifies, but never defeats, an amendment. Adoption of the same text as a rival amendment might entail defeat because Rules 90 and 130 provide that when "the adoption of one amendment necessarily implies the rejection of another amendment, the latter amendment shall not be put to a vote". This rule was adopted in 1949 (A/C.6/4/ SR.158, 11 Oct. 1949, paras. 10–1), in hopes of reducing the amount of time spent voting and limiting minority ability to obstruct by offering long strings of similar amendments. When it is unclear whether one amendment cancels another, the matter can be settled either by a vote rejecting the other amendment or by a motion to dispense with voting on further amendments.

Amendments can be used to change a proposal a bit, or to distort it so much that it means the opposite of what the original sponsors intended. In 1976 Israel, departing from some fifteen years' practice of not offering proposals on the question, offered a proposal on the situation in the Middle East. India, Malta, Senegal, Sri Lanka and Yugoslavia then introduced a set of amendments to include in the Israeli draft all the provisions relating to PLO participation in the Geneva Conference and Israeli withdrawal from lands occupied in 1967 that Israel was known to oppose. Since these changes seemed likely to be adopted and would have made the Israeli draft almost identical to the Arab-sponsored rival drafts, the Israelis withdrew it (A/31/ PV.89–90, 6 Dec. 1976, and PV.95, 9 Dec. 1976, para. 27; texts in A/31/Annex 29, Docs. A/31/L.24–7).

Though the formal rules allow for amendments seeking to delete any part of a proposal – anything from whole paragraphs to single words – the same result can be accomplished by requests for a separate vote on parts of a proposal. Using motions to vote on parts has two advantages over amendments to delete. First, an amendment to delete can be debated at length, but Rules 89 and 129 provide that a motion to vote on parts can be discussed by only two delegates favoring the separate vote and two opposing. Second, adoption of an amendment to delete requires a larger majority. Deletion must be supported by a simple majority in committee and a simple or two-thirds majority in plenary (depending on whether the motion applies to an "important" question). The part of a proposal or amendment affected by a request for a separate vote will be dropped unless the relevant majority votes to maintain it. In cases where the simple majority rule applies, this does not greatly affect the total needed for deletion. When the two-thirds rule applies, it means that one-third plus one of the members can drop a provision on a separate vote, but two-thirds would be necessary to drop it on an amendment to delete (as demonstrated by maneuvering on US amendments to a resolution on apartheid in A/39/PV.98–99, 14 Dec. 1984). Hence, requests for votes on parts are the preferred tactic.

Requests for separate votes on parts of proposals are a common feature of Assembly proceedings, ranging from 40 to 130 a session as noted in Table 3.3. Most are accepted without demur. When objections are raised, they are usually defeated. Such requests serve any of several purposes: altering the content of a proposal before it is adopted, indicating different degrees of support or opposition to parts of a proposal, or simply delaying proceedings.

Many proposals have been altered by successful deletions of parts on separate votes. In 1969 a Costa Rican motion led to a vote deleting the words "neo-nazi" from a description of intolerance-breeding movements. This permitted the Declaration on Measures against Intolerance to be read as condemning all forms, not just those associated with right-wing political movements as the Soviet bloc wanted (A/24/PV.1829, 11 Dec. 1976, p. 13; a similar motion had failed in committee on the close vote of 17 to delete, 18 to retain, with 11 abstentions, A/C.3/24/SR.1712, 24 Nov. 1969, p. 361). A vote to delete the words "and expansionism" in the eighth preambular paragraph to the Declaration on Elimination of Racism showed that the Assembly was not ready in 1969 to equate Zionism with racism (A/C.3/18/SR.1225, 9 Oct. 1963, p. 58).

In most cases, and particularly when stable two-thirds majorities exist, votes on parts of a draft do not affect their fate. Yet motions for separate votes may be made so that delegations can indicate different opinions on various parts of the draft before them. Often this involves showing that a delegation had objections to only one part though it will ultimately abstain on the whole resolution. Several Western delegations used this device in 1961 to object to a paragraph in the draft on activities of the United Nations Special Fund calling for it to consider establishing a service to help developing countries find the most appropriate sources of foreign aid (A/C.2/16/SR.777, 6 Dec.

Table 3.3 Motions to Change the Order of Voting

Session	Adopt by consensus	Adopt by vote	Reject by vote	Reject by consensus	Withdrawn	Total
2nd	6	2	1	1	0	10
4th	8	3	6	2	0	19
6th	9	2	4	1	1	17
8th	0	6	6	0	0	12
10th	0	1	1	0	1	3
12th	2	2	1	2	1	8
14th	4	2	1	0	2	9
16th	2	6	1	0	1	10
18th	3	0	2	0	0	5
20th	3	2	0	0	0	5
22nd	3	1	1	1	0	6
24th	1	2	2	0	0	5
26th	6	1	2	1	1	11
28th	1	0	0	1	0	2
30th	0	1	3	2	1	7
32nd	3	0	0	0	1	4
34th	0	4	0	0	1	5
36th	1	0	1	1	0	3
38th	1	0	0	0	0	1

(*Note:* this includes both motions to change the order of voting and arguments about whether an amendment should be defined instead as a rival proposal.)

Source: General Assembly Official Records of plenary and main committee meetings in sessions indicated.

1961, p. 344; texts in A/16/Annex 22, Doc. A/5058, para. 38). Many delegations indicated reservations about the second sentence in draft Article 24 of the International Covenant on Civil and Political Rights in the same manner. The whole paragraph read:

> All persons are equal before the law and are entitled without any discrimination to equal protection of the law. In this respect, the law shall prohibit any discrimination and guarantee to all persons equal and effective protection against discrimination on any ground such as race, colour, sex, language, religion, political or other opinion, national or social status, property, birth, or other status.

The first sentence was adopted by a vote of 72 to 0 with 4 abstentions, the second by a vote of 57 to 2 with 17 abstentions, and the whole article by a vote 72 to 0 with 5 abstentions (A/C.3/16/SR.1102, 13 Nov. 1961, p. 211).

Occasionally a separate vote allows a delegation to indicate that it supports some idea while rejecting the proposal as a whole. In 1963 the Soviets indicated support for the Committee of 24 and mediation efforts in Oman by voting in favor of specific budget lines relating to them while rejecting the section of the budget in which they appeared because the USSR objected to the inclusion of funds for special missions relating to the Congo operation (A/C.5/18/SR.1059, 16 Dec. 1963, paras. 4–6). Similarly, a number of delegations indicated acceptance of the idea that states should settle their disputes through peaceful means by voting in favor of paragraph 3 while voting against the whole of a Soviet draft condemning "preparations for a new world war" directed against the West (A/4/PV.262,1 Dec. 1949, p. 438). This practice is so widespread that even a delegation in favor of retaining a particular part may request a separate vote on it (A/C.1/24/PV/1709, p. 11, rejecting the argument that only delegations opposed may make such a request).

Finally, requests for separate votes may simply stem from a desire to impose delay, secure a long series of rejections and then make loud complaints about the operation of "automatic majorities". The United States has not used this particular device, but the Soviet Union used it quite frequently in the early sessions – on one occasion calling for votes on eighteen different parts of a single resolution (Hovet, 1960, p. 21).

Both permitting separate votes on pieces of proposals ranging in size from several paragraphs to single words and permitting the prevention of such votes by a simple majority have important political ramifications whenever alignments on a proposal are unclear. Separate votes are a means by which individual delegations can indicate specifically those parts of a proposal they oppose the most. Second, a determined minority can use separate votes to modify proposals if the majority behind them is not solid on the point they are challenging. Preventing separate votes is a way of keeping the proposal intact. This maneuver has greatest importance in plenary when a two-thirds majority is needed for adoption. A wobbly majority can assure that the compromise it has worked out remains undisturbed by refusing to grant requests for separate votes. As Robert O. Keohane noted in the mid-1960s:

Preventing a vote on parts may permit a cohesive majority or near-majority to impose its will and still emerge with a final resolution that is opposed by a few states. This result occurs because many delegations that oppose particular parts of a resolution may be reluctant to oppose the entire measure because of the universally-accepted shibboleths that compose its major portion. Thus, the parliamentary battle in the General Assembly ... often takes the form of an elaborate ritual in which supporters of a resolution attempt to bury controversial passages in layers of rhetoric to which few states can object and then manipulate procedure so that the resolution must be adopted *in toto*. After the resolution has been safely adopted, the controversial passages are sure to be resurrected by their sponsors.

(Keohane, 1967, p.233)

A stable majority, particularly one numbering at least two-thirds of the members, can easily protect its proposals from modification by separate votes on parts. It need not reject the request for a separate vote because it can be confident of the result. This is seen in the closer analysis of votes to deny such requests shown in Table 3.4. Relatively few denials have occurred in situations where the alignments on a proposal followed strictly along stable majority/other members lines. Most have occurred when an *ad hoc* majority on a particular issue needed to protect itself from defections. Another increase occurred between 1960 and 1964 when infighting among fluid coalitions was particularly intense.

In the plenary, votes on amendments and separate votes on parts have a further complication. Since 1949 Rule 84 has provided that

Decisions in the General Assembly on amendments to proposals relating to important questions, and on parts of such proposals put to the vote separately, shall be made by a two-thirds majority of the Members present and voting.

This means that arguments about the majority needed for the adoption of a decision can be applied to the adoption of amendments and parts as well. This makes it more difficult to adopt amendments and easier to delete provisions, favoring the elimination of existing provisions over the substitution or addition of new ones. More than in committee, therefore, plenary consideration of "important" questions is influenced by the draft or drafts before the meeting. In 1961 the two-thirds rule prevented the

Table 3.4   Requests for Votes on Parts

Session	Requests	Denied	Denied by stable majority
2nd	53	5	1
4th	97	4	0
6th	128	4	1
8th	89	5	0
10th	64	2	1
12th	61	6	n.a.
14th	110	5	n.a.
16th	91	15	n.a.
18th	48	7	n.a.
20th	82	3	1
22nd	72	4	0
24th	123	5	1
26th	71	4	0
28th	48	4	0
30th	38	2	1
32nd	19	2	0
34th	59	1	0
36th	32	0	0
38th	32	0	0

Source: General Assembly Official Records of plenary and main committee meetings in sessions indicated.

adoption of amendments to a resolution on aid to Palestinian refugees that would have given the UN Conciliation Commission for Palestine an explicit mandate to protect Palestinian property rights, shifting its character away from mediator to advocate (A/16/PV.1086, 20 Dec. 1961, pp.1146–7). Not until 1975 was a UN body, the Committee on the Exercise of the Inalienable Rights of the Palestinian People, created to advance the Palestinian cause (Resolution 3376 [XXX]). In 1960 and 1961 decisions that resolutions contemplating the recommendation of sanctions against South Africa needed a two-thirds majority for adoption led to the deletion of all passages referring to sanctions on separate votes (A/15/PV.981, 13 April 1961, paras. 123–4; A/16/PV.1067, 28 Nov. 1961, para. 105). This proved only a short respite for South Africa however. In 1962 the Assembly decided that separate votes would not be taken, which assured that the recommendations for sanctions were adopted (A/17/PV.1165, 6 Nov. 1962, paras. 25–33).

Consensus Decisions

The consensus rule is simply the latest development in a long Assembly tradition of seeking wide agreement on many questions. Habits developed under the unanimity rule, and the traditional international law doctrine that rules are effective only when they have the express or tacit consent of states, both kept the Assembly from going too far in a majoritarian direction. Though, as shown in Table 3.5, voting was the normal method of making decisions before 1964, only twice were more than 2 percent of the resolutions adopted by a simple majority in any session.

Table 3.5 Adoption of Assembly resolutions, 1946–63

Session	Total*	Without a vote†	Unanimous‡	Two-thirds majority	Simple majority
1st	113	89 (78.8)	4 (3.5)	19 (16.8)	1 (0.9)
2nd	81	47 (58.0)	1 (1.2)	32 (39.5)	1 (1.2)
3rd	129	52 (40.3)	3 (2.3)	71 (55.0)	3 (2.3)
4th	108	23 (21.3)	10 (9.3)	75 (69.4)	0 (0.0)
5th	144	29 (20.1)	10 (6.9)	103 (71.5)	2 (1.4)
6th	121	19 (15.7)	7 (5.8)	92 (76.0)	3 (2.4)
7th	122	27 (22.1)	2 (1.6)	92 (75.4)	1 (0.8)
8th	106	30 (28.3)	0 (0.0)	75 (68.8)	1 (0.9)
9th	108	27 (25.0)	1 (0.9)	80 (74.1)	0 (0.0)
10th	93	37 (39.8)	2 (2.2)	54 (58.1)	0 (0.0)
11th	131	41 (31.3)	1 (0.7)	88 (67.2)	1 (0.8)
12th	109	42 (38.5)	3 (2.8)	62 (59.9)	2 (1.8)
13th	126	52 (41.3)	3 (2.4)	69 (54.8)	2 (1.6)
14th	128	43 (33.6)	9 (7.0)	75 (58.6)	1 (0.8)
15th	148	68 (45.9)	14 (9.5)	65 (43.9)	1 (0.7)
16th	130	68 (52.3)	6 (4.6)	55 (42.3)	1 (0.8)
17th	131	67 (51.1)	9 (6.9)	55 (42.0)	0 (0.0)
18th	125	71 (56.8)	2 (1.6)	52 (41.6)	0 (0.0)

(*Note:* percentages shown in brackets.)

*Totals here are larger than official UN figures because resolutions distinguished by a letter (e.g., 1191A and 1191B) are counted separately.

†Resolutions listed as adopted without a vote or unanimously.

‡Resolutions adopted on a vote in which there were no negatives or abstentions.

Source: Djonovich, 1973–8, "Numerical Tables of Votes."

Dispensing with a formal vote is an old Assembly practice. Except in the period 1949–54 (the height of the Cold War), at least one-third of Assembly decisions were made in this way. The shift to consensus thus was not the adoption of a completely new practice, but represented a more precise explanation of and rationale for an existing one.

This evolution was encouraged or assisted by a number of developments. The rise of regional and other groups as vehicles for negotiation and consultation made wider informal discussion possible. Increasing membership and agenda led many members to accept informal negotiations and wider pre-submission discussion of proposals as essential tools for completing business in the allotted time. However, the most important reason for accepting the consensus rule was its usefulness in bridging gaps between the control of votes in the Assembly and the possession of power outside.

The consensus rule was first applied explicitly to substantive questions in the Committee on Peaceful Uses of Outer Space in 1962 (on earlier development of consensus in other international and UN bodies, see Cassan, 1977, pp. 463–7; Lacharrière, 1968, p. 11). As Soviet ambassador Zorin, who had worked hard to get the rule adopted, explained:

> The decisions taken in this committee and in its subcommittees must represent a common agreement among the members ... in other words, they must be taken without a vote because only in that way is it possible to exclude the possibility of seeing decisions adopted by a mechanical majority of votes that are in the interest of some particular group of states.
>
> (A/AC.105/SR.1, 27 Nov.1961, p. 29)

Soviet reasons for wanting a consensus rule are obvious, for it meant they would have to be consulted rather than outvoted; American reasons for accepting it need explanation. In 1962 the Soviet Union and the United States were the only states active in space. Each realized that the other could prevent effective application of any international rules for space that it did not like. This meant the United States could not simply vote the rules it wanted regardless of Soviet desire and have them effectively govern the use of space. By this time, too, the US wondered how long it could continue to raise Assembly majorities on any issue. Third World states accepted the consensus rule, despite the weakening of majoritarian norms it represented, because they realized that only rules supported by both superpowers would be applied in space. Accepting consensus meant increasing the likelihood that space issues would be discussed in the Assembly where the Third World had some voice, rather than outside where it probably would not.

The second significant development occurred in 1964, when the entire nineteenth session of the Assembly was conducted on a consensus basis. With the superpowers arguing over whether Soviet nonpayment of peacekeeping expenses should mean loss of its vote in the Assembly, the other members sought a way to continue work without causing either to wreck the organization (on the "Article 19 Crisis", see Russell, 1966; Hoffmann, 1968; Wilkinson, 1968; Stoessinger, 1977, ch. 7; Franck, 1985, pp. 82–6). An agreement worked out among the outgoing president of the 18th session (Carlos Sosa Rodriguiz of Venezuela), the incoming president of the 19th (Alex Quaison-Sacky of Ghana), the Soviet and United States chief delegates and the chairmen of the five regional groups provided that the 19th session would meet but transact only the business that could be accomplished by general agreement without taking formal votes (remarks of Secretary-General in A/19/PV.1286, 1 Dec. 1964, paras. 7–8). The 19th session was able to elect members to all UN bodies that would have vacancies at the beginning of 1965 and to pass fourteen resolutions on various subjects (A/19/Supp.15). Though some observers dismissed the agreement as an expedient justified only by the need to save the organization (e.g., Charpentier, 1966, pp. 875–6), the proceedings of the 19th session showed delegates that a fair amount of business could be accomplished by consensus even in the most heated atmosphere.

At the same time use of the consensus rule spread through the Assembly's main committees and subsidiary bodies. It was formally adopted for the Special Committee on Friendly Relations and Cooperation among States, first set up in 1963 to draft a comprehensive statement of the rights and duties of states. It was also adopted for the Special Committee on Peacekeeping Operations – which had to bridge continuing East–West differences after the Article 19 Crisis had been resolved by an agreement that peacekeeping would be financed from voluntary contributions rather than the regular budget, and the Committee on Peaceful Uses of the Seabed. In 1971 the Special Committee on the Rationalization of the Procedures and Organization of the General Assembly endorsed using consensus though did not recommend its adoption as a general rule:

The Special Committee considers that the adoption of

decisions and resolutions by consensus is desirable when it contributes to the effective and lasting settlement of differences, thus strengthening the authority of the United Nations. It wishes to emphasize that the right of every member State to set forth its views in full must not be compromised by this procedure.
(A/26/Supp. 26, Doc. A/8426, Sept. 1971, para. 28; also noted in A/520/Rev. 13, 1979, Annex V, para. 104).

Since 1970 the Assembly has followed the line laid down in the late 1960s. It has been willing to have subsidiary organs, such as the UN Development Program or the Disarmament Commission and Committee, operate under a formally specified consensus rule (Sohn, 1974; Cassan, 1977, pp. 467–85), but has left consensus an informal practice in main committees and the plenary. This is important, because it means that when efforts to attain consensus fail, or when a majority does not care to seek consensus in the first place, the formal majoritarian rules can be invoked freely.

The transition toward greater use of consensus began slowly. North–South divisions on economic matters led to many votes. Only in the aftermath of the highly contentious sixth special session in 1974 did both Western and Third World states reconsider their positions and shift to more accommodating positions. Between 1976 and 1984, as Table 3.6 shows, some three-fifths of the Assembly's decisions were taken without a formal vote.

This consensus rule is a new development, standing somewhere between the unanimity rule used in most international meetings before the Second World War and the majority rule adopted for the Assembly in 1945. As the practice of deciding by consensus was being accepted, there was much discussion about just how much agreement a consensus represents. The longest public discussion occurred in the Special Committee on Peacekeeping Operations, where the French, Czech, Hungarian and Romanian members insisted that it should mean unanimity among committee members. This closely followed the older Assembly practice, which defined "unanimity" as adoption without any negative votes or abstentions, even if the total number of positive votes was less than the whole membership (see discussions in, e.g., A/4/PV.242, 16 Nov. 1949, para. 117; A/14/PV.846, 5 Dec. 1959, paras. 37–41, 96–9, 163–4, 167; or A/16/PV.1118, 27 June 1962, para. 1112). Others felt that wide agreement should exist, but that consensus should not be equated

Table 3.6 Adoption of Assembly resolutions, 1964–84

Session	Total*	Without a vote†	Unanimous‡	Two-thirds majority	Simple majority
20th	150	75 (50.0)	4 (2.7)	69 (46.0)	2 (1.3)
21st	136	63 (46.3)	3 (2.2)	68 (50.0)	2 (1.4)
22nd	139	59 (42.4)	14 (10.8)	64 (46.0)	1 (0.7)
23rd	142	57 (40.1)	15 (10.6)	69 (48.6)	1 (0.7)
24th	158	64 (40.5)	5 (3.2)	87 (55.1)	2 (1.3)
25th	160	58 (36.3)	2 (1.2)	98 (61.3)	2 (1.2)
26th	180	55 (30.6)	11 (6.1)	114 (63.3)	0 (0.0)
27th	177	56 (31.6)	12 (6.8)	109 (61.6)	0 (0.0)
28th	181	73 (40.3)	4 (2.2)	104 (57.5)	0 (0.0)
29th	187	95 (50.8)	5 (2.7)	85 (45.5)	2 (1.1)
30th	215	119 (55.3)	4 (1.9)	89 (41.4)	3 (1.4)
31st	251	158 (62.9)	3 (1.2)	90 (35.9)	0 (0.0)
32nd	262	158 (60.3)	6 (2.3)	98 (37.4)	0 (0.0)
33rd	274	155 (56.6)	5 (1.8)	113 (41.2)	1 (0.4)
34th	299	185 (61.9)	0 (0.0)	113 (37.8)	1 (0.3)
35th	317	187 (59.0)	0 (0.0)	128 (40.4)	2 (0.6)
36th	333	193 (58.0)	1 (0.3)	138 (41.4)	1 (0.3)
37th	345	190 (55.1)	2 (0.6)	152 (44.1)	1 (0.3)
38th	323	178 (55.1)	0 (0.0)	145 (44.9)	0 (0.0)
39th	350	201 (57.4)	0 (0.0)	149 (42.6)	0 (0.0)

(*Note:* percentages shown in brackets.)

*Totals here are larger than official UN figures because resolutions distinguished by a letter (e.g., 1191A and 1191B) are counted separately.

†Resolutions listed as adopted without a vote or unanimously.

‡Resolutions adopted on a vote in which there were no negatives or abstentions.

Source: Djonovich, 1973–8 (through 28th session); A/29/PV.2233–326; A/30/PV.2351–444; Annex of the Supplement to General Assembly Official Records reprinting all resolutions and decisions (31st–39th sessions).

with unanimity in either small committees or the Assembly as a whole (A/AC.121/SR.1, 22 April 1965, p. 4).

The issue arose in the General Assembly itself during 1970. South African delegates objected to clauses in the Declaration on the 25th Anniversary of the United Nations that condemned racism and endorsed armed struggle against colonialism. Initially they wanted to express their opposition by calling for a vote and then voting against the Declaration. Other members, who wanted it adopted without a vote, appealed to the South Africans to withdraw their request for a vote. The South Africans did, but only after receiving assurances that no one would assume the Declaration enjoyed unanimous support (A/25/PV.1880, 22 Oct. 1970, paras. 151–66). By 1974 all the elements of a definition were in place and there was no difficulty writing the rules for the World Population Conference. These specified that the conference should "reach decisions on the basis on consensus, which is understood to mean, according to United Nations practice, general agreement without a vote, but not necessarily unanimity" (E/5472, 3 April 1974, Annex; approved by ESC Resolution 1835 of 14 May 1974).

More recently the Assembly has made a distinction between adoption "by consensus" and adoption "without a vote" or "without objection", Though having the appearance of hair-splitting, the distinction is significant for diplomacy in the UN. A resolution adopted "by consensus" is one based on negotiations involving every delegation to some extent and showing that all identify positively with the project to some degree. A resolution adopted "without objection" or "without a vote" (the two terms being treated as synonymous) follows from a less inclusive pattern of negotiation showing that some delegations merely take note of a project. They do not oppose, but are not inclined to participate actively in it. This is still a wider agreement than a resolution adopted by vote. Even if opponents content themselves with abstentions, the mere fact of calling for a vote means that one or more delegations have strong objections they want to express publicly (A/C.6/35/SR.75, paras. 2, 9–17; interview with a member of the UN Legal Office, 23 December 1981).

This hierarchy of formulas for adoption of decisions allows groups and individual delegations to indicate the seriousness of disagreement relatively precisely, both to proponents of the resolution and to each other. These indications tell proponents how far they can go and how fast. Such nuances show up most vividly in instances where multiple resolutions are adopted on the same topic. For instance, Western governments have individually signalled how far they would go in action against South Africa by allowing the adoption of essentially humanitarian projects like the UN Trust Fund aiding exiles without a vote, abstaining on calls for sanctions and voting against such notions as endorsement of violent overthrow of the South African government. A similar pattern appears in resolutions about Israel, where a split between United States and European positions has become greater since 1974.

Shifts of position also tell everyone how solidly a group supports or opposes a given proposition. The large number of abstentions on resolutions about the future of Eastern Timor warned leaders of the Third World coalition that this was a divisive issue that should not be pursued too much. The shift of moderate African states from abstaining on the more radical Arab proposals about Palestine put everyone on notice that a new alignment had been forged. Similarly, Western European delegations have signalled their countries' differences with US policy not only in statements but by shifting voting patterns toward non-objection and abstention rather than flat opposition on most resolutions endorsing PLO positions or condemning specific Israeli policies.

The consolidation of regional and other groups has permitted another elaboration of the term "consensus". Today it is also taken to mean agreement among most states in each of the five regional groups or the main interest groups affected by the particular decision. This aspect of the definition was illuminated clearly during 1967 debates on intervention in the Special Committee on Friendly Relations and Cooperation among States. In that summer's meetings, the African, Asian, Latin American and Eastern European members presented a joint draft of articles on intervention. This met with intense opposition from Western delegates on grounds that it made no distinction between ordinary diplomatic representations and coercion. The Latin Americans, with their long history of interest in defining intervention broadly, wanted to bring the draft to a vote and have it adopted anyway. The other three groups of sponsors hesitated, accepting the Western argument that taking a vote would violate the agreement on procedure adopted in 1966. The Latin Americans then indicated their unhappiness with the situation by refusing to join in accepting any other drafts before the committee. The others reacted to this situation by continuing discussion but deferring adoptions of drafts presented until the following year (reflected weakly in A/AC.125/SR.79–80, 18 Aug. 1967; detailed account in Munves, 1970, pp. 155–6). It also appears constantly in economic issues, where "consensus" effectively means agreement between the Third World and the West.

This regional or interest elaboration makes consensus a more exacting requirement than that of a two-thirds majority. First, it means that no region can be left out completely, as is now possible in a two-thirds vote. In the current 159-member Assembly, 54 constitute a blocking third. None of the regional groups can muster that number on its own, though the Africans come closest with 51 (see Table App. 1). Second, all doubters must agree that their objections are minor and would lead only to abstention if a formal vote were taken. Since the consensus rule supplements, but does not supersede, the majority rule, any state with a strong objection has the right to force a vote. If opponents are few in number, they know in advance that they will lose the vote and see the decision adopted anyway. However, by forcing a vote they deny the proponents the extra moral and symbolic weight that now attaches to decisions adopted by consensus.

This requirement for broader agreement means that minority rights are better protected under the consensus rule. If supporters of a proposal place high value on obtaining consensus, any minority except a tiny one composed of pariah or very insignificant states can prevent the adoption of a decision. The majority may then go ahead and adopt the decision by a vote, but this means forgoing the moral and symbolic advantages of consensus. Yet some observers read the situation very differently. They believe that the regional groups, particularly Third World ones, exert strong pressures on all members to accept whatever position the group adopts and that is politically almost impossible for the West to oppose any Third World initiative – particularly one with Eastern backing as well (e.g., Schwebel, 1979, p. 309). Such fears seem exaggerated. States can force votes if they will insist on what they believe. Though the Third World hoped to get the Charter on Economic Rights and Duties of States adopted by consensus at the twenty-ninth session, a vote was taken because Western states continued to oppose it (A/29/PV.2315, 12 Dec. 1979, pp. 41–5).

Further, the process of reaching consensus entails lengthy negotiations resulting in modifications of the original draft. At the 7th special session in 1975 the Third World proposed that money for development be transferred automatically from rich states to poor through distributing extra SDRs to poor states, giving them funds from the IMF Trust Fund being raised by gold sales, favoring poor countries in the distribution of revenues paid to the international agency proposed for controlling deep seabed mining, levying special taxes on extraction of all nonrenewable resources in poor countries and having rich states reimburse to poor ones that portion of tariff revenues accruing on imports orginating in poor states. The comprehensive program adopted at the end of the session in Resolution 3362 (S–VI) endorsed only the first two ideas, which had already been widely discussed and largely accepted in the IMF. The others were not mentioned; the resolution contained only a promise that other methods for automatic transfer would remain a topic for negotiation (United Nations, 1975). Such modification of drafts is common practice (see list in Puchala, 1983). In fact, it is so widespread that some observers feel the Assembly is capable of producing nothing but platitudes and decisions so vague that members can interpret them in many, often conflicting, ways (e.g., Gregg, 1981, pp.63–4).

Though consensus first developed to bridge East–West gaps in the Outer Space Committee and performed the same function in discussions of disarmament, peacekeeping and friendly relations, today it is used most often to bridge South–North gaps of votes and resources. In 1964 Raul Prebisch, the Chilean economist who served as UNCTAD's first secretary-general, advised:

> Clearly, there is no immediate practical interest served by adopting resolutions by a simple majority composed of developing countries that do not enjoy support from developed ones, because the implementation of these recommendations depends on their acceptance by the latter.
> (E/CONF.46/SR.141, vol. 2, p. 629)

In most instances the Third World majority continues to follow this advice since the gap between votes and resources that inspired it still exists.

Summary

No matter how it adopts a decision, the General Assembly remains a majoritarian organ where each member state has one vote. When efforts to reach a consensus fail, the majority can always force a decision by shifting from informal practice to formal rules and taking a vote. Whether this is wise depends on the context, but the fact remains that decisions cannot be prevented by a minority.

Charter rules allow the adoption of most decisions by a simple majority but require two-thirds approval of resolutions relating to security questions, elections to other principal UN organs and the budget. This has greatly affected the politics of coalition-building. While a simple majority, such as the anticolonial alignment of African, Asian, Latin American and Soviet bloc states operating between 1954 and 1960, can make most decisions, only the larger two-thirds coalition can hope for secure control. This complicates efforts to maintain control because the coalition has more members to keep happy. They may be kept happy on many issues with symbolic stands, but will also want some material benefit. The implications of this complication will be examined further in Chapter 7.

Consensus decision-making presents some problems of coalition management for both minorities and majorities since they need to decide which compromises are or are not acceptable. In the main, however, consensus is a procedure for attempting to reconcile differences and arrive at a decision all can accept, if not positively endorse. Consensus owes its prominence both to long-standing international tradition that states are subject only to those directives they impose on themselves and to the fact that control over votes in the Assembly does not correlate perfectly with control over capability in the international system. Lacking control of ancillary institutions capable of enforcing resolutions on states, the Assembly majority must secure implementation by persuasion rather than by coercion. The full implications of this fact will be discussed in Chapters 5 through 7. Before that, however, Chapter 4 will examine the changing patterns of negotiation and debate in the Assembly. These activities, particularly negotiation, produce the proposals finally adopted or rejected, so form an integral part of the decision-making process.

Chapter Four

Consideration of Proposals

Decisions seldom appear ready-formed. Virtually all of them are preceded by a period of discussion permitting examination of relevant information, evaluation of competing proposals and negotiation of compromises to create wide enough support for formal adoption. Sometimes this process occurs behind closed doors, and hints of what occurred can be gleaned only by rumor or media leaks. Sometimes all or part of this process occurs publicly. The General Assembly, like the League Assembly before it, derives much of its importance from the fact that it provides an open forum for discussion of issues, something the international system lacked before 1920.

Public debate, even if conducted as a ritual after supporters and opponents have decided their attitudes toward a proposal, serves a number of important functions. For supporters, it provides a chance to explain the rationale for the decision and their vision of the consequences that are intended to follow from it. To the extent that groups or individuals not members of the decision-making body must cooperate in implementing the decision, this provides guidance to them. It also allows appeals to sympathetic individuals and groups who might then seek to influence opponents. For opponents, public debate offers a chance to appeal both to the wider political system and to future decision-makers. All political systems provide many examples of arguments once rejected being accepted later because conditions change, initial decisions prove less effective than expected, or participants in the political process change their minds.

Negotiations among contending factions within decision-making bodies are seldom public. Yet the general style of negotiations is usually known and exerts influence on the political system by setting the tone of inter-factional competition. A political system in which factions shoot it out in the palace is very different from one where factions bargain and leave each other alive to bargain again another day.

Negotiating patterns in the Assembly are based on continual bargaining. They have evolved over time to accommodate a growing membership, a growing agenda, the development of regional and caucusing groups and changes in the relation between control over votes in the Assembly and possession of capability outside. As in the adoption of decisions, the Assembly has two patterns of debate and negotiation. One, consisting of extensive private negotiation and short public debate laying out basic positions, is usually associated with adoption by consensus. The other, consisting of less private negotiation and more public debate (often including sharp attacks on others), is usually associated with adoption by vote. In most cases, therefore, it is possible to gauge the character of the decision-making process by the type of public debate being carried on.

Negotiation

Like all large bodies, the General Assembly has both formal debates and informal discussions. The informal discussions make the formal business flow more easily by providing a channel for reaching understandings about the procedures to be used at a particular moment or on a particular question, drafting more widely acceptable versions of proposals, or working out the tactics to be pursued in securing passage of one's own or defeat of an opponent's proposal. In national legislatures, these informal discussions occur within and between party caucuses; in the General Assembly they occur within and among the regional and other groups.

In the 1940s most delegates took a very formalistic view of Assembly proceedings. Though certain clusters, like the Latin American group, the Arab states, the Soviet bloc, the Commonwealth, or the Nordic states, did consult among themselves, inter-group consultations were rarer. Difficulties over procedure were seldom worked out beforehand; they were raised and debated at length in formal meetings. While representing carry-overs from older diplomatic practice, this formalistic style of debate was also encouraged by the Cold War. Neither the US-led majority nor the Soviet bloc minority saw much use negotiating on many of the issues raised in the Assembly. Rather, it was a forum for presenting contrasting world views. The Soviet bloc took advantage of any device for obstruction the rules permitted, in part to assert its views and in part to persuade home opinion that its position as an embattled minority in a hostile world required extensive defensive measures. Tactics of obstruction encouraged counter-tactics on the other side.

By the mid-1950s Assembly debates had become less formalistic. Rule changes, some endorsed and some bitterly opposed by the Soviet bloc, had made many forms of obstruction more difficult. Regional and caucus groups took root. Inter-group consultations on procedural problems became common as Secretariat efforts to encourage informal consultations began to bear fruit (interview with Oscar Schachter, a member of the Secretariat from 1944 to 1976, January 1983). Many procedural questions were worked out in advance, and more questions were being settled in subcommittees and working groups.

After the reshuffling of regional groups occasioned by the rapid increase in membership during the early 1960s, the regional groups came to play a more prominent role in informal negotiations. This was particularly true for the Third World groups since many members were unable to send a large delegation to New York and had to depend on the group for a good deal of information and advice. The constant increase in membership, reaching 99 in 1960, 125 in 1968 and 154 in 1980, together with the ever-expanding agenda also enhanced the groups' role. Individual consultation on every question was clearly impossible; the groups provided a handy way to consult with clusters of members simultaneously. The groups' importance was also boosted by the rough correspondence between regions and significant political divisions in international politics. The Eastern European group on one side and the Western European and Other group on the other closely reflected the Cold War East–West division. Those two groups, but mainly the Western, on one side, and the African, Asian and Latin American groups on the other, closely reflected the North–South cleavage that became more important after 1960.

The rising importance of the groups and the wider use of consensus as a rule for decision-making have greatly changed the way in which proposals are prepared. Until the late 1960s it was normal for contending clusters of sponsors to prepare drafts on a question and formally present them early in the proceedings. The rule that proposals were voted upon in chronological order encouraged early submission. This was a way to gain priority for one's own version should later efforts at drafting compromises fail. Only after formal submission did the sponsors indicate their actual intentions. If they were ready to make deals with others,

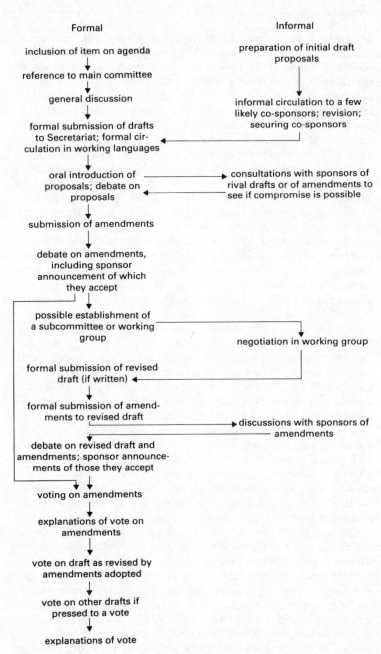

Figure 4.1 Consideration of draft resolutions, 1950–1970

they either withdrew their draft in favor of another or agreed that their draft should be sent with others to a subcommittee or working group charged with writing a proposal that would command general support. If they were not interested in compromise, either because they already had a majority or because they wanted their views on record anyway, they pressed for a vote on their proposal as it stood. In many instances members were able to identify the proposal enjoying widest support early in the proceedings. It then became the focus of others' efforts to modify the decision on it.

The typical process of the 1950s and 1960s is illustrated in Figure 4.1.

On highly political questions, there were always multiple proposals. For instance, the Special Political Committee received at least three draft resolutions on questions relating to Palestinian refugees in the 1960s. The Western draft, which was generally submitted first, dealt mainly with the mechanics of aid and reaffirmed paragraph 11 of Resolution 194 (III), which provided that

the refugees wishing to return to their homes and live at peace with their neighbors should be permitted to do so at the earliest practicable date, and that compensation should be paid for the property of those choosing not to return and for the loss or damage to property which, under principles of international law or in equity, should be made good by the Governments or authorities responsible [a provision understood as applying to both Arabs and Jews uprooted in 1948].

The Afro-Asian draft did much the same, except to carry an endorsement of the refugees' right to return unconditionally as a way to express both sympathy with the Arabs and disapproval of Israeli policy. The third draft, written by a number of Arab states, sought to increase the pressure on Israel by appointing a UN custodian for refugee property in Israel. Until 1967 discussions produced a compromise between the Western and Afro-Asian drafts. This compromise would be adopted by a wide majority, and then the Arab draft rejected. Between 1968 and 1974 the Western and Afro-Asian drafts were both adopted, but the Arab one still rejected (proceedings summarized in *UN Yearbook*, 1960, pp. 188–9; 1961, pp. 157–9; 1962, pp. 141–2; 1963, pp. 59–61; 1965, pp. 221–4. 1966, pp. 181–5; 1967, pp. 261–6; 1968, pp. 281–93; 1969, pp. 234–9).

A similar pattern marked the 1957 discussion about creating a

UN-administered fund for capital loans to developing states. The idea had been kicking around in the Second Committee for several years when India and other Afro-Asian states proposed that such a fund, under the name Special UN Fund for Economic Development (SUNFED), be established as of 1 January 1960. Though some of the smaller Western states agreed, the major aid donors, particularly the United States, did not accept the idea. The United States then submitted a proposal to create a special projects fund within the already-established Expanded Program for Technical Assistance as a way to delay SUNFED. In the ensuing debate, US delegates said their draft was meant not as a substitute but as something that could be done while the problem of raising funds for SUNFED were studied further. This did not persuade proponents of SUNFED, who noted that a lack of Western will was the root of the fund-raising difficulties. Even so, a small program appeared better than none. Both sides then agreed on a consolidated draft establishing the EPTA fund while continuing discussion of SUNFED the following year (summarized in *UN Yearbook*, 1957, pp. 139–43).

There were occasional exceptions to this pattern of multiple proposals. On something technical like the reports of the EPTA fund in 1958 and 1959, delegates held a general discussion and quickly agreed on a resolution that commended the work involved and encouraged its continuation (summarized in *UN Yearbook*, 1958, pp. 100–3; 1959, pp. 109–14). In 1960 a 44-state Third World draft calling for the establishment of a UN Capital Development Fund was recognized immediately as the most widely supported draft. Other ideas were submitted as amendments to it rather than as separate proposals (*UN Yearbook*, 1960, pp. 285–7). Most debates on human rights issues in the 1950s and 1960s were based on drafts prepared in the Commission on Human Rights (*UN Yearbook*, 1954, pp. 203–8; 1962, pp. 313, 347–9; 1964, pp. 346–52.

In the 1970s the exceptions became the rule. The appearance of multiple proposals became a sign that consensus was not being sought or that attempts to reach consensus had failed. Even the formal submission of amendments indicated that negotiations had broken down or that the previous understanding had been rendered obsolete by events. This growth of informal consultations was also encouraged by problems in securing all sponsors' agreement to amendments as their numbers grew. Jacobsen (1970, p. 252), whose results are shown in Table 4.1, has calculated that the average number of co-sponsors increased steadily in the first twenty-one sessions.

Table 4.1 Cosponsorship of Draft Resolutions

Sessions	*1–3*	*4–6*	*7–9*	*10–12*	*13–15*	*16–18*	*20–1*
Initial	1.4	2.1	4.1	6.0	7.2	12.6	14.4
Revised	1.3	2.3	5.5	6.1	7.5	13.5	18.9

Since all co-sponsors must accept an amendment before it can be deemed "friendly", the process of negotiating improvements to a formally introduced text was becoming rather cumbersome. Shifting to a pattern in which drafts were discussed informally and submitted only toward the end of negotiations meant avoiding the amendment process entirely in most cases.

A successful exercise in consensus building during the 1970s and early 1980s took one of the two main forms. In the first, shown in Figure 4.2, one proposal is submitted at the end of informal discussions.

In the second, shown in Figure 4.3, drafts are submitted earlier, but withdrawn in favor of revised versions after consultations indicate the changes needed to win consensus.

Discussions leading to passage of Resolution 3362 (S–VII), on "Development and International Economic Cooperation," at the 7th special session in 1975 provide a good example of the first pattern. Before the session assembled on 1 September 1975 the Group of 77 had prepared a comprehensive working paper setting forth all of its proposals. This was circulated to other groups early enough that the European Community was able to prepare and announce its position before the first meeting. The United States took longer, announcing its position only on the first day of the session. Negotiations to forge a common draft based on these various proposals were taken up in "contact groups" consisting of 27 states chosen by the three Third World regions and 12 states chosen by the West. As usual in discussions of economic issues, Eastern Europe gave verbal support to Third World positions while disclaiming any obligation to contribute financially on the grounds that underdevelopment was a consequence of capitalism and Western imperialism. Thus, it played no significant role in the informal discussions. One of the contact groups dealt with issues of trade and resource transfers while the other handled industrialization, technology, food problems and questions of restructuring UN economic and social programs. Through the five weeks while informal talks proceeded, formal

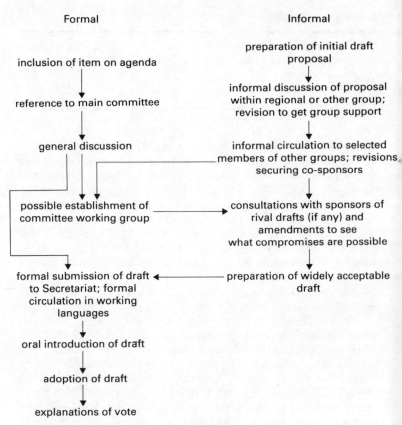

Figure 4.2   Usual process of drafting consensus resolutions

meetings were devoted to a general discussion of all the economic
questions before the session. These informal negotiations, which
were particularly intensive in the last two and a half weeks, led to
generally acceptable compromises. These were written into an
omnibus draft resolution, which was adopted without a vote on
16 September. Delegations set out their views for the record in
explanations of vote, either then or at an earlier meeting of the *ad
hoc* committee (A/S–7/PV.2349, 16 Sept. 1974, paras. 33–108;
negotiations described in United Nations, 1975).

Stable majority coalitions have never had a monopoly over the
initation of proposals. It is possible for others to press initatives
that win general backing. For example, in 1974 the Netherlands,
Austria, Ireland and Sweden presented a proposal that the

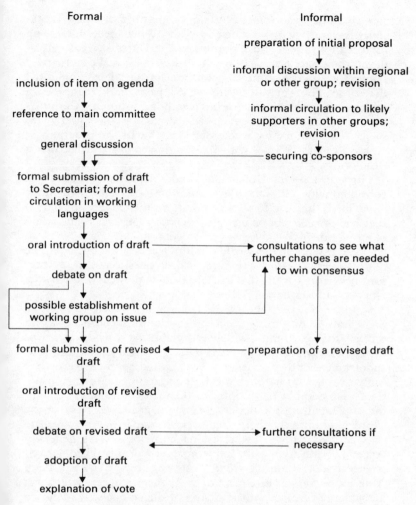

Figure 4.3 Alternate process of drafting consensus resolutions

General Assembly ask the Fifth UN Congress on the Prevention of Crime and the Treatment of Offenders, which was to meet at Geneva in September 1975, to draft a set of rules that would protect prisoners against torture. The four initiators had worked out a draft before the 29th session of the Assembly met in September, and circulated it among likely supporters. Without much difficulty, Bangladesh, Costa Rica, Jordan and the Philippines quickly agreed to become co-sponsors. This was a good

sign, because endorsement by a good number of Third World
states is necessary to building consensus. When the item came up
for debate in the Third Committee, the Dutch delegate introduced the draft. At this point 10 other states, 8 Western and 2
Latin American, became co-sponsors. Further debate indicated
that some minor revisions were needed, particularly to meet Iraqi
criticism that the proposal seemed to bypass the UN Commission on Human Rights. A revised draft was then presented,
which was adopted by a vote of 111 to 1 with 2 abstentions in
committee and 125 to 0 with 1 abstention in plenary, becoming
Resolution 3218 (XXIX).

Through 1975 the Dutch and Swedes kept the issue alive and
consulted with others to coordinate a three-part campaign on the
issue. First, they had to prepare a draft for the Congress. Second,
they had to keep tabs on how the Secretary-General's solicitation
of governments' views was proceeding. Third, they had to
coordinate work in the World Health Organization on an outline
of principles of medical ethics relevant to questions of protecting
prisoners from torture that had also been requested for use by the
Congress in Resolution 3218.

At the Congress, the Netherlands and Sweden shepherded
their draft Code through, accepting minor amendments along
the way to make it more widely acceptable. At the 30th session of
the General Assembly, the two initiators decided that a general
endorsement of the Congress's work would not be enough; they
sought explicit adoption of the draft declaration on torture in one
General Assembly resolution and then a second outlining steps
for implementing the declaration. Both proposals went to the
Third Committee, where they were debated together. Debate
showed that with a few revisions both ideas were generally
acceptable. Meanwhile the implementation proposal had secured
twenty-five co-sponsors from Western Europe, Asia and Latin
America. Here, in a nice piece of symbolism, Greece, which had
just emerged from the dictatorship of the colonels, was chosen
to introduce the draft formally. Informal consultations, particularly with Eastern Europeans, produced further refinements
of the text. These changed the preamble so it was clear that states
would pursue "international cooperation" rather than provide
for "international action" because the Soviet bloc felt the latter
was too strong a term. A revised draft was formally submitted on
28 November; the draft was adopted by consensus. Both proposals were adopted by consensus in the plenary, becoming
Resolutions 3452 (XXX) and 3453 (XXX) respectively (Kaufmann, 1980, pp. 150–4; A/C.3/30/SR.2159–60, 14 Nov. 1975;

SR.2165, 20 Nov. 1975; SR.2166, 21 Nov. 1975, paras. 63–6; SR.2167–8, 24 Nov. 1975; SR. 2172, 28 Nov. 1975, and A/30/Annex 74).

On certain symbolic issues particularly dear to the Third World majority only one draft proposal is presented. There, however, the similarity with negotiations leading to consensus ends. While sponsors and their regional groups consult among themselves, they undertake few discussions with likely opponents. Debate indicates clearly that compromises will not be made. Some amendments may be accepted by the sponsors or adopted on a vote, but those that seem to stray too far from the sponsors' intentions will be rejected. Then the decision is adopted by a vote. Explanations of vote will indicate that there are few areas of underlying agreement between proponents, opponents and abstainers.

Today consideration of most questions relating to South African apartheid policy and the future of Palestine follow this pattern. The discussions of Palestine in 1975, before the situation was complicated by Egyptian–Israeli peace talks, provide a good example. Debate was held in plenary to assure maximum publicity; ten meetings being needed for the speeches. The tone of debate was set early by a very hard-line speech from the PLO observer. Two draft resolutions were presented on the question. The first, sponsored by forty-seven Third World states, called on the Security Council to take measures to ensure that the Palestinians were able to exercise their right to self-determination (a criticism of US support for Israel), called on all UN bodies and conferences to invite the PLO to participate in all discussions on the Middle East on an equal footing with other states in the area, requested the Secretary-General to inform the co-chairmen of the Geneva Conference on the Middle East (the USSR and the USA) of this desire and to take all steps necessary for securing the PLO an invitation to that conference on an equal basis with the participating states, and requested the Secretary-General to report to the Assembly on developments at the next (31st) session.

The sponsors accepted a few minor revisions before seeing the draft adopted as Resolution 3375 (XXX) by a vote of 101 to 8 with 25 abstentions. The other draft, sponsored by fifty-five Third World and Eastern European states, was even tougher on Israel. After explicitly reaffirming the previous year's Resolution 3236 endorsing Palestinian self-determination and naming the PLO as its authentic agent, it went on to express "grave concern" over the lack of progress toward implementation of the Palestinians' rights to self-determination, national independence, sovereignty and to return to their original homes, and to create a "Committee on the Exercise of the Inalienable Rights of the Palestinian People" to propose steps for implementing Resolution 3236. The committee was to report by June 1976, and the Security Council was asked to consider its proposals as soon afterward as possible. Here was a resolution that could be read as endorsing the PLO's desire to destroy Israel and that sought to put pressure on the United States by asking for Security Council action. After some debate and no revisions, this proposal became Resolution 3376 (XXX) by a vote of 93 to 18 with 27 abstentions. Here, 14 Latin American states, 8 pro-Western African states and Fiji joined the West in opposing or abstaining because the draft did not refer to Israel's right to exist. China and Iraq announced non participation to indicate their refusal to endorse the Geneva Conference or Security Council Resolution 242 (A/30/PV.2399, 10 Nov. 1975; A/30/Annex 24; the whole course of proceedings summarized in *UN Yearbook*, 1975, pp. 242–5).

Where a question inspires sharp divisions of opinion but there is no clear majority at the start, the older pattern of rival drafts is likely to reappear. However, the use of informal discussions has reduced the number of drafts formally submitted to the Assembly even in these cases because clusters of sponsors will try to amalgamate drafts before proceeding. The number of amendments offered formally has also declined as delegates discuss their differences in advance.

No matter which pattern is used, Assembly negotiations today are exercises in coalition-building channeled through the regional and other groups. The main difference between patterns is that attaining consensus requires securing wider support and entails more compromise. Yet even raising a simple majority requires finding some seventy-eight states willing to vote in favor of a proposal. It is difficult to negotiate with seventy-eight others all at once, making the groups an indispensable element of Assembly life. At the same time, states, even middle-ranking powers, have to delegate at least some portion of the negotiating to others. This is not unprecedented in international politics, but it is far more widespread now that it ever has been. In traditional theory and bilateral practice, each state negotiates only for itself. In contemporary multilateral practice states have to trust one another. It is possible to remain outside the process of compromise and dissociate from the result, but this carries costs. The Eastern European group is discovering that excuses for non-involvement in international economic discussions are wearing thin, and that non involvement itself poses some problems for efforts to encourage the East–South ties it so often talks of fostering as an alternative to "capitalist exploitation" (Bielawski, 1981, gives a Polish exposition, and Cutler, 1983, a United States analysis of the ideas). The Nixon administration seems to have grasped the point between 1974 and 1975, and US delegates came to the 7th special session far more ready to talk than at the 6th. The net result is that diplomats have begun to learn some of the skills of caucusing and delegating that mark the behavior of legislators. This makes diplomacy very different from what it traditionally has been.

Debate

Assembly debates can create great confusion for outside observers – including government officials back home. The most active debaters are seldom the most active negotiators (Alger, 1968). Often, though not always, the most active debaters are fringe elements. As Donald Puchala put it, "the weakest members shout the loudest, the most radical seek the most attention, and the most paranoid are the most critical" (1983, p. 344). Thus the tenor of debate may not reflect the opinions of most of the membership. Further, debate is often a poor prior indication of a decision's content. To the extent that the negotiators and the debaters have different views, the product of inter-group consultations will reflect the former's deals. There can thus be a large gap between themes advanced in debate and the content of decision. Finally, most Assembly debates are not exchanges between supporters and opponents; many are simply a series of set speeches leaving the listener to discern areas of agreement or disagreement.

Despite their limitations, and the fact that the amount of formal debate has decreased as the use of informal negotiation has grown, debate still serves a number of purposes. Within the Assembly, formal debate reaffirms the principle of sovereign equality by affording all members an opportunity to present their views, permits the tentative floating of ideas which may form the basis of decisions later if others take them up, permits comment on broad questions of principle which might get ignored in the more focused informal negotiations, and allows expression of conflict independent of items on the agenda. Outside the Assembly, formal debate is also important. It, not the informal negotiations, receives media attention and shapes outsiders'

impressions of the Assembly. It also provides an opportunity to
appeal to broader publics, government officials not participating
in Assembly work and later governments by offering rationales
for the decisions made or votes cast. Of course, the effect of these
appeals depends on the openness of governments and societies to
them. Third World states have relied heavily on this device in
their campaigns to end colonialism and to foster a new set of rules
for international economic relations. Finally, formal debate is
essential to campaigns of vilification or embarrassment; without
it the target, third states and attentive publics would not understand the reasoning behind the condemnations.

Statements made in formal debate can also constrain a government's later statements or actions. Though new governments,
particularly those coming to power by coup or revolution, often
want to demonstrate discontinuity with their predecessors by
adopting new policies, established governments tend to prefer
consistency. Continuing old policies is easier than inventing new
ones. Consistency is widely viewed as a sign of skillful and
knowledgeable policy-making. To the extent that attaining a
particular policy goal requires maintaining a certain image, later
statements and acts must be consistent, or at least compatible,
with the assertions put forward. Thus, if the Soviet Union is
preaching "peaceful coexistence", it gets further by conciliatory
approaches than by invading neighboring states. Western arguments that "the time is not ripe" for beginning certain aid
programs were always weakened by Third World beliefs that the
money would be forthcoming if the political will were present. In
most circumstances it is difficult for a government openly to
disavow an earlier statement, particularly if that statement is
widely known or strongly worded. Thus, most governments
cannot abate their criticism of South Africa lest the South African
government decide they have given up on the issues of Namibia
and apartheid.

Assembly rules of procedure divide formal debate into three
phases: (1) general discussion of the item or group of items
focusing on the problem, broad approaches to it and its significance, (2) detailed examination of the particular proposals and
amendments submitted on the question and (3) explanations of
vote setting out the reasons a delegation supports, opposes, or is
ambivalent about the decision reached. When the Assembly
proceeds by consensus, the first and third segments of debate are
held in full, but the second will be shortened, or even disappear,
because details are discussed informally. Only an oral introduction of the proposal and a brief explanation of its terms are

sure to remain because the rules require oral introductions before voting. Explanations of vote then take on particular importance because they provide the only opportunity for public comment on the exact terms of the decision made. When the Assembly proceeds by majority rule, all three phases occur in full.

The rules and their interpretation also permit pairs of small groups of members to pursue conflicts without placing them on the agenda. Both the lack of an effective rule of relevance and the right of reply permit all delegates to make polemical and even vituperative remarks about other countries, their governments, or their governments' policies. Though distracting, these devices do permit the expression of differences between states in a relatively non-destructive way.

Though the rules provide that delegates may be called to order for extraneous remarks, presiding officers soon concluded that attempting to enforce this was counterproductive. As Paul-Henri Spaak explained in 1948:

> In the Assembly as it exists today, it is difficult to stop an orator once he has begun to speak. A prudent president does not attempt to do so, because if he is unfortunate enough to stop the orator, the rules of procedure are invoked with extraordinary promptness, and instead of gaining time one loses it in the ensuing discussion as to whether the orator is discussing the question properly, whether he is really following the rules of procedure, whether he is well within his rights, or whether he has really touched upon the subject of the question. It is better, therefore, to let him go on.
>
> (Spaak, 1948, pp. 608–9)

The length, but not the intensity, of rhetorical excess has been curbed by generally agreed time limits for many types of speeches. Perhaps, too, the poor reception accorded the more outrageous behavior at the 15th session, of which Nikita Khrushchev's shoe-banging remains the most famous, encouraged some restraint.

The right of reply permits delegates whose country, government, or government's policy is the target of rude remarks to respond. Initially it was intended as a mechanism for allowing delegates who felt their country or government had been insulted or their own remarks were misrepresented to respond after the list of speakers had been closed. Almost at once, however, it became a device for "jumping the queue" and replying at once even if the list were still open. The practice of allowing the delegation inspiring the reply a short response also grew rapidly. These responses sometimes remove misunderstandings but often consist mainly of equally rude remarks about the other. Sometimes, as with African responses to South African speeches or Arab ones to Israeli speeches, the right of reply is used to create an impression that the target is extremely isolated. If also intended to cow the target delegation, it is an unsuccessful tactic; both South Africans and Israelis gave as good as they got. At other times, two states pursue a running polemic through the plenary and all the main committees. Ethiopia and Somalia in 1977, Cambodia and Vietnam in 1979, and Iran and Iraq since 1981 provide particularly good examples. Since 1979 these exchanges have been limited in number and length, and placed at the end of meetings. This has not ended them, but limits the extent to which pairs of quarreling states can interrupt the flow of Assembly business.

Majorities in all deliberative bodies are tempted to impose limits on debate so they may more expeditiously proceed to decisions. Yet a streamlining of rules governing Assembly debate occurred much less because of majority maneuvering than because of general recognition that the combination of rising membership and lengthening agendas made greater efficiency imperative. Even members of the Soviet bloc, extremely sensitive to any change that would curb their rights of expression because of their minority position in the Assembly, admitted this point. In 1971 the Polish delegate noted that:

> Members of the UN must retain the right to express themselves fully on agenda items allocated to main committees. On the other hand, the Organization now had 127 members, and all of those wishing to speak should be given an opportunity to do so. Situations frequently arose in which this was not possible, and some limitation on the length of statements was then obviously desirable in order to facilitate the more efficient use of the available time.
>
> (A/AC.149/SR.14, 17 May 1971, p. 27)

This steamlining of procedures occurred slowly, through the adoption of incremental changes in the rules. In 1949 all delegations agreed to accept limits on the number of speeches made in procedural debates, usually two speeches in favor and two opposed to the particular motion before the Assembly. Though Soviet bloc delegates had made the most of the older lack of limits, they accepted the idea because it would limit both majority and minority equally (A/C.6/4/SR.150, 1 Oct. 1949, para. 99). Additionally, it would spare the minority a drawn-out public humiliation as ten or twenty majority speakers opposed their motion. Over vehement Soviet bloc objection, a change making it easier to dispense with plenary debate on items already debated in a main committee (by holding debate only when one-third of the members requested rather than by dispensing with it when two-thirds agreed) was also adopted (Werners, 1967, pp. 151–2, explains the tangled history of this rule; 1949 debate in A/C.6/4/SR.146–8, 29 Sept.–1 Oct. 1949). However, even the Soviet bloc soon found merit in the change because it freed considerable amounts of plenary time, which was then used to debate items for which the majority wanted special publicity. Since first the anticolonial and then the Third World majority usually wanted to discuss issues more embarrassing to the West than to itself, the Soviet bloc was content.

Other devices for streamlining debate were accepted, but slowly. Most delegations feared partisan use of any rules, so were prepared to adopt only those devices that appeared to impinge equally on all. By 1953 explanations of vote in plenary were limited to ten minutes, but no such limit applied in main committees until 1979 (A/2402, 26 June 1953, para. 30; A/34/ Annex 8, Doc. A/34/250, para. 4). Members had tacitly limited themselves to one speech each in the plenary general debate. By 1963 the press of numbers was great enough that they agreed to limit such speeches to thirty minutes (A/26/Supp.26, Doc. A/8426, Sept. 1971, paras. 146–7). Among other things this keeps general debate to its traditional three weeks' duration, allowing the plenary to take up other issues by mid-October.

The list of speakers had always been used to regulate the order in which presiding officers called on delegates. In 1971 members agreed to use it as prod to earlier decision about whether and when to speak by closing it at the end of one-third of the meetings tentatively allocated to discussion of the item or group of items at hand (A/26/Supp.26, Doc. A/8426, Sept. 1971, para. 202; A/26/PV. endorsed in Resolution 2837 [XXVI], para. 2).

The 1960s also witnessed efforts to reduce the amount of time lost while individual delegations pursued private conflicts through the right of reply. Though this right is a safety-valve all delegations cherished, most also realized that with the press of numbers the interruptions would have to be curbed somewhat. The first step occurred in 1962, when the President of the 17th session (Muhammad Zafroulla Khan of Pakistan) ruled that all of the seventeen African delegations wanting to reply to a South

African speech should wait until the end of the meeting (A/17/ PV.1128, 24 Sept. 1962, pp. 68–70). The controversial nature of many of the items handled in plenary, combined with the persistent tendency for a series of African delegations to reply to any South African speech and a series of Arab delegations to do the same after any Israeli speech, led to an agreement to postpone all rights of reply to the end of plenary meetings (proposed in A/24/Annex 8, Doc. A/7700, para. 17; adopted in A/24/ PV.1758, 20 Sept. 1969, para. 147).

Discussions of rationalizing the Assembly's procedures in 1971 led to further proposals, but none of them was adopted until 1979 when membership of 149 and an agenda of 140 items had brought the Assembly to the verge of breakdown. First, members agreed to limit themselves to one ten-minute explanation of vote per resolution, to be delivered either in plenary or the relevant main committee. Delegates have occasionally gotten an extra minute or two when explaining on behalf of a group (e.g., A/37/PV.48, 30 Oct. 1982, pp. 98–100). Only if a delegation changes its vote may it deliver an explanation in both places (proposed in A/34/ Annex 8, Doc. A/34/250, para. 5; adopted in A/34/PV.4, 21 Sept. 1979, p. 151). Second, each delegation is now limited to two rights of reply per agenda item per meeting, the first ten minutes long and the second five (proposed in A/34/Annex 8, Doc. A/34/250, para. 6; adopted in A/34/PV.4, 21 Sept. 1979, p. 151). The additional agreement that replies and responses to replies will be given only at the end of a meeting also means that other delegates may leave without risk of missing any substantive business or engage in informal discussions with others.

Much streamlining of debate has occurred as a by-product of the shift to greater reliance on regional groups and informal negotiations. Prior consultations now settle many points that would have inspired long procedural debates in the early sessions. Even when efforts to reach consensus fail, informal negotiations reduce the number of draft resolutions and amendments submitted, so reduce the amount of time spent debating the specifics of proposals before the meeting. The grouping of similar items for simultaneous debate leads to more multiple interventions in general discussions than was formerly the case, but to fewer speeches overall since the number of interventions by each delegation seldom equals the number of items in the grouping.

The limits of Assembly interest in efficiency can also be seen in proposed changes that were not accepted. Secretary-General Lie's 1952 proposal that the list of speakers be closed as soon as all the delegates who had signed up already had spoken was rejected as impractical by most delegations. They were aware that delays in receiving instructions from home accounted for many of the delays in signing up (discussed in A/C.6/7/SR.347–8, 11–12 Dec. 1953). Nor did members adopt the Special Political and Fourth Committees' 16th session remedy for gaps caused by delegates not ready to speak when their turn came. These committees, under a Bulgarian and a Liberian chairman respectively, simply assumed that the unprepared had decided not to speak (announced in A/SPC/16/SR.227, 2 Nov. 1961, para. 21; and A/C.4/16/SR.1278, 2 Feb. 1962, para. 50). An attempt to apply the same rule in the First Committee was rejected (A/C.1/PV. 1240, 4 Feb. 1962, paras. 35–6). The idea was not taken into general practice except late in the 26th session when the Assembly was hurrying to complete work before 20th December. Again, concern about a lack of timely instructions and the difficulties facing small delegations attempting to cover several simultaneous meetings led to rejection. Nor have delegations ever accepted the idea of limiting themselves to one speech in each general discussion of an agenda item. Though the President hesitated before allowing a second Soviet speech in debate on the return of Axis war criminals in 1947 (A/2/PV.102, 31 Oct. 1947, p. 522), the right to multiple interventions was well established by 1955 (e.g., A/C.3/7/SR.443, 12 Nov. 1952, para. 34). This resistance became stronger as items were grouped, and differences in the timing of instructions or desires to highlight positions on certain items in the cluster made multiple speeches necessary more often.

Besides these general restrictions, Assembly rules also permit limiting debate on particular occasions. Delegates or presiding officers may propose limiting the number of speeches by each delegation in particular debates, the length of each speech, or the closure of debate. On the whole, delegates are loath to apply special limits to particular debates.

This reluctance to interfere with member rights of expression shows most vividly in the treatment of motions to close debate. First, motions to close debate do not necessarily bring discussion to an immediate end. Assembly rules have no provision for moving the previous question – that is, calling for an immediate vote on the motion under discussion – so the adoption of a motion to close debate can be followed by the introduction of further amendments, short comments on the text of the proposal, or motions to suspend or adjourn the meeting (e.g., A/SPC/16/SR.227, 2 Nov. 1961, para. 21; A/C.4/16/SR.1278, 2

Feb. 1962, para. 50; and A/C.1/16/PV.1240, 14 Feb. 1962, paras. 35–6). Second, in many cases where it looks like some members are trying to impose closure on others, motions to adjourn, which have priority over nearly all other motions (Rules 77 and 119 give them second place after motions to suspend the meeting), will be accepted instead. Delegates have always preferred adjournment to closure since it permits informal discussions for heading off unfriendly maneuvers or clearing up misunderstandings without forcing the meeting to move into the voting process. Closure motions have also become less frequent with the acceptance of time limits on speeches and greater reliance on informal negotiations in the preparation of draft resolutions.

Motions to close debate have seldom been numerous; they usually number fewer than fifteen per session. As Table 4.2 shows, many are withdrawn after other members object, or are headed off by motions to suspend or adjourn the meeting. Nor, as Table 4.3 shows, have stable majorities been the main source of motions to close debate. Thus, it has not been used to suppress minority rights of expression, although that potential always exists. Stable majorities are also rather selective about the issues on which they propose closure. The US-led majority used closure on Cold War issues like Korea, the civil war in Greece and individuals' eligibility for aid from the International Refugee Organization. The Third World majority has used closure mainly on questions relating to development, decolonization, or racism.

Though the Assembly usually respects individual members' right to speak, the rules have been used on occasion to constrain or silence particular members. The worst abuses are recent. In 1973 the Ethiopian chairman of the Second Committee ruled against a motion that the Portuguese delegate be prevented from speaking in a general discussion of world economic conditions; the twenty delegations involved then resorted to the older method of protesting Portuguese colonial policy by walking out (A/C.2/28/SR.1526, 5 Oct. 1973, paras. 42–4). The abuses that now occur apply to the pariah states. Though exceptions, such incidents stand as a warning that particularly unpopular members may not have their rights respected. The Assembly's refusal to accept South African delegates since 1974 is thus, among other things, a maneuver to silence them completely. This aspect of the credentials argument was made clear at the resumed 35th session in March 1981. South African attempts to raise a point of order early in the first plenary meeting were effectively stopped by an

African group motion to suspend the meeting until the Credentials Committee reported with the expected recommendation that South African delegates not be seated (A/35/PV.102–3, 3 Mar. 1981).

Summary

A growing membership and agenda would have forced the Assembly to move away from its rigidly formal and easily obstructed early practices. The Cold War provided some impetus for speeding the trend by heightening Soviet bloc intransigence and US-led majority impatience. By 1971 concern that the Assembly be able to conduct its business was general; even members of the Soviet bloc were prepared to admit that unless all

Table 4.2 Motions to Close Debate

Session	Total	Agreed by consensus	Agreed by vote	Rejected	Withdrawn	Headed off	Ignored
1st	31	14	6	7	4	0	0
3rd	49	6	24	11	2	4	2
5th	16	6	7	2	0	1	0
7th	7	5	2	0	0	0	0
9th	12	4	2	3	1	0	2
11th	8	1	4	1	1	1	0
13th	25	11	7	3	4	0	0
15th	19	7	6	3	2	0	1
17th	12	2	5	3	1	1	0
19th	n.a.	n.a.	n.a.	n.a.	n.a.	n.a.	n.a.
21st	11	3	3	0	3	2	0
23rd	24	7	7	8	0	2	0
25th	13	3	6	1	0	2	1
27th	7	4	1	0	0	2	0
29th	6	1	3	0	0	1	1
31st	5	3	0	2	0	0	0
33rd	3	0	3	0	0	0	0
35th	8	0	7	0	0	0	1
37th	0	0	0	0	0	0	0

Source: General Assembly Official Records of plenary and main committee meetings in sessions indicated.

Table 4.3 Closure Imposed by Stable Coalitions

Session	Total motions	Successful motions	Imposed by a stable majority
1st	31	20	3
3rd	49	30	11
5th	16	13	3
7th	7	7	2
9th	12	6	0
11th	8	5	n.a.
13th	25	18	n.a.
15th	19	13	n.a.
17th	13	7	n.a.
19th	n.a.	n.a.	n.a.
21st	11	6	0
23rd	24	14	1
25th	13	9	1
27th	7	5	0
29th	6	4	2
31st	5	3	0
33rd	3	3	0
35th	8	7	0
37th	0	0	0

Source: General Assembly Official Records of plenary and main committee meetings in sessions indicated.

members showed some self-restraint the rights of expression each so prized would be eroded.

Happily for the members, the general shift toward greater explicit reliance on consensus encouraged the wider use of private negotiations between regional groups as a method of refining proposals. This permitted omitting or shortening the phase of debate devoted to detailed examination of draft resolutions and removed many of the occasions for procedural wrangling. Even when proposals are adopted by a formal vote, inter-group consultations decrease procedural battling by reducing the number of competing proposals brought forward.

On the whole, the Assembly respects members' rights of expression. The available procedural devices for limiting or ending debate have not been used by majority coalitions to silence minorities. They have on occasion been used to silence particular states. So far this has been applied to South Africa and, to a lesser extent, Israel. While both, South Africa far more consistently, have encouraged this by intransigence, the incidents provide troubling precedents which could be used against others later.

A similar shutting-out can occur in the process of informal negotiations. When consensus is not, or is no longer, being sought the majority can omit serious discussion of proposals with likely opponents. Just as in debate, where delegations can decide not to speak, single delegations or groups of delegations can choose to remain aloof from informal negotiations. The United States and other Western states seldom participate in the Committee of 24 deliberations leading to most of the broad resolutions on colonial issues. The Soviet bloc never participates in informal negotiations on economic development issues. In each case, a group voice is lost. While each group has good reasons for its behavior, the result is a set of resolutions drafted without reference to its views.

The shortening of debate about specific proposals has permitted using relatively greater amounts of public debate time for polemical exchanges or mutual insults. While both allow members to let off steam and pursue bilateral conflicts without seeking decisions about them, the relative prominence of these activities helps contribute to the Assembly's poor public image in many countries.

Debate, negotiation and adoption of resolutions together form the decision-making phase of Assembly activity. Yet even securing a decision completely consistent with the initial demands does not guarantee a state or group of states that the outcome they seek will be attained. A decision directs that values be distributed or redistributed in a certain way, but does not itself guarantee that the addressees, whether political institutions or other actors in the political system, will act as directed. Securing action is the next step in the political process, implementation. The implementation of General Assembly resolutions is the subject of Chapters 5 through 8.

Chapter Five

The Assembly and Member States

Securing a favorable decision does not end the effort required to turn demand into outcome. The decision must be acted upon to have real political effect. This gives opponents of all or part of the decision a last chance to prevent or modify outcomes by obstruction, selective action, or inaction. Even in a well-integrated domestic system, where there are central administrative and enforcement agencies having the material resources and moral legitimacy needed for securing compliance from individuals and groups, the implementation of decisions remains a process fraught with hazard (e.g., Pressman and Wildavsky, 1973; Bardach, 1977; Grindle, ed., 1980). The hazards are even greater in international politics given the anarchical nature of the system.

The politics of implementation differs greatly depending on whether a decision is deemed binding on the addressees, or simply a recommendation. If a decision is binding, addressees are expected to act consistently with it. If it is a recommendation, then addressees are free to accept or ignore it as they choose, and the politics of implementation necessarily includes a greater amount of post-decision effort to persuade or induce them to act. Binding decisions will be treated in this and the next chapter; recommendations in Chapter 7.

The politics of implementation also differs according to whether a decision is addressed to member states or to other UN bodies. Decisions addressed to member states are expected to affect their conduct directly. Decisions addressed to other UN bodies sometimes affect their internal workings, but more often are meant to affect member states' conduct indirectly by altering the context within which they act. A decision to increase the number of people working in the UN Office of Public Information affects the speed and efficiency of its operations, but directly concerns states only in so far as they must pay for the extra salaries involved or are beneficiaries or targets of UN–sponsored publicity. A decision to add a new UN aid program or to convene a global conference has greater effect on states since it alters the web of institutions providing aid or creates an opportunity for changing the set of ideas states use in approaching existing or emerging international issues. This difference is great enough that binding decisions addressed to member states will be considered in this chapter and those addressed to UN bodies in the next.

The UN Charter gives the Assembly binding authority in eight areas, three of which apply to direct relations with member states: (1) designation of the states and other entities entitled to participate in Assembly or Assembly-sponsored activity, (2) approval of the regular UN budget and apportionment of assessments among members and (3) approval of Trusteeship Agreements and any alterations thereto (except in the case of territories designated Strategic Trusts). States may also agree to accept individual Assembly decisions as binding in particular cases.

On a strict reading of the Charter, all other Assembly resolutions directed to member states are recommendations. However, an annual meeting of representatives from nearly every state in the world also functions as a forum for debating what principles, norms, rules and procedures ought to guide world politics generally or individual conduct on some particular issue, such as the use of the oceans or respect for human rights. It was thus not long before governments and legal scholars began discussing the place of Assembly resolutions in the development of international law. Though often couched in unfamiliar technical terms, this is an important debate. If most states ever decide that Assembly resolutions are a separate source of international law, this will be a vast extension of Assembly authority.

Decisions about Participation

The Assembly makes a set of binding decisions having some material and great symbolic effect when it decides who may participate in its activities. These decisions allow it to comment on two questions: what entities should be considered states, and what set of people their governments. Both are questions of status that have traditionally been settled in the international system by each existing state, applying relevant rules of international law. States still make their own decisions for bilateral relations, but the General Assembly determines who participates in many UN activities. These decisions can then affect bilateral relations by indicating which entities and regimes enjoy broad international acceptance.

The power to admit a state to membership in the United Nations is shared between the Security Council and the General Assembly. The Assembly cannot act until the Security Council recommends that a state be admitted, yet admission does not occur until the Assembly approves. Though the Assembly could reject an application, it has not so far. However, the Third World majority made clear that neither Rhodesia under Ian Smith nor the black "homelands" created and given quasi-independence by South Africa would be accepted, deterring them from applying. In one area, Assembly pressure has brought positive action by the Security Council. While the Soviet Union long held out against US-led-coalition pressures to admit certain states but not others, neither it nor the other permanent members held out for long against Third World pressures to admit every state – no matter how small. The UN did not adopt the League practice of barring states on grounds that they were too small to fulfill all the obligations of membership. Rather, an open approach was accepted. This gave symbolic confirmation to Third World beliefs that independence should be the future of all colonies and extended the Charter norms protecting weak states from depredations by the strong to a larger number of entities.

However, the Assembly can be used to endorse or reject claims to statehood when issuing invitations to UN-sponsored conferences. During the Cold War, much East–West sparring occurred over the issue of whether "all states" or only "members of the United Nations or the specialized agencies" should be invited to the various diplomatic conferences held under UN auspices. The Soviet Union insisted on an "all states" formula in order to secure invitations for East Germany, North Korea and North Vietnam. The United States insisted on the more restrictive formula so the Soviet bloc could not acquire any form of UN acknowledgement of their status (e.g., A/C.2/14/SR.602–4, 26–7 Oct. 1959, and SR.606, 29 Oct. 1959; A/C.3/21/SR.1407–10, 28 Oct.–1 Nov. 1966). The issue disappeared in the mid-1970s only when the two Germanies recognized each other's statehood and were admitted to the UN simultaneously, when North Vietnam imposed unification on the South in 1975 and the unified state was admitted to the UN, and when North Korea achieved parity with South Korea by a grant of observer status in 1973.

The Assembly can also endorse various claims to statehood or other international status when it grants a nonmember state, an intergovernmental organization, or a "national liberation group" observer status. Initially observer status was limited to states not members of the United Nations, entities that could be defined as states like the Vatican, or regional international organizations. Until the 1960s observer status had a Cold War aspect, with the US-led majority granting observer status to its half of divided countries while denying status to the Soviet bloc half. In this way, the impact of Soviet vetoes against membership was partly overcome. In the late 1960s the Third World majority began extending observer status to African "national liberation groups" recognized by the OAU, such as the Patriotic Front in Rhodesia (Zimbabwe) or Frelimo in Mozambique. In most cases, this constituted Assembly endorsement of independent statehood for the territory involved; in the Rhodesian case it meant Assembly endorsement of a change of government as a precondition for international acknowledgement of a territory's independence. This helped the groups broaden their international contacts beyond Africa and gave them a quasi-governmental status difficult to accord under the traditional international law of recognition. This was reinforced by Third World efforts to assure these groups wide participation in the specialized agencies and UN-sponsored international conferences. A similar desire to enhance a group's international position was obvious in the 1974 decision to grant observer status to the Palestine Liberation Organization.

The 1960s and 1970s also brought an increase in the number of intergovernmental organizations given observer status. The Organization of American States, the Commonwealth Secretariat and the Arab League had enjoyed such status almost from the start. After 1965 they were joined by the European Community, the Council for Mutual Economic Assistance, the Islamic Conference, the Organization of African Unity, the Latin American Economic System, the Agency for Cultural and Technical Cooperation, the Afro-Asian Legal Consultative Committee and the African, Caribbean and Pacific Group (organization of the developing states parties to the Lomé Convention with the European Community). This has reinforced those organizations' claims to be important international actors in their own right by permitting them to address the Assembly through their own staff rather than through Assembly delegations of their own members.

Not only are there more observers today, but the privileges of observer status have increased. Until about 1970 observers could attend debates, receive all UN documents and occasionally address main committees. These privileges were expanded in the 1970s because the Third World majority wanted to give extra legitimacy to the liberation groups. From 1971 their requests to address the plenary were granted when issues of particular concern to them were taken up only in the plenary meetings (e.g., A/31/PV. 41, 26 Oct. 1976, pp. 7–12). They also began to be more active in main committee debates (compare A/C.6/28/ SR.1447, 26 Nov. 1973, where the Swiss observer's request to participate led to lengthy discussion, and A/C.6/32/SR.14, 11 Oct. 1977, para. 18; SR. 18, 14 Oct. 1977, paras. 64–9; and SR.19, 17. Oct. 1977, para. 6, where they speak routinely). By the late 1970s observers were occasionally allowed statements in reply or after the adoption of decisions (e.g., A/32/PV.42, 21 Oct. 1977, para. 249; A/32/PV.73, 17 Nov. 1977, paras. 245–50; A/32/PV.57, 4 Nov. 1977, paras. 158–69). The shift to greater reliance on informal negotiations has allowed those observers who are so inclined to participate in private talks and have a hand in the writing of proposals (interviews with members of several delegations, 1982–3). This has meant that the older distinction between members and observers have been greatly reduced (Suy,1978; interview with C. Clyde Ferguson, 1981). The Third World majority does not adopt any proposal on Palestine lacking PLO endorsement,and the PLO observers help draft most of them. Though the national liberation groups were the intended beneficiaries, some of the intergovernmental organizations – particularly the European Community and the Council for Mutual Economic Assistance – have taken good advantage of their new opportunities.

The Assembly has greater influence when questions relate to who is the government of a particular state. Here it does not share power with the Security Council. Rather, it can act directly by using the procedures for verifying delegates' credentials. In traditional diplomatic practice, envoys sent by one government to another bear papers signed by their head of state, head of government, or minister of foreign affairs attesting that they are authorized to negotiate and make agreements on behalf of their state. The General Assembly, like the League Assembly before it, maintains this traditional practice, with the modification that credentials are addressed to the Assembly through the Secretary-General. At the start of each session the Assembly appoints a Credentials Committee to examine the credentials to be sure they are in order and report to the plenary. This is supposed to be a routine matter of making sure the proper authorities issue the credentials and that the delegates named are those who actually participate in the session, but it can be turned to endorsing or rejecting the sending regime's claims to be a government in two ways.

The most common occasion for contention is the arrival of two delegations sent by rival regimes. Since each member state may be represented by only one delegation, the Assembly must necessarily make a choice, a choice with strong political implications. Between 1950 and 1971 the Assembly spent part of most sessions debating whether delegates from the Republic of China or the People's Republic of China should be seated. Though by traditional rules for recognition of government the Peking government's delegation ought to have been seated once its control of most of the country was clear, the Korean War and later political events led the United States and and a number of its allies to oppose seating those delegates and insist on leaving the Taipei delegates in place. Those who supported the Peking government's claim thus phrased their challenge as a challenge to Taipei's right to represent China in the Assembly. This long debate went through several phases, each determined by the strength of the coalition put together by the United States. Until 1954 challenges were rejected in the Credentials Committee and not brought to the plenary. From 1954 to 1960 the plenary accepted General Committee recommendations that the matter would not be discussed, either in the Credentials Committee or as a separate agenda item. From 1961 until 1971 the matter was debated as a separate item. Since the United States could not be sure of victory otherwise, it persuaded other members to define the matter as an important question and then raised a blocking third. The issue was finally resolved only in 1971 as the United States itself was shifting away from its former hostility to the People's Republic. The Assembly rejected the argument that the question was "important", and by a simple majority adopted an Albanian motion providing not only that PRC delegates be seated as "the only legitimate representatives of China to the United Nations," but also that ROC delegates be "expelled forthwith" (Resolution 2758 [XXVI]). This prevented adoption of the "two Chinas" solutions being discussed by United States and other delegates (Note, 1971, pp. 480–4). The Assembly has had to make choices between rival delegations on four other occasions. In 1960 rival delegations appointed respectively by President Kasavubu and Prime Minister Lumumba of the then

Republic of the Congo (now Zaire) arrived in New York. The rules provided no way out, since heads of state and heads of government were equally entitled to issue credentials. Understandably, no one thought each might send a different delegation. With Zaire on the verge of civil war, the Assembly's decision was a serious political choice that could influence the outcome. At the time, most members supported Kasavubu's delegation (A/15/PV.911–12, 7–8 Nov. 1960; PV.917–24, 18–22 Nov. 1960; A/15/Annex 3, Doc. A/4743). Once seated, a Western–Third World coalition was able to keep them in place, which became important when justifying the UN Congo operation. In 1962 the Yemen civil war produced rival delegations, one sent by the newly proclaimed republic and the other by the previously ruling monarchical government. The Assembly accepted the republican delegates (A/17/PV.1201–2, 20 Dec. 1962; *UN Yearbook*, 1962, pp. 148–9), giving them the international advantage. In 1973 some Third World and Eastern European delegations proposed seating delegates from the Khmer Rouge "government in exile" then based in China but managing guerrilla campaigns in Cambodia rather than the republican delegates sent by Lon Nol. Supporters of the latter, led by the United States, were able to defer the question at both the 28th and 29th sessions. By the time the 30th session met in September 1975 the Khmer Rouge ruled all of Cambodia, and its delegates were seated without challenge (A/28/PV.2141, 5 Oct. 1973; A/29/PV.2320, 16 Dec. 1974; A/30/PV.2351, 16 Sept. 1975). Cambodia was also the subject of the fourth argument, running since 1980. As a protest against the Vietnamese invasion and imposition of a government subservient to itself, the ASEAN states persuaded a majority of the Credentials Committee to recommend seating the Khmer Rouge (Pol Pot) delegates anyway. The Soviet bloc then took the matter to the plenary, where both its proposal to seat the Heng Semrin delegation and the Indian proposal – which delegations from the ASEAN states knew was really a Soviet idea (interviews, 1983) – to leave the Cambodian seat open were both rejected. Despite some rumblings of Western European intentions to shift votes in 1982 (New York *Times*, 23 June 1982, p. 6), the coalition supporting continued seating of Pol Pot held despite continued challenge on behalf of Heng Semrin's delegates (A.34/PV.2–4, 16–22 Sept. 1979; A/35/PV.34–5, 13 Oct. 1980; A/36/PV.3, 18 Sept. 1981; A/37/PV.42–3, and PV.45, 25–6 Oct. 1982). At the 38th session in 1983 challenge was confined to verbal protest unaccompanied by any motion to leave the Cambodian seat open (A/38/PV.34, 24 Oct. 1983).

The Assembly can also be used to question the legitimacy of a state or government. It cannot invoke the most extreme measure and suspend or expel a member state, since Articles 5 and 6 of the Chamber specify that such action may be taken only after the Security Council recommends it. However, the credentials procedure can be used to question the legitimacy of a government even when it is not immediately challenged by domestic opponents.

Such activity began with the reaction of an *ad hoc* Western, Latin American and Afro-Asian majority to Soviet suppression of the Hungarian Uprising in November 1956. The Credentials Committee report had not yet been received, which gave the *ad hoc* majority a chance to decide that the Assembly would "take no action" on the credentials of representatives sent by the new Kadar government. This decision was repeated at every regular, special and emergency session until 1962. That year the Hungarians asked the UN Legal Counsel about the situation and he advised the Assembly that Hungarian credentials were in order and ought not be handled in that way (*UN Repertoire*, Supp. 3, 1: 211; Werners, 1967, p. 76). Though hostile, the material consequences of this action were kept very small. First, the *ad hoc* majority went along with the Credentials Committee's practice of reporting only on the very last day of the session, which ensured that Hungarian delegates could participate in the Assembly's work because Rule 29 provides that "Any representative to whose admission a Member has made objection shall be seated provisionally with the same rights as other representatives until the Credentials Committee has reported and the General Assembly has given its decision." This doctrine was also used in 1983 to shunt aside a United States challenge to the credentials of delegates appointed by the Bishop government of Grenada after its overthrow and consequent US intervention long enough to permit the new government elected afterward to decide on appointments (A/38/PV.40, 2 Nov. 1983, pp. 3–5). Second, the eventual decision to "take no action" was interpreted as allowing participation because it fell short of outright rejection (Bailey, 1960, p. 47, for Hungary; presidential interpretations in A/25/PV.1091, 11 Nov. 1970, para. 286, and A/26/PV.2027, 20 Dec. 1970, paras. 254–5, for the early challenges to South African credentials). In 1973 a number of members led by Senegal and Tanzania attempted unsuccessfully to challenge the credentials of those members of the Portuguese delegations actually residents of Portugal's African colonies (A/28/Annex 3, Doc. A/9179, Add. 1). Portugal included them as a symbol of its contention that colonial peoples could be accepted as fully Portuguese if they qualified for *assimilado* status. The Africans, of course, denied the relevance and justice of the idea.

In 1974 the Third World took by far the most controversial step in this series of challenges when it decided to reject South Africans' credentials and interpret this as barring South African delegates from participation in Assembly work. The challenge itself had begun back in 1965, when the Africans took a leaf from the US book and secured a plenary decision to "take no action" on South African credentials by a vote of 53 to 42 with 9 abstentions (A/20/PV.1407, 21 Dec. 1965, pp. 74–5; A/20/ Annex 3). At the 25th and 26th sessions the decision was modified to read "approve all credentials except those of the representatives of South Africa" (A/25/PV.1903, 13 Nov. 1970, para. 132, and A/25/Annex 3; A/26/PV.2027, 20 Dec. 1971, paras. 249–50, and A/26/Annex 3). At the 28th session in 1973 the Group of 77 won adoption of an amendment to the Credentials Committee report stating that the Assembly "rejects the credentials of the representatives of South Africa" (A/28/PV.2141, 5 Oct. 1973, para.44, text in A/28/Annex 3, Doc. A/BUR/L.700). The President (Leopoldo Benites of Ecuador) did not interpret this as barring South African participation because of doubts about whether the Assembly could make such a decision when only one delegation claimed to represent a particular member since this might be tantamount to suspending South Africa's membership. At the 29th session in 1974 South African credentials were rejected by the more decisive vote of 98 to 23 with 14 abstentions (A/29/PV.2248, 30 Sept. 1974; Resolution 3206 [XXIX]). A General Assembly resolution then asked the Security Council to consider expelling South Africa from the United Nations, but a combined British, French and United States veto prevented any action. The Africans then sought their goal of ousting South Africa by other means, asking the President (Abdulazziz Bouteflika of Algeria) to rule on the meaning of the earlier vote rejecting credentials. He ruled that it meant the South African delegates could not participate in Assembly work, a ruling upheld by a vote of 91 to 22 with 19 abstentions when Western delegates raised a formal challenge (A/29/PV.2281, 30 Sept. 1974, paras. 12–86). From 1975 through 1978 South Africa decided that there would be no use trying to send delegates to any session, but tried at the 34th session in 1979, and at the 8th emergency session in March 1981 (which convened to discuss Namibia). On each of those occasions South African credentials were rejected, and the delegates were not allowed to participate

(Resolution 3200 [S–VI]; reports of the Credentials Committee in A/34/Annex 3, A/35/Annex 3 and A/E–12/Annex).

The Third World majority, this time under Arab inspiration, has also considered applying the same measure against Israel. Though for a time it appeared likely to happen at the 36th session in response to Israel's invasion of Lebanon in June 1982, the Arab states decided not to press forward. United States threats to cut off budget contributions and refrain from active participation in the Assembly, plus moderate Arab calculations that such a move would be silly at a time when an Arab summit had endorsed the latest United States peace proposals and was waiting for an Israeli response, prevented such a move. Later Iranian attempts to raise the issue won little support (A/38/PV.34, 24 Oct. 1983, pp. 27–43).

Assembly decision about status have direct effects only within the Assembly and its subordinate bodies. As will be seen in Chapter 6, other UN bodies do not necessarily take them as a guide, though they generally follow Assembly decisions about which contender rules a particular state (see below, page 179).

However, these decisions do carry important indirect effects. Access to the Assembly also permits full participation in the "corridor contacts" by which many states gather information, make trades of support on issues in or outside the Assembly and conduct a variety of bilaterial discussions. Ostracism, in contrast, severely limits what a government can do directly, though it may be able to have its positions expressed and its interests protected by friendly governments with access. While Assembly decisions do not affect bilateral relations or alter the immediate material circumstances of those in favor or disfavor with the majority, they do create a climate making it easier or harder to build and maintain contacts or support abroad.

Control of the Regular Budget

General Assembly decisions can commit member states to paying for a variety of UN activities. Article 17 of the Charter provides that:

1. The General Assembly shall consider and approve the budget of the organization.
2. The Expenses of the Organization shall be borne by the Members as apportioned by the General Assembly.

Both sides of the budgetary process, determining the amounts to be allocated to various activities and the size of each member's contribution toward the total amount decided upon, have caused constant controversy. Though some observers have viewed the conflict as a large fight over a trifling sum (e.g., Stoessinger, 1961, p. 3), governments have as generally recognized the argument for what it is: a dispute over who may exact what sums from whom for what purposes.

Through the Article 19 Crisis in 1964 most arguments about the size and uses of the regular UN budget followed East–West divisions. The Soviet bloc, conscious of its minority position, worried about US-led attempts to use the UN for Cold War purposes. Generally distrustful of international organizations anyway, the Soviet bloc has sought to keept the budget as small as possible and to minimize the extent to which its own members would have to pay for UN activities that clearly served Western interests, such as UNEF I or attempts to investigate the situation in Hungary after November 1956. However, a number of the most important arguments, particularly those about financing peacekeeping, also pitted Western states against one another. While France never went as far as the Soviet Union in the Article 19 Crisis, it also withheld payments and supported the idea that peacekeeping should be financed separately from the regular budget.

Early conflict over the budget was limited in three ways. First, the US-led coalition was not united, which imposed internal restraints on the majority. Second, arguments occurred within a general climate of budgetary restraint that permitted accommodating opponents on details without challenging the principle of collective financial responsibility too openly. The arguments did not pose the question of a huge budget versus a small one, but a relatively small budget against a smaller one. This Western preference for budgetary restraint showed up most clearly in the determined Western effort to define most economic aid activities as voluntary, with money raised by separate negotiations rather than through the regular budget. Third World countries did not challenge this disposition too sharply because of their own divisions and their focusing greater attention on the political issues of decolonization. Finally, budget decisions were, though to a decreasing extent as years passed, self-assessments by those with the ability to pay. Western countries did accept a certain amount of technical aid activity within the regular budget to accommodate other members of the US-led coalition before 1955 and to maintain Third World support on Cold War issues afterward, but kept considerable control over the budgetary process.

Despite the influx of newly independent Third World members in the 1960s, arguments about the size and uses of the budget remained relatively muted. This issue was joined not in the Fifth Committee, but in the Second where proposals for UN aid agencies were debated. Some Third World members pressed for funding them through the regular budget, but most realized that Western governments would not agree to this. Since the absolute levels of multilateral and bilateral aid were increasing well ahead of the global inflation rate, Third World pressure was having some effect on outcomes anyway. At the same time, an informal coalition of Britain, France, the United States and the Soviet Union was lobbying quietly but effectively for slower growth in the UN budget (Finger, 1984, p. 455), while the Third World was not ready to push the issue hard.

The climate of argument changed greatly in 1973. That summer the Algiers Summit of the Nonaligned shifted the Movement away from stressing neutrality in the East–West conflict to focusing on creating a "New International Economic Order" that would redress North–South economic inequalities. The NIEO package hammered together at Algiers assembled previous Third World demands, added some new ones aimed at increasing Third World influence in international economic decision-making and packaged the whole in blistering anti-Western rhetoric. All this might have remained a rhetorical exercise but for the 1973 oil crisis. The OPEC interruption of supply, followed by a quadrupling of oil prices, forced Western countries to pay more attention to Third World countries. It also heartened other Third World countries by providing the spectacle of a group able to gain wealth at the expense of, and exert clear political leverage over, the West. "One, two, many OPECs" became a popular slogan of the new assertiveness.

This new assertiveness changed arguments over the UN budget by increasing the attention given to the issue of automatic transfers from industrial to developing states. Various mechanisms were suggested, but few attracted much Western support. At the same time, global economic changes were reducing the flow of aid funds. First, added inflation brought about by the sudden rise in oil prices put the industrial countries into a deeper recession. Even those countries that continued to meet UN targets for aid (then 0.7 percent of GNP) were providing less because their GNP's fell. However, recession made a number of countries more reluctant to give aid. This mood was also reinforced by debates going back into the late 1960s about whether aid programs as then conceived really did anything for economic development. Significant segments of Western opinion had come to question their effectiveness, dampening enthusiasm even among those who felt the recession should not be an excuse to cut aid. Second, and in the short run more important for the UN budget, Assembly adoption of the resolution equating Zionism with racism touched off vehement opposition in the United States. When the US Congress decided to express the nation's displeasure by reducing US contributions to the voluntary UN aid programs, some Third World states increased their efforts to use the UN regular budget as a mechanism for transfers by putting more aid programs within it (Meagher, 1983, p. 112).

The idea was quickly accepted by the Third World coalition as a whole. Between 1978 and 1980 that coalition used its votes to increase the technical aid components of the UN and specialized agency budgets from $19 million to $41 million (Meagher, 1983 p. 114). Even allowing for inflation, this was a formidable increase, and came at a time when the industrial states were again suffering recession worsened by the 1979 oil price increase. For many Western countries, dissatisfaction was increased by the use of regular budget funds for meetings open only to Third World states. The United States also opposed the use of regular budget funds for Secretariat activities on Palestinian affairs, which it views as irremediably anti-Israel, and for meetings of the Preparatory Commission drafting detailed seabed mining regulations to supplement the 1982 Law of the Sea Convention.

The rate of this increase bothered the Western Europeans, many of whom sympathized with Third World desires for automatic transfers. It also caused another attack on the UN budget in the United States Congress. This led first to an attempt during 1979 and 1980 to delete all assessments for technical aid from US payments. Though defeated by narrow margins both times, this initiative forced the Carter administration to take a tougher stance than it might otherwise have done, and encouraged the Reagan administration's anti-UN attitudes. Congressional anger at continued budget increases led to a tougher measure in July 1985. This provides that unless the UN and the specialized agencies move toward weighting votes by size of assessment for the making of budget decisions by January 1987, the US will pay no more than twenty percent of the regular budget (Eckhard, ed., 1985, p. 150).

Though the United States is the most outspoken, other major

contributors are also perturbed by recent trends. By 1980 Western governments caucused regularly on budget matters. In 1982 an *ad hoc* coalition including the US, the USSR, Japan, and several Western European states served notice to the Secretary-General and the Fifth Committee that they would accept no increases in the regular UN budget beyond what was necessary to compensate for inflation. Despite differences of opinion on specific budget measures, this coalition continues to press for restraint in spending.

The character of budget arguments has thus shifted from an East–West to a North–South confrontation. They are also intensified by the fact that there is less agreement between those with the resources and those with the votes. In essence, the Third World coalition is seeking money from others, and those others are refusing to pay very much more. Each side blames the other. One Third World delegate summed up the situation as follows:

> We have always shown restraint because we are aware that too much spending can kill the goose that lays the golden egg. The problem is that now it is no longer their goose, the developed countries no longer care whether it lives or dies.
> (Quoted in Washington *Post*, 26 December 1982, p. A28)

For their part, the Western and Soviet bloc delegates see few signs of restraint, a mood encouraged by the fact that some Third World delegates have reacted to the new pressures for restraint by voting additional programs (Puchala, ed., 1982, p. 152).

Determining who pays what share of the money needed to finance the budget has always been a source of controversy. Assessments are determined in the Fifth Committee, acting with the advice of the Committee on Contributions, a group of ten specialists acting in their individual capacity. While the committee provides an analytical base for formulas apportioning assessments, the final decisions are reached by delegates ready to modify the specialist advice as political needs seem to require.

In 1946 assessments were initially figures on a scale based on a member state's national income and per capita income, with deductions for wartime dislocation and relative access to the needed foreign currency (US dollars). A strict application of this formula would have assessed the United States for 49.89 percent of the total, but US delegates got this reduced to 38.89 percent for 1946 and then in increments to 33.33 percent in 1954 with arguments that it would not be healthy for the UN to depend so heavily on one member for its finances (Stoessinger, 1961, p. 8).

At the same time, extremely poor states were all assessed at a minimum rate of 0.04 percent of the total and given a "low per capita income allowance" permitting those with per capita GNPs of less than $1,000 relief from 40 percent of the base assessment (Resolution 69 [I]). These decisions meant that a larger burden was placed on the middle powers, particularly as Europe recovered from the Second World War. Western European grumbling was limited because the size of the budget remained small; Soviet bloc grumbling that the formula overestimated the size of their national and per capita incomes persisted. Even so, Canada and the Western European members sought to protect themselves from too heavy a share of the budget by a rule, first accepted in 1948, that no member should have to make a per capita budget contribution larger than that made by the United States (Resolution 238 [III]). The Soviets protected themselves to some extent later by releasing figures that understated their capacity to pay under UN formulas (Franck, 1985, p. 259).

In the first decade and a half of the UN's existence, then, arguments about assessments featured some East–West conflict and a good deal of bargaining within the US-led coalition. Extremely poor members had minimal payments, the United States had a ceiling, and other industrial states had limits derived from the per capita contribution rule. This pattern of argument did not change even with the influx of Third World states in the early 1960s. Most of them were assessed at the minimum rate, so the issue was not pressing. In 1961 the assessments were apportioned such that fifty Third World states (half the membership at the time) together paid less than 3 percent of the total, the United States one-third, Britain, China (Taiwan), France and the USSR another third, and another fifteen industrial states some 20 percent (Stoessinger, 1961, p. 12).

The arguments about financing the UNEF I and Congo peacekeeping operations, which led to the Article 19 Crisis, did not feed into the main debate about assessments for several reasons. First, payments for both were calculated on special scales with complicated provisions for voluntary contributions to compensate for shortfalls. Second, it was tacitly agreed that contributions for peacekeeping would be credited to separate accounts to which the obligation to pay was waived for those who insisted hard enough.

Though Third World membership exceeded two-thirds of the total after 1961, the unified Third World coalition developed only later. For most of the 1960s, therefore, arguments over assessments continued along the lines developed earlier. The budget remained small enough, and the complications of overhauling the assessment formulas great enough, that few wanted to tackle the issue. Instead, incremental adjustments remained the rule.

Serious arguments broke out in the 1970s as the United States sought a further reduction in its assessment and Third World countries sought to reduce their burdens through either lowering the minimum rate or delaying the upward adjustments that followed from increased income. The first round, in 1972, was relatively quiet and received little public attention. The United States contribution was lowered to 25 percent, at a time when calculation strictly according to capacity to pay would have meant a 38.4 percent assessment (Franck, 1985, p. 256), while that of the poorest members was reduced to 0.02 percent (Resolution 2961B [XXVII]). While the admission of East and West Germany provided new contributors able to make up the resulting shortfall, an ancillary argument showed that the old intra-Western arguments about relative contributions were being joined by some OPEC states.

These reductions had the effect of shifting more of the burden to states with medium–level per capita incomes. This led to some intriguing alignments. In the 1972 scale of assessments, Canada, Denmark, Kuwait, Sweden and the United Arab Emirates all became eligible for reductions based on the per capita rule. The three Western nations waived the reduction, but the two Arab states accepted it (Meagher, 1983, p. 119). The following year a number of other Third World states urged the Committee on Contributions to study the matter and report on whether the rule should be kept. In 1974 the committee advised dropping the rule, a decision adopted in the Assembly by a vote of 101 to 7 with 13 abstentions (Resolution 3228 [XXIX]). The opponents were all OPEC members, who would have been eligible for reductions under the rule. Kuwait expressed their views most clearly when it argued that wealth based on a depletable resource should not be treated in the same way as wealth derived from a broad industrial base (A/C.5/29/SR. 1647, 22 Oct. 1974, para. 27)).

The whole issue of how to adjust assessments to account for the great changes in the world economy sparked intense debate after 1976, the first year in which new oil income figured in the calculation of assessments. At the time, assessment formulas were based on an average of the total and per capita national income of each member in the most recent three years for which statistics were available. The assessments figured in 1975, to apply in 1976, were based on figures from 1972–4. Having lost the protection of the per capita rule, OPEC members and a few others wanted to scale down or defer the increases. This put them in opposition to other developing states, which complained that continuing to use the 1974 scale would unfairly burden countries whose economies had suffered the most. It also inspired United States and Soviet opposition.

Hard bargaining within the Group of 77 led to a series of compromises. OPEC members received relief in the form of changing the base period for calculations from a 3- to a 7-year interval (1969–75 for the 1978 scale), allowing them to defer feeling the full effects of new oil income. The poorest members got the minimum assessment reduced to 0.01 percent (Resolution 32/29). In 1981 the populous developing states were able to shift part of their burden to the less populous by raising the ceiling for the "low per capita income allowance" to $2,100 and increasing the relief to 85 percent of the assessment (Resolution 36/321A). In return, OPEC members and some of the newly industrializing countries got upward assessment deferred further when the base period for calculations was lengthened to ten years (A/38/Annex 11, Doc. A/38/11). Between 1975 and 1982, China used its influence to win a reduction of its assessment from 5 percent of the budget, a figure assumed by the Nationalist government in 1946 despite the fact it exceeded China's fair share, to 0.88 percent (Franck, 1985, p. 258). Industrial state discontent was fanned by several decisions adopted in 1984. The Assembly accepted a scheme for limiting the amount an assessment could be increased from one scale to the next that heavily favored developing states. It also raised the low per capita income allowance to $2,200 and permitted additional relief for any developing state assessed above the minimum 0.01 percent of the budget that is burdened by high external debt or other serious economic problems. A separate formula assures that the few developing states that might otherwise have to accept higher assessments to help make up the resulting shortfall (Kuwait, Libya, Singapore, and Venezuela) will not be affected (Resolution 39/247B; Eckhard, ed., 1985, p. 151).

The result of all this bargaining is a UN budget that still weighs most heavily on the industrial states. Under the 1977 scale, the 117 Third World members together paid 11.73 percent of the budget; under the 1978 compromise scale, 10.96 percent (US delegate's remarks in A/C.5/32/SR.22, paras. 24–5). In the scale to be used for 1983–5, the 125 Third World members are assessed 9.86 percent of the total (calculated from Resolution 37/125). This situation has promoted an unusual unity of perspective between the superpowers. Both regard the newest scale as grossly unfair and are suspicious of all efforts to change the method of calculating assessments. The Soviets charge that the Third World members had managed to shift about $68.5 million of the budget on to the industrial states by 1982 (A/C.5/37/SR. 7, 8 Oct. 1982, p. 7). Among industrial states, mutual jealousies are probably less serious now than in the past. On strict calculations of ability to pay, the US contribution would now stand at 27 percent, so the one-quarter ceiling is less of a distortion than it used to be. Soviet efforts to underestimate income are limited by the fact that the USSR is widely assumed to have the world's second largest GNP. This forces it to use figures that will yield an assessment at least equal to that of Japan, the state with the world's third largest GNP (see discussion in A/C.5/37/SR.8, 8 Oct. 1982). In the 1983–5 scale, this meant assessing Byelorussia, the Ukraine and the USSR together at 12.22 percent, and Japan at 10.32 percent (Resolution 37/125).

Delegates realize, however, that this too is a temporary solution. The Committee on Contributions is still trying to find a formula that can be applied with reasonable objectivity and be accepted widely. Both developing countries paying at rates above the minimum and industrial countries remain unhappy. Whether they can form an effective coalition for change depends on the extent to which Third World solidarity is weakened.

Arguments about budgets and assessments show that no group of states is anxious to take up financial burdens. Eastern and Western disinclination to pay the sums desired by the Third World appears not only in debate on the regular budget but also in the discussion of voluntary contributions for particular aid programs. An individual government may be enthusiastic about a particular program, but the rapid rise of these budgets – from $400 million in 1970 to some $2,000 million today (Luard 1983, p. 678) – has created general resistance to further expansion. Arguments about the scale of assessments show that Third World members are also interested in avoiding paying. Discussions of both assessments for the regular budget and contributions to voluntary programs also show that the more prosperous Third World countries, like industrial states, prefer directing aid through bilateral or regional channels. These countries lobby hard to avoid being identified as "donors" in most UN programs. They have been willing to accept that status in programs where votes are weighted by contribution, such as the International Fund for Agricultural Development (IFAD), but not in others (Weiss, 1983, p. 668, discusses their views regarding the Substantial New Program of Action for the 1980s for the Least

Developed Countries). They have also lobbied successfully to limit upward revision of their assessments for the regular budget.

This general desire to minimize or shift financial burdens also shows up in two other ways: slow payment of assessments and withholding funds altogether. Slow payment is an old habit in the United Nations; at any given moment at least two-thirds of the members are behind in their payments (see, e.g., UN Doc. ST/ADM/SER.B/252, 12 March 1982). Occasionally slow payment stems from a real economic crisis or an inability to secure enough US dollars (though the UN is authorized to accept some payments in other currencies, US dollars remain the organization's preferred currency). For many countries, however, slow payment is simply a convenient habit, a habit so strong that every year a number must be reminded that if they do not pay something soon the Article 19 provision for losing their vote in the Assembly could be applied (e.g., A/34/PV.1, 8 Sept. 1979, para 14). This habit of slow payment causes the Secretariat many problems as it shifts money from account to account in an effort to meet the UN's obligations (Report of the Secretary-General on the Financial Emergency of the United Nations, Doc. A/C.5/37/15, 13 Oct. 1982). This situation has become more serious since 1982 when the United States changed its policy and joined the slow payers. When only $30 million of a $180 million assessment has arrived by the end of September (Franck, 1985, p. 263), the cash flow problems get serious indeed. This pattern of slow payment affects the voluntary programs even more acutely; many such programs have had to be cut back severely as promised contributions failed to arrive (Puchala, ed., 1984, and Eckhard, ed., 1985, make constant reference to such programs).

More troublesome, since the money is unlikely ever to arrive, are decisions to withhold assessments for political reasons. More than twenty-seven members are withholding specific contributions for political reasons (Eckhard, ed., 1985, p. 152). Arab states, France and the Soviet Union have long withheld assessments for peacekeeping operations. Other countries have other targets. In 1982 the United States decided to withhold funds equal to its 25 percent assessment for certain activities (Puchala, ed., 1983, p. 152). The UN budget thus represents a standoff. The Third World majority can vote various sums, but cannot collect them from unwilling payers. The only penalty for non-payment is the provision in Article 19 of the Charter that a member owing the equivalent of two years' assessments may be denied the right to vote in the General Assembly. Both the applicability and the seriousness of this penalty are severely limited.

Many states are unlikely to have the penalty applied against them. Article 19 itself permits the General Assembly to waive it when the nonpayment stems from circumstances beyond the member's control. Any developing country, particularly one of the least developed, can always make an argument that will win majority support. It is true that individual members have lost their vote for short periods of time (e.g. Central African Republic in A/37/PV.4, 25 Sept. 1982, p. 62), but so far they have been able to raise enough money to get their arrears below the two years' level fairly quickly (in the Central African Republic example, that government came up with enough one week later; see A/37/PV.14, 5 Oct. 1982, p. 2). Though the Third World majority may tolerate these temporary deprivations of vote so that the weapon is available against others (such as the Soviet Union, which would have hit the two years' level on 1 January 1986 but for a payment in July 1985 averting that situation until 1988 [Eckhard, ed. 1985, p. 152], it seems doubtful that a long-term deprivation of vote would be accepted so easily. It is also difficult to apply Article 19 to a superpower. As both the Article 19 Crisis of the mid-1960s and Assembly reaction to United States threats to withhold all contributions if Israeli delegates were expelled from the Assembly show, it cannot be applied to any member able to wreck the UN in return.

The range of application is also limited to the regular budget. Article 19 cannot be invoked for missing contributions to voluntary programs. This is why so much energy goes into defining what will or will not be financed from the regular budget and what from the voluntary funds.

Additionally, the penalty is not very severe. It extends only to loss of voting rights in the Assembly. This does not mean suspension of membership or expulsion from the UN, nor does it affect the right to vote in any other UN body. It does not prevent a delegation from participating in Assembly debates and informal negotiations. Since the Assembly now adopts more than half of its decisions by consensus, loss of voting rights is less significant than it would have been in the 1940s.

This situation led Harold Macmillan to argue in 1961 that budgetary obligations meant little in the UN:

> There is the compulsory subscription and the voluntary subscription. The only difference between them is this: the compulsory one is the one that you do not have to pay if you do not

want to, and the voluntary one is the one that you need not pay
unless you wish to.
        (Parliamentary Debates, House of Commons, 5th Ser.,
                vol. 651, p. 755; also quoted in Claude, 1963, p. 850)

Though containing an element of exaggeration, this points up the
important fact that there are limits to members' willingness to
pay. The recent rate of increase, from $1.2 billion for the years
1980–1 to $1.6 billion for the years 1984–5 (compare Resolu-
tions 34/320 and 38/326), has been too great for many. This
mood is only strengthened by the fact that requests for voluntary
contributions have risen and the regular budgets of specialized
agencies have increased from $300 million in 1970 to over $1,000
billion today (Luard, 1983, p. 678). The need to compensate
for inflation accounts for some of the increase, but most of the
large contributors think the Secretariat has been too generous
with its calculations of the amounts thus required. Further a
steady increase in the number and remuneration of Secretariat
positions and in expenses for travel and acquisition, rental, or
maintenance of premises gives critics of waste plenty of reason
for dissatisfaction. This mood is likely to be increased by a
Cuban-inspired initiative calling for reports about the effects of
inflation and monetary instability on UN finances. Many
Western observers view it as the prelude to a campaign for higher
assessments on Western members (e.g., Jackson, 1983, p. 157).
    It is true that the UN's regular budget is a relatively small sum
in a world where one F-18 fighter-plane costs $35 million, where
Iraq owes France $7.15 billion, where Service Corporation
International, a medium-sized firm, raised some $48.3 million in
a February 1983 stock offering, or where Kuwait's 1982 oil
revenue was about $11 billion. Though the total appears trivial,
specific budget allocations often are not. To a national liberation
group having difficulty spreading its message inside or outside
the country, assistance from the UN Office of Public Information can make a great difference. Thus, the approximately
$180,000 a year that the UN has allocated to dissemination of
information about Namibia ($175,000 in 1977; see A/32/8/
Add.4, 1 Nov. 1977, p. 3) vastly expands SWAPO's resources.
Programs giving exiles access to education abroad also cost
relatively little, but permit the training of a counter-élite ready to
play a role in its country's development once the existing regime
is overthrown. The regular budget supports a number of
administrative structures, such as the staff of the UN Development Program, which then work to keep particular issues before

governments and encourage the continued flow of voluntary contributions supporting the program undertaken. In certain respects, then, the regular budget represents "seed money" having a wider political and economic impact than a look at the figures might suggest. Even if growth of the budget stops, controlling the use of this "seed money" helps the majority influence the selection of issues for international attention and the terms under which they are considered.

Trusteeship Agreements

The UN Charter established Trusteeship as the institution through which the international community would supervise the administration of those League Mandates not yet brought to independence, any colonies taken from Axis states at the end of the Second World War and any other colony voluntarily placed within the system. Except in the case of "Strategic Trusts" (only the US-administered Trust Territory of the Pacific has this designation), where the Security Council had this task, administering states held authority under terms of a Trusteeship Agreement approved by the General Assembly. All such agreements provide that the administering state will apply in the Territory various multilateral treaties and, unless it has good reasons for doing otherwise, recommendations of the UN or the specialized agencies relating to attainment of the basic goals of Trusteeship – namely, promoting peace, development of the territory to self-government or independence and respect for human rights (Lauterpacht, 1955, pp. 116–19). The agreements also reaffirmed the administrator's obligation to report on conditions in the Trust Territory and on measures taken to implement UN recommendations that have application there. It also specified some other measures that the administering state undertook to implement.

The General Assembly has maintained the view that administering states must carry out the terms of the agreement, and has by and large succeeded in imposing independence as the sole goal of the Trusteeship system. In the case of Namibia, the Assembly decided, and the ICJ agreed, that its power of supervision over Trust Territories and League-era Mandates (an extension of the Charter brought about after South Africa refused to place South West Africa under the Trusteeship System; see ICJ opinion endorsing this in *International Status of South West Africa, ICJ Reports*, 1950, p. 128) includes dismissing the administering state if it persistently fails in its obligations (*Legal Consequences for States of the continued presence of South Africa in Namibia [South West Africa], notwithstanding Security Resolution 276 [1970], ICJ Reports 1971*, p. 16). So far the physical action necessary to get South African administration out of the territory has not been taken, but there are some indications that the South Africans have begun to accept the idea that they will have to leave.

The anticolonial and Third World majorities were never able to exert much influence over the Trusteeship Council. Article 63 of the Charter specifies that the permanent members of the Security Council are also members of the Trusteeship Council and that it should have an even balance of members administering and not administering Trust Territories. These provisions meant that it was hard for any Assembly majority lacking adherents among the Big Five or the administering members to control the Trusteeship Council.

In any event, the Trusteeship Council was never the central forum for discussions of decolonization. The fact that most colonies were kept outside Trusteeship meant that the main debates occurred in the Assembly's Fourth Committee where Chapter XI of the Charter, the Declaration on Non-Self-Governing Territories, became the vehicle for Assembly initiatives on the subject.

Special Agreements

There is an additional category of binding Assembly decisions not mentioned in the Charter. The twentieth-century proliferation of informal methods of agreement among states includes using Assembly resolutions for this purpose. To be used as the basis of a binding agreement, a resolution must meet two conditions. First, it must not involve a matter on which the Charter defines Assembly resolutions as having only recommendatory value. Second, the text of the resolution or statements made in the relevant public debates must include clear indications that the states involved accept the resolution as binding.

Most frequently this method is applied to specific questions. A large group of resolutions, such as Resolution 1991B, which defined a regional allocation of seats on the Economic and Social Council, set forth agreements about how to interpret the Charter or the rules of procedure. In at least two cases, states have used the same device for settling a substantive issue. The 1947 Peace Treaty between Italy and the Allies provided that if the parties could not agree on how to dispose of Italy's colonies in direct negotiations, they would refer the question to the General Assembly and do whatever it decided. They failed to agree, so took the issue to the Assembly in 1949. After considerable debate, the Assembly decided in Resolution 289 (IV) that Libya should become independent by 1 January 1952, that Italian Somaliland should be put under a UN Trusteeship administered by Italy for ten years and then become independent, and that a five member UN commission should visit Eritrea to ascertain whether the people wanted to join Ethiopia or preferred some other future. The parties then implemented these decisions (*Everyman's United Nations*, 5th edn., 1956, pp. 129–32, 269). Similarly, the transfer of assets from the League of Nations to the United Nations was effected by a General Assembly resolution. Paragraph 2 of Resolution 24 (I) specifically stated: "The General Assembly records . . . that those Members of the United Nations which are parties to the League Covenant assent by this resolution to the steps [transferring the assets] contemplated below."

Members can also agree to give binding effect to a resolution stating general principles or rules. Before the Assembly adopted the Declaration of Legal Principles governing the Activities of States in the exploration and use of Outer Space (Resolution 1962 [XVIII]) in 1963, the United States, Soviet and Canadian delegates said that those countries would respect the principles therein contained. This resolution had resulted from a consensus draft expressing ideas that had been winning support for several years (A/C.1/18/SR.1342–6, 2–5 Dec. 1963, and in particular SR.1342, p. 159[USA], SR/1342, p. 161 [USSR], and SR.1346, p. 161 [Canada].

Other Binding Decisions

Legal scholars have long debated the question of whether the Assembly makes any other binding decisions. They accept the existence of what Detter calls "external administrative rules" (1965, pp. 114–15), decisions that regulate the relations between an international organization and its member states. These specify how to comply with Charter provisions (such as registration of treaties as provided in Article 102) or regulate routine detail (such as the Economic and Social Council rules on granting consultative status to nongovernmental organizations). However, legal scholars disagree about whether any wider legislative authority exists.

Proposals to grant the Assembly legislative authority over member states were rejected at the San Francisco Conference (Russell, 1955, pp. 754–76). Instead, the Charter provides that General Assembly resolutions on matters other than internal UN operations are recommendations to the members. None the less, some international lawyers are sympathetic to the idea that certain resolutions may be viewed as creating binding obligations for members. Though this discussion is aimed in part at assuring that supporters of a resolution act in conformity with it, the real object of attention is states initially opposing the resolution. It may be assumed that states supporting it will help implement a resolution to the limits of their capabilities, though a sense of obligation helps prevent inattention or half-hearted effort. The willingness of states opposing a resolution to help implement it cannot be assumed. The prod of legal obligation is meant to get them to act, or at least not to obstruct.

A number of international lawyers have argued that the Uniting for Peace Resolution (Resolution 377 [V]) forms the basis of binding Assembly decisions now that it has been accepted by all members (Casteñeda, 1969, pp. 81–107, argues that use of the procedure by states initially opposed to it amounts to their acceptance). This resolution allows the General Assembly to make two types of decision binding on the members. First, approval of collective measures releases members from their normal obligation to avoid resort to force, or discrimination in trade, communications, financial transactions, or other activities violating treaties to which they may be parties with the target state (weakly by Lauterpacht, 1955, p. 115; Casteñeda, 1969, pp. 107–16; Schreuer, 1977, p. 118). This means that the target cannot resist collective measures by treating them as violations of the Charter or other international treaties. This precludes invoking the normal rules of state responsibility to secure an end to the measures and, in certain circumstances, reparations for damage caused by them (on the general law of state responsibility, see Brownlie, 1979, ch. 20). Second, the Assembly can create UN peacekeeping forces or truce observation groups to supervise withdrawal of armed forces from foreign territory or police cease-fire lines. Though the creation of a such a force or group could be considered simply another example of creating a subsidiary organ, the strong and immediate material consequences involved lead members to look at such decisions very carefully and to do so only when there is very wide agreement that the work should be undertaken.

However, it is well-established that a state need not contribute troops, money, or assistance to Assembly-ordered measures unless it wishes. In addition, national contingents of troops lent for the operation serve only if they are also acceptable to the state or states where they will be based (Higgins, 1969). States may incur political opprobrium, but not legal responsibility, if they ignore Assembly calls to join in a boycott or contribute to military measures against a particularly unpopular target. Similarly, the target incurs political costs but not legal responsibility by resisting Assembly measures or Assembly appeals to desist.

In instances where the Charter requires a defined action in certain circumstances or the functioning of UN programs requires previous factual determinations, Assembly findings that the requisite circumstance of fact exists may bind member states. The most widely accepted and widely discussed example concerns Article 73 of the Charter, which provides in part that

> Members of the United Nations which have or assume responsibilities for the administration of territories whose people have not yet attained a full measure of self-government ... agree to transmit regularly to the Secretary-General for information purposes, subject to such limitations as security and constitutional considerations may require, statistical and other information of a technical nature relating to the economic, social, and educational conditions in the territories for which they are respectively responsible other than Trust Territories.

Like other legal rules, this one may be regarded as containing a hypothesis and a statement of consequences to be attached if the hypothesis is true. Here, the hypothesis is that a member administers a non-self-governing territory, and the consequence is a requirement to submit information to the Assembly about that territory. Nowhere does the Charter define what constitutes a "non-self-governing territory" or list the territories to be considered as such. Application of the rule requires deciding which territories are non-self-governing, and Assembly majorities have always claimed that this was within the Assembly's competence. This was true even during the era of the US-led majority, but the insistence was greatly intensified in the early 1960s as the Third World majority formed. Though virtually all members endorse the Assembly's authority to decide which territories are non-self-governing, the Assembly has not always been able to enforce its definitions. It can hear individuals from the territory as "petitioners" in the Fourth Committee and the Committee of 24. It can debate and pass resolutions about the territory. However, a recalcitrant colonial power cannot be forced to make the required reports. This was proven between 1956 (the year Portugal was admitted to the UN) and 1974 when Portugal refused any information on its colonies on the grounds that they were integral parts of Portugal rather than non-self-governing territories (*UN Yearbook*, 1956, pp. 290–1). Nor does the Assembly definition by itself assure a quicker passage to independence or self-government, since that depends on the actions of states.

Assembly definitions in three other areas are also accepted as binding by virtually all states. For purposes of initiating debate, the Assembly determines whether some matter is an international question or falls within a state's domestic jurisdiction (see above, pages 21–3). It also specifies which states are eligible for the various UN assistance programs operating for the benefit of developing states, least developed states, land-locked developing states, states most seriously affected by the rises in oil prices since 1973 and states victims of natural disaster. Finally, the Assembly makes binding determinations in the application of its rules of procedure. In all, the Assembly's authority to make binding determinations for matters other than UN operations is very limited. In the legal literature, Article 73 is usually the only example offered (e.g., Schachter, 1963, p. 187; Casteñeda, 1969, pp. 117–38). This does not mean that the Assembly refrains from making determinations of fact. Many resolutions are devoted to such matters as condemning human rights violations in particular states, advocating various changes of policy, or condemning states still maintaining relations with pariah states. However, these determinations are matters of politics, not law. They are not applying a particular legal rule; rather, they are attempts to put pressure on the state addressed. Assembly determinations about human rights might have served a legal function, but the whole process has become so politicized as to have no credibility.

Controversies about the Assembly's authority to deal with specific international situations or to make determinations of fact are minor compared to those surrounding the effects of Assembly resolutions purporting to establish principles, norms, or rules for member state's conduct. This larger debate arises from the ever-present tension between the need to ensure continuity of legal rules and obligations, so that the actors may form stable expectations regarding their own and others' behavior, and the need to ensure sufficient flexibility that rules and obligations may be modified as the needs or desires of the community change. Stability is assured in most legal systems through a careful statement of the rules, whether by codification in statutes or treaties or by explanation of customary law in court decisions and specialist writings. Flexibility is assured through procedures allowing a centralized revision of rules.

In domestic legal systems, new legislation constantly replaces old, and new court decisions elaborate upon or adjust doctrines accepted in old ones. Hierarchical relations between the legislature and the courts, and between national and local authorities, ensure that changes are consistent with one another. The decentralized character of the international system makes maintenance of the balance between stability and flexibility more difficult. Changes in international law occur through the writing of new treaties, particularly multilateral treaties on general subjects, or through the processes of assertion and counter-assertion, action and reaction, that lead to the modification of customary law. Either method takes a long time; the latter is particularly drawn out and subject to great uncertainty owing to disagreements among the specialists about when customary rules may be said to have gained or lost validity (see the different formulations in Hudson, 1950, p. 26; D'Amato, 1971; Sohn, 1973, pp. 50–3; Bos, 1977, pp. 25–32). Those legal scholars and statesmen most impatient with the relatively slow traditional processes of change in the international legal system – whether from dissatisfaction with the existing rules, belief that the pace of 20th-century change requires more efficient mechanisms for bringing law up to date, or both – have been very interested in using Assembly resolutions as a mechanism for hastening legal change. Since nearly all states are represented in the Assembly and it can discuss virtually any matter of international concern, it seems an obvious forum for making general understandings about rules and obligations.

So far, however, even those scholars most sympathetic to the idear that General Assembly resolutions can be used for writing new rules of international law have stopped short of claiming that the General Assembly has already acquired a legislative role (e.g., Schachter, 1963, pp. 184–6; Falk, 1966, pp. 790–1; Bleicher,1969, p. 447; Elias, 1972, pp. 71–6; Sohn, 1973, pp. 50–53; Joyner, 1981, pp. 452–3). The farthest any will go is a claim that the process of inter-group negotiations establishes a faster method of creating customary law. Whatever the theoretical desirability of such authority, legal scholars realize that the attitudes of government still determine the legal weight of Assembly resolutions.

Most governments remain wary of attributing any general

legislative authority to the Assembly. This was expressed clearly in 1974 during a Sixth Committee debate about creating a special committee to study the role of the International Court of Justice in resolving disputes between states. The Congo, Ivory Coast, Kenya, Kuwait and Mexico proposed adding a paragraph to the preamble of the resolution creating the committee that would have read:

> Considering also that the International Court of Justice should take into account those developments in international law reflected in declarations and resolutions adopted by the United Nations General Assembly.
>
> (A/29/Annex 93, p. 2)

Other delegates had not wished to get into a discussion of the sources of international law, but felt compelled to address the matter once it was brought up. After objections had been expressed, the five sponsors of the amendment and the eighteen sponsors of the main draft resolution met informally and drafted a paragraph acceptable to all. This new paragraph read:

> Recognizing that the development of international law may be reflected, inter alia, by declarations and resolutions of the General Assembly which may to that extent be taken into consideration by the International Court of Justice.
>
> (A/29/Annex 93, p. 2; the eighth preambular paragraph of Resolution 3232 [XXIX])

Despite the fact that sponsors of the amendment denied they intended to say General Assembly resolutions were a source of binding rules (Mexican remarks in A/C.6/29/SR. 1486, 28 Oct. 1974, paras. 4–11) and accepted this modification of their handiwork, other delegates criticized even this formulation. The Brazilian, British, Bulgarian, Byelorussian, Chilean, East German, Hungarian, Israeli, Japanese, Soviet, Turkish, Ukranian and United States delegates gave explanations of vote running from regret that the paragraph had been included to statements that had it been put to a separate vote they would have opposed it (A/C.6/29/SR.1492, 5 Nov. 1974, paras. 4–49). Only one delegation, the Algerian, expressed support for the paragraph (SR. 1492, para. 43).

Debate was joined again briefly when the United States adopted unilateral deep seabed mining legislation in 1979. Since the Law of the Sea Convention was not yet opened for signature, a number of governments and legal scholars argued that the US move was illegal because it violated the "common heritage" principle established in the General Assembly's Declaration of Principles governing the Seabed and the Ocean Floor, and the Subsoil thereof, beyond the Limits of National Jurisdiction (Resolution 2749 [XXV]). In 1980 an informal committee of Third World diplomats and legal specialists argued that since the Declaration had been adopted by consensus, it represented "instant customary law" (letter of the Group of Legal Experts on the Question of Unilateral Legislation, reprinted in UNCLOS III Official Records, 8: 80 [1980]).

This notion met with strong resistance, however. A number of delegations had foreseen the possibility of such arguments in 1970, and specifically denied that the Declaration could be viewed as anything more than a pointer of the direction in which negotiations were expected to follow (A/C.1/25/PV.1799, p. 1 [United Kingdom], and PV.1798, p. 6 [Soviet Union]). H. S. Amerisinghe of Sri Lanka, later president of UNCLOS III, and Raynoldo Galindo Pohl of Peru, then chairman of the Assembly's Seabed Committee, both pointed out that the Declaration was a statement of moral aspiration rather than of law (A/25/PV.1933, p. 21, and A/C.1/25/PV.1871, p. 3, respectively). Other governments have admitted this tacitly. With completion of the Convention in 1982, arguments against US and other (see Puchala, ed., 1984, pp. 104–6; and Eckhard, ed., 1985, p. 102) moves toward unilateral or "mini-treaty" deep seabed mining have cited the Convention rather than the Declaration (e.g., Resolution 39/73).

Another, albeit minor, indication of similar caution came from the UN Secretariat and the normally vehemently anti-Israel Committee on the Exercise of the Inalienable Rights of the Palestinian People in 1980. When they published a study on "An International Law Analysis of the Major United Nations Resolutions concerning the Palestine Question" (Doc. ST/SG/SER.F/4 of Sept. 1979), a prefatory note was added identifying the authors and stating that neither the Secretariat nor the Special Committee necessarily endorsed the authors' opinion that those resolutions were legally binding on member states. The Israeli government commissioned a rebuttal, which was also circulated by the Secretariat (Doc. A/35/316 and Annex, 3 July 1980).

This negative conclusion does not mean that Assembly resolutions lack all legal significance. Governments, no less than legal scholars, agree that the terms of resolutions and the statements made in debates over their adoption form part of the evidence about states' attitudes toward particular rules. Assembly debates and decisions thus help actors and observers determine which customary rules retain or have lost validity and indicate which of the possible revisions to existing customary or treaty rules enjoy the widest support. Assembly resolutions and debates thus supplement more traditional forms of evidence, with the advantage of offering a good deal of information in a relatively short time.

Most authorities agree that proving a particular custom is part of international law requires showing that (1) there is concordant practice in a matter of international relations over a considerable amount of time, (2) this practice does not meet with objections from other states and (3) the practice has come to be viewed as required by international law. General Assembly resolutions and debates offer a good deal of evidence about how states define and view particular rules. They are not good indications of practice since states often say one thing in the Assembly and behave differently outside. Even so, Assembly debates may include discussions of behavior and provide states not heretofore faced with the need to act with an opportunity to comment on the practice.

Assembly resolutions can be used as either positive or negative evidence of a rule's inclusion in international law. Positive evidence would show that states accept and abide by the rule. Negative evidence would show that a rule still lacks or no longer enjoys the acceptance and obedience of states.

Certain negative answers are easy to prove. The mere fact of repeated Assembly debates and resolutions on an issue can help disprove assertions that some matter is "essentially within the domestic jurisdiction of states." For instance, it is now difficult to argue that human rights questions fall within domestic jurisdiction, even though this was largely true until 1945. The proof begins with Articles 55 and 56 of the Charter. Here states agreed by treaty that attainment of "universal respect for and observance of human rights and fundamental freedoms for all," was to be one of the aims of the UN, and that they would "take joint and separate action in cooperation with the Organization" for attainment of that purpose. Subsequent Assembly action has two important legal meanings. First, it assures that Articles 55 and 56 are not among those parts of the Charter that might be considered "dead letters" for lack of invocation. Second, since the debates have involved most states in the world and it is clear that all accept the idea that the Assembly has competence to pass resolutions on human rights (though some object on occasion to

their content), they provide good grounds for assuming a customary rule that binds even those few states that are not parties to
the Charter.

Other negatives are harder, but possible, to prove. Assembly
discussions and resolutions show that many states reject the
pre-1945 idea that compensation for private property taken by the
state must be paid quickly, in hard currency and cover the full
value of the property. While the principle of compensation has not
been challenged, many states assert that the total may be adjusted
to account for various types of "excess profits" and other abuses,
and paid in the form of bonds or shares in joint ventures with the
newly state-owned local company. Though state practice (including the acceptance of particular compensation offers by private
corporations and their home governments) has been the most
important indicator of this change, Assembly discussions have
been useful because they allowed states not involved in compensation controversies to express their views.

Proving the positive proposition, that some rule is accepted as
part of international law, is more difficult. Not only do scholars
disagree about when the proposition has been proved, they disagree about which types of Assembly resolution provide useful
evidence. Some separate the legally significant from the legally
insignificant by the generality of the text. Some stress the type of
statement made in the text and in related debates. Some stress the
size, or the size and distribution, of the majority supporting the
resolution. Others stress the number of times the resolution is
cited in later resolutions. In short, there is no commonly accepted
standard for identifying the most valuable evidence.

A resolution is good evidence for international law when it
repeats a rule that appears to have been accepted in state practice
using language indicating that the states supporting the resolution accept it as binding. For example, Resolution 95 (I) sets forth
the definitions of war crimes, crimes against the peace and crimes
against humanity adopted for the Nuremburg Trials, and records
that the Assembly "affirms the principles of international law
recognized by the Charter of the Nuremburg Tribunal and the
judgment of that Tribunal." Similar language appears in Resolution 96 (I) on the crime of genocide, which the International
Court of Justice later said proved that the principles underlying
the 1948 Genocide Convention "are principles which are recognized by civilized nations as binding on States, even without any
conventional obligation" (*Advisory Opinion on Reservations to the
Convention on the Prevention and Punishment of the Crime of Genocide, ICJ Reports*, 1951, p. 23).

Resolution 217 (III), the Universal Declaration of Human Rights, provides a stark contrast. Here, governments were extremely cautious. The resolution itself states that the General Assembly

> Proclaims this Universal Declaration of Human Rights as a common standard of achievement for all peoples and all nations, to the end that every individual and every organ of society, keeping this Declaration constantly in mind, shall strive by teaching and education to promote respect for these rights and freedoms and by progressive measures, national and international, to secure their universal and effective recognition and observance.

This caution was also evident in debate, where only the Belgian, Chilean, French, Lebanese and Panamanian delegates said they viewed the rules contained in the Declaration as binding, and that usually with reservations about some of them (A/3/PV.180–3, 9–10 Dec. 1948).

In most cases evaluating the legal weight of a resolution is not easy because it expresses new ideas rather than preexisting rules. Governments generally take a cautious attitude toward resolutions, particularly those stating general principles and called "declarations". Many declarations are not left standing alone; they are quickly supplemented by treaties setting forth the same ideas in greater detail. This shows that states do not place great weight on the declarations, and still prefer the more traditional methods of making international law. If a treaty does follow, then its rules are binding on the parties and may, if conditions are right, eventually bind non-parties as well (see comments in ICJ Judgment in the *North Sea Continental Shelf Cases, ICJ Reports,* 1969, p. 4). Yet many declarations are not followed by treaties. Their legal weight must be assessed by other tests.

The legal weight of a resolution depends heavily on the majority supporting it. Few legal scholars maintain that size alone qualifies the special majority. Most agree that there must be few opponents and that the opponents must not include states with the material capability to overturn the rules by themselves (e.g. Falk, 1966, p. 783; Schachter, 1963, p. 186). Thus, for instance, resolutions laying down rules for conduct in space have little value without both United States and Soviet support. Soviet writers in particular have stressed the importance of consent from all major groups of states involved. They argue that General

Assembly resolutions may attain the force of law when they are supported by states of the world's two social systems ("socialist" and "capitalist") and do not violate the UN Charter (Tunkin, 1974, pp. 164–72; Hazard, 1977, pp. 19–21; Grzybowski, 1983, pp. 866, 869). Many others now argue that the majority must include most states of the five main regional groups and/or of those groupings representing different interests on an issue, such as industrial and developing states on economic matters. Most governments accept some variant of this view, and give greater weight to resolutions adopted without strong objection by any and with affirmative support from most states in the regional and affected groups.

In assessing whether such a majority exists, particularly when the Assembly adopts a resolution by consensus, it is necessary to go beyond the bare statistics of the vote to the text of the resolution and the statements made in debate. Some resolutions, such as Resolution 3314 (XXIX) on the definition of aggression, contain vague formulations of key points because any precise formulation would have destroyed all chances of its adoption (a consideration frequent enough that Arrangio–Ruiz, 1972, p. 485, believes even less credence should be given to general declarations than to other Assembly resolutions). For those seeking legal rules, such statements have little value. Others, such as Resolution 1653 (XVI) declaring that the use of nuclear weapons should be considered illegal, are not supported by a genuine consensus, since one important group of directly affected states (here those possessing such weapons) opposed them.

While the existence of widespread agreement on a reasonably specific rule is a reason for giving one resolution greater weight than another, its full weight cannot be established until states have an opportunity to act on what they said. In the case of Resolution 1962 (XVIII) on outer space, the superpowers and other states undertaking space activities have generally respected its terms and incorporated most of its rules into a treaty. In the case of the numerous Assembly resolutions on nonintervention, it must be concluded that the consensus in the Assembly means very little because states of all regions and sizes have continued to intervene in others' affairs.

Some writers have argued that sufficient repetition of the same rule, particularly if coupled with repeated citation of particular resolutions, provides evidence that that rule has become part of international law. This argument is particularly popular with Western advocates of human rights and Third World advocates of self-determination, who view the many citations of the

Universal Declaration of Human Rights and the Declaration on
the Granting of Independence to Colonial Countries and Peoples
(Resolution 1514 [XV]) respectively as having made them part of
international law.

It is easy to understand the attraction of this idea. First, it
provides a test of states' opinion over time. A rule asserted once
and then forgotten is not very important in current legal arguments. Second, it provides a test easy to apply. It is necessary
only to take collections of the Assembly's resolutions, which are
widely available, and count the number of times a particular rule
is asserted or a particular resolution cited (Bleicher, 1969, offers
examples of the quantitative tests that might be used). Evaluating
the effect of repetition would be easier if governments stated at
some point that an oft-repeated rule has become part of international law. Occasionally such a proposition is given treaty
form, evidence that a new rule exists at least for the states parties
to the treaty. For example, condemnations of apartheid have
been supplemented by the Convention on the Suppression and
Punishment of the Crime of Apartheid, to which sixty-five states
had become parties by the end of 1981 (*Multilateral Treaties
deposited with the Secretary-General: status as of 31 December 1981*,
UN Doc. ST/LEG/SER.E/1 of 1982). In most cases, however,
the issue is left unclear.

Again, the test of actual behavior must be invoked. A rule
more often violated than respected is not an effective rule of law.
It may be an exhortation, a moral standard, or a maxim
urging prudence, but it can hardly be viewed as a legal obligation.
The evidence of words must be compared to the evidence of
deeds. Only if the two are consistent is there good reason to
presume that a rule exists. Thus, the rule that colonialism must
end appears well established. Not only has Resolution 1514 been
cited time and time again, but the behavior of states shows that
they accept the rule (as noted in the ICJ *Advisory Opinion on the
Western Sahara, ICJ Reports*, 1975, p. 12). Former rulers have, on
the whole, been willing to see colonies (that is, territories
separated from the metropole by a body of salt water) attain
independence. Other states have not sought to acquire new
colonies. This can be seen very vividly in a recent conflict.
Argentina presented its attempt to capture the Falkland Islands as
a move to recover territory wrongly taken from it in the
nineteenth century; Britain presented its successful effort to retain
them as a vindication of the Islanders' right to self-determination.

In sum, though most General Assembly resolutions are not
binding, they all enter into the stream of legal discourse. Those

relating to a specific situation provide little evidence about general rules. Others, made once and then forgotten, have little effect even if they discuss general rules. Yet others come to play a prominent part in legal discourse. No one test assesses their weight completely. All the elements discussed – their text, the statements made in debates, the size and distribution of the majority supporting them and the number of later assertions of the rules they contain – go into determining their weight. Yet in the end, the resolutions themselves provide only part of the evidence. They must be supplemented by an examination of the actual behavior of states when faced with situations covered by the rule. Resolutions persistently contradicted by behavior are not strong evidence for the existence of a legal rule.

Summary

Assembly decisions bind member states in three areas: (1) determination of who may participate in Assembly and Assembly-sponsored activities, (2) approval of the regular UN budget and apportionment of assessments among member states and (3) establishment of conditions under which an administering state rules a Trust Territory. Additionally, states may agree in advance to accept a particular Assembly resolution as binding.

Questions of participation arise in most acute form when two or more delegations claiming to represent the same state arrive in New York. Though traditional international law rules encourage acceptance of whatever regime actually controls the state, the empirical question is not always easy to answer. Beyond that, the members know that any Assembly decision takes sides so have a strong incentive to apply other criteria to their choices. The only Third World innovation in this regard has been use of the credentials procedure to deny participation to governments when no rival delegation has appeared. Though much groundwork was laid in Western, Latin American and Nonaligned reaction to Soviet intervention in Hungary, the Third World coalition took the leap increasing the actual as well as the symbolic consequences to the point where Assembly action approached suspension of membership.

Budget questions have always received great attention. Spending decisions allocate a small but real set of resources, while assessment decisions determine who will provide those resources. Arguments about spending have usually pitted majority against minority, though until the 1970s these arguments occurred within a context created by the realization that no industrial state, East or West, wanted the total budget to grow too large. This realization thus muted the East–West and early West–Third World arguments. After 1973 the struggle intensified as the Third World majority sought to use the regular budget to assure a level of resource transfer that most industrial states refused to support. The old consensus limiting the regular budget by placing both peacekeeping and economic activities in voluntary budgets was breaking down.

Arguments about assessments have been more diffuse, pitting different groups of states against each other at different times. These have usually been arguments between those who would pay less and those who would pay more under alternative formulas. Here the main divisions were within the West until 1973 and within the Third World afterward. OPEC states' positions merely confirm the rule that the Third World coalition, like other groups, will accept a large UN budget only if others do most of the paying.

The extent of Assembly authority in the Trusteeship System was never matched by its range. The authority was broad, but the system applied to relatively few territories. Effective action in colonial issues required that Assembly majorities enhance the advisory Assembly role foreseen in the Charter provisions on other non-self-governing territories.

The charter allows for *ad hoc* agreements that particular resolutions will be deemed binding. Even at fifty-one members the Assembly was too unwieldy to be used for the definitive settlement of disputes, so this has been a minor aspect of Assembly activity.

Though they did not do so at San Francisco, states could agree to accept the General Assembly as a global legislature. Despite some interest in this idea among some legal scholars and a few Third World governments, most governments still reject it. Most states, including the more revisionist members of the Nonaligned Movement, prefer to confine the Assembly to recommendations. This does not prevent assertions that certain recommendations have acquired the authority of law through repetition, but means that the question can be treated on a case-by-case basis more amenable to members' control. Thus, even North–South arguments about principles, norms and rules focus more on their content than on the method by which they are created, revised, or supplanted. Arguments about method reflect differences mainly of emphasis. The Third World coalition, with its weak capabilities and its great desire for change in existing rules, wants a larger Assembly role in making international law since it is in control. Other states prefer a smaller Assembly role.

Since its binding authority over member states remains so limited, the Assembly must be used in other ways to exert influence on their conduct. One way is to approach the problem indirectly, by commanding or attempting to command other UN bodies to act in ways that will encourage desired or discourage undesired member activity. Obviously, the success of such efforts depends on the extent to which the General Assembly can be used to control the rest of the UN system, the subject of Chapter 6.

Chapter Six

The Assembly and the Rest of the UN System

The General Assembly's authority or influence over other parts of the UN system gives a controlling majority, particularly a stable one, opportunities for creating a UN system it prefers and influencing the context within which states and other actors operate through the activities the system undertakes or avoids. The UN Charter delineates spheres of differing Assembly authority over other UN bodies. Sometimes this authority extends to giving direct instructions or influencing another body by changing the size or composition of its membership. At other times it consists simply of making recommendations.

The Charter gives the Assembly binding authority over UN bodies in three areas: (1) the election of states to serve as nonpermanent members of the Security Council, elective members of the Trusteeship Council and members of the Economic and Social Council; (2) the establishment of staff regulations governing appointment, promotion, conditions of work and standards of conduct for members of the Secretariat, and the allocation of tasks to the Secretariat's various units; and (3) the establishment, selection of members and allocation of tasks to subsidiary bodies of the Assembly. Finally, the General Assembly can be used to influence the rest of the UN system by making recommendations about how that system should be structured and should operate.

Elections

The Security Council, the Economic and Social Council, the Trusteeship Council and the International Court of Justice are all defined in the Charter as "principal organs of the United

Nations" and assigned particular tasks independently of the General Assembly. Yet Assembly majorities can exert some influence over the three Councils and the Court through the Assembly's power to elect their members. The extent of this influence varies widely, depending in part on Charter provisions and in part on informal practices that regulate the conduct of elections. Charter provisions set two conditions: the majority needed for election and the special qualifications, if any, required of candidates. The most significant practice is that dividing available places among the regional groups in the Assembly.

Article 18(2) of the Charter provides that elections to any of the three Councils are "important questions" requiring a two-thirds majority. This means that a coalition comprising only a simple majority cannot control the result on its own. Article 10 of the ICJ Statute provides a different rule for the Court. Judges are elected when they receive support from an absolute majority of the General Assembly and Security Council voting simultaneously. The veto does not apply in the Council, but abstention and absence are both counted as equivalent to negative votes in these elections. An Assembly majority of less than two-thirds can determine the Assembly vote if all members come and vote, but can determine the whole election only if its members also comprise 9 of the Council's 15 members.

Other Charter and ICJ Statute provisions constrain Assembly majorities by limiting the number or type of candidates. Article 23 of the Charter limits Assembly influence on the Security Council significantly. It provides for five permanent members – Britain, China, France, the USSR and the USA – each with the right to defeat substantive decisions by its own negative vote. The nonpermanent members chosen by the Assembly serve two-year terms, and by custom are not immediately re-elected. They have a group veto if all hold together since the Charter requires that 9 (until 1963, 7) positive votes are required for a decision. An Assembly majority lacking connection with a sympathetic permanent member can provide itself a veto if it is able to elect its own members to all the nonpermanent seats. Whether it can do so or not depends on the informal rules that divide seats among regional groups.

Article 86 of the Charter establishes rules that make it hard for Assembly majorities to influence the Trusteeship Council. All member states administering Trust Territories and all five permanent member of the Security Council are automatically members of the Trusteeship Council. The Assembly elects only that number of additional members needed to ensure an even balance between administering and non-administering members. Since few states held Trusteeships, this meant elective members were always a small minority. The US-led coalition did have to control, but only because it included so many permanent Security Council members and administering states. The *ad hoc* anticolonial majority of the late 1950s and early 1960s could not control it since the administering states needed only one more vote to have a majority. The Third World majority would have been in the same position. Yet it never got a chance to try controlling the Trusteeship Council. The attainment of independence by many of the Trust Territories meant that there were only two administering states in 1963. They were more than balanced by permanent Security Council members, so there were no elections after that year (*UN Repertoire*, Supp. 3, vol. 3, pp. 216–19). Had the Trusteeship Council been serving an important function in the general decolonization process, the Third World majority would have sought Charter amendments allowing it to elect more members. However, the Committee of 24 was already the main arena of activity and the Third World had secure control there since places were allocated on a formula giving each regional group a share of seats roughly proportional to its size in the Assembly.

Article 61 of the Charter allows Assembly majorities to exert strong influence over the Economic and Social Council. There are no reserved seats or special qualifications; the Assembly elects all members. The extent of influence over the Council thus depends on the informal division of seats among regional groups.

Article 10 of the ICJ Statute attempts to place limits on Assembly influence additional to that of sharing the election with the Security Council. Continuing procedures used in the League to elect members of the Permanent Court of International Justice, candidates are selected not by governments but by panels of international lawyers designated by governments for that purpose. These panels, usually with four members, consist either of the national group of lawyers designated for service on the Permanent Court of Arbitration established by the Hague Convention of 1907 or, for states not parties to that Convention, of lawyers appointed to make the nominations. While governmental influence over the process remains, it is made somewhat less direct than if nominations came directly from the justice or foreign ministry. Rules that candidates be highly qualified specialists and that elected judges serve staggered nine-year terms also attempt to raise barriers against political deals. They do not prevent all politicking (Kelsen, 1950, pp. 468–9), but do mean that the politicking has to be conducted with some degree of subtlety and that where a government allows professional groups an independent voice that voice can be heard (e.g., election of R. R. Baxter to the Court in 1978, Schachter, 1980, p. 891).

For the Security Council, the Economic and Social Council and the International Court of Justice, the formal rules have been modified by understandings allocating quotas of seats to each of the five regional groups and providing that groups will accept one another's nominees. These understandings have ensured a certain level of minority representation. Whether this minority representation prevents majority control has depended on the voting rules and the size of the body involved. Though the Security Council was enlarged in 1963, the increase was not sufficient to give the Third World a majority of the seats. The ICJ has never been enlarged. Only with the Economic and Social Council has enlargement permitted majority control. Yet this represents little change since all seats on that body were always elective and always allocated on a formula roughly corresponding to the composition of the Assembly.

The allocation of regional quotas began in 1946 as a way of dividing electoral spoils among 51 member states in a reasonable amount of time. At that time, there were no clear political alignments among the members. The anti-Axis coalition appeared to be holding together, and differences of opinion about postwar international issues had not produced clear lines of cleavage. With no way to identify "political parties", the members agreed to fall back on League of Nations custom and divide themselves by rough geographical or affinity categories. Thus, seats on the Security Council and the Economic and Social Council were divided among the British Commonwealth and several rough geographical divisions as shown in Table 6.1 (*UN Repertoire*, 2: 8 and 3: 193; Assembly membership from Hovet, 1960, ch. 1).

Once adopted, this geographical tradition became deeply rooted. First, it ensured that all parts of the world would be represented in the UN's highest Councils, marking a break with what many members felt had been the overly European focus of the League. Second, it quickly became a way in which Assembly minorities could assure themselves of some representation in other bodies. This calculation became prominent in early discussions of Security Council elections, when the Soviet Union maintained that "Eastern Europe" should be defined to include only the pro-Soviet Marxist–Leninist states in the area, not such states as Greece, Turkey, or Yugoslavia that the US-led majority

Table 6.1   Distribution of Council seats in 1946

	SC (6 elective)	ESC (18)	Assembly (51)
Latin America	2 (33.3%)	4 (22.2%)	20 (39.2%)
Asia and Mideast	1 (16.7%)	1 (5.6%)	10 (19.6%)
Commonwealth	1 (16.7%)	2 (11.1%)	5 (9.8%)
Eastern Europe	1 (16.7%)	3 (16.7%)	5 (9.8%)
Western Europe	1 (16.7%)	3 (16.7%)	6 (11.8%)
Big Five		5 (27.8%)	5 (9.8%)

sometimes elected to Eastern European seats (Bailey, 1960, p. 39.
Today Yugoslavia is in the Eastern European group for most
elections). Third, it led to pressure for the enlargement of other
organs so that their composition would reflect the regional
balance in the Assembly. This last idea had little support before
1955; Latin American proposals to enlarge the Security Council
and the Economic and Social Council so they could become
"more representative of the Assembly" were rejected (A/
Jt.C.2&3/SR.30–3, 19–23 Oct. 1948, pp. 53–82).

Even after geographical allocation of seats was accepted, there
remained problems of assuring that members would actually
vote for states of the region supposed to have the seat. Initially
this was done informally, with each group telling others privately of their choices, and the others complying. Yet difficulties
continued. In the early 1960s, as discussions about enlarging the
Councils began again, the Afro–Asian group expressed dissatisfaction about its relatively small representation by contesting
Eastern European seats (Bailey, 1960, pp. 165–6; *UN Repertoire*,
Supp. 3, 2: 7). The Eastern European group, seeing this as
another US-led attack, insisted that some system of assuring a
region's hold be created.

This second round of discussion yielded results that gave both
the Third World and the Soviet bloc what they wanted without
making Western acceptance impossible. The Security Council
was enlarged to 15 by adding 4 new elective seats while the
Economic and Social Council was enlarged to 27. The seats were
then distributed on the formulas shown in Table 6.2.

Third World states thus moved far toward attaining their
preference that the regional composition of the Councils closely
reflect that of the Assembly (e.g., Libya in A/18/PV.1211, 23
Sept. 1963, para. 51; Burma in PV.1216, 25 Sept. 1963, para. 87;

Table 6.2   Distribution of Council seats in 1963

	SC (15)	ESC (27)	Assembly (113)
Afro-Asian	5 (33%)	12 (44%)	58 (52%)
Latin America	2 (13%)	5 (19%)	22 (19%)
Eastern European	1 (7%)	2 (7%)	9 (8%)
Western	2 (13%)	3 (11%)	19 (17%)
Big Five	5 (33%)	5 (19%)	5 (4%)

Nepal in PV.1218, 27 Sept. 1963, para. 119; Guinea in PV.1220, 30 Sept. 1963, paras. 158–9; Sudan in PV.1227, 3 Oct. 1963, para. 34; Tanganyika in PV.1231, 7 Oct. 1963, para. 22). These distributions allowed a united Afro–Asian–Latin American bloc to control the Economic and Social Council and to prevent decisions in the Security Council. Minority regions, particularly the Soviet bloc, gained assurances of some representation. The regional allocation of seats was put in writing and included in an annex to the resolution authorizing enlargement (Resolutions 1991 A and B [XVIII] for the Councils and 1990 [XVIII] for the General Committee). Once the enlargement went into effect, ballot papers provided for voting region-by-region and specified that voting for a non-regional state would make that part of the ballot invalid (example of a ballot in Bailey, 1960, p. 65). Western acceptance was eased by the fact that neither the veto nor the "permanent members' convention", under which the Big Five were automatically elected to most other bodies, was attacked. The latter allowed both East and West, but particularly the West, greater than proportional representation on other bodies.

Since 1963 arguments over the size of the Councils and the extent to which their composition should closely reflect that of Assembly have continued. Despite some informal attack (members' refusal to elect China to any body from 1960 until Peking's delegates were seated in 1971), the permanent members convention has persisted. Its implications were reduced in the early 1970s when the Third World majority pressured the affected regional groups (Eastern European, Asian and Western European and Other) into accommodating the Big Five within their allocations. This caused few problems in the Economic and Social Council and the larger subsidiary bodies, but did cause serious arguments over allocation of seats in several of the smaller ones (see below, page 213).

Table 6.3 Distribution of economic and social council seats in 1963 and 1971

	1963*		1971	
Region	ESC (27)	GA (113)	ESC (54)	GA (131)
Africa	} 12 (44%)	} 59 (52%)	14 (26%)	42 (32%)
Asia			13 (24%)	33 (25%)
Latin America	5 (19%)	22 (19%)	10 (19%)	24 (19%)
Eastern Europe	3 (11%)	10 (9%)	5 (9%)	10 (8%)
Western	7 (26%)	22 (19%)	12 (22%)	22 (17%)

*In 1963 but not in 1971 Africa and Asia were allocated seats together. The 1963 calculations also reflect the situation if the Big Five are put in their respective regions, a rule adopted only in 1971.

Table 6.4 Regional composition of ESC and General Assembly in 1980

Region	ESC (54)	Assembly (154)
Africa	14 (26%)	51 (33%)
Asia	13 (24%)	39 (25%)
Latin America	10 (19%)	30 (19%)
Eastern Europe	5 (9%)	11 (7%)
Western	12 (22%)	23 (15%)

The impact of these developments can be seen by comparing the composition of the Economic and Social Council after its 1963 and 1971 enlargements, as shown in Table 6.3 (Resolutions 1991 B [XVIII] and 2847 [XXVI]).

This comparison also points out the fragility of each change, at least as long as the Assembly grows continuously. With the addition of another thirteen members by 1980, the proportions had been disturbed, as shown in Table 6.4.

Were the Security Council and the ICJ to be enlarged, a united Third World would also be able to control them by providing a majority of the members. At present the distribution of seats among regions means that a unified coalition of Third World members can prevent decisions. Though the Third World coalition would like to expand its influence, it has had to accept the current situation because enlargement would require amending the UN Charter or the ICJ Statute (to which the same procedure applies).

Debate on enlargement since 1960 has pitted Third World states against both Western and Soviet bloc ones. China supported Third World positions in the 1970s, but may be discovering the virtues of small bodies and the veto. The interplay among the three groups has determined when and to what extent the various principal organs have been enlarged.

Both Western and Soviet bloc states accepted enlargement of the Security Council in 1963 because the allocation of seats left the Third World short of control. Even if all of the Big Five abstained, the African, Asian and Latin American members could not assemble the nine votes necessary for a decision on their own. The 1963 enlargement of the Economic and Social Council did place that body under Third World control. This did not bother the Soviet bloc, which preferred that situation to control by the US-led majority. Western states also accepted it. First, the Third World was not yet a united coalition so there was room for thinking that internal divisions would continue and be played out in that body as well. Second, some observers thought enlargement would encourage greater use of the Council by Third World states, which had just bypassed it to set up UNCTAD. They thought that the bypassing had stemmed from the fact that in the older 18-member Council, the Third World held 7 seats, a number insufficient to exert much influence. However their expectations were not fulfilled.

The fates of the Councils diverged in the 1970s. All proposals to enlarge the Security Council have met united Western and Soviet bloc opposition. Individual Third World delegations still press the idea, but most understand that enlargement will never be accepted (Puchala, ed., 1983, p. 141). In 1971 the Economic and Social Council was expanded again, to fifty-four members. This permits a large number of countries to participate in its work, but has not eroded Third World preferences for dealing with economic issues in organs of the whole membership.

The International Court of Justice has occasionally aroused Third World ire, but so far has not been the object of a campaign in favor of enlargement. This stems mainly from the highly specialized nature of the Court's activities and the fact that states can almost always avoid it. The fate of the Court depends less on the politics of the Assembly than on the continued unwillingness of states to submit most of their disputes to third party settlement. On those occasions when the Court is asked to give advice to another UN body, the majority controlling that body can influence the outcome to some extent by the way it frames the question. The Court may not stay fully within the constraints thus established, but must address the points raised by the question.

Creation of Subsidiary Organs

Article 22 of the Charter specifies that "The General Assembly may establish such subsidiary organs as it deems necessary for the performance of its functions." This allows it to create, rearrange, or abolish a whole array of committees, expert groups and study panels. Though the Charter is silent on this point, the Assembly also convenes special conferences to discuss particular questions or to draft multilateral treaties. Article 62 authorizes the Economic and Social Council to call such conferences on issues within its competence. Since its competence and membership are less broad than those of the Assembly, the Assembly has simply assumed the right to call conferences on its own. Though such conferences are not subsidiary organs in the strict sense, since the Assembly cannot change their agendas later or abolish them before they have completed their tasks, they do provide another way in which the majority can initiate international discussion of some matter. An Assembly majority is thus able to create a whole range of bodies – temporary committees of experts or states, standing committees, committees of the whole, gatherings of all member states to deal with particular problems, or new UN operating agencies.

Subsidiary bodies of the Assembly have a number of effects. First, they permit the Assembly to do more work. An *ad hoc* or special committee has more time to go into the details of an issue. Since subsidiary organs can meet between sessions, they can also function at a time when fewer issues are competing for delegates' attention.

Second, they can be used to channel Assembly debates and decisions in predetermined ways. Bodies like the Committee of 24, the Special Committee on the Exercise of the Inalienable Rights of the Palestinian People, the Committee against Apartheid, or the Human Rights Commission's Ad Hoc Working Group on the Human Rights situation in Chile, are created with definite mandates to suggest how the Assembly can act to best attain an already-determined goal. Sometimes states opposed to that goal have been able to frustrate such bodies by non-cooperation. The Soviet Union's and Hungary's refusal to give any information or permit visits to Hungary condemned to futility all the UN committees and representatives on the Hungarian question. Chile also used the same tactic with UN bodies investigating its human rights record for a time (Puchala, ed., 1981, p. 116). Similarly, the nuclear weapons states frustrated Third World purposes in 1973 when none agreed to participate in the Ad Hoc Committee on the World Disarmament Conference and all but the Soviet Union refused to participate in the Special Committee on the Distribution of Funds released as a Result of the Reduction of Military Budgets (Finley, 1977, pp. 182, 202). Disarmament debates went forward, but under revised terms. Much of the time, however, opponents have difficulty stopping or slowing action because a body can almost always manage to make some sort of report or recommend some sort of action. If the issue is one on which a majority of members feel strongly, such as colonialism in the 1960s or apartheid today, stopping such activities is impossible.

A "committed" subsidiary organ may create problems for the Assembly. In most cases, its membership will not reflect the balance of opinion in the whole Assembly. States having doubts about the goal tend not to seek membership, or to leave when the majority on the subsidiary body appears to be ignoring their views. The subsidiary body, then, comes to consist mainly of states very enthusiastic about the goal and likely to propose ambitious programs toward it. Since Assembly majorities are reluctant to disavow the work of subsidiary bodies they also control, this permits the enthusiasts to set the tone and pace of debate and decision. This is one of the processes by which moderate members of the Assembly are pressured into accepting more extreme views. This process is even more powerful if parallel efforts occur in regional or caucusing groups to which members of the majority belong. Decisions of the Committee of 24 or the Special Committee against Apartheid guide the Assembly much like the chairman's drafts guide the evolution of Nonaligned Movement declarations (on the Nonaligned, see Corea, 1977; Shaplen, 1979; Misra, 1981).

Third, all subsidiary organs, not only those committed in advance to a particular viewpoint, affect the timing and form of international discussion on the issues they consider. Creation of the UNCTAD allowed developing states to focus and intensify discussions about international economic questions not only because it was a conference of the whole, but also because its mandate was defined to mean almost exclusively North–South issues. The UN Environmental Program served not only to mark international concern about the effects of pollution; it permitted governments and transnational groups particularly worried about the problem to spread their views through a regularly convoked forum. The Outer Space Committee reminds the superpowers and other states with active space programs that all states have an interest in outer space, and will assert a right to help determine the rules for space activity. Expert groups can be used to focus attention on some new issue or, more frequently, to revive flagging interest. For example, the Brandt Commission was established to examine world poverty at a time when the developing states feared that the industrial ones were losing interest in the problem.

The notion that the composition of other bodies should reflect that of the Assembly has been applied to most subsidiary organs. This permits an Assembly majority able to control elections in enough of the regional groups to extend its control to the subsidiary body. Making the subsidiary body proportional to the Assembly is easy when it is a new creation. When it has existed at a certain size for some time, enlargement requires more negotiation. Though a two-thirds majority can decide both the number and allocation of seats on its own, such decisions come slowly because effective activity requires agreements with minorities or because the majority itself is divided on the question. Establishing or increasing the membership also runs up against trade-offs between proportionality to the Assembly and size. Unless the "permanent members convention" is ignored completely, a subsidiary body must have thirty members to reflect the regional balance in the Assembly. Yet thirty is well above the size that most specialists in administration regard as efficient. If a subsidiary body is to serve as an additional negotiating forum, like the Committee of the Whole on North–South negotiations or the Committee on the Peaceful Uses of Outer Space, efficiency is less important. If it is to perform some coordinating function, like the UN Council for Namibia, or provide specialist advice, like the Committee on Contributions, then efficiency is a more important consideration.

Under the US-led majority, Assembly subsidiary organs tended to be small. A few, like the International Law Commission, had 15 or more numbers, but most had less than 10. While the "permanent members convention" held in those numbering more than 10, there were no other set formulas for distributing seats.

The tradition of distributing seats in subsidiary bodies by set regional allocations arose after the 1955 influx of new members.

Table 6.5 Distribution of ILC seats in 1956

	ILC (21)	Assembly (80)
Afro-Asian	5 (23.8%)	27 (33.8%)
Latin American	a 4 (19.0%)	20 (25.0%)
	b 5 (23.8%)	
Eastern Europe	2 (9.5%)	9 (11.2%)
Commonwealth	a 1 (4.7%)	
	b 0 (0.0%)	
Western Europe	4 (19.0%)	19 (23.7%)
Big Five	5 (23.8%)	5 (6.3%)

It was most popular among Latin American members, since their twenty made them the largest group in the Assembly, and the Soviet bloc, which saw in it a way to assure itself some representation. Readiness to accept set formulas was expressed most clearly in the 1956 enlargement of the International Law Commission from 15 to 21. As shown in Table 6.5, negotiations resulted in a formula allocating 20 seats and alternating the 21st between Latin America and the Commonwealth (A/11/Annex 59, Doc. A/3427, para. 13).

Consolidation of the Third World majority led to further demands that the composition of subsidiary bodies reflect that of the whole Assembly. Occasionally this has meant insisting that the subsidiary body consist of the entire UN membership, as with the Committee of the Whole on North–South negotiations or UNCTAD. More often it has led to fairly large bodies, so that not only regional groups but sub-regional clusters can have continuous representation. Thus, the UNEP Council has 58 seats, allocated on the formula 16 African, 13 Asian, 10 Latin American, 6 Eastern European and 13 Western (Resolution 2997 [XXVII]); and the preparatory committee for the 10th special session (1st Special Session on Disarmament) had 78, allocated by the formula 19 African, 16 Asian, 15 Latin American, 10 Eastern European and 18 Western (A/35/PV.79, 3 Dec. 1980, para. 23).

The political reason for Third World desires that subsidiary bodies precisely reflect the regional composition of the Assembly is obvious. Subsidiary bodies almost always operate by simple majority, permitting a united Third World coalition to control them directly if their composition mirrors that of the Assembly. Such strict proportionality is not always attained, however,

Table 6.6　Distribution of seats on selected economic bodies in 1985

	UNCTAD Council		UNDP Board	
Industrial states	24		17	
Western		18		14
Soviet bloc		6		3
Developing states	31		19	
African		⎱ 22		7
Asian		⎰		6
Latin American		9		6
Floating				1
	55		37	

because the nature of the issue being handled requires balancing relevant interests instead.

This can be seen in the tripartite composition of the Eighteen National Committee on Disarmament, which includes the United States and 5 of its allies, the Soviet Union and 5 of its allies and 6 states outside either alliance system. This is a concession to the fact that many disarmament questions can be settled only with agreement between the two superpower alliance groups. Similarly, the political realities of economic negotiations require balancing a slight Third World majority (reinforced if the Soviet bloc sides with the Third World) with industrial state "over representation" in such bodies as the UNCTAD Council and the UNDP Board, as shown in Table 6.6.

Subsidiary bodies have grown larger for two reasons. First, most Third World states believe that as many states as possible should have an opportunity to participate in any subsidiary body. This belief is so strong that many are now created with a partly or wholly "open-ended" membership permitting any state to send representatives if it wishes. In other conferences and meetings on North–South issues, the general rule now is to appoint general committees and other bodies on a 3 Group of 77 to 2 Western to 1 Eastern ratio (Weiss, 1983, pp. 666–7). Second, the notion that a particular regional group "owns" its seats is so strong that it is far easier to add new places than to reallocate existing ones. The Soviet bloc has long insisted that a region's representation may not be reduced without its consent, while tensions between

Africans and Asians over which group should have how many "Afro–Asian" seats led to Asian insistence on separate allocations in the early 1970s. Though a divided Western group gave up one seat to Asia so that China could be accommodated on the Economic and Social Council in 1971 (A/C.2/26/SR. 1445–46, 14–15 Dec. 1971 and A/26/PV.2026, 20 Dec. 1971, para. 19), the norm holds on most occasions. An extra seat was added to the Committee on Contributions to accommodate China (Resolution 2913 [XXVII]; A/C.5/27/SR.1512, 12 Oct. 1972, paras. 42–52). The Soviets complained after the election of one more Westerner and one less Asian than informally agreed to the International Law Commission in 1976 (A/31/PV.68, 12 Nov. 1976, paras. 17–26), where balloting by individual allows such possibilities. The situation was righted the following year when a Western member died and an Asian was elected to serve out his term (A/32/10, 8 Sept. 1977, para. 4). The Indian proposal to break the long dead-lock between Colombian and Cuban candidacies to the Security Council in 1979 by electing a non-Latin-American state was universally rejected (A/34/PV.118, 2 Jan. 1980, pp. 21–5).

However this custom is not the only reason the Third World majority has not refrained from changing the composition of subsidiary bodies as it pleases. First, the Third World needs to keep the East and West interested in the UN, so has to give them some role. Second, strict proportionality is not necessary for control of most subsidiary bodies; holding a majority of the seats suffices. Third, both the membership growth since 1975 and the most likely future growth favor Asia over Africa and Latin America since, barring secessions, the greatest source of likely new states is the Pacific island groups just coming to independence. Asian numbers have risen markedly in recent years, from 36 in 1975 to 41 today. This may make Africa and Latin America, like the Soviet bloc and the West, more interested in keeping what they have than in starting discussions of reallocation.

Regulating the Secretariat

The General Assembly and the Security Council acting together elect the Secretary-General. Since the veto applies, an Assembly majority must find a candidate acceptable to all five permanent members. At the same time, the permanent members must find a candidate acceptable to the Assembly majority. The truth of both statements was amply proven in 1981. The Third World majority was better able to insist upon election of a Third World national when a Chinese veto ended a Soviet–US effort to get Kurt Waldheim reelected as the "least unacceptable choice". United States vetoes forced Salim Salim of Tunisia, the candidate favored by many of the Nonaligned, to withdraw his candidacy. Javier Perez de Cueller of Peru was then elected as a compromise candidate.

All other members of the Secretariat are appointed and supervised by the Secretary-General. However, the Charter gives the Assembly the right to establish staff regulations, assign tasks, determine the broad outlines of Secretariat structure and exercise oversight. An Assembly majority thus possesses considerable influence over a civil service working directly for the United Nations. Since the secretariats of specialized agencies are appointed separately, Assembly majorities can influence them only when they also form a majority in the specialized agency involved.

Nearly every decision of the General Assembly creates a task for the Secretariat. The creation of subsidiary organs means that personnel must be available for such services as translation, reference, distribution of documents, provision of facilities and advice on procedure. Some decisions, like those instructing the Department on Public Information to disseminate accounts of conferences or prepare educational materials on such issues as racism, women's rights and disarmament, or those asking the Secretary-General to circulate a draft convention to governments and solicit their views, give an existing part of the Secretariat a new task.

Much of the time, Assembly majorities let the Secretary-General determine how to organize the Secretariat. Certain steps, such as changing the level of a particular post, adding additional posts, or establishing new units, require General Assembly approval because they affect the budget. Until recently Assembly majorities accepted the Secretary-General's proposals. This happened in part, of course, because astute Secretaries-General lobbied for support beforehand. However, arguments about the size of the budget have led both Western and Soviet bloc states to resist many of these proposals on grounds that the Secretariat is already too large and inefficient. Sometimes objections are political. United States objections to the establishment of the Secretariat Law of the Sea office in Kingston, Jamaica, on a permanent basis (US delegate remarks in A/C.5/38/SR.20, 27 Oct. 1983, para. 11) were part of a broader campaign to prevent the adoption of the 1982 Convention so long as it contains its current provisions on deep seabed mining.

The Assembly can step in at any time, and has often done so. The establishment of the UNEF I peacekeeping force meant creation of Secretariat structures to supervise the operations. While many of the detailed arrangements were left to the Secretary-General, Assembly impetus lay behind his acts. The Third World not only insisted upon the creation of staffs to serve both UNCTAD and UNIDO but ensured that they consisted of Third World nationals committed to Group of 77 goals of economic change. The Third World has also taken a step avoided by the US-led majority. While the latter created "committed" subsidiary bodies of the Assembly and provided them with Secretariat services, it never created a unit of the Secretariat committed full-time to taking a side in a particular conflict. The Third World majority took this step in 1977 when it created the Special Unit on Palestinian Rights.

The post-1974 discussions about the structure and operation of the whole UN system of economic and social programs have included a major program of restructuring the Secretariat. Some members, particularly the major providers of UN funds, had complained for years about the constant growth, confusing organization and inefficiency of the Secretariat. A majority got interested in the issue only when it was linked to a broader discussion of how the UN as a whole could be reorganized to better serve as a negotiating forum and executing agency for programs aimed at securing the "New International Economic Order."

Reorganization of the Secretariat formed only one of eight points in the initial restructuring program, but proved the easiest to accomplish since changes could be made without necessarily adopting Western or Third World preferences on either the broader restructuring or the substantive economic measures to which it was related. In 1977–8 two major steps were taken. First, the Third World desire to increase the organizational prominence of development-related activities was partly satisfied by creating the post of Director-General for Development and Economic Cooperation as the second ranking member of the Secretariat. By a further understanding, the post was reserved to a Third World national whenever the Secretary-General is from an industrial country and vice versa (Meltzer, 1978, p. 998). However, the Director-General's role remains somewhat undefined because he lacks clear authority over the various UN development-related programs. Second, the huge Department of Economic and Social Affairs, long a target of reformers' criticism, was greatly reduced after Western European opposition prevented its complete dismemberment. In the end, three new units – one for system-wide research, planning and programming, one for managing technical assistance activities and a third for monitoring the implementation of resolutions adopted by the General Assembly, the Economic and Social Council and special global conferences – took over some functions while others were devolved to the regional economic commissions and the UNDP resident representatives in the individual countries (*UN Yearbook*, 1978, pp. 450–4).

These reforms have not ended the habits of bureaucratic sprawl, duplication and inefficiency that plague much of the UN system. Continuing argument over the relation of the wider restructuring effort to substantive changes on economic issues has slowed negotiations on further steps. Member-state and Secretariat resistance to any moves threatening bureaucratic "turf" has also torpedoed many proposals. States have sought to preserve their hold on particular posts, so generally resist outright abolition of any existing unit. The Group of 77 has been reluctant to see any change in the current UNCTAD staff, which functions mainly as the secretariat for the 77. The European Community resisted dismantling the Department of Social and Economic Affairs because the head is traditionally a Frenchman (Meltzer, 1978, p. 1015).

While negotiations on restructuring proceed, member states are continuing to focus considerable attention on the overall composition of the Secretariat staff. The Assembly, working through the Fifth Committee, has always viewed its authority to approve staff regulations as including the right to suggest the considerations that should be taken into account when recruiting or promoting staff. All Secretaries-General have asserted their right to have the final say over individual appointments and promotions, but realize that the Assembly's wishes cannot be ignored and accommodate them as much as possible.

While verbally endorsing the need for efficiency, competence and integrity in staff members, the Assembly has always pressed the Secretary-General to give great weight to geographical considerations. The US-led majority, beginning with a Secretariat composed largely of its nationals (Bailey, 1964, p. 74, notes that two-thirds of the Secretariat were British, French, or US nationals in 1946), expressed interest mainly in hiring staff of nationalities not yet represented on the Secretariat. The Third World majority, dealing with a Secretariat it deems overloaded with nationals of industrial countries and accustomed to quotas for seats in other UN bodies, shifted focus. It sought a more diverse composition at all levels, and took particular interest in ensuring that developing state nationals filled a larger proportion of the top posts. This drive became more focused after 1974, and was symbolized in Algerian foreign minister Bouteflika's remark that "the only thing left now to decolonize is the Secretariat" (quoted in Jackson, 1983, p. 159).

The idea of giving each member state a precise quota of the staff was rejected from the start, but Secretary-General Lie did accommodate members' views by establishing a more flexible system of "desirable ranges". Under his scheme, certain Secretariat posts (in 1980 it covered only 2,729 of the 23,624 posts at Headquarters; A/35/528, 24 Oct. 1980, Table A and Annex, Table 9) would be allocated to nationals of members in proportion to their state's contribution to the regular UN budget, with a 25-percent variation up or down from that number allowed to permit flexibility of recruitment, and a minimum of four posts per member. In 1962 the method of calculating "desirable ranges" was modified after small state complaints that a contribution-based calculation ran contrary to the sovereign equality of the members. The Fifth Committee was unable to agree on a scheme, so accepted Secretary-General U Thant's decision to calculate ranges by a formula that gave each member a minimum of five positions, then weighted for both population and share of the regular budget (Bailey, 1964, p. 82). In the early 1970s the minimum was increased and another adjustment made to weight population more heavily. Only in 1974 and 1975 did debates over the formula take on a clear North–South overtone. Some developing states challenged the existing formula on grounds that the categories used in reporting statistics lumped industrial and developing states together, and still laid too much stress on contributions to the regular budget (A/C.5/29/SR.1661–5, 13 Nov.–16 Dec. 1974, *passim*; A/C.5/30/SR.1742–62, 18 Nov.–6 Dec. 1975, *passim*). The categories have not been changed, but the formula was revised in 1976 and 1980 to weight population and membership more heavily. The 1980 formula is 57.2 percent assessments, 35.6 percent membership and 7.2 percent regional population. The Third World majority hopes to have the formula treat membership and contribution equally by 1986 (Jackson, 1983, p. 161). Even without further changes, some developing states will receive additional allocations as their contributions to the budget increase.

These continuing pressures have led to a broader recruitment of the Secretariat. As Table 6.7 shows for those posts subject to the "desirable range" system, the percentage of posts held by different groups of states has changed greatly since 1946.

Table 6.7 Distribution of Secretariat posts subject to the "desirable range" system

Region	1946	1960	1965	1970	1975	1980	1984
Africa	less than 1%	2.2%	9.7%	9.6%	11.1%	13.3%	16.0%
Asia and Far East	7%	14.7%	15.6%	16.9%	14.5%	14.8%	16.3%
Eastern Europe	7%	17.9%	17.5%	12.2%	11.5%	10.9%	10.1%
Western Europe	32%	24.7%	19.7%	22.7%	23.9%	23.6%	22.2%
Latin America	4%	6.4%	8.2%	9.1%	8.6%	8.6%	8.6%
Middle East	less than 1%	2.0%	3.7%	4.7%	5.0%	4.9%	4.8%
North America and Caribbean	50%	32.1%	25.6%	22.8%	23.5%	22.4%	20.7%
Others*	—	—	—	—	1.8%	1.6%	1.1%

*Stateless persons and nationals of nonmember states.

The 1946 figures include the whole Headquarters staff; later figures only posts subject to geographical distribution.

Source: Bailey, 1964, p. 78; A/15/Annex 60, Doc. A/C.5/833, p. 2; A/6077, 27 Oct. 1965, Table B; A/8156, 12 Nov. 1970, Table C; A/31/154, 19 Aug. 1976, Annex, Table 2; A/35/528, 24 Oct. 1980, Annex, Table 3; A/39/453, p. 19.

Having nationals anywhere in the Secretariat is helpful, but governments also want to see sympathetic individuals in policy-making positions. Pressure along these lines began after Resolution 2359A (XVII) of 1967 called for separate reports on the nationality of the top staff. By 1975 Third World efforts to expand its collective hold on top posts was in full gear. Resolution 3417A (XXX) made preambular complaint that developing states comprise 73 percent of the membership but industrial state nationals hold 64.5 percent of the top Secretariat positions. Here, too, successive Secretaries-General have sought to meet Assembly desires while avoiding the imposition of strict quotas. Table 6.8 shows that these efforts have yielded changes; however, they are still not as great as the Third World would like.

The pressures to distribute posts more widely have also contributed to a shift in the nature of appointments. The Charter assumes that the Secretariat will be a career service. In the early 1950s the United States did not object to a career service *per se*, but did insist on extending security checks to citizens already working for the United Nations as well as those seeking appointment. This made others wonder just what the United States

Table 6.8 Distribution of highest Secretariat posts

Region	Positions				
	1965	*1970*	*1975*	*1980*	*1984*
Africa	10	19	28	47	58
Asia and Far East	23	36	50	69	84
Eastern Europe	30	38	36	34	42
Western Europe	46	64	87	95	93
Latin America	7	17	26	29	38
Mideast	3	10	18	25	26
North America and Carribbean	35	54	58	63	61
Other	2	5	4	4	1
	156	243	307	366	403

Source: UN Yearbook, 1966, p. 928; A/8156, 225, 12 Nov. 1970, Table G; A/31/154, 19 Aug. 1971, Annex, Table 5; A/35/528, 24 Oct. 1980, Annex, Table 6; A/39/453, p. 20.

government really believed. Eastern European governments were perfectly clear about their preferences; they never hid their dislike of the career concept (see, e.g., remarks of A. Roshchin in A/4776, 14 June 1961, p. 11). Yet for many years most members supported the career concept. Secretary-General and General Assembly basically agreed that while short-term appointments had uses, people hired on them should never exceed more than one-fourth of the whole Secretariat (A/17/PV.1199, 19 Dec. 1962, p. 1194; A/5377, 18 Dec. 1962, paras. 16, 40).

Hammarskjöld had admitted that short-term appointments could assist in adjusting the composition of the Secretariat to reflect changing UN membership. His successor U Thant took this further as Third World demands for a redistribution of posts grew. By 1969 more than 34 percent of the professional staff were appointed on a short-term basis (A/7745, 5 Nov. 1969, p. 11). In 1975, 38.4 percent of the professional staff held such appointments (Doc. A/10184, 28 Aug. 1975, Annex, Table 9). The proportion has continued to rise as individuals recruited on a career basis in the late 1940s and early 1950s reach retirement age and are replaced by individuals on fixed-term appointments. With 80 percent of new professional appointments for a fixed term (A/8156, 12 Nov. 1970, Table D; Franck, 1985, p. 112), it will not be long before the Secretariat becomes a 25-percent-career and 75-percent-short-term-appointment service. This amounts to a general disavowal of the career service concept.

Besides insisting on the general "desirable range" for its nationals within the Secretariat, member states also exert pressure to have the Secretary-General appoint or not appoint certain persons to the staff. Virtually all governments insist on being consulted before one of their nationals is appointed. Some, like the Western governments, allow the UN to recruit their nationals directly, reviewing only after the Secretary-General has made a selection. Others, like those in the Soviet bloc, permit selection only from a list of candidates they present to the Secretary-General (Stoessinger, 1977, p. 3).

In many cases, individual countries have come to view specific posts as "their property" and succeed in having them filled continuously by one of their nationals. Each of the Big Five traditionally has a national among the Under Secretaries-General. Poland has long kept a hold on the post of Under Secretary-General for Conference Services (Puchala, ed., 1982, pp. 142–3). All the major contributors to the regular budget either have nationals in certain posts continuously, or trade off a vacancy in one post for an appointment to another of equal importance (Franck, 1985, p. 110). Among other members, some posts are earmarked for individuals from a certain region, a practice that received formal Assembly endorsement in 1980 at Third World insistence (Resolution 35/210). The strength of these notions can be seen in African dismay at Secretary-General Perez de Cuellar's decisions to replace the Ghanaian serving as Director-General for Development and Economic Cooperation – despite the fact that this was required by understandings reached when the post was created (see above, page 167) – and the Sierra Leonean serving as head of the personnel department (*The Economist*, 4 June 1983, p. 55).

Even where a post is not earmarked, appointment or promotion often depends on representations from the permanent mission of the individual's country or regional neighbors. This sort of lobbying is so widespread that most staff members now believe that "a successful career in the United Nations is contingent, above all, on 'contacts', 'knowing someone' and having pressure applied by members of their national mission to the United Nations" (*Personnel Questions: Report submitted by the Staff Unions and Associations of the United Nations Secretariat*, 1980, p. 11, circulated as UN Doc. A/C.5/35/17; also quoted in Franck, 1985, p. 114).

Both the desirable range system and these more specific pressures reduce the role of merit in initial appointments and promotions. Of the two, the specific pressures are the more insidious because they constrain choice far more than would any general quota. Successive Secretaries-General have found it difficult to resist the specific pressures partly because they are so pervasive and partly because resistance would consume political capital that might be needed for other things. Though the idea of specific post allocations has never been endorsed by the Assembly, member conduct has made it a widespread fact. Secretariat posts have thus become another item in the log-rolling that marks Assembly politics.

Structuring the UN System

While the Charter laid out a basic structure of the UN system in 1945, changes in world politics and the interests of members have inspired constant tinkering, usually by adding on new pieces. This tinkering can occur either by formal amendment of the Charter or by decisions that stop short (or can be interpreted as stopping short) of altering any structural feature established by the Charter.

Assembly majorities have always found amending the Charter difficult. Article 108 of the Charter stipulates that an amendment becomes effective only when ratified by two-thirds of the member states, including all of the Big Five. Both the US-led and the Third World majorities could muster the needed two-thirds if all members ratified the projected change. However, the fact that one or more of the Big Five have always been outside the Assembly majority has made Charter amendment almost impossible. Amendments to enlarge the Security Council once and the Economic and Social Council twice are the only ones that have been adopted in the UN's forty year history.

However, much rearranging of the UN structure can be accomplished by ordinary Assembly resolutions. They can be used to create new bodies, initiate treaty-making exercises that result in the creation of new specialized agencies, merge or abolish old bodies and lay down guidelines for relations between different parts of the UN system. Yet other rearrangements can occur tacitly. For example, the Economic and Social Council never served as expected, and its functions were taken over by the General Assembly (Gordenker, 1983, p. 23). Both of these processes of change can be controlled by Assembly majorities.

There were complaints about sprawling bureaucracies and uncoordinated efforts even in the 1950s, but restructuring the UN system was not a major issue for the US-led coalition. Its ventures were restricted to occasional campaigns for greater economy and efficiency and the creation of some new bodies to handle new issues, such as the International Atomic Energy Agency and the Commission on Human Rights. In the era between stable majorities, some (mainly Western) members continued to worry about economy and efficiency. Yet *ad hoc* coalitions were busy adding a proliferation of new bodies to deal with concerns dear to Third World states (such as the Committee of 24 or UNCTAD) or to address emerging issues (such as the Committee on Peaceful Uses of Outer Space). Organizational sprawl continued during the first decade of Third World control as a result both of Third World pressures for favorable fora and sympathetic operating agencies and of several Western decisions to concede a new UN body rather than a substantive position. By 1970 the result was a maze that confused everyone.

Though the Jackson report (*A Study of the Capacity of the United Nations Development System,* Doc. DP/5, 1969) included recommendations on changing the organization of the UN system, restructuring did not become a serious issue until the mid-1970s. Third World countries saw it in part as an element in the broader effort to secure a New International Economic Order. They also saw it as "the first real opportunity they have had, as relative newcomers to membership in the United Nations, of participating in the shaping of the system in an area of fundamental importance to them" (remarks of the Jamaican delegate on behalf of the Group of 77 in A/32/PV.109, 20 Dec. 1977, para. 33). At the same time, both Eastern and Western states were ready to discuss restructuring because they felt it was imperative to cut waste, reduce organizational sprawl and slow the growth of bureaucracies and budgets.

All these concerns feed into a two-track discussion about restructuring. The first, carried out mainly in the Special Committee on the Charter of the United Nations and on the Strengthening of the Role of the Organization, deals with improving the UN's ability to prevent or end wars and promote peaceful settlement of disputes. The second, carried out initially in the Ad Hoc Committee on UN Restructuring and, after 1977, in the various bodies identified as needing overhaul, deals with improving the UN's ability to serve as a negotiating forum and operational agency for economic and social programs.

Individual members have long expressed concern about the UN's ability to function in both areas and advanced proposals to remedy the perceived ills. On the political-security side, such expressions include adoption of the "Uniting for Peace" Resolution and later interpretations further expanding the role of the General Assembly, elaboration of techniques for peacekeeping pioneered by Dag Hammarskjöld and proposals to create UN mechanisms for mediation. On the economic side, they include the creation of such bodies as UNCTAD, the UNDP and the Jackson Committee. However, neither side of the problem received sustained attention from an Assembly majority until linked to its major substantive concerns. On the political-security side this happened in the late 1970s as impatience with Western vetoes of proposals to condemn South Africa and Israel merged with an older drive to increase Third World influence over the organization. Concurrently on the economic side, UN restructuring became part of a broader program intended to make the United Nations a more effective instrument for attainment of the New International Economic Order. Viewed in this light, both efforts are part of a broader Third World drive to maximize the role of the General Assembly in, and hence its own influence over, the rest of the UN system.

Third World efforts to reduce the Security Council's role further date back to the early 1970s. In 1972 thirteen Nonaligned states proposed outright abolition of the veto. Other Nonaligned initiatives included proposals to limit the veto to the most serious actions, such as the creation of peacekeeping forces, to abolish permanent memberships of the Security Council, or to enlarge the Security Council to nineteen members on a regional formula giving Third World states enough seats to be able to form a majority without help from smaller Eastern or Western states.

Though few Third World states have explicitly linked the proposals to abolish or limit the veto and to enlarge the Security Council, the combination clearly indicates the goal: Third World control of the Council approaching the strength of its control of the Assembly as closely as possible. As more states, particularly among the Latin Americans, joined the Nonaligned Movement in the 1970s and its members established more effective mechanisms for cooperating in the Security Council (described in Jackson, 1983, ch. 8), the drive for control intensified. However, it may have passed its peak. The same proposals are made, but increasingly obvious Third World divisions have reduced the energy behind them. Greater divisions among the Nonaligned have made cooperation in the Security Council more difficult. In fact, elections to the Security Council have become one of the most public manifestations of Nonaligned divisions. Since 1979 the Latin American group has not been able to agree on candidates for its vacancies on the Council three times, forcing elections into the Assembly in 1979–80, 1982 and 1984 (A/34/PV.47, 26 Oct. 1979 and PV.120, 7 Jan. 1980, pp. 21–5; A/37/PV.36, 20 Oct. 1982, pp. 6–21; Rubins, 1984). The African and Asian group also failed to agree on all candidacies in 1984 (Rubins, 1984). (Similar divisions have marked elections to the Economic and Social Council as well as other bodies; see General Assembly records for sessions since 1980.)

This effort also came up against unyielding Western and Soviet objections. Though China often sympathizes with Nonaligned initiatives, the other four permanent members remain adamantly opposed to enlarging the Council or abolishing the veto. The four also see dangers in proposals to limit the veto. They know that the preamble of a resolution or the authorization of an ostensibly procedural step like sending a fact-finding mission can be used to condemn or endorse the conduct of a particular side, then be used as a precedent for further action.

In response to this opposition Third World states turned to proposals that would strengthen the Assembly at the Council's expense without amending the Charter. One possible route lies in greater use of emergency sessions. The seventh emergency session shows the possibilities clearly. The Nonaligned decided in 1979 that it would seek an emergency session the next time the United States vetoed a resolution on Palestine. The United States provided the occasion on 30 April 1980, but the emergency session was not even requested until July. The session ended with the adoption of a formula whereby it could be reconvened at any time, a procedure used to call four meetings in 1982. The eighth emergency session on Namibia also convened in leisurely fashion.

Another route for asserting influence lies in ensuring that the Security Council does not meet to consider any crisis that would divide the Third World majority. This is difficult since the Security General or any Council member can request a meeting. Some Third World observers have argued that Third World control of the Security Council agenda is strengthened by the fact that permanent members have traditionally refrained from requesting meetings and generally refrain from sponsoring proposals (e.g., Nicaraguan Foreign Ministry, 1983). Yet there have been many instances of permanent members doing both either directly or through proxies. The Big Five have not yielded any of their rights even though they may have decided in the past to exercise them infrequently. Yet another possibility lies in deriving an Assembly right to lay down guidelines for Council activity from the fact that the Council must submit an annual report on its activities. This, too, has not proceeded very far.

Once restructuring discussion shifts away from determining the relative influence of General Assembly and Security Council to other subjects, Third World unity breaks down. Proposals to strengthen the Secretary-General's role as mediator, create a new Commission on Good Offices and Mediation, or merge existing fact-finding bodies do not command broad Third World support. Since most of these ideas also arouse opposition in East or West, none seems likely to be adopted soon (*UN Yearbook*, 1979, p. 161; Puchala, ed., 1984, pp. 146–7).

The economic side of the restructuring debate is a more wide-ranging discussion involving relations not only between the Assembly and the Economic and Social Council, but also between the Assembly and specialized agencies, between member states and UN agencies providing aid or services and between central UN bodies and the regional economic commissions. Most of this involves changes that do not require amending the Charter. Here, the Third World's majority's influence is constrained by the need for Western agreement so that funding will continue. The Soviet bloc also provides some constraints by opposing any changes that require amending the Charter or enlarging the regular UN budget (attitudes of groups noted in A/32/34, 13 Jan. 1978, Annex 1).

This side of the discussion has been split into eight issues: (1) the role of the General Assembly, (2) the role of the Economic and Social Council, (3) the coordination of efforts in various UN negotiating fora, (4) the role of the five regional commissions, (5) the financing and coordination of operational activities, (6) the reform of planning, budgeting and evaluation procedures, (7) the improvement of interagency coordination and (8) the reorganization of the Secretariat better to perform economic and social tasks.

Though the Ad Hoc Committee on UN Restructuring was able to agree on a series of steps in 1977, their implementation has been delayed by continued disagreements about the goals and paths of change. Third World states, particularly the Non-aligned, have pursued the vision of a General Assembly-directed system resting on steady finance and ensuring that all parts of the UN system cooperate in securing the substantive goals of the New International Economic Order. Western states are interested in reforms that will streamline the system and make its programs more efficient, but resist linking reorganization to the NIEO or reducing the autonomy of specialized agencies and negotiating fora (such as GATT) where they have greater informal influence than in the Assembly. Soviet bloc states are interested in changes that will save money or reduce Western influence, goals that often pull them in opposite directions.

At the same time, virtually all members want to be sure that UN programs do not escape their control while a coalition of organization officials and particularly sympathetic members seeks to protect any body threatened with abolition. Determining the future of UNCTAD poses particularly difficult problems. Though established as a negotiating forum, its secretariat has always served as a research and proposal-drafting group for the Group of 77. This activity has made it what one UN official calls "a trade union" (quoted in Meltzer, 1978, p. 1018). Western governments do not perceive it as a good negotiating forum, so would like to move that activity elsewhere. The United States even proposed a series of small consultative groups to deal with specific issues, a disaggregated approach anathema to the Third World. The result is stalemate. Not only are the Third World and the West at loggerheads, but many within the UN system doubt that UNCTAD as currently organized could do a good job. The results of UNCTAD VI did nothing to reduce that doubt, though recent measures taken by the Grenadan acting director have inspired some optimism (Eckhard, ed., 1985, p. 157).

Efforts to increase centralization through new Secretariat planning, programming and evaluation units and merging all twenty-five special fund programs except UNICEF into a single UN Development Authority have also bogged down. Western countries have agreed to the merger on efficiency grounds so long as it does not include the UNEP and the World Food Council. Third World countries have tried to link this to rules ensuring the allocation of funds according to priorities set by the General Assembly and greater autonomy for the five regional commissions.

Any effort to increase central coordination of and General Assembly authority over activities of specialized agencies, particularly the GATT, IMF and World Bank group, meet intense resistance. Most comes from Western governments. They are anxious to preserve their relatively greater influence in those agencies. They also want to maintain the traditional sectoral approach to activity so that they can better resist Third World linkage strategies. Yet serious resistance also comes from agency officials loath to lose their own realms of autonomy. (Meltzer, 1978; Krishnamurti, 1980; and Meltzer, 1983, describe these debates.)

The restructuring debates are simply struggles among groups of states eager to create a set of machinery more favorable to their interests. The Third World coalition could end the discussion at any time simply by voting resolutions embodying most of the steps it favors. It cannot alone transform the Economic and Social Council into another organ of the whole since that would require amending the Charter, but could do everything else. The fact that it has not suggests not only that it fears inspiring serious obstruction from the West but also that it is more internally divided than the public debates suggest. Division has manifested itself in Secretariat–delegate coalitions to preserve certain units; it may extend to other questions as well.

The Assembly and the Specialized Agencies

Though the restructuring debate goes on, Assembly–specialized agency relations remain the loose association they have always been. This looseness shows in two ways. First, the Assembly has no obligation to consult them when considering matters within their competence. Though the Assembly usually does, proposals to change the rules of procedure to mandate such consultation have failed (the scant notice given a 1961 proposal described in Ghanaian remarks in A/C.2/21/SR.1067, 11 Nov. 1966, para. 18; a 1968 proposal was laid aside after short debate in A/C.2/23/SR.1229–30, 25 Nov. 1968, and A/C.2/24/SR.1283, 18 Nov. 1969). Second, Assembly resolutions and decisions are not binding on the specialized agencies. The agencies are notified of all Assembly decisions, but take them into account in their work only when their own executive councils or governing assemblies adopt them. Thus, UNESCO's plenary assembly has not accepted and never cites the 1974 "Zionism is a form of racism" resolution in its work (interview with UNESCO staff member, 1983; also see, e.g., the General Conference's "Declaration on Race and Racial Prejudice" of 17 December 1978); and in October 1982 the IMF decided to approve a $1.1 billion loan to South Africa despite an Assembly appeal that it not do so (New York *Times*, 22 October 1982, sec. 4, p. 9). Though the Assembly has urged that both Israel and South Africa be denied participation in agency work, the record is uneven, with some agencies accepting the idea and others rejecting it (see lists of membership in *UN Yearbook*, 1983, part II).

Specialized agencies' independence stems from an independent basis for existence in their own constituent treaties, procedures for admitting members, budgets and income and staffs. It is also supported by the politics of policy-making in member states. States are represented in the General Assembly by foreign ministers and diplomats, but in the specialized agencies by ministers and personnel of the ministries dealing with the substantive issues handled in each agency. Thus, delegates to the World Health Organization tend to come from the public health ministry, to the Food and Agriculture Organization from the agriculture ministry, to the International Telecommunications Union from agencies in charge of telephone and broadcasting services and so on. Though the head of state or government can impose uniformity of policy on the various ministers, they do not accept subordination to one another. The head cannot pay attention to every problem, and generally has to allow, if not encourage, each minister to regard matters within his ministry as his business and matters outside as other people's business. This compartmentalization is being weakened by the growth of interdependence and increased awareness that each issue has ramifications for others, but ministers and delegates still attend different international meetings with their minds focused very much on what is happening in their own sphere. Thus, the other ministers representing their states in the specialized agencies will not automatically defer to views expressed by the foreign minister in the General Assembly.

This domestically rooted bureaucratic tendency is further encouraged by the different nature of debate in the Assembly and in the specialized agencies. The General Assembly discusses questions at a high level of generality where values, beliefs and ideologies are often more important than the precise nature of the problem at hand. The specialized agencies deal with issues at a more detailed level where operational decisions must be made and where more attention is given to specific situations. The interest is not as much in formulating broad general principles as in seeing how health can be advanced, or agriculture made more productive, or educational materials more effective. Specific circumstances and material interests of particular states thus come into play more often, leading to debates where problem-solving is usually more important than striking general poses or asserting theories. The contrast is not absolute; specialized agencies are capable of windy debates and political battles. Yet the difference is great enough that the agencies do not always subscribe to or follow up on ideas adopted in the Assembly.

An Assembly majority cannot, therefore, influence a specialized agency directly from the Assembly. Rather, it must rely on coordination among delegates in the relevant agency. This has been easy to obtain on certain symbolic issues (such as treatment of South Africa or Israel), but hard to obtain on specific issues once differences in national interest come into play. The same thrust toward revising existing international rules, campaigning against "colonial" or "neocolonial" abuses and increasing Third World influence over decisions exists in all UN bodies. The results differ agency by agency because of different mandates, voting rules and negotiating situations.

Summary

Assembly majorities can use that body to influence the UN system in several ways. They can influence the activities of some principal organs through the Assembly's power to elect members. They can directly control activity by the Secretariat or subsidiary organs of the Assembly. They can use Assembly authority to carry out a considerable amount of formal and informal restructuring of the UN system. They can try to influence specialized agency activities through recommendations.

Authority over the Secretariat and Assembly subsidiary organs provides the strongest channel for extending majority control. It can be used to bypass an uncongenial principal organ, as in the case of creating UNCTAD rather than using the Economic and Social Council. It can be used to initiate a new area of UN activity, as in establishment of the UN Industrial Development Organization or the UN Environmental Program. It can be used to alter the definition of particular issues, as in creation of the Committee of 24 or the Secretariat Unit on Palestinian Rights. The extent to which these UN system activities then influence member states' conduct depends on the content and context of the decisions made. Neither the Secretariat nor the Assembly's subsidiary organs have any more direct authority over member states than does the Assembly itself.

The effect of restructuring depends on the measures taken. Assembly majorities that do not include all of the Big Five cannot make decisions that require amending the Charter. They are unable, for instance, to abolish the Economic and Social Council or to create a strictly hierarchical relation between the General Assembly and the specialized agencies. However they can do other things, like redistribute authority between Headquarters and regional or local UN offices, assign new tasks to the

Secretariat, or merge existing aid programs, that have real effect on members.

The strength of Assembly majority influence over other principal UN organs varies greatly. For the Third World coalition, it was nonexistent with the Trusteeship Council, but this caused no anguish since that Council was playing such a small role in the decolonization process. It is low with the Security Council and the International Court of Justice because of limitations on the power of election, the relatively small size of those bodies, which prevents the full application of ideas that their composition should reflect the regional balance in the Assembly, and – for the Security Council – the veto. It is greater with the Secretariat because Assembly control over the budget on which the Secretariat exists allows great influence over appointments. It is also great with the Economic and Social Council since all members are elected and decisions there are taken by a simple majority.

Assembly majorities still have great difficulty influencing the specialized agencies directly. This posed less of a problem for the US-led coalition since it also had high influence in the individual agencies. Its relatively modest reform goals and strong acceptance of the sectoral approach to activity also meant it had few great objections to what the agencies were doing. The lack of hierarchical relation between General Assembly and specialized agencies poses a real problem for the Third World coalition. It is usually not as influential in an individual agency as in the Assembly, and would like to erode the sectoral approach so the agencies can be better mobilized to serve its revisionist goals.

To the extent that Assembly majorities can guide UN system activity, they can influence member states in two ways. First, many UN activities impinge directly on states by providing benefits such as aid funds, new information, or access to expertise they lack at home or by framing binding rules for particular interactions, such as International Atomic Energy Agency safeguards or International Maritime Organization rules on safe navigation at sea. Second, the rest of the UN system can be used to exert indirect influence through appeals and recommendations. This activity can capture states' attention and encourage negotiation, but is no more significant to producing outcomes than General Assembly recommendations. It rests on the same sort of symbolic and material incentives to action as do Assembly recommendations, which are the subject of the next chapter.

Chapter Seven

Assembly Recommendations and International Relations

The fact that a particular Assembly decision has the formal status of recommendation does not deny it all value. It does mean, however, that implementation must rest on foundations other than a perceived legal obligation to act as instructed. This requires framing decisions in ways that appeal to the moral conceptions, material interests, or both, of governments and other entities. A decision need not appeal equally to all; implementation will be effective as long as those motivated to act have sufficient resources to bring about the desired result. Of course, the resources sufficient for producing the desired outcome vary greatly from case to case, depending on the difficulty of the action requested and the amount of active opposition that has to be overcome. Opposition can be handled in two ways: by the application of power great enough to overwhelm it, or by the use of symbolic images to neutralize it. Assembly majorities have always used both methods, though the balance between them has changed over the years.

Symbols and Implementation

All deliberative bodies use words to influence conduct. Words explain what outcome is desired. Words also help motivate action by appealing to addressees' sense of moral right or wrong. Given the anarchical nature of the international system, Assembly majorities must rely heavily on such appeals since the Assembly can offer so little material inducement and threaten so little material deprivation. In Assembly decisions, as in those of national and local deliberative bodies, symbolic politics takes two forms. In the first, members state or restate principles, norms, or ideas that they believe do or should govern interactions generally. In the second, members seek to alter attitudes and behavior in specific situations by endorsing or condemning particular actions or positions.

When the Assembly states general principles and norms, as in the Declaration on the Granting of Independence to Colonial Countries and Peoples, or rules for activity in a particular field, as in the Declaration of Peaceful Uses of the Seabed, those members supporting the decision hope to see its precepts guide daily conduct. The precepts thus endorsed may be new at the time, like the Universal Declaration of Human Rights, or they may be reaffirmations of old ideas, like the long string of resolutions condemning intervention. Later resolutions reaffirming earlier statements may be intended as reminders of existing rules or steps in a campaign to secure wider acceptance of new ones. Many appear to be majority exercises in self-reassurance that despite considerable behavioral evidence to the contrary the rule does in fact exist. Weak states' constant reaffirmations of the ideals of nonintervention and noninterference are good examples, because both norms are constantly being violated by strong and weak, Western, Eastern and Third World states alike.

Principles, norms and rules have a number of political effects. At the very least they force governments to explain nonconforming conduct. If a government is loath to face international criticism on a particular matter, it may well alter policy. The British seem to have decided fairly early that large-scale repression of colonial rebellions would not be accepted in the post-1945 world, and the French came to the same conclusion after the Algerian War. Standards can also increase the likelihood of conforming conduct if governments adopt them into bureaucratic routines. When they do, decisions to violate must be made consciously and are likely to be challenged internally before acted upon. States conforming to accepted standards also have a strong defense if their conduct is questioned by others. In most cases they need simply point to the standard. Occasionally two standards may clash, but they are still in a strong position because accusers must then show why one standard should yield to the other in that particular case.

States violating standards have a difficult time unless they can show that they are conforming to a more important standard or that the particular circumstances justify their conduct. The Tanzanian government laid itself open to charges of intervention when it sent troops to overthrow the Idi Amin regime of Uganda in 1978, but was not criticized then, partly because Amin had earlier launched an attack on Tanzania but mainly because he was such a murderous tyrant that his ouster was viewed as a positive good no matter how accomplished. Neither United States attempts to justify intervention in Vietnam in the 1960s and early 1970s nor Soviet attempts to justify intervention in Afghanistan since 1979 have won much international support; too many governments reject the arguments put forward in each case.

Standards can also help sort out conflicting claims, legitimating one more than others. This has been particularly clear on colonial issues. As Patricia Wohlgemuth noted in 1963:

> Not the least among Unted Nations contributions to the case of the Portuguese territories is confirmation of the issue as a nationalist struggle for self-determination. Discussion focuses on the African population in the territories and virtually precludes consideration of the white settlers, the more numerous *mestizos*, and the few Africans who have chosen to "be" Portuguese. International debate is thus automatically structured to the disadvantage of Portugal, for the moral issue has long since been settled in favor of self-determination.
>
> (Wohlgemuth, 1963, p. 44)

Assembly resolutions can also affect evaluations of issues or situations by propagating theories of causation. Even when those issues or situations are open to several interpretations, the cumulative weight of Assembly resolutions may tip thinking toward one interpretation at the expense of others.

Majorities should be aware that a weak theory will not aid their cause in the long run. The US-led majority came to accept a world-view separating democratic "good guys" from communist "bad guys", but the heavy stress on political competition between the superpower blocs ignored things that many member governments believed were equally important. When the Soviet Union shifted policy from confrontation with the West to overtures to the Third World, its support for ending colonialism and fostering economic development made the whole theory less credible. For weak states hoping to avoid being dragged into superpower conflicts and anxious to discuss a variety of other issues, the Soviet shift made it easier to demand more from the United States. As new states with no experience of the Soviets but plenty of bad experience with the West joined the UN after

1955, the old notion lost appeal. Similarly, Arab efforts to discredit Israel were weakened, not strengthened, by attempts to equate Zionism with racism. Western states reject this equation vehemently, and even the more moderate Third World states have difficulties with it. Much of the current United States discontent with the Assembly rests on a belief that Third World views of the world are hopelessly skewed by Marxist or Fabian socialist notions (Moynihan, 1975) or by a reflexive anticolonialism seeking explanations of all current ills in colonial or neo-colonial terms (e.g., Jackson, 1983).

Yet any theory that attracts wide governmental following, no matter how weak it may be intellectually, cannot be ignored while that following remains large or powerful. Most Assembly members are weak states extremely sensitive to attempts at any form of outside influence. This shows up in many ways. The Assembly (or at least the Third Committee) is one of the few places in the world where substituting the words "alien subjugation" for "foreign influence" in the text of a draft resolution could be called without irony a "minor change" (secretary of the committee announcing a translation error in A/C.3/37/SR.18, 21 Oct. 1982, para. 8). Third World states have devoted considerable energy since 1960 to the passage of Assembly resolutions stating that foreign economic influence is as onerous a limit on the freedom of weak states as direct colonial rule or armed intervention, and that independence without strong local government control over the economy is no real independence. While it is easy to point out the intellectual weakness of these ideas, the political climate of suspicion against foreign firms (particularly privately owned ones based in market economy states) is too strong to be ignored by any government or business firm.

Assembly statements about specific situations may be attempts to manage conflict by reminding contestants of the need to settle differences without resort to force or suggesting ways to reduce, if not settle, their differences. Assembly majorities can tap a rich set of symbols for this purpose, ranging from specific provisions of the Charter to general images of the folly of war. However, such statements may also register majority decisions to take sides by endorsing one party or condemning the other. Here, too, a wide range of symbols is available. Charter provisions, rules of international law, statements of what is just or fair and earlier Assembly resolutions can all be used in aid of a particular side.

The form of symbolic politics differs in each type of case. Attempts to foster the reduction or settlement of conflict address appeals to all parties evenly. Though individual members may have views about who is right or wrong, these do not get included into decisions. Rather, pressures are exerted in private discussions while public decisions appeal to both sides to negotiate or to accept mediation or to avoid acts that would worsen the dispute. Other members do not simply "hold the ring"; they try to separate and restrain the boxers.

Using the Assembly to take sides produces different appeals to the various sides or individual parties. Here, the Assembly praises one and condemns the other or makes statements that back one's case more than the other's. Of course, taking sides has different degrees of intensity. An African–Arab coalition within the Third World ensures that South Africa and Israel are routinely and continually condemned in the most scathing terms. Divisions among the Nonaligned meant that Turkey was condemned for invading Cyprus in 1974 and Indonesia for taking over Eastern Timor in 1975, but not in particularly harsh terms.

Coalition Politics and the Use of Symbols

The goals of different coalitions, their relative power outside the Assembly and their mechanisms for maintaining coherence all influence the way in which Assembly decisions are used. Goals and relative power can be related in four ways, as shown in Figure 7.1.

		Goals	
		Major change	Minor change or status quo
Power	Strong	a	b
	Weak	c	d

Figure 7.1 Possible relation between coalition goals and power

A coalition of strong states with status quo or reformist goals need not rely very heavily on symbolic politics. To the extent that it does, symbols are used to keep coalition members together, to encourage active roles in implementation and to preempt criticism by opponents. This does not mean that such a coalition will content itself with mild appeals. Though its goals are modest, its rhetoric may be immodest when it feels deeply threatened.

The US-led coalition provides an excellent example of such a coalition. Its modest goals allowed it to use the Assembly relatively sparingly. It produced somewhat fewer resolutions stating general principles and tended to compartmentalize issues, treating political norms like nonintervention as one thing and economic norms like open international trade as another. This does not mean that the members failed to see connections among the various realms, only that their world-view tended to divide issues into relatively autonomous areas. This was consistent with Western domestic political philosophy which tends to separate the state (that is, the governing apparatus) from society and the political from the nonpolitical. The prevailing conceptions sought to preserve wide areas of private and nonpolitical activity, with governmental and political activity viewed as providing a framework of order, rules and public goods necessary to fostering cooperation and keeping private interactions from getting out of hand.

This is not to say that the US-led coalition had no vision of the world other than protecting the status quo. In certain areas all or most of its members sought to change traditional features of international relations. US policy-makers shared the goal of creating an international system that would encourage democracy and free enterprise in a community of independent but mutually cooperative states. Most members agreed that ending colonialism was necessary to a just international order, but saw this as a gradual process in which the peoples of individual colonies would first be readied for independence. Additionally, they expected that the smaller colonies would usually opt for local self-government within a continued relation to the metropole rather than independence. This ending of colonialism would mean global acceptance of self-determination, a major normative change as compared to the nineteenth century. The US-led coalition also sought to change the traditional presumption that, massacre aside, the way in which governments treated their own people was a domestic affair. This general notion that peace and democracy depended on respect for human rights received great impetus from the Axis, whose conduct appeared to prove once and for all the proposition that there was a strong link between suppression of the people at home and aggression abroad. Both the UN Charter and Assembly decisions were used to promote new norms in this area.

The US-led coalition did employ some strident rhetoric on occasion. Most was inspired by Cold War conflict with the Soviet bloc, which offered a different and uncongenial vision of the world. Whether this vision is seen as an attack on democracy or on continued capitalist domination, it represented challenge to the basic tenets of international order held by the US-led coalition. This meant that Soviet efforts to advance their vision had to be combated with symbolic as well as material means. Assembly rhetoric provided part of the symbolic contribution.

On other conflicts, the Assembly was used in more conciliatory fashion. It might be used to endorse one side, but not in terms that cast the other as a pariah, since only the Soviet bloc was seen as having thoroughly revolutionary or otherwise unacceptable ambitions. This can be seen in early resolutions on the Arab–Israeli conflict, where the goal remained finding some way in which both Palestinians and Israelis could live in the same area, whether this meant two states or some form of federation (see Hurewitz, 1950, for the early history of this issue). Of course, this moderation was greatly assisted by early Soviet sympathy with Israeli aspirations, which persisted until 1956. It can also be seen in efforts to mediate in the Indonesian War for independence against the Dutch or the 1947 Kashmir dispute between India and Pakistan.

A coalition of weak states with far-reaching goals must rely very heavily on symbolic politics. To the extent that its goals cannot be obtained with its own resources, such a coalition must persuade others to use their resources. This means getting them to accept or at least to tolerate the goals, since no uncoerced rational actor will use its resources to further goals it does not support (except by accident). Symbolic politics are used, then, to persuade others that they ought to share the goals and help attain them. Such efforts can take any or all of three forms: showing how norms professed by the others mandate accepting the weak coalition's goals, appealing to the others' self-interest, or instilling guilty feelings.

The Third World coalition has used all three approaches to varying degrees. The nationalist and egalitarian symbols so prominent in Nonaligned and Group of 77 rhetoric have a strong place in Western political thought. This has made it hard for Westerners to oppose decolonization and exerts a strong pull on economic issues, particularly since the differences between equality of states and equality of individuals are seldom explored. Western governments and individuals who profess any form of socialism or Marxism tend to be very sympathetic to Third World leaders professing similar ideas. On occasion Third World analysts and governments have echoed the views of Western analysts who see international economics as a positive-sum game in which all can benefit from cooperative activity and certain changes in the rules (Gordon, 1978). Such arguments have not been prominent in Third World group rhetoric. This stems in part from the number of influential leaders in the Group of 77 and the Nonaligned who view international economics as a zero-sum game, and in part from the fact that the high level of abstraction in much of the General Assembly debate makes it difficult to specify what interests would be furthered by what actions. Most appeals to interest have been negative, focusing on the possibility of organizing more commodity cartels or the dangers of political instability stemming from continued lack of progress. These negative appeals had strong effect in 1974–5, but have less today as the commodity cartel scenario seems very unlikely. Except among adherents of Marxist (though a few classical Marxists like Warren, 1980, maintain Marx's view that colonialism hastened economic development), neo-Marxist or dependency theories of the world economy, Westerners are not now attracted by arguments that the Third World's current lack of development is the West's fault. Worse, such arguments tend to backfire; fear that making any concession will be seen as acceptance of the guilty verdict has slowed down some Western governments' responses. Further, the different rate of economic progress among Third World states suggests that some of the blame for current difficulties rests on bad decisions on the part of some Third World governments – a point advanced by the Japanese for some time (Fukai, 1982, p. 76) and more recently by Secretary-General Perez de Cuellar (New York *Times*, 13 July 1983, p. A7). Whatever their difficulties in making decisions because of outside pressure, a growing number of Third World governments are beginning to admit that they have the main responsibility for dealing with their own problems (e.g., paragraph 6 of the Declaration on the Critical Economic Situation in Africa, Annex to Resolution 39/29).

A rational-actor model suggests that Third World governments should drop the guilt arguments and focus instead on common norms and interests. However, a number of factors maintain the prominence of guilt rhetoric. First, the slowness of Western response leads to extreme frustration and encourages its continued use. Second, both the Nonaligned and the Group of 77 were built on an anticolonial ideology that cannot be abandoned too quickly. Third, the normal tendency of organizations to modify their ideologies slowly is powerfully reinforced by the necessities of coalition maintenance and the internal workings of those groupings. The internal strains of both the Group of 77 and the Nonaligned are becoming great enough to make cooperation difficult. Blaming outsiders is a handy way to keep these strains from going too far and splitting the coalition. The US-led coalition held together far longer on Cold War issues than on any other because of this phenomenon; the Third World coalition now uses calls for a New International Economic Order and campaigns against Israel and South Africa in the same way. Finally, the inherited anticolonial ideology, plus the fact that Western countries happen to be on the other side of the issues of greatest concern to the Third World, allows the more radical members of both the Group of 77 and the Nonaligned to campaign for continued attacks on the West. Or, as one diplomat from a Nonaligned state has been quoted as saying, "While the running dogs of the USSR are proud of being running dogs of the USSR, the running dogs of the Unites States have their tails between their legs" (quoted in Jackson, 1983, p. 189). Until lately, the radicals were more organized than the moderates and able to push both Group of 77 and Nonaligned in a more anti-Western direction than set by the existing organizational ideology.

A strong coalition with sweeping goals would combine features of US-led coalition and Third World use of the General Assembly. It would employ the Assembly mainly to legitimize its own views, but also use fairly strident rhetoric because it wanted to overturn or greatly revise the previously existing international order. An alliance between the Soviet bloc, Third World Marxist–Leninist states and other radical elements of the Nonaligned would, if they ever became sufficiently numerous, be such a coalition. Were they in control, the General Assembly would be used to provide the doctrinal justifications for actions the majority was taking to revamp the world.

The extent to which a weak coalition with modest goals could use the Assembly would depend, as in the Third World case, on the goals of the strong. If their goals were also relatively modest, the Assembly would be a forum for serious, but relatively calm, discussion of differences and for the registration of ensuring agreements in the form of resolutions or draft treaties. Conflicts between individual states would be treated as unfortunate incidents to be settled. Though there would still be some competition for influence, this would be less intense than in the current ideology-fueled competition between the superpowers. The UN would then work as an institution for mediating conflict and encouraging cooperation much like the San Francisco Conference hoped. If, however, the strong wanted greater changes, the weak would have considerable difficulty protecting themselves.

The General Assembly would be used to legitimize weak state views, but would be a pitiful shield against a concerted program of revolution or revisionism sponsored by a coalition of strong states. The Third World coalition realizes this intuitively; hence some members' fears of "superpower condominium" when the United States and the Soviet Union moved into a period of relatively good relations and began cooperating on a wider variety of issues in the mid-1970s.

Maintaining a controlling coalition and, when needed, gaining the additional support needed for the effective implementation of decisions involve choices among strategies linking and separating issues. The choice of strategy depends not only on the goals and material resources of the coalition, but also on its leaders' perception of which strategy will work best. The US-led coalition preferred to split issues. In part this stemmed from its members' relative happiness with the main principles of the postwar order, which made change a matter of tinkering here and there. But it also stemmed from its leader's perception that different members could be kept in the coalition only by being permitted some of what they wanted. The US-led coalition thus acted more like a coalition government in a domestic political system. Each of the sub-groupings got some of what they wanted in return for supporting others in some of what they wanted. The material resources of the coalition were great enough that it could afford some defections and still implement or get relatively far in implementing its decisions. Further, the US-led coalition found control of the General Assembly useful, but not always essential since it had plenty of other resources.

The Third World coalition views its situation very differently. Lacking very many other advantages in world politics, it has tended to place a very high value on controlling the General Assembly and, if possible, the wider UN system. This requires sticking together. As one African diplomat put it, "Such weight as we carry depends on whether we act as a group. Alone, Zaire or Uganda count as nothing, unlike the United States or Britain" (quoted in New York *Times*, 30 January 1982, p. 4). While some Third World states are getting to the point of counting for something, most are so small they never will. The tendency to cluster in the group will persist for them. Sticking together, in turn, is aided by linking issues and reducing them to fairly simple propositions all members can endorse. Even when an individual member feels that some decision goes too far, it is likely to accept it both to maintain group unity and because demanding more than is really desired often serves as a useful negotiating play.

Very few of the Nonaligned have publicly criticized any Non-aligned decision; only Burma has expressed thorough discontent by leaving the Movement altogether.

Any weaker party seeks to link issues so that it can trade whatever advantages it has in one area for concessions on the other (e.g., Nye and Keohane, 1977, pp. 30–2). However, there are many kinds of issue-linkage. In most bilateral negotiating, it takes the form of trades on two fairly specific questions, such as more aid for continued use of base facilities. The dynamics of coalition maintenance have led leaders of the Third World coalition to adopt a very different pattern of linkage in the General Assembly, which consists of aggregating many individual abstract propositions into a larger overall package. This process not only produces grand packages, such as the New International Economic Order or the New World Communications and Information Order, but inflates their individual components as well. Development of the concept of "permanent sovereignty over natural resources" provides a good example.

The notion of "permanent sovereignty" was first advanced in the late 1950s as one of several ways in which governments of developing states could strengthen their hand in dealings with transitional corporations and other foreign investors, by reducing the likelihood that those corporations or investors would gain help from their government if they got into a conflict with the government of a state where their assets were located. Initially efforts to promote the idea of "permanent sovereignty" did not get far because of strong Western opposition. Third World states did get the Human Rights Commission to take up the matter in 1958, but could not win enough support in the Assembly as it was then constituted to secure its mention in any resolutions. Only in 1960, when it was clear that the US-led majority could no longer control all decisions and many new African and Asian states keenly interested in the idea had joined the UN, was it included in the operative part of a resolution. Paragraph 5 of Resolution 1515 (XV) recorded the Assembly's recommendation that "the sovereign right of each State to dispose of its wealth and natural resources shall be respected in conformity with the rights and duties of States under international law." Western states were able to accept this formulation because they believed the reference to international law meant that the norms of nondiscrimination and the full compensation for takings of foreign-owned property would still apply in cases of nationalization.

In succeeding years developing states pushed the balance of texts away from those older norms toward interpretations more favorable to their own interests. Resolution 1803 (XVII) of 1962 began with an insistence that

> the right of peoples and nations to permanent sovereignty over their natural wealth and resources must be exercised in the interest of their national development and of the well-being of the people of the State concerned.

Succeeding paragraphs emphasized that foreign investment should be regulated by the national law of, and by agreements "freely entered into" by, the host state, Compensation in case of nationalization was to be "appropriate" and, in a precariously balanced phrase, "in accordance with the rules in force in the State taking such measures in the exercise of its sovereignty and in accordance with international law."

The 1962 definition was reaffirmed in resolution 2154 (XXI) of 1966. The body of the resolution then endorsed measures for strengthening national control over foreign-owned enterprises, particularly through training local personnel to manage them and increasing host-state equity participation in the venture. Developed states were asked to transfer capital, technology and know-how, and to refrain from lowering commodity prices by selling noncommercial stockpiles. Commodity cartels were endorsed as a way of "ensuring the exercise of the permanent sovereignty" over the natural resources of developing states.

In the Charter of Economic Rights and Duties of States, Resolution 3281 (XXIX), adopted over Western objections in 1974, the concept had been broadened to include other forms of wealth, and the idea of host-state control over foreign investment strengthened. Article 2(1) of Chapter II said that "every State has and shall freely exercise full permanent sovereignty, including possession, use, and disposal, over all its wealth, natural resources, and economic activities." The rest of Article 2 then set out a wide-ranging definition of the mechanisms for exercising this "full permanent sovereignty".

Responses to General Assembly Decisions

Governments and, to the extent they are addressed, other actors consider a number of factors when deciding how to respond to an Assembly recommendation. Obviously, they consider whether or not they think the recommendation appropriate to the matter. Opponents will think it inappropriate, but it is also possible that some supporters of the general goal will think a particular resolution inappropriate because they feel it suggests a poor way to gain the goal or a line of action that makes the goal harder to attain. Both supporters and opponents are influenced by the legality of methods used to secure the decision and by the size, composition and solidity of the majority supporting it. Finally, responses will depend heavily on the balance of costs and benefits to each individual addressee of complying or not complying.

The political impact of an Assembly resolution depends heavily on the extent to which governments and other actors view its terms as appropriate. Governments often ignore those parts of resolutions that seem extraneous to the matter at hand. In an extreme case, a government may claim that the extraneous references vitiate the whole resolution. This has become the Western mood faced with resolutions on, for instance, women's rights that devote paragraphs to condemning racism, colonialism, imperialism and apartheid. On the other side, supporting governments may regard the extraneous references as necessary because opponents are ducking the issue and have to be reminded of it as often as possible (e.g., editorial comment on Western objections to Assembly requests that the IMF deny loans to South Africa, *The Weekly Review* [Nairobi], 5 November 1982, p. 5).

Sometimes the whole resolution raises strong objections. Western objections that Resolution 3379 (XXX), the "Zionism is a form of racism" resolution, improperly equates a nationalist movement to racist theories have colored its response not only in the Middle East context inspiring the resolution but in all Assembly discussion of the problem of racism. That objections go beyond a belief that the resolution unfairly singles out Israel can be seen from Western European responses. The European Community has taken a more pro-Palestinian stance on Middle East issues than the United States, but objects just as vehemently to equating Zionism with racism during human rights discussion.

A state's opposition to a decision may be greater and will be harder to overcome if it has legal objections to the terms or the mode of adoption. The Soviet bloc has tended to regard most criticism of its activities at home as infringements of domestic jurisdiction and has rejected them out of hand. Such arguments were the bloc's main line of defense when the Assembly attempted to discuss the Hungarian situation in the late 1950s. France rejected the Assembly's call that the island of Mayotte be joined with the Comoros on grounds the Assembly ought not ignore the freely expressed wishes of the people when they opted by plebiscite to remain a French colony rather than join the Republic of the Comoros (French remarks in A/31/PV.39, 21 Oct. 1976, paras. 6–14; a stance maintained to this day).

There are, however, few formal legal objections to Assembly resolutions that can be regarded as making them void *ab initio* (e.g., Osieke, 1983, esp. pp. 248–65). The Assembly has a long tradition of sharp procedural maneuvers, none of which has yet been deemed so great an irregularity as to void the resolution. The only thing that might lead the Assembly to such a conclusion is fraud or massive confusion in voting. Confusion has been handled on occasion by taking a second vote (e.g., A/C.6/7/SR. 310, 24 Oct. 1953, para. 60 – SR.311, 27 Oct. 1952, para. 73, and A/C.3/4/SR.238, 30 Sept. 1949, paras 50–52; general discussion in A/10/Annex 51, Doc. A/2977, paras. 79–93), and fraud is rare (the claim of fraud in A/34/PV.90, 10 Dec. 1979, pp. 23–5, being one of the few on record; Gross, 1983, discusses a possible last-minute change of vote on another issue). The use of consensus has made voting less important and so has further reduced the occasions on which such objections might be raised. The Assembly's broad competence to deal with issues limits objections based on lack of competence to two: that the resolution refers to the merits of a situation or dispute being actively discussed by the Security Council at the time of passage, or that the resolution constitutes intervention in matters "essentially within the domestic jurisdiction" of states. As already noted, (see pages 18–23), the Assembly has found ways to limit the range of both exclusions to the point that very few resolutions would be voided on those grounds if there were some international process of judicial review.

Governments may claim that the terms of a properly adopted resolution should be ignored because they violate the Charter, international law, or a treaty obligation. This might be difficult when a resolution discusses customary law, for supporters would probably argue that adoption of the resolution proves that the alleged rule is not or is no longer customary law. If the resolution is recommending sanctions against a particular state threatening the peace or commiting aggression, supporters can plausibly argue that the need to maintain peace or punish aggression justifies those particular violations of other treaty obligations.

In many circumstances, a majority impressed by the minority's legal objections changes the text to remove those objections before the resolution is adopted. If the majority is not impressed by the minority's objections, it will pass the resolution anyway.

The international legal system being as decentralized and fragmented as the international system it serves, the legal disagreement between supporters and opponents is likely to persist until one or the other side changes its views on the matter.

Governments pay great attention to the size, composition and solidity of the majority supporting a particular resolution. A large majority has always been considered more valuable than a small one. Governments can count and will not view a resolution passed by a bare majority as being a statement of "world opinion". It is precisely the thinness of the majorities involved, showing that the Third World is split on the issue, that permits Morocco and Indonesia to continue their efforts to annex the Western Sahara and Eastern Timor respectively. In 1981 resolutions on those subjects were adopted by votes of 76 to 9 with 57 abstentions and 54 to 42 with 46 abstentions respectively (A/36/PV.70, 27 Nov. 1981, pp. 22–3, 29). In 1984 there was no resolution on Eastern Timor (UN Press Release GA/7095, 21 Jan. 1985), and that on the Western Sahara was adopted by a vote of 90 to 0 with 42 abstentions (A/39/PV.87, 5 Dec. 1984, pp. 22–3). Even the fact of a large numerical majority might not impress opponents. If that majority consists solely of the controlling coalition, opponents are likely to dismiss its efforts as products of an "automatic voting machine". This was true of the Soviet bloc before 1955 and has been true of Western states, particularly the United States, since 1970.

The fact that the Assembly commands neither a bureaucracy and police force nor wide moral authority means that majorities which do not include states with the material capability to implement resolutions will not get very far along the path from decision to outcome. Such a majority can assert standards as much as it likes, but those standards will have little effect unless states with the capacity to act abide by them. It can set forth its preferred solutions to particular conflicts or specific crises, but the lack of material power will make their attainment unlikely.

If the decision is meant to become a rule of international law, then the agreement of all great powers is important. This can be seen vividly in a negative example. In 1961 the Assembly adopted a resolution stating that use of nuclear weapons should be deemed illegal by a vote of 55 to 20 with 26 abstentions. This resolution has been mentioned in some scholarly studies, but it is not cited by governments because the opponents included all the states then possessing nuclear weapons except the Soviet Union. This political and doctrinal insight has been incorporated into the definition of consensus, which is now held to mean suppport or

acquiescence by most states, including all powerful ones, in all
five regions of the world.

The solidity of the majority behind a decision also affects
reactions to it. A minority faced with a majority barely able to
hold itself together has a wider field of maneuver than one faced
with a solid majority. This can be seen even in two issues of great
interest to the Third World: South Africa and the Arab-Israeli
conflict. The Arab–African alliance that drives Third World
decisions on both issues to all-out confrontation has been able to
hold together better on South Africa than on Israel. This became
apparent in 1977 when the previously–existing Arab split into
moderate and hard-line groups widened as the former supported
Egypt's decision to initiate peace negotiations with Israel and the
latter attempted to cast Egypt as a pariah for doing so. Arab
disarray meant that the Third World coalition lacked steady
guidance on the issue, except when Israel re-united the squab-
blers temporarily by an action like annexing the Golan Heights.
The Africans remain united in opposition to South Africa (in part
by ignoring the fact that neighboring states must come to certain
accommodations on economic and security issues), so continue
to drive a Third World coalition ready to defer to their wishes on
the question.

A minority dealing with a majority barely holding together on
some question may not only oppose the resolution but may hope
to split the majority. This may permit securing the express or,
more likely, tacit retreat from certain resolutions. Repudiation
of resolutions dealing with general principles, norms, or rules is
unlikely, but splitting the majority is useful none the less.
Success can mean that the campaign to broaden or sharpen the
principle, norm, or rule will slow down or end. The minority
may even be able to join with one part of the now-split majority
to steer the discussion and later resolutions in directions it prefers.
This can be seen in Assembly discussions of human rights, where
the Universal Declaration emphasized individual and political
rights far more than the Soviet bloc wished. The US-led coalition
split on the issue in 1950. The Soviet bloc was then able to make
common cause with African, Asian and Latin American
members and with their help steer greater attention to group and
economic rights in the mid-1950s. Thus even before the Third
World coalition had coalesced, Assembly discussions were
emphasizing group and economic rights over individual and
political ones.

The solidity of the supporting majority is particularly
important when decisions are adopted without a formal vote.

Supporters will claim that the lack of a vote indicated that no government objected to the text. Opponents will challenge this, either to deny moral weight to the resolution or to forestall follow-up resolutions going further in the same direction. The opponents will look beyond the fact of adoption without a vote to the text of the resolution and to statements made in debate or explanation of vote. They will seek to exploit all evidence that vague passages paper over continuing disagreements. They will also stress the importance of objections stated in debate. The "Program of Action on the Establishment of a New International Economic Order" (Resolution 3202 [S–VI]) provides a good example. Third World governments like to point out that it was adopted without a vote, so represents consensus. Western governments sought in various ways to deny that there was any consensus. The United States delegation called it a "false consensus", while others, such as the Japanese, contented themselves with reservations to many of its major ideas, such as the indexation of commodity prices to compensate for inflation in the industrial countries or the particular definition of permanent sovereignty over resources it incorporated (statements in A/S–VI/PV. 2229, 1 May 1974, para. 21–PV.2231, 2 May 1974, para. 68). In some cases, such opposition can deflect a majority from a given point. In others, it simply means that the majority will still seek a decision but the minority will be ready to force adoption by a vote, destroying any possibility of claiming there is consensus on the issue. This happened at the 29th session when the Group of 77 sought to follow up on its success at the sixth special session with consensus adoption of a "Charter of Economic Rights and Duties of States" embodying similar ideas. This time Western states forced a vote, which has made the charter less politically influential than would otherwise have been the case.

Supporters must pay attention to these indications as much as opponents, for just as they are signs of hope to the latter they are signs of danger to the former. A coalition of any size that wishes to remain in control of developments must prevent defections, either by slowing down the campaign or by providing members with sufficient satisfaction on other issues to buy their continued support.

Solidity is particularly important if supporters hope to emphasize a particular resolution by referring to it in subsequent resolutions on the same or other questions. Though the legal and moral value of re-citation has been diluted by a growing tendency to re-cite many resolutions in ever-growing preambles, certain resolutions have been given extra prominence in this way. The

Universal Declaration of Human Rights, the Declaration on the Granting of Independence to all Colonial Countries and Peoples, the Declaration on the Elimination of all forms of Racial Discrimination, the Declaration of Principles governing Friendly Relations and Cooperation among States and the Declaration of Economic Rights and Duties of States are among the most frequently cited resolutions. Even if it does not sway opponents, re-citation shows that the principles are still supported by many members, so cannot be viewed as the accidental product of some ephemeral alignment.

In some situations, the difference between the size of the expected majority and the size of the majority actually attained may be important. When elections were still settled by formal ballot, some members used abstention as a way to indicate disapproval of a state nominated by a particular group. Today this effect is seen mainly with resolutions condemning states for their actions. The best-known recent example is Assembly condemnation of the Soviet invasion of Afghanistan. The Soviets knew that a majority would condemn them, but expected it to be thin enough to have little political impact. They were dismayed when a large number of Third World states, prominent among them members of the Islamic Conference, decided to vote in favor of the condemnation rather than abstain (New York *Times*, 15 January 1980, p. 1).

As in other areas of human endeavor, the likelihood of an Assembly decision's being implemented depends in part on the action requested. Just like individuals, governments find it easiest to comply when little or no action is required or when the acceptance of a particular standard would not harm their material interests. A situation where low benefits are balanced by low costs make acquiescence easy, and in the General Assembly acquiescence is almost as good as active support. If costs rise but benefits stay low, action becomes harder to get. If costs and benefits both rise, the likelihood of action depends on the ratio between them. When benefits outweigh costs action can still be elicited; when costs outweigh benefits this becomes very difficult.

Situations of low cost and low benefit have supported all Assembly coalitions, whether the US-led coalition, the cross-cutting anticolonial majority of the 1950s, or the Third World coalition. Most states were not asked to do anything in East–West confrontations other than condemn the Soviet Union at a time when the Soviets were not offering much material incentive to do otherwise. The members of the anticolonial majority were asked to lend verbal support, but not to run grave risks or spend material resources on anticolonial struggle. Most Third World states can accept group positions on many issues because the issue involved has few material implications for them or is asking the industrial states to extend benefits. They will not lose tariff revenues if a generalized system of trade preferences is adopted or find their nationals' patent royalties reduced under the more far-reaching schemes for technology transfer.

As costs rise, action follows only if benefits rise more. These benefits may be moral or psychological as well as material. Even with their way eased by UN financing of extra costs involved, most governments find participation in peacekeeping expensive. Some do it anyway because they gain rewards either from helping states with which they wish to maintain good relations or from building a reputation as a relatively impartial state willing to assist in the maintenance of international peace. Canada, India and the Scandinavian states have been particularly interested in cultivating such a reputation. For Finland, up in the north of Europe next to the Soviet Union, such activities are particularly attractive since they allow it to project widely an image as a neutral and independent state.

In fact, such moral and psychological pay-offs may support a higher and more consistent rate of activity than would material benefits alone (see discussion of "norm-oriented behavior" in Hardin, 1982, pp. 103–8, 216–19). Most Western governments extend aid to developing states mainly for material reasons, which leaves it highly vulnerable to reduction when calculations of self-interest change as well as when assessments of its effectiveness in bringing about development shift.

A resolution that recommends extensive or expensive action, such as a peacekeeping operation or an aid program, will not be implemented unless actively supported by states possessing the material resources necessary to the task. This does not mean it is necessary to get all the strong or wealthy powers to support the resolution or to act afterward. However, the amount of resources needed may depend on the depth of opposition. If a great power, or some other state with enough resources to affect events in the region or issue involved, vehemently opposes, the supporters will need more resources. This can be seen in the career of the First UN Emergency Force in Sinai. The Soviet Union was not keen on the idea, but let it go ahead since others were ready to act. At the same time, the force's activities were constrained by the desires of the states involved in the conflict. Israel refused to allow its troops on Israeli territory, so they were limited to patrolling on the Egyptian side of the border. When the Egyptian government wanted them out in 1967, they had to go. Even if the Secretary-General had not been obliged to terminate the force in this situation under agreements recorded in the resolution creating it, the Egyptian army would have been strong enough to push it out of the way. Few states would have been willing to make this costly for Egypt by threatening or applying sanctions. Similarly, verbal Soviet support for UN aid programs has not always been followed by contributions. Since UN aid programs are financed almost exclusively by voluntary contributions, this stance has let the West, and more recently some of newly industrializing and OPEC states, determine the tempo and extent of those programs.

The extent to which an Assembly decision is implemented depends on the aggregate balance of decisions to aid or hinder the attainment of the outcome specified. If supporters are better able than opponents to organize cooperative or parallel action to attain their preferences, the decision will be implemented, at least in part. If, however, opponents organize more effectively, the decision will not be implemented. The decentralization of the international system means that both supporters and opponents must organize this action on their own; they cannot rely on some preexisting central mechanism to do it for them. The ways in which supporters and opponents go about this are suggested by the theory of collective action (Russett and Sullivan,1971, suggest ways to apply it to international relations; Hardin, 1982, provides a concise summary of the theory).

This theory begins with the assumption, amply supported in empirical studies of behavior, that in most situations where individual actors make separate choices the activity needed to secure some collective goal will either not occur or fall short of what is needed to obtain the full result desired. A group wanting to provide itself with some collective good or avoid some collective bad must then find ways to overcome this inherent problem. The theory suggests the sorts of mechanism available, the likelihood that any or all of them will be used by a particular group of states and the likelihood that they will work in a given situation.

Assembly decisions pose problems of collective action because the benefits of the outcome can usually be enjoyed even by states that do not contribute to its attainment. This being the case, states have strong incentives to let others bear the burden of creating the outcome. Yet as soon as some start shirking, the outcome becomes less likely either because the efforts of those who do contribute falls short of what is needed or because the contributors decide there is no use contributing when others are not. There are several ways in which states can try getting around this problem.

First, the problem may not arise in a particular case because one powerful member is so interested in the outcome that it will provide all the necessary action itself. Such a situation characterized the US-led coalition's activity in Korea. The United States was so interested in preventing a reunification of Korea imposed by the North Koreans that it was ready to carry out the whole military action itself. It wanted allies not for their material contributions but for legitimization of the activity as a collective security effort. In such situations, the rest of the group can simply rely on the strong member to act. Whether the strong member's action succeeds in creating the desired outcome depends on the strength and actions of opponents. In the Korean case, opponents were able to prevent the wilder dreams of taking over the North, but the United States met its main goal of preventing North Korea from overrunning South Korea.

A group without an overwhelmingly strong member may be able to organize collective action if it is small enough that members (1) gain more individually from providing the good than it costs them to contribute to the joint effort and (2) can monitor each other's activity well enough to prevent any from failing to act. This means that advantages will accrue to relatively small groups of like-minded states. The level of UN aid programs is still set largely by the OECD states, which use that organization as a way to monitor each other's performance. Though now running into difficulties, OPEC benefited from relatively small size and large gains to be had from acting together. Later, as members began taking the higher oil price for granted and began seeking greater revenues for themselves, OPEC shifted to a single-provider pattern, with Saudi Arabia increasing or decreasing its production as needed to attain group goals on price. The degree of advantage enjoyed by the small like-minded group depends, of course, on the relative organization of others. Several results are possible. One small like-minded group may find its efforts cancelled by a similar group which prefers a different outcome. It may find its efforts overwhelmed by a more powerful single state. It may be able to overcome the resistance of a less powerful small group. Finally, it may not meet any real resistance because the numerous opponents are unable to organize effectively.

A large group of states may be able to act effectively as a group if it can induce action by providing members with separate individual benefits in other areas. These benefits may be material, such as confidential information on the latest developments in weapons technology or prospecting data from satellite recon- naissance, or they may be psychological. In large part the Nonaligned Movement is an attempt to keep a large number of states on similar paths of action by giving their leaders the psychic rewards of belonging to a larger whole. The formation and maintenance of a large group require that some set of members provide leadership. This may consist of finding and raising issues popular among the members, such as the Algerian role in formulating the Nonaligned's New International Economic Order proposals in 1973–4. Or it may consist of offering others side-payments to induce cooperation. The OPEC states have sought to defuse tensions arising from energy issues by increas- ing their aid to others. In this way, OPEC hopes to keep the oil-importing LDCs focused on efforts to get concessions from the West rather than making futher demands on them. Though these processes of leadership also occur in small groups, the effort required from leaders in large groups is greater because of the larger number of members involved.

Occasionally, collective action occurs as a by-product of efforts to attain individually beneficial outcomes. Most medical research is supported by individual states concerned about health of their own people. However, the scientific norm of open publication means that results become available to foreign governments and become part of an improvement in global health standards. This is not always a perfect mechanism. In the health example, problems affecting the populations of poor countries unable to support much research may not be covered by that of others. Though they benefit from the published research, they do not benefit as much. This leaves them relatively worse off, so highly interested in mechanisms to assure greater attention to these neglected areas. Yet this continuing gap should not be allowed to obscure the fact that many of the problems covered in current national research efforts, such as the causes and cures of diseases afflicting the elderly, the impact of nutrition on health, or the effects of various chemicals used in industrial processes, are as relevant to the poor countries as to the rich ones. Similar patterns probably apply in many technical areas, which is one reason why Assembly decisions in these areas focus so much on the gaps rather than on the bigger picture.

In some cases, too, collective action may be promoted by educational or propaganda efforts aimed at getting the noncontri- butors to act or getting opponents to change their preferences and come to support the desired outcome. Coalitions in the Assembly have always relied heavily on this sort of activity, which is simply another way of looking at the uses of symbolic politics.

Obviously, a large group can overcome barriers to collective action if it sets up an organization charged with providing the good after securing contributions from each member. A government is one such organization, and the one usually favored in the domestic context because it can enforce tax payments and other necessary compliance. International organizations are another. Budget assessments can become a mechanism for securing the needed resources and permitting easy identification of noncontributors. Therefore, even if the Third World coalition had the resources to implement the changes it desires, it might still support having a larger UN budget and a greater UN role in operational activities if those resources were spread among a fairly large number of states.

Several factors determine who will prevail in any contest of competing group activity between supporters and opponents of a decision. Obviously, capability is important. A large group of weak states cannot overcome a small group of more powerful ones. Yet capability is not the only relevant consideration. The relative unity of contending groups and the relative intensity with which different actors desire outcomes also help determine the result.

Differences in the level of unity and organization of the group can override differences in capability. The Third World coalition has been able to gain concessions from the West because the West has not maintained a completely united front on all issues. There are important differences in the approaches of individual Western states to particular economic issues, and the Nonaligned have learned how to exploit these. Similarly, the anticolonial coalition saw its preferences prevail because they were shared by many governments and groups in the West.

The intensity with which groups, or individual members of groups, desire an outcome is also important. The PLO intensely desires implementation of the many Assembly decisions endorsing Palestinian statehood. Yet other members of the Third World coalition feel less intensely about the issue. For Asians and Latin Americans, it tends to be a distant problem. For Africans, it strikes a little closer to home because of the analogies made between Israel and South Africa, but it still comes relatively far down in their list of concerns. Arab states vary in attitude. At times, such as 1967 or 1973, a considerable number ready to put their armies on the line can be found. At other times, such as June 1982, they are more concerned about other things. Since the PLO is less powerful than Israel, which cares equally intensely about the issue, Israeli preferences have tended to prevail. If a large coalition of Arab states were to care enough long enough to fight a long war, then Israel would be in serious trouble.

Summary

Most Assembly decisions are recommendations. Their political effect depends on the addressees' response to their symbolic appeals for action by supporters or restraint by opponents. Thus, their political effect is indirect; they seek to mold action by affecting the context in which governments and others make their choices. With supporters, the symbolic appeals are meant to further encourage action helping secure outcomes with which the addressee is already sympathetic. With opponents, the symbolic appeals are meant to prevent action hindering outcomes or perhaps even reduce opposition to the outcome by appealing to their self-interest or their moral beliefs.

Governments' responses to an Assembly decision depend in part on their reaction to Assembly proceedings surrounding its adoption. They pay close attention to the breadth and apparent solidity of the coalition supporting the decision. They also respond to the dynamics of coalition formation and maintenance that encourage a majority to use particular symbols or particular styles of decision.

Decisions adopted by a narrow or shaky coalition are far less persuasive than those adopted by a wide and solid one. Opponents are not likely to be impressed by a narrow vote or a vague decision that clearly papers over disagreements among supporters. Rather, they are likely to view such situations as invitations to obstruct the outcome while continuing to press their views in hopes of breaking down the coalition. Lukewarm supporters are also less likely to act if the decision seems to have a narrow or insubstantial political base. They are likely to reflect further on the reasons for their lack of enthusiasm and defer action until they decide whether the reasons for desiring an outcome really outweigh the reasons for not desiring it.

The dynamics of coalition formation and maintenance affect the symbolic content of decisions and so influence addressees' response to them. The US-led coalition held together by disaggregating issues. Its leading members' tendency to prefer disaggregation was reinforced by the fact that only by keeping things separate could the log-rolling that held the coalition together continue. Except on Cold War issues, where an all-out ideological contest with the Soviet bloc mandated strident rhetoric, the symbolic appeals were universalistic but measured. Nothing encouraged supporters or opponents to feel urgency except when warfare had broken out and UN mechanisms were being used to control or stop it. Outcomes were approached gradually and piecemeal. The Third World coalition has a very different style. Both its leading members' philosophical preferences and the coalition's internal dynamics encourage linking issues. Not only do individual issues, such as information questions or the role of women in society, acquire broad definitions, but the individual issues are all linked to the grand overarching concepts of anticolonialism and a New International Economic Order. The appeals remain universalistic, but have an across-the-board stridency lacking in the 1940s and early 1950s. This encourages both supporters and opponents to share a sense of urgency. While the urgency of opposition is highest in the United States, other Western countries share the mood when faced with particular formulations of particular issues. The Soviet bloc, too, has found elements to oppose in Third World demands.

Conditions outside the Assembly have greater effect on governments' responses to Assembly decisions. The nature of the appeal being made or its likely implications are evaluated independently of how it came to be adopted. The relation of control over Assembly decisions and ability to create or influence outcomes outside necessarily affects the implementation of decisions. Finally, individual governments consider the costs and benefits of compliance or noncompliance on a case-by-case and individualistic basis.

Obviously, governments react to the content of a decision. They support or oppose some decisions more than others. Western countries differ greatly in their opposition to specific Third World initiatives on Middle East issues, but all vehemently oppose the 1975 decision defining Zionism as a form of racism. The Soviet bloc supports general calls for a new international economic order, but is happiest about those parts emphasizing the role of state guidance in the economy and least happy about those parts entailing new demands on the UN's regular budget. Third World countries support any general appeal to self-determination, but disagree among themselves about how to define the rights and wrongs of such situations as Moroccan efforts to annex the Western Sahara, Indonesian annexation of Eastern Timor, or the Falklands dispute. Thus, a government's activity in a particular instance cannot always be deduced from its general statements.

A coalition having ample resources for implementation can convert decisions into outcomes with greater ease than one that does not. Even a strong coalition meets with frustration, such as the US-led coalition's difficulties in Korea, but it finds the implementation phase far less frustrating than a coalition that can make decisions but must garner outside help for implementation. A weak coalition has two choices: retreating to propositions strong outsiders will help implement or relying more heavily on symbolic politics. Either is frustrating since the gap between initial aspirations and outcomes is large. How this frustration gets expressed depends on the goals of the coalition. One with moderate goals can probably live with it more easily since the gap is small. One with highly revisionist or even revolutionary goals is tempted to go further in rhetorical excess or to fall into complete cynicism because the gap is large. More likely, it will suffer heavy internal strain as some members decide that they should accept what they can get and work from there while others decide to keep the full revisionist or revolutionary fervor alive. This process will be accelerated if some members are able to improve their material position within the existing rules, and so come to view change as less urgent. Both dynamics afflict the Third World coalition today.

Though a truism, it bears repeating that governments, even more than individuals in domestic political systems, evaluate decisions in terms of what is in the outcome for them. The "what" may be moral; defense of a principle or procedure may be deemed important in its own right. Yet the continued decentralization of the international system encourages perspectives focusing on the interests of one's own state or of its closest allies. Supporters are most likely to act if the costs of helping bring about the desired outcome are low compared to the benefits involved. Decisions that bring about small benefits at trivial costs or larger benefits at costs below that of the benefit are more likely to be implemented. Opponents face a slightly different calculus. An outcome with low costs may not inspire any great opposition, even if it could be stopped at a small outlay of effort. Governments generally have many issues competing for attention and have to allocate their limited resources to the more pressing matters. Thus, they are likely to pay far more attention to outcomes threatening high costs. Their tendency to obstruct the outcome actively depends on whether they think this can be done at an acceptable cost.

The fate of implementation efforts depends, therefore, on the balance between action furthering the goal and action obstructing it. This, in turn, brings up all the problems of collective action in decentralized social systems. The outcome will reflect the preferences of those most able to overcome the barriers to collective action and impose their preferences in the implementation stage.

The fact that governments consider action very much in the light of their individual interests means that the study of implementation cannot be left at this general level. A full understanding of what happens requires closer examination of the ways in which Assembly recommendations fit into the foreign-policy-making processes of individual states, the subject of Chapter 8.

Chapter Eight

Assembly Decisions in the Foreign Policy Process

Once adopted, General Assembly decisions become an element of the environment to which individual states respond in making their foreign policies. Therefore, their reactions depend not only on the broad patterns of incentives and disincentives to comply discussed in Chapter 7, but also on the way in which the decisions fit into or can be used to change the ongoing policy-making process. It is a truism that states pay attention to the Assembly and its decisions when they are compatible with national interests and ignore them when they are not. It is more interesting and significant to understand how states decide that particular decisions are or are not in their interest, and how they can be persuaded to change those assessments.

This understanding requires inquiry into several related subjects. First, the Assembly alters the web of personal relationships among policy-makers by providing another place for contact and interaction. Second, the regularity of Assembly sessions offers an opportunity for taking initiatives to those who wish and imposes a burden of responding on others. Clearly this affects the policy process by changing the timing and allocation of attention. The question of just how much the Assembly does this and to what effect needs more detailed specification. Third, Assembly decisions may parallel or supplement bilateral or small-group activity. They thus become a new element in relations among governments. The impact of this new channel of intergovernmental relations must also be assessed. Finally, it is important to see how Assembly proceedings and decisions affect the internal policy debates of states. Governments are not unitary, fully rational actors managing entities fully responsive to their commands and sealed off from all external influences. Rather, their decisions are affected by intra-bureaucratic arguments, trans-governmental coalitions, domestic and transnational activities by private groups and foreign governments' attempts to sway opinion. The Assembly can be used to further or influence all of these processes.

The Assembly and Personal Contacts

Governments interact with others in the Assembly mainly through the delegations they send to particular sessions and the year-round staff they maintain at their UN mission. Individual issues before the Assembly are often discussed in other inter-governmental fora, such as meetings of the Nonaligned, the OECD, the CMEA, or the European Community. There, too, governments work through delegations, which may or may not include the same people sent to the General Assembly. This means that the human element enters into Assembly proceedings and related discussions, just as it does in any political process. Impersonal forces such as material interest, the strength or weakness of a particular state, or accident shape much of govern-ments' behavior. Yet the fact that these forces affect politics only through the thoughts and actions of particular individuals holding responsible positions means that the effects of personal-ity cannot be ignored.

Personal relations among policy-makers affect Assembly pro-ceedings and governments' reactions to them in four areas: (1) relations of delegates and mission staff to their counterparts at home, (2) relations among delegates and Secretariat staff active in Assembly business, (3) relations of foreign delegates or Secreta-riat staff with government officials or influential private people they meet occasionally and (4) relations among officials and others affecting their countries' policy who do not participate directly in Assembly sessions. Though this last area belongs properly to the study of transgovernmental and transnational coalition building, it will be addressed here as a convenience.

Relations of the foreign ministry and other government departments at home with the Assembly delegation differ from country to country. Some governments keep their delegation closely instructed; others permit it a wide field of initiative. Some leave the same delegates in place for many years; others rotate them to other assignments after relatively short intervals. The combination of these possibilities yields patterns characteristic of different groups of states.

Soviet bloc governments tend to combine tight instructions and long tours of duty. This combination yields great discipline and a close familiarity with the ways of the Assembly that permits the cultivation of influence and skillful use of Assembly procedures. As the Third World majority formed in the mid-1960s, the Soviet bloc came out of its thick defensive shell and began to take more account of the flow of activity. Its diplomats changed from being essentially dour-faced messengers to skillful operators. They have learned to combine unyielding policy with good personal relations (e.g., New York *Times*, 29 December 1983, p. A1) and extreme stubbornness in private negotiations with public postures of reasonableness (Agena, 1982).

The governments of most Western states combine shorter terms of duty and close instruction from home based on prior consultation with the delegation. While the diplomatic services of most Western states have acknowledged the differences in multi-lateral and bilateral diplomacy by formally or informally splitting their diplomatic corps into a group spending most of its time representing the country in multilateral conferences and a group spending most of its time in individual embassies (interviews with several Western European diplomats, 1981–3), tours of duty at the Assembly still tend to be less than five years. Western delegates usually have more room for personal initiative than their Soviet bloc counterparts, but the need to coordinate a policy acceptable to numerous government agencies and attentive segments of the public limits what they can do on their own. The United States probably represents the extreme limit of this Western pattern. Its diplomatic service has not developed as much of a multilateral–bilateral split as others (Hollick, 1984, p. 521, argues that this stems from the far greater prestige of the regional bureaux controlling embassy assignments), and the proximity of Washington to New York, combined with large amounts of communications gear, permits up-to-the-minute instruction. Yet even in the United States there is plenty of room for personality to affect policy. Adlai Stevenson lost influence within the Kennedy and Johnson administrations because both presidents and many of their advisors felt he took too soft a line on various foreign policy questions, especially the Vietnam War (Finger, 1980, p. 154). A lack of direction from the top allowed Ambassador Kirkpatrick and Secretary of State Haig to follow contrasting lines of policy during the early phases of the Falklands Crisis in April 1982 (Finger, 1984, p. 453; Haig, 1984, pp. 268–9).

Third World governments tend to retain the same permanent

representative for long periods and to rotate even the subordinate members of delegations more slowly. While none can equal the record of Jamil Baroody, who was the chief Saudi delegate from 1945 through 1979, terms of a decade are common. The pattern of instruction depends heavily on the size of the state and its government apparatus. The smaller Third World states do not attempt to backstop their delegation and mission with a staff at home. Rather, they rely on the diplomats in New York to frame policy on any issue before the Assembly that does not directly affect the state's material interests. Many of these people are educated abroad, and most spend their whole career representing their country at one international meeting after another. So long as they retain the confidence of their political chiefs at home, they are left to frame policy within the guidelines of regional, Non-aligned, or Group of 77 declarations. Subordinate members of Third World delegations are a more mixed group. Some are emerging "stars" who will one day become head of the delegation; some are relatives of prominent people at home; a few are individuals the leaders want kept occupied abroad; most are simply career diplomats serving at the UN between other assignments.

The larger Third World governments, like those of Algeria, Brazil, India, Mexico, Nigeria and Saudi Arabia do not leave their delegates quite as much room for personal initiative in policy decisions. However, like their other Third World peers, they tend to remain on assignment a relatively long time and to spend most of their career abroad. Many also fit into the international Third World "old-boy network" more comfortably than into networks back home. Their international prominence gives them special influence at home on particular issues, giving them wide latitude to make policy on them (Hambro, 1976; Jackson, 1983, pp. 108–10).

This combination of long service and heavy reliance on the group means that Third World delegates' strongest personal ties are to other delegates and to Secretariat staff from their region. Personal considerations thus reinforce policy imperatives to express dissent from group decisions mildly – accepting adoption without a vote, voting with the group while expressing reservations in an explanation of vote, or abstaining. Even absence may be used as a way to register differences, though it probably stems more often from an inability to cover all meetings at once. Though no delegation has equalled Dominica's record of missing all roll-call votes taken in the plenary and main committees during the 37th session (Jackson, 1983, p. 138), many other

Nonaligned states have absence rates higher than 50 percent (see listings of roll calls in the Assembly Official Records).

Ties between Third World delegates and Third World nationals in the Secretariat tend to be relatively strong. Many of the latter, particularly in higher ranking posts, are former members of delegations or candidates actively sponsored by their country's mission. While the general effort to increase Third World representation at the higher levels has opened a greater variety of posts, Third World nationals still cluster in those parts of the Secretariat dealing with issues particularly dear to the Nonaligned and the Group of 77. Personal and institutional imperatives thus reinforce one another on budget matters as well, since both Third World governments and ambitious members of the Secretariat desire larger UN budgets. Secretariat members have traditionally engaged in budget lobbying, though they occasionally irritate some delegations in the process (e.g., US and Soviet complaints noted in Puchala, ed., 1982, p. 145 and US delegate remarks in A/C.5/36/SR.83, 18 Dec. 1981, para. 20).

Any permanent representative hoping for wide influence in the Assembly needs to maintain contacts at the higher levels of the Secretariat and have subordinates who have contacts at the lower levels (Hambro, 1976, p. 35). Clearly, ties of friendship assist this process. While these ties can be used to advance the personal career of an individual diplomat, they may also be part of larger state policy. In the 1950s when India was pursuing a policy of active leadership in the Assembly, it was also "overrepresented" in the Secretariat and turned this fact to account. As Rana noted, this high proportion of staff members gave India "an unrivalled access to the microscopic details which have gone a long way in bestowing it with the insight essential for exerting an influence that was more than purely technical" (Rana, 1970, p. 69).

Western activities follow a different pattern. For them, group coordination of policy is more difficult because of the more complicated pattern of decision-making at home. Delegates are always only one set of participants in ongoing policy discussions. They can advise, and may acquire some special influence by having greater knowledge of what will or will not be received well in the Assembly. Those delegates drawn from some interest group may be able to influence that group. Some head delegates may have extra influence because of their political prominence, something that happens more often with the Americans than others because the United States usually does not appoint a career diplomat as permanent representative.

The fact that the main outlines of policy emanate from a large bureaucracy buffeted by active legislatures, publics and interest groups makes Western coordination of policy in the Assembly hard. The European Community twelve have come to consult on more issues, but are not always successful at keeping ranks closed. The Western European and Other regional group in the Assembly coordinates only choices of candidates for elections since its members' positions on substantive issues are often fairly far apart. On economic issues, the most sustained coordination comes from the Group of Five, but it includes only Britain, France, Japan, the United States and West Germany (Crane, 1984, describes the Group's activity on debt and commodity issues in the late 1970s). The smaller Western states more sympathetic with Third World views do not participate in the Group of Five, but express their views in the wider Western European and Other group, the EC twelve, or the Organization for Economic Cooperation and Development (OECD) as well as in the Assembly.

The personal ties between Western delegates and Westerners serving on the Secretariat tend to be weaker. Though Western governments vet prospective staff for security reasons, they generally permit the UN to recruit directly and still prefer the older career model. The length of service has been reduced as the Secretariat has shifted to greater reliance on short-term contracts, but the individual Westerners recruited are often people who subscribe to the ideal of an international civil service independent of individual governments. While most Western governments lobby for posts and some even offer their nationals special inducements to serve (e.g., subsidies to make up for lower UN salaries or higher living expenses in New York; see Franck, 1985, p. 109), the Westerners remain a more separate group on the whole.

Though Western diplomacy depends far less on it, personality differences do affect policy in particular cases. Though the substance of US policy on most issues in the Assembly differed less from the Ford to the Carter administrations than the contrasting personalities and approaches of Daniel Patrick Moynihan and Andrew Young led many to believe, the Reagan administration's unilateralist preferences were highlighted by the confrontational style of Jeanne Kirkpatrick. British and United States cooperation in the Falklands Crisis was hampered by British suspicions that Ambassador Kirkpatrick was encouraging the Argentines to be intransigent.

The Soviet bloc's two main mechanisms for maintaining policy coordination depend little on delegate personality. One, which shows enough signs of weakening that General Secretary Gorbachev has issued stern warnings through *Pravda* (*The Economist*, 19 July 1985, p. 16), is the traditional Soviet leadership of its Warsaw Pact allies. This operates outside the Assembly and is influenced by personal contacts among national leaders. The second is the simple expedient of supporting the Third World coalition whenever so doing does not harm the bloc's material interests. Delegates and others make efforts to get the Non-aligned to take a position closer to Soviet bloc desires whenever possible. However even when that fails the Soviet bloc will usually support the current Third World position.

Personality has more influence in relations with other delegations or the Secretariat. The Soviet bloc tries to keep close relations with its members on the Secretariat by insisting that all bloc nationals be recruited through the home government and serve only for a short time. All bloc governments also keep tabs on their nationals in the Secretariat through security agents attached to the delegation. The Soviet Union and some others also require that all but the highest ranking of their nationals on the Secretariat live in their missions diplomatic compounds rather than in their own housing in New York. They, too, join in the pattern of circulating and influencing others to take positions more favorable to the Soviet bloc, and passing information home for use in policy-making.

While delegations and missions provide their country's main contact with the Assembly, other officials sometimes attend particular sessions or represent their country in international meetings dealing with issues also arising before the Assembly. Contacts with these people can affect Assembly politics. It is clear, for instance, that Western suspicion of Amadou-Mahtar M'Bow, the current Director-General of UNESCO, heightens the already-existing Western opposition to handling information issues in that organization (e.g., New York *Times*, 15 August 1984, p. A1; Crovitz, 1984).

Other transgovernmental contacts can also affect Assembly proceedings. This is probably most true with Western governments, since they carry on a more active pattern of transgovernmental politics than others. Yet other governments are affected as well. Egyptian unhappiness with Soviet policy and the conduct of Soviet diplomats and military officers in charge of Soviet–Egyptian relations was an important element in the shift toward negotiations wih Israel and *rapprochement* with the United States. This change of policy, in turn, greatly affected Assembly consideration of and decisions about the Arab–Israeli conflict. Transgovernmental coalition activity pervades all group efforts by the European Community twelve. These governments coordinate foreign policy through three overlapping mechanisms: the European Community Commission for issues over which the Community has authority (e.g., fishing or agriculture), the Committee of Permanent Representatives of member states to the EC Commission in Brussels and the Political Committee of foreign ministers managing the wider program of European Political Cooperation in external issues that arose in the 1970s. The Committee of Permanent Representatives, which has a staff consisting of officials seconded from various ministries at home, and the Political Committee often compete for influence, a regional reflection of the competition among ministries going on concurrently in each national capital (Wallace, 1973; Wessels, 1980).

The Assembly and the Allocation of Attention

Virtually all observers of world politics agree that the Assembly's public debates tend to force governments into taking positions on issues when they might prefer either to remain silent or to wait a while before making a definite statement. They have disagreed strongly about whether this is a good or a bad thing. At minimum, it forces governments to explain their policies in terms others will find reasonable. This helps create some level of common discourse despite the deep ideological divisions of the post–Second World War world. A good deal of hypocrisy remains, but governments are provided with a set of common symbols to be used in efforts to control behavior. This is why governments pay so much attention to the vocabulary of Assembly resolutions and try to hone it in the many general declarations adopted.

The need to explain policy also affects its timing and content. Observers of domestic politics have long been aware that certain ritual occasions for official statements, such as the opening day of a legislative session, the national holiday, or the day on which the budget is presented, force the pace of decision-making and impose deadlines that limit the field of maneuver. Assembly sessions have the same effect. If the Assembly devotes a special session to some topic, such as disarmament or development, then governments work hard to come up with proposals they can present. The projected date for the end of any session – regular or special – becomes the deadline by which compromise must be reached or the question deferred. When issues are raised unexpectedly, pressures for a statement can force decisions to be made in a very short period of time. Benjamin Cohen has argued that Assembly debates forced the United States to adopt a clearer policy on Indonesia in 1948 and on partitioning Palestine in 1947 than would otherwise have been the case (Cohen, 1951, p. 257).

Even when governments hope to avoid public debates, they may not be able to keep an issue out of the Assembly. When it looks like the Assembly will take up a question, pressures to settle the matter beforehand may become intense. Governments may then begin private efforts to settle the question before the Assembly meets, or at least before debate starts on the relevant item. This, however, is only one of many considerations and may not determine policy. Some observers thought calculations of this sort would push the United States toward putting serious pressure on Portugal to give up its African colonies in the 1960s and 1970s (e.g., Wohlgemuth, 1963, p. 51), but other things intruded and these predictions were not borne out by events.

In some cases, though, the value of avoiding Assembly debate may be considered high enough to drive policy. A desire to avoid the political costs of increasing castigation by the radical members of the Third World coalition, and an appreciation of the ways in which the issue gives them extra influence over the others, does lie behind Western efforts to bring out South African withdrawal from Namibia. The United States has also sought, successfully so far, to prevent formal discussion of Puerto Rico, though this requires considerable effort in bilateral discussions (Pastor, 1984; Franck, 1985, pp. 195–204).

Though many actions cannot be timed with any precision because they follow upon acts of others, some can be. Where that leeway exists, governments have timed certain actions to avoid or coincide with Assembly sessions depending on whether they expected a sympathetic or a hostile hearing. British and French planners initially hoped to mount the Suez operation during the summer of 1956. They then settled on late October in hopes that United States would be sufficiently distracted by its impending presidential election to stay uninvolved and that quick success would permit presenting the UN with a *fait accompli*. Israel tends to avoid major moves in the fall, knowing that the Assembly will not be sympathetic to anything it does. This does not shield it from criticism in other seasons, because an emergency session can be convened at any time, but does slow down the process and give the Israeli government a chance to finish whatever it is doing before Assembly pressures complicate the situation any further.

If the USSR was trying to avoid invading Afghanistan while the Assembly was in session, its calculations went awry because instead of breaking up for the year in December the Assembly had to reassemble during the first week of January 1980 to settle the long drawn out contest between Cuba and Colombia for the vacant Latin American seat on the Security Council. This meant that the emergency session could be assembled very quickly because heads of delegation were in New York rather than on their usual holidays. However, the Soviet Union may not have been worried about Assembly reaction at first. Its friends in the Nonaligned Movement were still actively seeking formal adoption of the thesis that the USSR is the "natural ally" of the Third World. Further, no one had protested at the time of the 1979 coup bringing Marxist–Leninists to power in that country. An accident of timing allowed quick expression of anti-Soviet feelings.

Some governments can act in the fall confident that the Assembly will support them. India moved forces into the Portuguese enclaves of Goa, Damao and Diu in mid-December 1961, just as the 16th session was winding up. India was confident that the Third World majority would endorse its view that continued colonial rule in those areas constituted "permanent aggression" rightly eradicated by force since Portugal showed no signs of negotiating on the question.

Public debate can make the resolution of problems or conflicts more difficult by forcing the articulation of half-formed policies or the freezing of governments' positions. This is most apparent in campaigns to condemn individual states. Even if some members would like to avoid further embarrassment by leaving the South African issue alone for a while the majority refuses to let it go for fear that even temporary silence would be interpreted as giving up. Subsequent modification of earlier stands or decisions, if its comes at all, must involve slight rewordings of earlier decisions or a tacit agreement to accept another solution without publicly admitting the fact. Latin American governments were very worried by the vagueness of early resolutions endorsing national liberation groups in Africa. By quiet discussions, they succeeded in getting later resolution written so that the endorsements applied only to groups recognized by the Organization of African Unity. This meant that groups supported by a single outside power would not enjoy the same legitimacy as the long-standing and widely supported groups formally recognized and aided by the OAU. Assembly acceptance of arangements whereby the people of Papua New Guinea decided to retain certain links with Australia was a low-key affair buried deep in the Committee of 24's report and the series of resolutions on individual colonial territories.

Finally, Assembly activity can affect the allocation of attention and resources across issues. Left to their own devices, the African, Asian and Latin American members of the US-led coalition would have devoted less time to Cold War issues. This can be seen most clearly in the efforts of some to create a third way between the superpowers starting at the Bandung Conference of 1955. The United States and Western Europeans for their part would have been happy with a lot less discussion of colonialism.

Unless the spotlight of condemnation falls on them for some reason, individual Third World governments are generally happy with the amount of time allocated to various issues in the Assembly. Collectively they control the agenda, and individually they can "tune out" by adopting the group position or failing to attend meetings. The industrial countries, particularly of the West, feel the effects of reallocation more since the dynamics of Assembly activity put them in the position of responding on most issues. On many issues, this represents a salutary erosion of particularistic attitudes. In some cases, though, it creates costly effects. For a Western state, avoiding condemnation can be expensive, not necessarily in terms of material side-payments but in terms of effort diverted and political debts incurred. As Pastor concluded on the Puerto Rico issue:

> The United States not only incurs a debt to these governments voting against Assembly debate, but these governments owe a debt to Cuba for putting the item on the agenda and transforming their vote into hard currency.
>
> (1984, p. 595)

Puerto Rico may represent an extreme case because the target is anxious to avoid all forms of condemnation, but similar dynamics are at work on other issues.

The Assembly and Intergovernmental Relations

The Assembly has four effects on intergovernmental relations. It can provide information about others' attitudes toward particular issues or proposed activities very quickly. It has forced states to make part of their foreign policies through the relatively new mechanism of regional and caucusing groups. It provides individual states with a stage for playing particular roles or projecting particular images of themselves. Finally, it provides an alternative to bilateral and small-group channels of diplomacy.

The Assembly affects the quantity and type of information available to governments. All governments, particularly those with large mission staffs, can use the Assembly (or the other permanent missions when it is not in session) to get a quick assessment of how others will react to particular ideas or actions. At least one Western European delegate has said that his country's policy on economic issues has been greatly influenced by Third World delegates' discussions of their countries' problems. These discussions thus parallel bilateral discussions between ex-metropoles and ex-colonies or between the European Community twelve and the Third World parties to the Lomé Convention. Another Western European delegate argues that if the United States wanted to know how others would react to its policy toward El Salvador in 1981, its mission would have been able to find out in about thirty minutes. Such information is particularly useful to governments that have few other channels for learning one another's attitudes. Of course, having information does not guarantee that it will affect policy or be used. It is doubtful whether any amount of information would have changed Reagan administration policy toward El Salvador, any more than advance knowledge that most of the Nonaligned would condemn it would have kept the Soviets from invading Afghanistan in December 1979. For most governments, the information available via the General Assembly or the permanent missions is unlikely to affect their broad goals or grand strategies, though it will affect the timing and tactics adopted. For some countries, though, information from other governments or international secretaries does affect policy more significantly. Many Third World governments lack diplomatic services and foreign policy staffs large enough to handle all the issues that come up in typical Assembly session. They thus rely on their regional group for policy ideas on issues where they lack a strong interest. They also use international staffs, particularly the UNCTAD secretariat, for developing ideas and writing early drafts of proposals.

Rothstein (1980, p. 5) argues that this means the international staffs dominate the early and middle stage of the North–South dialogue. Though this does happen, its continuance depends on congruity of interests between the staff and the Group of 77. When the two diverge, the Group of 77 does not hesitate to ignore the international staff involved (Weiss, 1983, describes the limited role of the UNCTAD secretariat at the 1981 Conference on the Least Developed Countries).

These habits affect Third World policies in a number of ways. First, they guarantee that those who are most intensely concerned about a particular issue exercise disproportionate influence. Such disproportionate influence is not unique to the Third World coalition; it happens in all politics because intensity means willingness to devote greater resources to a problem. The norm of Third World solidarity is sufficiently strong, however, that the less enthusiastic as well as those who might oppose can be put under severe pressure with accusations of betrayal. For instance, Antigua and Barbuda has invoked it in efforts to secure wide agreement to bring Antarctica to the General Assembly as a North–South issue. It has tried to deal with the inconvenient fact that several Third World states participate in the very regime it wants to replace by saying such things as:

> What is sad about this connivance between the Eastern and Western industrialized nations is that a handful of Third World countries are active participants with them in efforts to exclude other Third World nations.
> (Statement to a foreign ministers' meeting of the Organization of Eastern Caribbean States, 26 May 1983, quoted in Mitchell, 1983, p. 43)

Second, the number and complexity of issues encourages the drafting of very general proposals. Third, weakness forces members to adopt linkage strategies. Some, such as OPEC insistence that oil prices be discussed internationally only if they are linked to measures to stabilize the value of currencies (particularly the dollar), reflect traditional tactics of linking an issue where one has advantages to one where one does not, in hopes of attaining a better overall result than what would happen if each were negotiated separately. Others, such as the linking of Israel and South Africa, reflect the imperatives of coalition maintenance rather than calculations that the link will increase the chances of attaining a better outcome. Here, linkage is additive; in both areas the Third World is weak and wants similar outcomes. This is not a question of trading one outcome on South Africa for a contrasting one on Israel, but of trying to get preferred outcomes on both in the face of strong opposition against them. In this particular case, the additivity and the low probability of attaining the desired outcome in the short run mean that the issues can be used in this way without undue cost.

The net result is a form of intra-coalition politics that makes it as hard for the Third World coalition as a group to change policy as it is for even the most divided and interest-group-pressured Western government. Both the Group of 77 and the individual Western government arrive at policies through a long series of discussions leaving little energy for compromising with one another. Happily both have a measure of flexibility that does permit the last-minute small-group talks and compromises that mark so many Assembly discussions. The Western government has a hierarchical organization that permits the top leadership to impose its views when necessary. Though operating in terms of formal equality, both numbers and differing intensities of concern for different matters induce the Group of 77 to accept what its spokesmen accept in the small-group negotiations.

The existence of one group usually inspires the formation of others in self-defense. Existence of the Group of 77 has forced at least the major Western industrial states to coordinate their approaches to economic questions more than would otherwise have been the case. This means that many international negotiations go through several phases, often running simultaneously, in which an individual government settles on its own policy, adjusts it to the needs and preferences of its group and then refines it again in inter-group talks. International negotiation then becomes not the traditional bilateral seeking of a mutually acceptable bargain but a meeting of coalitions in which each coalition has to spend at least as much energy on maintaining itself as on finding an acceptable bargain with the others. Third World governments are more used to this sort of process, so have an advantage over industrial state governments of East or West which are less so. Most Third World governments, like the Eastern ones, have an additional advantage over the West in that they do not have to worry about dealing with well-organized and powerful domestic interest groups having foreign policy preferences of their own.

The Assembly's third effect on intergovernmental relations is its provision of opportunities to play various roles. This effect is particularly important for weak states because the Assembly gives them a wider choice of roles than has traditionally been available in world politics. Like domestic legislatures, the Assembly gives scope to members who excel at working out compromises, specialize in the details of particular issues, make or break coalitions because of their influence with others, or serve as gadflies raising new ideas or disrupting compromises in the name of principle. These supplement the traditional roles of world politics and open many to small states. While the role of great power may be played only by strong states, the Assembly allows a weak state to assume any other, including the traditional role of mediator. The net effect is greatly to expand the number of roles open to weak states.

Albanian activity demonstrates this point very well. Albania normally plays a small part in international politics, partly because of its small size and partly because its highly suspicious government maintains few relations with others. Yet in the 1960s and early 1970s Albania carved out a role for itself in the Assembly that commanded considerable attention from other members. In the 1960s this prominence stemmed largely from acting as a proxy for the People's Republic of China. China was not represented in the Assembly, and particularly during the "Cultural Revolution" the Albanians were the only ones maintaining close relations with China. Others therefore looked to Albanian pronouncements for clues to how China was reacting to events. But there was also an independent component, a conscious Albanian decision to take an "outsider" role. This was most apparent at the 19th session, when Albanian delegates tried to force votes that would have wrecked the understanding under which the session was meeting while the superpowers resolved their differences over the financing of peacekeeping. Albania even persisted in denouncing any form of cooperation between the superpowers as elements of a program to establish a global condominium even after the Chinese dropped that particular line in 1972. Albania's prominence declined greatly after the arrival of PRC delegates in the Assembly in October 1971, but it still plays the outsider role to emphasize its conviction that it alone remains on the true road to socialism (analysis inspired by Volgy, 1974).

India, too, used the Assembly to project a certain image and play a particular role, at least as long as Jawaharlal Nehru was prime minister. Though the world's second most populous state, India then lacked the material power to be a significant factor in traditional world politics. Indian statesmen sought to overcome this inconvenient fact by being conspicuous in Assembly proceedings. These efforts were most successful between 1955 and 1960, when India's position as one of the three acknowledged leaders of the Nonaligned Movement gave it great prestige. By 1965 India was less active in the Assembly. India had been disappointed by the Assembly's failure to side with it completely on the Kashmir dispute with Pakistan and stunned into a more openly power-politics-oriented policy after the Sino-Indian War of 1962. This shift was not a sudden conversion to a power-politics policy, but a scrapping of the earlier idealist rhetoric behind which India maneuvered as sharply as any other regional power. In addition, many of the newer member states were less inclined to accept its leadership, and changes of leaders at home had led to a shift of diplomatic style (Rana, 1970, describes these changes). Though the Indians still insist that "one-sixth of the world's population cannot be ignored" (interview with an Indian diplomat about his country's Antarctic policy, 1982) they are cutting a far less conspicuous figure in the Assembly than in the days of Krishna Menon.

Other governments use the Assembly not to capture headlines but to project a particular image of their country. Part of Canada's interest in peacekeeping lay in the opportunities it provided for pursuing a foreign policy and building an international image distinct from those of the United States without causing the latter to doubt its basic loyalty to the West. Though most Swiss still believe that their permanent neutrality bars participation in the Assembly, Austrian officials believe participation helps them reaffirm their neutral status by giving them opportunities to stress the role of general principles in foreign affairs and to demonstrate their readiness to help mediate disputes (Zamenek, 1961). Finland has used the Assembly to demonstrate that, contrary to some opinion, it is independent of the Soviet Union, without at the same time raising Soviet anxieties too much.

Another set of roles is created by providing services within the Assembly itself. An effective main committee chairman can enhance the prestige of his state. Delegates serving as chairmen of their regional group have extra importance during that time. The Assembly also gives extra prominence to the state that is serving as chairman of the Nonaligned or the Group of 77 because so many of its negotiations are discussions between West and South. Algeria found its normal efforts to be a leader of Third World opinion greatly enhanced in 1973–6 by being chairman of the Nonaligned and having its foreign minister serve as president of the 29th regular and 6th special Assembly sessions in 1974. Singapore has had a more prominent role in a number of international discussions than would be expected from an assessment of its material power because of the formidable talents of its chief delegate, Tommy T. B. Koh.

Finally, the Assembly, with its subsidiary bodies and special conferences, provides an alternative to the bilateral and small-group negotiating for a traditional in world politics. The

Assembly provides the best forum for dealing with issues of general concern arising out of the greater interdependence of states and interpenetration of societies. Issues of environmental protection, management of ocean activity, or regulation of transnational corporations could be discussed in smaller groups, but many aspects of them are most efficiently handled in a universal or near-universal one.

On other issues, the Assembly is simple one of many fora addressed simultaneously or sequentially. The Arab–Israeli conflict is carried out in bilateral and small-group interactions among the parties, interactions of parties and their respective superpower supporter, approaches of parties to other states able to provide significant material aid and attempts to gain wider sympathy in the Assembly. In such cases, the Assembly is used to reinforce or dilute the effects of other approaches. The Arab approach is a two-pronged effort to reinforce its own supporters while eroding United States support of Israeli policy. On the assumption that US relations with any single Arab state are unlikely to become important enough to erode the close US–Israeli tie, they have made joint efforts using appeals to segments of the American public, OPEC actions and Assembly appeals. Similarly, much foreign aid flows through programs sponsored by individual states or regional efforts by the European Community, Arab OPEC members, or the regional development banks. While the Assembly has created some UN aid programs, its main use lies is being a forum where recipient states as a group have more influence over decisions than donor states as a group and can exert more political pressure on donors, directly or through sympathetic segments of the public, than would be possible elsewhere.

Of course, the Assembly's proceedings and decisions also inspire considerable supplementary bilateral and small-group diplomacy. Individual states make bilateral approaches for support. Small groups coordinate initiatives to be presented first to regional groups and then to the whole Assembly. The campaign to prevent seating the Heng Semrin government's delegates as representatives of Cambodia is coordinated by the members of ASEAN. European Political Cooperation was greatly encouraged by EC member states' desire to increase Western European influence at the UN by having a common position on as many issues as possible.

The net result is a multi-tiered pattern of intergovernmental relations. Individual governments have a wide choice of bilateral, small-group, regional and global fora in which to discuss issues, pursue initiatives, seek support, or erode opponents' support. They can be used as alternates or supplements to one another depending on the nature of the issue at hand and a government's perceptions of which forum offers it the greatest advantages. The fact of multiple tiers also requires that governments develop a wider array of diplomatic skills and monitor developments at all tiers since they can easily affect one another. This is one of the elements that make foreign policy today a far more complicated thing than it was before 1914.

The Assembly, Governments and Other Actors

The Assembly and its decisions also affect the relations between governments and other actors in world politics. The Assembly gives some of the latter opportunities for contact that they would otherwise lack. Assembly decisions can enhance or inhibit nongovernmental actors' activities by granting or denying them a significant role in the formulation and implementation of decisions.

Almost all observers of international politics admit that a whole host of nongovernmental actors also involve themselves in world politics, though they disagree strongly about the significance of their activity. The Assembly offers many nongovernmental actors contacts with governments, particularly those of foreign states, and access to public attention that they would not otherwise enjoy. Transnational and some purely domestic nongovernmental organizations have "consultative status" with the Economic and Social Council, which permits their representatives to observe meetings, secure copies of documents, submit written communications and make statements to sub-organs like the Commission on Human Rights. Some intergovernmental organizations, the Roman Catholic Church, a number of African national liberation movements and the PLO have observer status in the General Assembly itself that permits them wide participation in main committee proceedings, occasional speeches to the plenary and access to the informal negotiating processes.

Though transnational activity existed before 1945, it has become much more prominent in the last two decades. The number of transnational corporations has increased, and they are now based in a larger number of countries, including India, South Korea and Singapore. The number of other transnational organizations has increased even more rapidly. In the UN, many of them have expanded their activity from maintaining contact mainly with the Economic and Social Council or relevant specialized agencies to wider forms of lobbying the Assembly or global conferences. It was possible to study the General Assembly without reference to nongovernmental organizations in 1960; it is not possible to do so today.

Formal contacts between nongovernmental organizations and UN bodies are supplemented by a whole range of informal ones. For all but the national liberation groups and the regional organizations having observer status with the Assembly, these are more important than the formal contacts. Transnational organizations have run meetings of their own parallel to several UN-sponsored global conferences and the Assembly's special sessions on disarmament. At the first special session on disarmament in 1978, representatives of 25 nongovernmental organizations and 6 research institutes were permitted to address the Assembly convened as a committee of the whole (Kaufmann, 1980, p. 94). Human rights groups have been very active in all aspects of UN work on the subject. Information that they publish is often cited by delegates in the course of debate.

Of all nongovernmental actors, national liberation groups have benefited the most from the Assembly's existence, from decisions to allow them formal status and from other resolutions. The strong anticolonial cast of Assembly resolutions granted them an automatic legitimacy in the eyes of most members, and made it difficult for most colonial powers to apply severe repressive measures or to refuse to discuss the issue (see discussions in Hoffmann, 1956; Wohlgemuth, 1963; Chang, 1972). This inhibition did not work in all cases, but did help speed the end of colonialism. The national liberation groups have been able to use the Assembly to mobilize support abroad and at home (Chang, 1972, discusses how various factions in South Yemen used or tried to use Assembly resolutions to bolster their domestic position). When they have been accorded observer status they have been able to take on an international role far beyond what rebels would have enjoyed under traditional international law.

Particular Assembly decisions can either enhance or diminish the position of nongovernmental actors. Again, the national liberation groups have enjoyed the greatest boost. The PLO, SWAPO, the ANC and the PAC have all benefited from Assembly decisions affirming the legitimacy of their resort to force, calling on specialized agencies to allow them participation in agency activity, inviting them to UN-sponsored conferences, including them among parties to some multilateral treaties negotiated under UN auspices, such as the 1982 Law of the Sea

Convention, and giving them various forms of financial assist-ance. On occasion the Assembly recognized the importance of other groups by general reference. Thus, resolution on South Africa routinely include paragraphs calling on private groups to aid in the anti-apartheid struggle.

The governments of most member states are not keen on seeing their citizens engaged in transnational activity. Many actively suppress or prevent it as part of larger efforts to prevent all forms of organized private activity within the state. The USSR, for instance, works to break up any privately organized group, such as the Helsinki Watch Committee set up among intellectuals in Moscow and other cities, and seeks to channel citizen energy into government-organized groups such as the official peace movement. Other governments place strong pressures on groups with actual or potential transnational ties to support official policy, the attitude of all Latin American dictatorships of whatever persuasion to the Roman Catholic Church.

Many Third World governments reserve special suspicion for transnational groups based entirely or mainly in Western states. This is clearest with transnational corporations. They are viewed as a large part of the problem on economic issues, and as a major obstacle to Third World aspirations. Since Western governments are not ready to impose the sort of control on their behavior Third World countries would like (which is not to say that all Western governments reject all controls), the Third World coalition has used the Assembly and other UN bodies as levers for control. This can be seen most clearly in the establishment of the UN Center on Transnational Corporations, which monitors their activities and drafts possible codes of regulations. Similar suspicions extend to foreign journalists. In part, these stem from Third World fears of the power of large Western news agencies and resentments of the way Third World news is often covered. Yet they partly have an independent base in reluctance to let foreigners inquire too closely into internal affairs. Similar sus-picions can extend to any group that a government feels is promoting alien ways or disrupting local affairs.

Such suspicions are not surprising. The governments of most UN member states are dictatorships which do not sympathize with private activity by their own citizens. Many of them particularly dislike the idea that their citizens might have contacts with or get support from people abroad. In some cases where severe repression at home has led dissidents to flee, foreign contacts are seen as making such flight easier. Even in states not ruled by dictatorial governments, political and social integration is often weak and the government apparatus barely able to cope with the demands of rapid industrialization. The governments of these states feel highly vulnerable to outside influences and are extremely sensitive to the possibility of outside pressures. The popularity of dependency theory is one index of these feelings. For the left, it provides an explanation of outside pressures and a call to get rid of them through social revolution. For the right, to the extent it has absorbed the ideas, it provides justification for measures strengthening the governmental apparatus and severely limiting the activities of foreigners.

Yet when the activities of transnational groups parallel what governments desire, even the most dictatorial welcome it. For instance, the London-based International Institute for Environment and Development organized conferences and press briefings that provided Third World governments with their main forum for raising challenges to the Antarctic Treaty system between 1975 and 1983 (Quigg, 1983, p. 168). The World Council of Churches' sponsorship of campaigns and boycotts against Nestlé and other firms selling baby formula paralleled governments' concerns about controlling transnational firms. Many transnational environmental groups assist governments by providing information and occasionally skilled personnel for particular activities.

Further, no government is averse to private and transnational activity that modifies other governments's positions in directions closer to their own. Few Third World governments have adopted the well-known Soviet bloc strategy of organizing and financing "front organizations" abroad, but all are aware of and appreciate various transnational activities. For instance, the International Coalition for Development Action (ICDA), an umbrella organization of some one hundred private lobbying groups in various Western states, generally takes positions fairly close to those of the Group of 77 on North–South questions. The ICDA serves as a coordinating mechanism for member group efforts to monitor the performance of their country's delegation at UNCTAD meetings, report on positions taken and lobby at home for changes in policy. Similar groups have emerged in the field of environment and human rights (Rodley, 1979; Archer, 1984). They are most effective when the conference's agenda parallels their concerns; they are less effective if that agenda crosses the concerns of several groups or includes issues around which no group is already organized (noted for the Conference on Least Developed Countries in Weiss, 1983, pp. 664–5).

This transnational activity is most prominent at Assembly-convened global conferences and special sessions devoted to a single issue. There is less at regular sessions because of the large number of issues involved and the cost of maintaining such activity on a sustained basis. However, such activity affects politics in the Assembly by reinforcing or weakening the solidity of different blocs of states and creating pressures on individual governments to change their positions.

The Assembly and its decisions also have some effect on the internal politics of states. The Assembly can be used for launching appeals to populations or particular groups within populations "over the head" of their government. It can also be used to mobilize preexisting sentiments in efforts to get governments to change policy. Finally, the government may use favorable Assembly decisions to build public support for its policy. Within governments, the Assembly and its decisions can affect policy by changing the attitudes of policy-makers toward world politics in general or toward specific issues that arise. They can also be used by politicians and bureaucrats seeking to change a policy that has already been announced or to head off one that has been proposed.

Many Assembly decisions represent efforts to raise popular and interest group support for the general norms asserted or specific programs undertaken by the Assembly and other UN bodies. Such landmark resolutions as the Universal Declaration of Human Rights or the Declaration on the Granting of Independence to Colonial Countries and Peoples were given wide publicity in efforts to enlist such support around the world. Both the Special Committee Against Apartheid and the Committee on the Exercise of the Inalienable Rights of the Palestinian People hold symposia and other gatherings to publicize their respective causes and forge links with sympathetic groups, particularly in the West. The limits to Assembly resources being what they are, such appeals are effective only when there is already a substantial popular following for the propositions being put forth.

Assembly decisions may also affect ongoing debates about national or local issues. Groups may well try to enhance their role in the debate by pointing to international support for their positions or international condemnations of positions taken by others. Groups trying to promote human rights through lawsuits have sometimes attempted to cite the Universal Declaration of Human Rights as evidence that their country accepts a particular norm. In virtually all cases courts have rejected explicit appeals to the Declaration, but its terms may have influenced courts' interpretations of national law in states that voted in favor (e.g., Skubiszewski, 1972; Schreuer, 1978). On the whole, however, national courts have preferred to rely on national law, treaties and customary international law.

Though some states are far more open to outside appeals and influences than others, the difference in effect of Assembly appeals to the public may not be very great. It is clear that in a state like China, where information is closely controlled, only those Assembly appeals the government likes will get publicity. In the West, particularly the United States, low public interest and low press coverage combine to limit the effect of Assembly appeals. Most people in most societies pay little attention to international affairs except in periods of crisis. The relatively small attentive public that follows foreign affairs may or may not pay great attention to the UN depending on how it views the UN. Those who find it particularly helpful or particularly harmful to their country's interests pay the most attention and seek to convert their less attentive compatriots to their views. As with other foreign news, news of UN activities tends to spread only when there is a crisis or some other dramatic event. As Geoffrey Goodwin noted in 1962:

> during most of its fifteen years' existence, so far as public interest in Britain in its political activities is concerned, the limited impact the United Nations has had on most of the major issues of peace and war has discouraged "public opinion" from waxing very enthusiastic – or bitter – about it; indeed, though a generally accepted part of international life, it has for long periods languished relatively unnoticed in a diplomatic backwater.
>
> (Goodwin, 1961, p. 581)

When they so desire, however, governments can ensure extra publicity for UN activity. In most cases this means publicizing the government's own stances in ways that make it appear to be defending the right. In 1951 a recently emigrated Polish official noted that the Soviet Union found the Assembly useful not only to speak to the rest of the world, but to help persuade its own population and those of Easter European states that it was the only defender of peace against US aggression (Rudzinski, 1951, p. 299). Similarly, the Soviet Union has used the 1975 "Zionism is a form of racism" resolution to give legitimacy to its domestic discrimination against Jews (Korey, 1978, p. 9). Third World governments publicize their speeches and Assembly decisions in efforts to maintain popular support. The United States government, too, used Assembly debates to raise popular support at home and abroad during the Cold War (Finger, 1980, pp. 80–1, on the activities of Henry Cabot Lodge).

Assembly decisions may also become part of a domestic political controversy when opposition groups use them to discredit the government. In South Africa in the mid-1940s and in Rhodesia in the early 1960s advocates of stricter racial discrimination defeated less strict opponents in elections confined to white voters. In both campaigns, the stricter group used the fact that the government attempted to defuse Assembly criticism with minor concessions as a sign that it would ultimately "sell out" and turn the country over to blacks (Mudge, 1967, pp. 61–7). Various decisions and mix-ups at the UN helped the Republicans portray the Carter administration as inept, overly inclined to accept Third World condemnation of the United States and insufficiently protective of Israel in the 1980 presidential election (Moynihan, 1980).

Finally, the Assembly and its decisions can affect intragovernmental arguments over policy. Many academic observers have attempted to assess the extent to which service as delegates in the Assembly affects policy-makers or diplomats' views and perceptions. Taken in general, the effects do not seem to be great. In a crisis, past and present delegates are not likely to differ from others in their assessment of threats or their choices of responses (Siverson, 1973, on Israelis and Egyptians during the 1967 War). In calmer times, delegates hold national views, but their exposure to others then makes them more sensitive to other countries' concerns and arguments (Ernst, 1978; Peck, 1979; Riggs, 1981). In countries where the top leadership seldom has spent much time in the Assembly or other UN activities, any attitude change produced by service in the Assembly affects the advice given, but not necessarily the processes of decision-making or the content of the decisions. For states where members of the top leadership have Assembly experience, the situation is probably different. Most Third World foreign ministers spend a fair amount of time at the Assembly (as well as at regional, Nonaligned and Group of 77 meetings), and many have previously been delegates. This is less common among the industrial states of East and West. Yet in individual cases, it is possible to trace shifts in attitude that did have an impact on foreign policy. Paul-Henri Spaaks's experiences with Soviet delegates helped turn him into a staunch advocate of Western defense coordination and the NATO alliance (Spaak, 1971, p. 109). Henry Cabot Lodge's discussions with Asian leaders persuaded him that nonalignment (generally called "neutralism" at the time) was not as terrible as other US policy-makers thought and that the United States should take a more sympathetic view of anticolonial initiatives (Finger, 1980, p. 79). To the extent that such individuals affect their countries' policies, the attitude shifts are politically significant.

Assembly endorsements, condemnations and statements of norms can all be used as ammunition in inter-agency and inter-branch arguments over policy. This may work in both directions. The British Labour Party, which in 1946 supported strong UN involvement in colonial issues, was very disenchanted with the tone of Fourth Committee debates by 1950. This meant a stiffening of British reluctance to handle such issues in the UN because Labour now moved closer to the Conservative Party, which had alwasy doubted the wisdom of extensive Assembly involvement (Fox, 1950, p. 200). In fact, it is generally agreed that any state being criticized constantly in the Assembly, be it Israel, South Africa, the Soviet Union between 1947 and 1950 (Mosley, 1966, p. 668), France between 1954 and 1964 (Duroselle, 1965, p. 695), or the United States today, will react against Assembly decisions. Domestically, this can undercut those politicians and officials who prefer decisions similar to those adopted by the Assembly and aid those who prefer a contrary policy.

Even the drift of Assembly debate can affect policy. If a government does not like being isolated, the knowledge that most states are prepared to accept some proposition can bring a shift toward what appears to be the general view. This may mean dropping opposition, but it may also mean expressing opposition in muted and modified form. Even when an individual government has not given its group a "blank check" by instructing its delegates to support whatever position the group takes (Rothstein, 1980, p. 7, argues that this is usually true for economic negotiations), discussions with the group can modify previous stands. The acquisition of new information may also lead to a change.

It is even possible, though difficult, to prove that the Third World tendency to lump large numbers of specific issues under a broader umbrella concept has as much to do with intragovernmental politics at home as with the maintenance of group solidarity against the industrial states (Krasner, 1981, p. 130, rejects this, but most detailed examinations of the Group of 77 do not disprove it). International negotiations on economic, ocean policy, communications policy and other issues proceed on two tracks. On the more general track, foreign ministers and other generalists hammer out principles that will provide a framework for the discussion of more technical issues and specific transactions. These more detailed discussions occur between specialists in the relevant ministries and their colleagues in other governments or private groups with which they want to make a deal. Just as in industrial state governments, the specialists often go their own way. Most Third World governments lack the large number of specialists both within and outside government that help policy-makers in industrial states monitor what particular agencies are doing and ensure that their decisions fit within general policy. Therefore, a combination of general guidelines and group consultations, even in the more technical multilateral fora, may act as a substitute. Even so, they do not always prevent specialists from acting on their own sense of priorities, a problem the industrial states also face.

In any event, this group caucusing affects only part of a state's foreign policy. It is important for aspects of policy handled multilaterally, but there is a vast realm of bilateral relations where each state stands more on its own. Most will avoid taking positions or making agreements that flatly contradict group policy on some important question, but bilateral relations remain a realm of each state for itself, particularly in times of crisis. This was shown dramatically in June 1982, when the PLO, which enjoyed wide verbal support in the Middle East, was unable to get much assistance against Israeli attacks. The initial confusion of estimates was so great that it took the Soviet Union nearly ten days to issue a two-sentence official statement condemning the Israeli attacks. Most decision-makers tend to separate the multilateral and the bilateral realms in their minds, much as they tend to separate one issue from another, if only because they are responsible for some things but not for others. This extends even to bilateral and small-group relations between industrial and developing countries, where the officials in charge of particular negotiations often know little about the state of the North–South dialogue and view it as a symbolic exercise not fully relevant to the pursuit of tangible advantages in bilateral dealing (Rothstein, 1980, p. 7). These mental separations reduce the impact of UN decisions even for intragovernmental policy discussions.

Summary

Assembly decisions and proceedings affect the foreign policy processes of member states in four ways. First, they alter the web

of personal contacts among those officials who have responsibility for foreign policy by providing an additional point of
contact. Second, they affect the amount and timing of attention
paid to particular issues. Third, by offering an alternative to the
bilateral and small-group relations traditional to world politics,
they add another dimension to intergovernmental relations and
afford greater opportunities for transgovernmental coalition
building. Fourth, they offer certain new opportunities for non-
state actors and for governmental attempts to appeal directly to
foreign publics and interest groups.

The influence of personality on policy is always difficult to
trace with any precision. It is possible, though, to show that
different groups of states are more or less able to take advantage
of the web of personal relations in the Assembly. Most Third
World states maximize use of Assembly networks while mini-
mizing the complications of home government/delegation relations by farming out large areas of policy-making and execution
to the delegation. This makes maintaining the Third World
coalition relatively easy since delegates do not have to worry all
the time about how agencies at home are reacting or that people
at home will be trying to undercut their efforts. The Soviet bloc's
practices tend to minimize the personal influence of all but top
leaders. Its insistence on close instruction from home does not
lead to particular difficulties in responding to development in the
Assembly since so much of the time the Soviet bloc aligns itself
with Third World positions. Western states have a complex
problem. Their delegates can use the Assembly network to some
extent, with the European Community twelve and the Scandinavians better at this than the United States. However, Western
delegates must also respond to a complicated policy-making
process at home, where legislative mandates, inter-agency com-
petitions and lobbying by interest groups have a stronger effect
on decisions than most of the advice given by the delegation.

The impact of reallocating attention has varied. Members of
the controlling coalition must accept some reallocation to keep
the coalition together. In the US-led coalition, this took the form
of trading attention on different issues: the NATO allies spent
more time than they wished on decolonization, group rights and
economic development, while the others spent more time than
they wished on Cold War issues and individual rights. In the Third
World coalition, the allocations seem to be additive: every
sub-group's particular demands are added to the rest to form the
final package whenever possible. Yet even with these intra-
coalitional patterns, the reallocation is not as severe as for

members of minority groupings. Though minorities can pursue initatives, they are usually "agenda-takers" rather than "agenda-makers". This is probably more true of the West now than of the Soviet bloc before 1955 because a larger proportion of Assembly time is given over to direct challenges of Western positions than was ever given to direct challenges of the USSR. On many issues, the Soviet bloc was able to advance positions gaining wider support, so was often spared being implicitly or explicitly labeled the source of most of the difficulty.

Providing an alternative to bilateral and small-group discuss-ions is probably the Assembly's most important effect on the policy process. In fact, it is almost possible to speak of a bifurcation between the multilateral and bilateral foreign policies of many states. Many issues before the Assembly, such as the "new world information and communications order", defining what acts constitute aggression, or defining which things should be included as individual or group rights, are handled mainly in multilateral fora. The politics of building and maintaining inter-governmental coalitions becomes very important to outcomes. Other issues, such as the future of Israel and Palestine, the operation of UN aid programs, or disarmament, are handled in bilateral or small-group fora as well. Multilateral and other discussions overlap and influence one another. On other issues, such as trade, technology transfer, or the management of world commodity markets, the overlap takes the form of broad discuss-ion of principles and general norms in the multilateral fora combined with the working out of specific deals in bilateral or small-group discussions. This can be seen clearly in West–South relations. The bilateral relations of any Western and any Third World country are not as conflict-ridden as the multilateral patterns of the Assembly might suggest. This stems in part from the fact that bilateral deals usually respond to very specific situations, whereas the generality of Assembly discussion makes it more abstract, and in part from the fact that countries do not link as many issues at once in bilateral as in multilateral relations. All this means that there is a far more complicated pattern of intergovernmental relations than ever before.

Finally, the Assembly affects the behavior and opportunities of nongovernmental actors, whether groups within single countries or transnational organizations of various types, acting for them-selves or attempting to influence government policies. On the whole, the Assembly is friendliest to national liberation groups, which are seen as proto-governments or proto-states that happen to lack their rightful status at the moment because of foreign interference, colonialism, or racism. The position of other non-governmental actors varies. Before 1955 there was little attention to such groups in the Assembly. Most of their activity occurred within specialized agencies dealing with matters on which they had some expertise. They did have consultative status with the Economic and Social Council for purposes of discussion on social and economic issues, while a few dealing with conditions in colonies had access to meetings of the Fourth Committee. On the whole, however, they were not active on issues before the Assembly. The situation changed in the 1970s. The Third World coalition had identified some nongovernmental actors, particularly transnational corporations, as threats that should be controlled. At the same time, umbrella organizations of national and transnational interest groups began taking an active interest in various "global issues" such as pollution, population control and food supply. Single-issue special sessions of the Assembly and Assembly-sponsored conferences became one of their favorite foci of lobbying efforts. To the extent that these groups took positions closer to those of the Third World than to those of the governments in their own states, the Third World coalition was happy to see them working. This greater activity by nongovernmental actors has added a further complication to the policy-making process for all states whose governments respond to public pressure and whose systems are open to foreign attempts to affect public opinion. This affects the West more than most Third World states and far more than the Soviet bloc, so it often adds to Western discomfort in the Assembly.

At this point, the impact of the Assembly in each of the four phases of world politics has been examined. The effects of its proceedings and decisions at both the international level and within individual states have been explored. It is time to put the pieces of the argument together, the task of Chapter 9.

Chapter Nine

The Assembly and World Politics

As a political institution, the General Assembly helps perform all the essential functions of a political system: socialization of individual actors, selection of individual actors for leadership roles, pursuit of transactions among actors, articulation of interests, aggregation of interests, adoption of decisions, application of rules and implementation of decisions. All political institutions both are shaped by and help shape the political system that they serve. In the case of the General Assembly, the high decentralization of the international system, which leaves most effective power and authority in the hands of states, and its low moral consensus, which encourages states to take a self-centered rather than a community-centered view of things, combine to restrict the effects of Assembly proceedings and decisions at every stage of the political process.

World politics remains as Secretary-General Waldheim described in 1975:

> A realistic assessment of the actual patterns of interstate relations reveals that many, if not most, of those relations continue to be handled bilaterally, that a relatively small volume of interstate activity is channeled through international organizations. Even in the case of problems recognized as global, there is a tendency to rely on restricted forums and groups of so-called "interested" countries, without reference to the more generally-accepted codes of behavior or co-ordination with activities carried on within the United Nations system.
>
> (*A New United Nations Structure for Global Economic Cooperation*, Doc. E/AC.62/9, May, 1975, p. 64)

This does not mean that the General Assembly is completely without influence; it does mean however, that such influence is limited. Yet the narrowness of the limits varies. The Assembly has greater influence on the international political system in some stages of the political process than in others.

The precise way in which Assembly proceedings and decisions affect world politics depends greatly on how the Assembly is being used and what decisions it produces. This, in turn, depends heavily on whether there is a stable coalition controlling the Assembly and, if so, on the goals and solidity of that coalition. If there is no stable majority coalition, the Assembly's impact is diluted as shifting *ad hoc* majorities pursue different goals on various issues. The Assembly's impact is greater when a stable coalition is able to pursue its vision across many issues for several years because the proceedings and decisions are then used to reinforce one another. To a lesser extent, the Assembly's impact on world politics also depends on the type of issue being considered at the moment. The Assembly is better suited to the consideration of generalities than of details, and has greater authority over the UN system than over member states. These differences influence the way in which coalitions use the Assembly.

Phases of the Political Process

The Assembly has greatest impact on world politics at the agenda-formation phase. Though only one of many political institutions operating at the group, regional and global levels, it can be used to supplement or reinforce activities undertaken elsewhere. Obviously, the Assembly does not control the whole agenda of world politics; much political interaction goes on outside it. However, the fact that it is difficult for even the most powerful state or group of states to prevent Assembly discussion of a particular matter once a majority decides to put it on the effective agenda means that the possibility of Assembly discussion must always be kept in mind. This has the effect of redirecting attention and energy to issues that some governments might prefer to ignore or to discuss elsewhere. The open agenda also gives advantage to those desiring to bring more states into the discussion of some matter over those seeking to restrict discussion to small groups.

The process of formulating the Assembly agenda has two effects on world politics independent of the nature of the issue or the identity of the controlling coalition. First, by being open only to states, the Assembly reinforces their position *vis-à-vis* other actors in the international system. It is states' concerns that get placed on the agenda and states' interests that form the basis of discussion and decision. This can be seen most readily in recent Assembly references to the activities of transnational corporations, which are routinely blamed for many of the woes of the Third World. It can also be seen in the shift of Assembly attention from the civil and political rights of individuals to the rights of groups and the need to assure better standards of economic well-being. Both of the latter are far less controversial among governments because their attainment assumes greater state action in society rather than the abstention required for the full play of civil and political rights.

Second, and more importantly, the Assembly creates a situation unusual even in domestic politics. The allocation of one vote to every state, the rule that the agenda is determined by a simple majority and the great numerical preponderance of weak states among the members mean the Assembly is an institution where the weak can form an alternative agenda and get the strong to pay attention to it. Even in the era of the US-led coalition, strong states found that they could maintain the support of weak ones only by making concessions. Giving the weak a large proportion of Assembly time for discussion of issues particularly important to them was one. The shift to the Third World coalition has not created a new situation in this regard; it has merely made the old one more obvious.

Agenda formation in the Assembly also affects the way in which interests are articulated in the international system by providing an additional choice of venue. It offers an instant global forum any state or group of states can invoke in efforts to secure support for their views or positions. Yet use of the Assembly is not compulsory. Some states avoid articulating very many demands in the Assembly because they anticipate a hostile reception. To the extent they do avoid it, the Assembly has not lived up to the hopes of those who believed it would serve as the "parliament of man". The international system remains one where issues of central importance – such as arms limitation between the superpowers – are as often discussed outside as inside the supposedly central institutions. This does not happen in national politics; at some point the central issues do make it to the agendas of the national legislature. Interest articulation thus remains less centralized in the international system than in many domestic ones.

Like other political institutions, the Assembly serves as both forum for seeking cooperative solutions and arena for pursuing conflict. This dual nature does not confuse the delegates or their superiors. It should not confuse anyone else either, since all political institutions serve both purposes. The low moral consensus in the international system means, however, that there are few limits to the verbal combat; the decentralization of that system means that the Assembly often seems more useful as an arena of conflict than as a generator of cooperation. The problem for outside observers is that the heat and dust of the arena have a way of hiding the quiet of the forum, resulting in a skewed impression of the Assembly's work.

The Assembly's pattern of agenda-making has also changed the pattern of interest aggregation significantly. A decision to handle an item inside rather than outside the Assembly changes the identities of those whose views have to be taken into account before arriving at a decision. A bilateral discussion, or one between a small group of "interested" or "like-minded" countries, means that the parties can focus on the views of a few. They may have to take the views of nonparticipants into account, for moral or (more often) prudential reasons, but the focus is on hammering out agreement within the group. A discussion in the Assembly, particularly one intended to inspire a consensus decision, requires accommodating a far wider range of views and interests.

Assembly influence in the decision-making phase is weaker but, when the performance of related political functions is taken into account, remains significant. Though the Assembly comes nowhere near to making all international decisions, its debates and negotiations have impacts independent of decisions and implementation. It is true that much of the attention paid to debates and negotiations stems from the knowledge that they usually lead to decisions, but governments also keep the separate effects in mind.

Assembly debate and negotiation are very important for the process of political socialization for governments. Just as individuals need to learn how to act in their national political systems, governments need to learn how to act in the international one. This is as true for established governments accommodating to change as for new governments just beginning to have foreign policies of their own. For the latter, the Assembly and the regional groups have been good places to explore the views and preconceptions of others, and acquire enough of the form of diplomatic discourse to be effective in bilateral relations as well. It is a place where their officials can seek the advice and opinions of others without publicity or revealing an obvious relation between the questions they ask and the uses to which they want to put the information acquired. They can also see diplomats from many states at work, and gain a sense of the cultural and other differences of others' styles. To the extent that the Assembly stresses multilateral issues and votes, it presents a somewhat misleading view of the international system. However there are enough confrontations, reminders of the importance of material power and examples of bilateral deals to hasten learning in areas where bilateral relations are the norm or power is more important. Socialization of the governments of new states was an extremely important function of the Assembly in the 1960s; since the number of likely new states has declined rapidly in recent years, it will be less important in the future.

Continued socialization of governments of old states will remain a function of the Assembly. Just as individuals must constantly learn as their domestic political system, the needs of their society, or their own interests change, so do states. This has been particularly true in the twentieth century given the pace of technological change and the revolution of expectations giving rise to the welfare state. The growing need for cooperation requires that states perfect new methods of negotiation and parallel activity. The Assembly is a good forum for discussing the problem so that all see its dimensions, and setting out the lines of action that are believed will best serve all states' needs. Socialization also includes the process of altering governments' attitudes on particular issues. Much of the Third World discussion of colonial and economic issues has been an effort (often assisted by nongovernmental actors in the West) to persuade other governments that the question is important and that existing standards of conduct are not widely accepted. Assembly encouragement of negotiation and peaceful settlement is an effort to persuade all states to settle conflicts without war by making suggestions and praising proper behavior.

It is true that confrontations may result in such perverse or confused messages that no learning results. Assembly activity on the question of Arab refugees can be viewed as an attempt to persuade the Israelis that remaining an occupier of the Arab lands taken in 1967 is unwise, to persuade the Arabs that it is unwise to try settling the refugees back into their original homes within Israel or to destroy Israel and to convince both sides that they will have to compromise (Forsythe, 1972, p. 711). Unfortunately, these efforts tended to get tangled in a lot of contradictory messages coming from UN bodies and a lot of nasty rhetoric coming from the parties and their supporters. In much of the debate, Arab and Israeli seem to be talking past one another and deriving from each other's speeches the most pessimistic conclusions about the other's intentions. Similarly, even segments of colonial state governments sympathetic to decolonization became prejudiced against the sort of rhetoric coming out of the UN and left it out of the process as much as possible.

Socialization occurs regardless of the coalition controlling the Assembly, though the identity of the coalition affects most of the lessons being imparted. Certain themes have persisted regardless of coalition. The most enduring theme of Assembly socialization applied to great powers might be summed up in Shakespeare's words,

> O, it is excellent
> to have a giant's strength; but
> it is tyrannous
> To use it like a giant.
> (*Measure for Measure*, Act II, Scene 2, line 107)

The effectiveness of socialization varies with the time, the message and the addressee. The particular impact of the Assembly consists of providing a forum where all states can join in and be subjected to the process, and in providing weak states with far greater possibilities for influencing the thinking of the strong than they have normally enjoyed in world politics.

Traditionally, the decentralization and low moral consensus of the international system have made it one where "clubs are trumps." The leading actors have been those states able to acquire and apply the greatest amounts of military and economic power. The Assembly itself has not changed that situation, but such twentieth-century developments as the spread of interdependence, the rise of mass interest in politics and the growth of the welfare state have created situations in which the older notions that states are unitary, rational actors mainly interested in security no longer apply. The Assembly is one of the places where these new developments are registered and their influence is brought to bear on state conduct.

The Assembly also permits states that otherwise would have little influence to take leadership roles, expanding the pool of potential international leaders beyond the ranks of the great powers. Sometimes, as with the "middle powers" and their peacekeeping efforts, others lead so that fragile understandings among great powers will be maintained. At other times, a great power lets another propose and shepherd its ideas through the Assembly process because identification of the idea with the real sponsor would make its adoption more difficult. Often the need for support allows relatively weak states that happen to be influential in a regional group to act much as party leaders domestically, making compromises and delivering the votes necessary to their adoption. Without the Assembly and the rest of the UN system, the North–South division of the world would not appear as prominent as it does. The South would have engaged the attention of statesmen and publics in the North only when Northern conflicts or Southern wielding of hitherto unsuspected economic power made the South materially significant. Northern attention waned with détente, the ebb of economic threat of commodity cartels and global recession, yet this process would have gone much further without the Assembly to keep attention focused on the issue.

Assembly negotiations have created a whole new set of ways for states to pursue transactions in world politics. These also give weak states more opportunities than they have traditionally enjoyed. The Assembly offers facilities for acquiring information and making contacts more widely and more quickly than would otherwise be the case. This is useful for all states, but particularly important to the weak or poor, which have trouble maintaining diplomatic missions in as many capitals as they would like and find UN Headquarters a useful supplement to those they do maintain. On occasion even the strong find UN Headquarters useful for hiding the fact that they are having discussions with some other state, lest a political storm erupt at home.

The Assembly, like other international organizations where votes determine the fate of proposals, encourages a new type of transaction, the trading of votes for votes or of votes for material favors. Neither idea is new to international relations. States often traded support on one issue for support on others. States also traded favors for statements of support. However, the Assembly provides a very clear form of such transactions and more opportunities for them than used to be the case. The number of such transactions will continue to depend on how badly a state wants support, but the Assembly increases the number of types of support that can be offered and the occasions on which it might be sought.

The Assembly encourages the use of another form of transaction, appeals to minority factions within foreign governments and foreign public opinion more generally for support. The public appeal is an old device in international politics; as long as there has been mass interest in politics (even in countries where this was not supplemented by mass participation in the political process) governments have sought to make such appeals. The Assembly simply provides a particularly convenient place for doing so. Even poor states which could not afford their own propaganda campaigns can use the Assembly, though its impact is limited by the low attention paid to its proceedings in most countries. A stable majority can also enlist the services of special Assembly committees or expert bodies created to assure arrival at the "right" answer, and the UN Secretariat.

The Assembly also serves as developer and publicizer of new techniques in multilateral diplomacy. Governments have learned to deal with one another in large groups, entrust key negotiations to selected group spokesmen and cope with rapidly evolving proposals on a host of issues simultaneously. Small governments cope by relying on their group; others modify their diplomatic procedures. The shift has posed different problems for different types of governments. Those with actively competing bureau-cracies and factions, active domestic interest groups and attentive publics find it harder to deal with these developments than others. It poses greater difficulties for open societies where foreign appeals can be heard and foreign governments or private actors link up with domestic actors to urge changes in policy. Closed political systems are not affected by appeals to the public, but the government may find itself divided and unsure of what to do because of developments in multilateral fora.

Assembly debates and negotiations also affect patterns of interest articulation. To some extent, they permit nongovern-mental actors, particularly the "national liberation groups" accepted by most states as having a legitimate cause, to play a part in raising and discussing international issues. It also encourages a larger number of states to articulate interests by providing many opportunities to participate in formal debates and informal negotiations. In this respect, then, the Assembly limits the power of the great because they cannot monopolize discourse. As a Swedish diplomat once put it, "small states like the Assembly because it is the one place where they can speak without being interrupted" (interview, 1983). The Assembly is particularly useful for the smaller members of alliances or other groups, who might otherwise go unnoticed. This is clearest in the case of the Soviet bloc. The smaller members generally follow the Soviet line, but the Assembly provides them with a forum where they can add their own elaborations or demonstrate the continued vitality of their national traditions by taking positions contrary to Soviet ones on some issues without appearing so disloyal that the Soviets decide to act against them.

The Assembly also affects the articulation of interests by helping forge a common international language of discourse. Governments know that they cannot advocate racism, genocide, colonialism, or the indiscriminate use of force because Assembly debates have shown that none of these positions is regarded as legitimate today. They must thus make an effort to present their interests and demands within the terms of the common discourse, and if they cannot their demands are not likely to win much sympathy. The Western Sahara question provides an interesting example. The Spanish government decided by 1975 that it could not justify continued Spanish rule over the area, and announced its intention to withdraw. The question then became whether Morocco and Mauritania could assert their old claims to it, or whether the local population would be deemed a "people" having its own right to self-determination. Mauritania has given up trying to assert its claim; Morocco and the local populations persist, with the Assembly unusually divided on the issue. Had the claimant been any but a neighboring Third World state, the local population's right to self-determination would have been accepted without question at once. The Falklands War provides another example. The Argentine government was not able to justify its invasion as a vindication of some oppressed people's right to self-determination; the Falklanders had long indicated their preference for continued British rule.

The General Assembly has increased the importance of large-scale coalition building as a method of interest aggregation. Coalition building is not foreign to world politics, though before the twentieth century it tended to be restricted to relatively small groups of states for limited, usually military, purposes. Traditionally states aggregated interests in bilateral or small-group discussions among those considered most interested in or most able to affect outcomes in the matter at hand. The large number of relatively unconcerned or weak states were not often consulted; it was assumed that they would acquiesce in the result. Within the Assembly, the one-state/one-vote rule, particularly when combined with rising membership and lengthening agendas, forced creation of more efficient mechanisms. Regional and other caucusing groups developed, much as did parties in national political systems, to meet that need. Thus, the General Assembly requires members to supplement the traditional methods of diplomacy, featuring a resident mission with diplomats acting on instructions from their own government, with newer methods of regional groups and caucusing ahead of time, which look something like the parties developed to co-ordinate activity among members of national legislatures.

The General Assembly has two patterns of coalition building. When consensus is sought, all the main regional groups have a hand in the negotiations. One or more might take a less promi-nent role, as in economic discussions where the Eastern European group accepts whatever result the Group of 77 reaches in its discussions with the Western industrial states; but since no decision can be deemed a consensus without all groups at least acquiescing, even the least active must be taken into account. When confrontation is pursued, either from the start or after efforts to reach consensus fail, propositions are not so widely discussed. The less active will be taken into account only if their opposition would prevent raising the required majority. The wishes of likely opponents will not be taken into account very much, though the majority may try to weaken the opposition by splitting it. Most attention will be paid to forging an agreement that will hold together as large a majority as possible in the cirumstances of the particular case. Since many Assembly dis-cussions deal with issues where the developing states face off against the industrial ones, confrontations are likely to result in the African, Asian and Latin American groups outvoting the West. Yet even in confrontations on other issues, there is a strong tendency to base coalitions on the regional groups and use the organizational mechanisms they provide.

Using the Assembly for aggregation of interests clearly favors states over other actors. Though some of the national liberation movements act almost like states, they are widely viewed as governments-in-formation; this disturbs the state-centered char-acter of Assembly workings very little. The interests of other international organizations are taken into account only in so far as the members insist. Members of NATO, the Warsaw Pact, the Organization of African Unity, the Organization of American States and the European Community have generally united to protect their organizations' interests in the UN. Members of the Commonwealth have a mixed record; at least in the early years India felt that most of its demands would receive a more sympathetic hearing in the Assembly (Carter, 1950, p. 249), and others did not insist on intra-Commonwealth discussions. The interests of other nongovernmental actors are taken into account only in so far as Assembly members decide that they should be. On the whole, Assembly is hostile to transnational corporations,

though Western insistence on their right to existence has channeled this hostility into regulation rather than attempts at
destruction. The Assembly is ambivalent about other nongovernmental groups, sometimes praising and sometimes condemning them. There is a general concern for individual rights,
but in practice human rights discussions stem more often from
calculations of political advantage than from concern with the
status of individuals.

To some extent the Assembly helps reinforce the fragmented
way in which states aggregate interests in the international
system. Weak states as a group generally find it advantageous to
bring issues to the Assembly because they can expect a sympathetic hearing. Strong states, which cannot always expect sympathy or prefer small-group talks, tend to settle their problems
among themselves. This was true even during the era of the
US-led majority; the Soviet Union made it clear that serious
discussions could not include the US-dominated Assembly, and
the United States found it easier to handle a number of matters
more privately. The Eastern and Western alliances both settle
their intra- and inter-group issues outside the Assembly. Individual states, no matter how weak, will keep issues out of the
Assembly if they fear an unfavorable response. These calculations
mean that the Assembly will not become the sole channel for
aggregation of interests in world politics.

In the adoption of decisions, the Assembly's influence is less
wide. It makes only a few decisions; most are made elsewhere.
Even so, it has fundamentally changed rule- and decision-
making in the international system. Its majoritarian rules allow
weak states as a group direct control over a set of international
decisions. Even when the consensus rules are used, Assembly
practice requires that the decisions be supported by most weak
states. This has proven a major gain to the weak states, which
have been able to shift in some instances from (willing or
unwilling) silent acceptors to active rule-makers.

Traditionally weak states influenced international decisions
indirectly, either by getting a great power to endorse their views
or by providing sufficient resistance to a strong power that the
latter decided that the effort to get compliance would outweigh
the gain. Portugal, a relatively weak state, retained its colonial
empire in the late-nineteenth-century scramble for colonies
largely because Britian decided it was better to protect Portuguese possession than to add to the stock of areas open for new
claims. Switzerland was not invaded during the Second World
War for both reasons. Initially German commanders knew that

Switzerland could mount formidable resistance to any invasion and felt that leaving Switzerland neutral was worth more than trying to conquer it. Before they could change their minds, the Allies were winning the war, and German attention had to focus on defense rather than on further invasions. Individual weak states still exercise influence in this way today, but the General Assembly gives weak states as a group an opportunity to control some decisions directly.

This has been true no matter what coalition controls the Assembly. From the very beginning most of the Assembly's members have been weak states conscious of their interests as weak states. In the era of the US-led coalition, weak-state assertiveness was muted by the need to have strong-state support for many propositions, by the fact that most of the small states agreed with the United States on many issues, and by residual habits of deference. As the "new states" of Africa and Asia flooded into the Assembly, the situation changed. Many weak states now had strong disagreements with the United States as well as with the Soviet Union, and residual habits of deference quickly fell away as they were perceived to be artifact of the bad nineteenth-century system of international relations. When weak states themselves forged the controlling Third World coalition in 1964 the only limit on weak state assertiveness was the need to have strong state support for implementing most material decisions. The symbolic content of Assembly decisions has taken on a stronger weak state tinge, but the major themes discussed were raised and made the subject of decisions even in the late 1940s.

The Assembly offers weak states as a group more influence over the process of formulating international law than they have traditionally enjoyed. Assembly debates permit them to comment on the legal rights and wrongs of any situation and to present their views about which rules do or should govern particular types of interaction. Though the weak cannot make international law themselves, neither can the strong, because the Assembly permits the weak to show that a rule advocated by the strong does not enjoy general acceptance.

The need to raise majorities for making decisions has the effect of modifying even strong government's policies. In 1954 Hans Morganthau described this effect as applied to the United States in these terms:

> The relationship is different between the predominant power and those nations which cluster around this core [of Western European and Commonwealth states supporting the United

States in the Cold War] in ever-changing combinations to make up the two-thirds majority of the General Assembly. For these nations are less exposed to pressure from the predominant power, and, hence, have a freedom of maneuver that is gainsaid to the members of the core. They can abstain or even vote with the Soviet bloc without jeopardizing their national interests as they see them. Since without their votes there can be no two-thirds majority, it is for the predominant power to redefine its interests in order to make them acceptable to these nations, and to adapt its policies to their preferences.

(Morganthau, 1954, p. 82)

Ernest Haas argued that the Assembly is a "deflector" of policy, forcing states to accept less-than-preferred outcomes in order to prevent the adoption of the most unfavorable decision (Haas, 1956, p. 256). Though he believed this would apply only in a world divided into Eastern, Western and neutral groups as long as East and West remained locked in intense competition, the idea has wider relevance.

There are limits to this "deflection", however. First, the Assembly has little effect on governments' long-term goals. Governments of weaker states might find it expedient to revise expectations, but governments of the strong can indulge the belief that they will gain everything they want. No government espousing an ideology promising that "history is on its side" is likely to view short-term disappointments as disasters irreparably harming long-term goals; such ideologies give their holders great tenacity and patience. Since the imperatives of coalition politics in the Assembly do alter what is attainable in the short-term, they can change tactics and the priorities given to attainment of individual national goals. These short-term changes may then alter long-term goals, though most alterations occur as change leads to a redefinition of interests or as experience indicates that the goal is too ambitious, too modest, or less relevant to the state's needs than formerly believed. Second, the range of Assembly decisions is limited. Many decisions in world politics continue to be made in bilateral, small-group, or regional fora, or in interactions among the great powers.

Even in areas where it makes decisions, the Assembly has the support neither of central institutions capable of enforcing its decisions nor of a shared sense of legitimacy that would induce widespread voluntary compliance. An Assembly majority must thus worry about a wider variety of difficulties in implementation than its counterpart in a national legislature. It must itself possess or enlist the power necessary to implement a decision. It must be sure not only that opponents do not obstruct, but that supporters act. The Assembly cannot offer many material incentives or disincentives to members; most of its appeals are confined to the symbolic realm. Material incentives can be supplied only by powerful members of the majority coalition acting outside the Assembly.

It is often difficult to hold the majority together long enough to secure effective implementation. The barriers to effective collective action on the part of an Assembly majority are usually formidable, even when the necessary action is relatively costless. The same central institutions that hold opponents at bay also serve to ensure that supporters contribute resources for implementation. Lacking them, the Assembly majority has to create some alternative mechanism. This is difficult unless a few powerful ones with sufficient resources are ready to act.

Assembly influence in the implementation phase of politics is strong only in those areas where it can command the obedience of member states or other parts of the UN system. With member states, this authority is restricted to determination and apportionment of the regular UN budget, determination of the entities eligible to send delegates to Assembly or Assembly-sponsored meetings, supervision of Trusteeship and any other issue on which the affected member states agree to give the Assembly authority. With other UN bodies, this is restricted to selection of members for some of the seats on other principal organs, control of Assembly subsidiary bodies, general supervision of the Secretariat and restructuring of the UN system that does not require amending the Charter or any of the separate agreements establishing the specialized agencies. Assembly majorities can exert important influence over the UN system; they have great trouble exerting much direct influence over member states.

The Assembly's role in applying and enforcing rules in particular situations is weak, even when the Assembly has been used to make the rule. When rules refer to internal UN operations, the Assembly's decisions about how they should be applied are binding. Thus, the Assembly could prevent continued South African participation and permit wide PLO participation despite opposition from some very strong states. The enforcement of internal decisions usually is not a problem either, though the enforcement of those costing a lot of money maý be difficult. The creation of peacekeeping operations is always followed by negotiations on financing because states are free to opt out of paying despite the fact such costs nominally form part of the regular budget. The situation is more stark for most UN aid programs, which are financed entirely outside the regular budget.

When, however, rules refer to situations outside the UN, the Assembly can condemn, praise, exhort, or discourage all it wants, but the effect will depend on the political calculations of the states being addressed. A state whose allies support its position, whose government is united on the question and whose public supports the government is unlikely to be affected by Assembly decisions. Only if allies put on serious pressure, the government divides and opponents of existing policy win the bureaucratic competition for control of policy, or an outraged public forces a shift, will the Assembly decision have an effect. A strong state can continue to oppose even by itself; a weak one will need friends. If the friends begin to waiver, then even a united weak state may have to change course.

Realizing this, Assembly majorities do not often present states with a choice between surrender or defiance. They know that defiance and exposure of the Assembly's weakness are the most likely result because only when their own interests require will states take action to enforce an Assembly decision on another. The vast amount of time devoted to confrontation with Israel and South Africa obscures this fact. On the whole, Assembly majorities prefer to act as they did in the Bangladesh–India dispute over Ganges waters, pursuing private negotiations and urging peaceful settlement without specifying any terms that would prove unacceptable to either side.

The application and enforcement of rules on questions external to the UN thus proceed much as they always have in international relations, through pressures, recruitment of supporters who will act if needed and, on occasion, self-help. The Assembly affects these traditional processes by creating general rules or making specific statements that legitimate some actions and delegitimate others. This tends to affect third states the most, by coloring their attitudes and encouraging or discouraging them from helping one or another side in a confrontation.

The Assembly's role in the implementation of other decisions is much the same. If the decisions refer to the creation of new UN bodies to undertake new tasks, then action will follow. The extent and effectiveness of the action will depend heavily on the cooperation member states give to the new body, but the mere creation of an international staff ensures that the issue remains alive and that some inquiries are pursued. If decisions refer to cooperation in the specialized agencies or outside the UN system entirely, then the Assembly becomes again encourager and discourager having effect only as the decisions enter into the political calculations and foreign policy debates of member states. Again, the strength of Assembly exhortation depends heavily on the size and composition of the majority behind it. Without consensus, the Assembly majority can claim very little moral weight for its decisions, as can be seen in the different fates of resolutions adopted at the 6th and 7th special sessions on economic development.

Coalitions

The General Assembly, like a national legislature, can be controlled by a stable majority coalition able to exert its influence in all phases of Assembly work, or contested among shifting *ad hoc* coalitions on different issues. The existence of a stable majority makes different features of the Assembly's overall impact on world politics more or less visible. The existence of a stable majority also imposes a clearer pattern on Assembly politics, sharpening the reactions of majorities and minorities alike to proceedings and decisions.

Majority coalitions may be distinguished by the nature of their goals, their solidity and the relation of their strength within the Assembly to their possession of capability in the wider international system. Many combinations of these characteristics are possible. Historically the Assembly has known two stable controlling coalitions: the US-led coalition of 1947–55 and the Third World coalition that has controlled the Assembly since 1964.

The two coalitions have had different goals. Members of the US-led coalition had created the UN and the wider postwar international order. While some of the Latin American members disagreed on certain economic issues, all endorsed the general liberal internationalist visions underlying the Charter. African and Asian members wanted a quicker end to colonialism than the Western European ones, but the latter agreed with the general goal. Therefore, the US-led coalition used the General Assembly, like the rest of the UN, to legitimize and strengthen the postwar order, to continue certain reform efforts begun in the Charter – such as elaboration of the notion of human rights – and to defend it against the alternative vision promoted by the Soviet bloc.

Most members of the Third World coalition attained independence after the postwar order was created. Even in areas where their substantive complaints are mild, this fact leads many to desire change simply because they do not like living in a system they had no role in creating. However, the members range from mildly revisionist to frankly revolutionary in their preferred visions of the international order. They agree on several broad propositions, such as the need to end all remnants of colonialism in international relations, to eradicate white racist regimes and to revise the rules for international transactions in such fields as trade, flows of news and information, or the transfer of technology to get rid of patterns that appear to give the West undue advantage. It is becoming clear, however, that they do not agree on more detailed propositions on particular issues. Even so, the Third World coalition still uses the General Assembly and the rest of the UN system to challenge many aspects of the current international order.

Both the US-led and the Third World coalitions have faced problems of maintaining coherence. It is difficult to say that one's problems were more severe than the other's, though circumstances have allowed the Third World coalition a longer period of dominance. Both coalitions have faced the problem of having to maintain a relatively large size – two-thirds of the UN membership – in order to have the fullest control over activities and decisions. As studies of coalition politics show, maintaining this large membership requires greater expenditure of resources in side-payments, symbolic appeals, or log-rolling to keep that two-thirds content. Each coalition has faced different problems in maintaining control over two-thirds of the votes, and has used different methods to do so. These in turn have affected Assembly proceedings and decisions in varying ways.

The US-led coalition included one superpower, several second-rank states, several regional powers and a large group of weak states. It also included both industrial and developing countries in its ranks. The interests of members thus went in several directions at once. The coalition dealt with this fact by trading support between issues. The weak members supported the West in the Cold War while the stronger members accepted norms protecting the weak, decisions pushing the pace of decolonization and efforts to tackle the problems of economic development. Since the UN had a relatively small membership and agenda, prior consultation and informal negotiation were less frequent than they became later. In particular, the US-led coalition never developed the extra-Assembly mechanisms for reaching coordinated positions ahead of time that would be developed later by the Third World coalition. This allowed for public airing

of intra-coalition differences, as in the early 1950s when the
African, Asian and Latin American members forced inclusion of
"self-determination" as one of the rights covered in both International Covenants on Human Rights despite US and Western
European objections. Traditions of consultation and informal
negotiation that might have eased the problems of coalition
management (or at least pushed them behind the scenes more)
were just developing when the coalition began to be swamped by
the influx of new African and Asian members. The Latin
Americans would have joined the Afro-Asians at some point,
given the common interests stemming from relative weakness
and lack of industrialization. The influx of new members meant,
however, that the US-led coalition was unable to command
two-thirds of the votes well before that happened. It lost its
secure vote advantage in 1955, though a firm Afro-Asian–Latin
American coalition was not forged until 1964.

Initially the Third World coalition had a far easier time
maintaining itself. All members were relatively weak in global
terms, though some were regional powers. All members were
also developing states. Most had experienced colonial rule and/or
racial discrimination. Many also faced serious challenges to
building an effective state apparatus and instilling a positive sense
of national identity among their populations. The Afro-Asian
members also desired to remain outside superpower conflicts.
The strength of these common feelings went far to paper over
differences of position between the more and less revisionist
members of the coalition. Both the Group of 77 and the Nonaligned came to be used for the extra-Assembly coordination of
coalition positions. While the coalition would often change
position when it began serious discussions with the West, there
was less public disagreement among Third World states because
the coordination mechanisms were used to ensure that potentially
divisive questions did not appear on the Assembly's effective
agenda.

Today both the differences and the coordination machinery are
more visible. The Nonaligned was transformed into an effective
mechanism in the period 1970–6, particularly after the 1973 oil
embargo. At the same time, the resulting increase in oil prices
exacerbated differences among Third World states. The
economic divisions between oil exporters, oil-importing non
industrial states and newly industrializing states attaining success
under the existing international economic rules became greater.
The increasing stress on economic issues in the Nonaligned
during the 1970s probably helped create a situation where the

open expression of greater political differences became common. Several Third World states came under Marxist–Leninist rule, sided openly with Moscow in East–West conflicts and sharpened the old radical–moderate differences within the Nonaligned. In many cases, these governments pushed neighbors in a more pro-Western direction. With the failure of other attempts to create commodity cartels, the oil weapon that once united the Third World now divides it as oil importers find their economies under stress as much from fellow Third World states as from dealings with the West. Economic divisions were also exacerbated by different rates of success in industrialization.

Severe as these divisions are, they have not yet led to a complete breakdown of the Third World coalition. In part, this is due to the continued activity of the Group of 77 and the Nonaligned, buttressed by the norm of group solidarity *vis-à-vis* outsiders. Yet the 1983 Nonaligned summit showed that it may be harder to drive the coordination mechanisms now as moderates and radicals openly contend for influence. The radicals still have the advantages of greater coherence and confidence, but they are not now riding herd over the Movement the way they did when Cuba was chairman. Despite divisions, the Third World coalition is able to hold on because members still agree on several broad propositions and because there is no clear alternative coalition to which the discontented may defect.

The next few years are likely to see the Third World coalition limp along, trying to bury disagreements by keeping them out of the Assembly or taking very vague general positions. The anti-Western bias to which so many US and some European observers object will remain, since the issues that unite the Third World are those where the contrast with Western positions is greatest. However, once discussion gets beyond generalities to specifics, intra-Third-World divisions surface. This can be seen in such matters as comprehensive North–South negotiations, the law of the sea, or UN restructuring, where intra-Third World differences are at least as responsible for the results (or lack of results) as West–South confrontations. By 1985 this trend had proceeded far enough that coalition formation in the Assembly was a more fluid process than it had been five years before, though not so fluid as to duplicate the situation between 1955 and 1964.

Perceptions of the Assembly's effectiveness or ineffectiveness in world politics have depended more on the relation between control of votes within the Assembly and possession of relevant capability outside than on anything that occurs in the Assembly itself. The US-led coalition made the Assembly look like a highly significant institution in world politics not only because it chose to define its role broadly and to legitimate traditions of wide Assembly competence, but also because it possessed the capability to turn most Assembly decisions into effective outcomes. Further, the US-led coalition did not have to use the Assembly too hard and thus expose its limitations; it had a full range of other channels in bilateral, small-group and regional relations. The Assembly supplemented and complemented these nicely, making it look like an integral part of the machinery.

The Third World coalition took over the precedents for Assembly importance created by the US-led coalition, but attempted to use the Assembly for ambitious goals it lacked the capability to attain. Most group progress came from playing the United States off against the Soviet Union whenever the super-powers saw influence in the Third World as important to their general competition, using or threatening to use the oil weapon, or appealing to sympathetic segments of Western opinion able to sway their governments' policies. Individual weakness led Third World states to stress banding together and placing most of their efforts in those global fora where the voting rules gave them the greatest influence. Bilateral and small-group channels led to some influence, though most regional ones did not include direct contact with the industrial states possessing the resources neces-sary to attainment of most Third World goals. The Third World's relative lack of resources and the existence of alternative channels expose the limits of Assembly influence. Now its activi-ties often seem to run against rather than parallel discussions in bilateral, small-group, or regional channels.

Both the lack of other fora and frustration with what appears to be Western foot-dragging on many issues lead the Third World coalition (or at least the more radical members, which have often led Assembly efforts) to use the General Assembly harder than did the US-led coalition. This is seen in many areas, such as the wider use of conflicts over status, greater reliance on committed subsidiary organs, greater efforts to forge a hier-archical relation between the General Assembly and the specia-lized agencies and the harsher rhetoric used in many resolutions. Yet this hard use helps expose the limits of Assembly influence on world politics. As they appear more clearly, some in the Third World are left as discontented with the UN as some in the West, though for different reasons. While the pattern of hard use may recede as individual Third World states acquire other chan-nels of influence and the coalition continues to fragment, it is likely to mark Assembly proceedings and decisions for the rest of the 1980s.

Issues

Reflecting both its place in the wider UN system and its stronger influence over UN bodies than over member states, most General Assembly activity has always been devoted to such "internal" matters as determining the regular budget, staffing, filling places in UN bodies, or preparing for special international conferences. As shown in Table 9.1, such activity accounted for 57 to 87 percent of the resolutions passed at any one session, with the usual level somewhere between 60 and 70 percent under the US-led coalition. Under the Third World coalition, this proportion has been somewhere between 54 and 76 percent, usually between 55 and 65 percent.

As a global deliberating body, the Assembly appears well suited to discussing the general principles and norms that do or should govern international relations. Considerable debate time is devoted to such questions, but the number of resolutions attempting to state principles or norms is restricted by two considerations. First, many such statements take the form of an international treaty and are discussed at diplomatic conferences rather than in the Assembly itself. While the Assembly formally endorses and recommends the adoption of many of these treaties after they are produced, others, particularly if written under the auspices of a specialized agency or a non-UN body such as the International Red Cross, are less likely to be recommended to states in an Assembly resolution. Second, the number of general statements is restricted by the fact that making too many (particularly on the same issue) may reduce the effectiveness of all by introducing conflicting principles or norms. Thus it is not surprising that, except at the 5th session, such statements have never accounted for more than 5 percent of Assembly resolutions.

The Assembly is equally well adapted to discussions about applying principles and norms to particular situations. Occasions for such discussion arise constantly, and a larger number of resolutions does not necessarily decrease their effectiveness (though a large number may indicate that states are ignoring the principle or norm involved). Such discussions can take two forms: (1) praising or condemning particular states by name, or (2) making general statements without naming particular states or making reference to particular controversies. In the Assembly, naming states is a sign that the majority is taking sides in a particular conflict, so those resolutions will be considered separately below. Making general statements is quite common. These include such statements as a desire that industrial states raise development aid to 1 percent of their GNP, a wish that states improve cooperation in the suppression of hijacking, or that they continue to respect the right to "permanent sovereignty over natural resources." The US-led coalition devoted anywhere from 5 to 15 percent of Assembly resolutions to such statements. Reflecting its broader goals and greater weakness, the Third World coalition devotes 15 to 20 percent of Assembly resolutions to them.

Despite the "Uniting for Peace" procedures, the Assembly is too large to function as a good mediator. Mediation tends to require quiet approaches by individuals or small groups of states or policy-makers rather than the glare of public debate. The Assembly can be used to encourage such efforts by indicating that "world opinion" favors settlement or by authorizing UN peacekeeping forces or other activities to assist in conflict management or resolution. Decisions urging settlement of disputes or committing UN resources to aiding it only once (in 1956) accounted for more than 10 percent of the Assembly's resolutions. Since the amalgamation of the Third World coalition in 1964, they have never accounted for more than 6 percent, though with a difference that committing UN resources to such efforts has increased as a proportion of this activity. Here again, the Third World coalition's tendency to use the UN system harder appears.

Slightly more attention has been given to using the Assembly to take sides in a conflict. Its status as the main global political forum makes it an ideal place for attempts to alter the balance between conflicting sides by seeking support from states not directly involved. Both the US-led and the Third World coalitions have used the Assembly for this purpose, usually devoting somewhere between 10 and 20 percent of resolutions to this activity. Though it got off to a slow start, the US-led coalition was using some 6 to 8 percent of all resolutions to commit the UN system to some activity that implied siding in a conflict after 1952. The Third World coalition also got off to a slow start, since in the era between coalitions this sort of activity had dropped to 3 or 4 percent of all resolutions. Yet between 1970 and 1981 it normally devoted between 6 and 10 percent of resolutions to it. In the last three sessions, this proportion dropped to 4 or 5 percent.

Table 9.1 Types of Resolution adopted at regular Assembly sessions

session	declarations	apply norms	UN internal	urge settlement	take sides	UN mediation	UN side	total
1st	3 (2.7)	18 (15.9)	88 (77.9)	2 (1.3)	2 (1.8)	0 (0.0)	0 (0.0)	113
2nd	2 (2.5)	9 (11.1)	56 (51.9)	3 (3.7)	2 (2.5)	0 (0.0)	9 (11.1)	81
3rd	5 (3.9)	17 (13.2)	84 (65.1)	5 (3.9)	8 (6.2)	0 (0.0)	10 (7.8)	129
4th	3 (2.8)	18 (16.7)	62 (57.4)	7 (6.5)	18 (16.7)	0 (0.0)	0 (0.0)	108
5th	13 (9.0)	9 (6.3)	87 (60.4)	13 (9.0)	19 (13.2)	0 (0.0)	3 (2.1)	144
6th	6 (5.0)	18 (14.9)	81 (66.9)	4 (3.3)	10 (8.3)	0 (0.0)	2 (1.7)	121
7th	6 (4.9)	8 (6.6)	74 (60.7)	8 (6.6)	16 (13.1)	1 (0.2)	9 (7.4)	122
8th	2 (1.9)	12 (11.3)	69 (65.1)	7 (6.6)	7 (6.6)	3 (2.8)	6 (5.7)	106
9th	1 (0.9)	13 (12.0)	75 (69.4)	2 (1.9)	6 (5.6)	2 (1.9)	9 (8.3)	108
10th	0 (0.0)	6 (6.5)	61 (65.6)	5 (5.4)	11 (11.8)	2 (2.2)	8 (8.6)	93
11th	1 (0.8)	12 (9.2)	77 (58.8)	9 (6.9)	19 (14.5)	7 (5.3)	6 (4.6)	131
12th	2 (1.8)	5 (4.6)	79 (72.5)	6 (5.5)	11 (10.1)	3 (2.8)	3 (2.8)	109
13th	1 (0.8)	9 (6.3)	93 (73.8)	9 (7.1)	10 (7.9)	2 (1.6)	3 (2.4)	126
14th	1 (0.8)	17 (13.3)	85 (66.4)	5 (3.9)	14 (10.9)	2 (1.6)	4 (3.1)	128
15th	3 (2.0)	23 (15.5)	92 (62.2)	5 (3.4)	12 (8.1)	8 (5.4)	5 (3.4)	148
16th	3 (2.3)	19 (14.6)	82 (63.1)	5 (3.8)	11 (8.5)	6 (4.6)	4 (3.1)	130
17th	6 (4.5)	14 (10.5)	90 (66.7)	3 (2.3)	13 (9.8)	4 (3.0)	3 (2.3)	133
18th	3 (2.4)	17 (13.6)	85 (68.0)	1 (0.8)	11 (8.8)	2 (1.6)	6 (4.8)	125
19th	0 (0.0)	0 (0.0)	12 (85.7)	1 (7.1)	0 (0.0)	1 (7.1)	0 (0.0)	14
20th	5 (3.3)	14 (9.3)	99 (66.0)	5 (3.3)	19 (12.7)	1 (0.7)	7 (4.7)	150
21st	4 (2.9)	19 (14.0)	92 (67.6)	2 (1.5)	9 (6.6)	2 (1.5)	8 (5.9)	136
22nd	3 (2.2)	22 (15.8)	96 (69.1)	1 (0.7)	9 (6.5)	4 (2.9)	4 (2.9)	139
23rd	3 (2.1)	18 (12.7)	96 (67.6)	1 (0.7)	16 (11.3)	1 (0.7)	7 (4.9)	142
24th	7 (4.4)	22 (13.9)	107 (67.1)	2 (1.3)	16 (10.1)	2 (1.3)	3 (1.9)	158
25th	8 (5.0)	25 (15.6)	97 (60.6)	0 (0.0)	15 (9.4)	4 (2.5)	11 (6.9)	160
26th	5 (2.8)	35 (19.4)	107 (59.4)	2 (1.1)	18 (10.0)	4 (2.2)	9 (5.0)	180
27th	5 (2.8)	26 (14.7)	114 (64.4)	1 (0.6)	15 (8.5)	4 (2.3)	12 (6.8)	177
28th	7 (3.9)	35 (19.3)	106 (58.6)	1 (0.6)	15 (8.3)	4 (2.2)	13 (7.2)	181
29th	6 (3.2)	38 (20.3)	106 (56.7)	4 (2.1)	16 (8.6)	6 (3.2)	11 (5.9)	187
30th	5 (2.3)	36 (16.7)	131 (60.9)	6 (2.8)	17 (7.9)	7 (3.3)	13 (6.0)	215
31st	5 (2.0)	46 (18.3)	146 (58.2)	3 (1.2)	26 (10.4)	7 (2.8)	18 (7.2)	251
32nd	1 (0.4)	47 (17.9)	150 (57.3)	3 (1.1)	29 (11.1)	8 (3.1)	24 (9.2)	262
33rd	5 (1.8)	44 (16.1)	158 (57.7)	3 (1.1)	36 (13.1)	14 (5.1)	14 (5.1)	274
34th	8 (2.2)	44 (14.7)	172 (57.5)	1 (0.3)	36 (12.0)	15 (5.0)	23 (7.7)	299
35th	5 (1.6)	45 (14.2)	191 (60.3)	2 (0.6)	41 (12.9)	8 (2.5)	25 (7.9)	317
36th	6 (1.8)	50 (15.0)	194 (58.3)	0 (0.0)	54 (16.2)	15 (4.5)	14 (4.2)	333
37th	7 (2.0)	66 (19.1)	187 (54.2)	4 (1.2)	51 (14.8)	15 (4.3)	15 (4.3)	345
38th	2 (0.6)	68 (21.1)	174 (53.9)	3 (0.9)	44 (13.6)	16 (5.0)	16 (5.0)	323

Note: Percentages shown in brackets.
Source: Author's classification based on texts published in *General Assembly Official Records*, supplement of resolutions and decisions.

This may reflect weakening cohesion or simply a temporary lack of new ideas.

While the development of consensus has reflected both the need for greater efficiency and the different power resources of the two controlling coalitions, the proportion of resolutions adopted with and without a formal vote also differs by the type of issue involved. Consensus has always been used most in decisions about ordinary UN activity. Except in the years 1949 through 1954, at least half of such decisions have been made without a vote. Many receive only perfunctory attention in debate, particularly if they amount only to postponing the issue another year. Rather, members seem to want to get most of these matters out of the way so that they can focus on the more controversial operational issues, such as the size of the budget, and the substantive issues before the Assembly.

Most decisions stating general principles or norms or applying them to particular types of situation have been adopted by vote. While attempts to forge consensus have become more common in recent years, these have not always been successful. Almost every such statement contains language that one or more members deem sufficiently objectionable to merit a vote, even if only to abstain. This is directly related to legal doctrines attempting to buttress the role of the Assembly in the making of international law. Governments rightly believe that if they permit the adoption of some normative statement by consensus, they will later find objecting to those parts they dislike difficult.

Although also representing a small number of resolutions, most decisions related to mediation or committing UN resources to conflict management are also adopted by vote. This stems in part from Soviet bloc objections to virtually all peacekeeping activity, which leads those members to insist on votes so that they may dissociate themselves from the activity (especially when it gets expensive or appears to serve Western interests). It also stems from the fact that a call for mediation can usually be viewed as helping one side more than the other if partisans look hard enough, leading friends of the side that feels disadvantaged to register objections. Only in the late 1970s did the number of such decisions taken by consensus reach half the total on a sustained basis.

The fact that decisions taking sides or committing UN bodies to aid one side of a conflict are taken by vote is not surprising. It is surprising, however, that a considerable proportion of decisions committing UN bodies to aiding one side, some 30–50 percent in the 1970s, have been taken by consensus. On closer examination this is readily explained; these decisions represent commitments to programs of humanitarian aid. Western members have used accepting these by consensus to demonstrate that in the cases of Portuguese colonialism, Rhodesia and South Africa they do not approve of those regimes and in the case of Israel they do not approve of all its policies while maintaining strong objections to most of the proposals for dealing with those governments or countries that emanate from the radical members of the Non-aligned or the Soviet bloc.

This issue-based pattern of differences in the use of consensus overlies the coalition-based increase in the use of consensus-decision-making techniques. Consensus remains most frequently a device for expediting ordinary UN business so that members may focus on more important issues. The main increases in the use of consensus have come in the areas of applying norms, where it is now possible to come to general agreement on how familiar norms should be applied in many situations, and in the area of committing UN resources to conflicts.

Whatever the future of the Third World coalition, then, the General Assembly will continue to have considerable influence over the agenda of world politics. It will continue to be used for producing a set of decisions that commit UN bodies to particular activities and attempt to move member states in directions preferred by a majority. Though it will continue to make many decisions, the impact of these decisions on the actual outcomes of political interactions in the international system will remain weak.

Again, whatever the future of the Third World coalition, the treatment of different types of issue will not change too much. Most decisions will still deal with internal UN questions. Side-taking will remain easier than conflict management in a body of almost 160 members as long as those members remain seriously divided by ideology and different degrees of happiness or unhappiness with the international status quo. Assembly debates will continue to be more useful for focusing on global issues and general points rather than on local questions or details of specific interactions. The Assembly will also continue to reinforce the position of states as central actors in world politics though its global conferences will provide new opportunities for lobbying by nongovernmental organizations.

However, some aspects of Assembly politics will change as coalitions evolve. Both the content of decisions and the strength of attempts to use the Assembly as a revisionist force in world

politics will change if the Third World coalition continues to
fragment. It is possible that in the 1990s politics in the Assembly
will return to the conditions prevalent between 1955 and 1964
when *ad hoc* coalitions controlled proceedings and decisions on
different issues. In that case, Assembly rhetoric on most issues
will cool down, and the tendency to link as many issues as
possible by insisting on the need for "new international orders"
of similar characteristics across them will also decrease.
Assembly majorities may well remain revisionist, but the differences in degree of revisionism among Third World states will
make the thrust appear more ragged than it did in the 1970s. It
may even turn out in retrospect that the neo-conservative–
isolationist alliance now directing United States policy toward
hostility and confrontation in the UN is a lagged response, more
relevant to the Third World rhetoric and activities of the mid-
1970s than to those of the 1980s. Yet that alliance may help
perpetuate the very habits it deplores by providing the fragment-
ing Third World with rallying points that help it maintain
cohesion a while longer.

Appendix

An Overview of the General Assembly

This Appendix examines the basic features of structure and procedure for readers unfamiliar with the General Assembly. It will describe the flow of work at a regular session, the formal and informal role of Assembly and main committee officers, the role of delegates and the functioning of regional and other groups. Much of the information also applies to special and emergency sessions, though they do not elect separate officers (those of the preceding regular session continue to serve), the agenda is usually deemed adopted when a majority of the members agrees to holding the session, and main committees do not meet if the members decide to create an *ad hoc* committee of the whole or work in specially appointed informal negotiating groups instead.

Work at a Regular Session

By custom, a regular session of the Assembly lasts thirteen weeks, beginning the second Tuesday in September and ending about 20 December. It is possible to add a few extra weeks in the spring or summer by resuming the session or calling a special session, but the press of other international meetings (see schedules of UN-sponsored meetings in Annex I of the annual report from the Committee on Conferences) is now so heavy that member states do not really want to have too many extra meetings. While the time available has remained constant, both the number of members to be heard and the number of items to be discussed have increased, making the management of time all the more important. The membership has tripled, going from 51 states in 1945 to 159 in 1985. The agenda has more than doubled,

Preliminary Phase

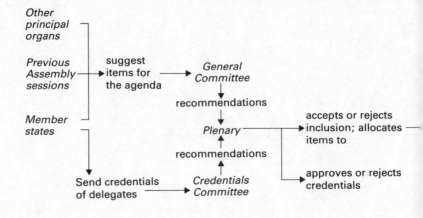

Substantive Phase

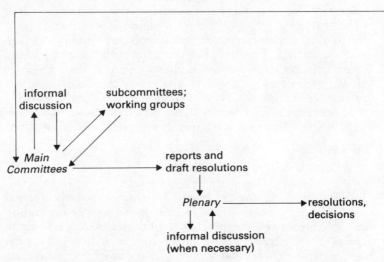

Figure App. 1 Work of a regular assembly session

going from 64 items in 1946, few of which were divided into sub-items, to 143 in 1985, most of which were divided into sub-items.

The flow of business at a regular session of the General Assembly has two phases, a preliminary "housekeeping" phase and the substantive phase of considering and making decisions on the various questions before it. This flow can be diagrammed as shown in Figure App. 1.

Preliminary Phase

The Assembly's first order of business is to select the officers who also comprise the General Committee and members of the Credentials Committee so that they can get to work immediately. While waiting for their reports, the plenary begins its first item of substantive work, the General Debate. This is somewhat outside the main flow of Assembly business since it does not lead directly to the adoption of any decisions. Rather, it is a three-week opportunity for each delegation to express its government's views on the general state of the world, questions proposed for the Assembly agenda and particular concerns of its own. Main committees meet to select the rest of their officers. The General Debate is interrupted as needed so that the plenary can hear and decide upon the General Committee's recommendations about the inclusion of items in the agenda and its allocation to main committees and the Credentials Committee's suggestions regarding the acceptance or rejection of credentials.

The General Committee has 29 members: the President of the Assembly, the 21 vice presidents and the chairmen of the seven main committees. The President and chairmen serve in their individual capacity, meaning that they turn over the task of representing their country to another member of their delegation and take on an institutional role. The vice presidencies are the domain of states, meaning that if the head of the particular delegation is not available, any of that state's representatives may sit on the General Committee or substitute for the President in presiding over the Assembly when asked. Since 1957 the distribution of seats on the General Committee has been governed by understandings written into the annex of the resolution adopting the successive enlargements of that group (1957, 1963 and 1978). Today the presidency (which rotates annually among the five regions) and the 21 vice presidencies are divided: Africans 6, Asians 5, Eastern Europeans 1, Western European and Others 2, Latin Americans 3 and permanent members of the Security Council (China, France, the USSR, the UK and the USA) 5 (Annexes to Resolutions 1191 [XII] and 33/138). Formally, this is done by pretending there are 22 vice presidencies and then deducting one from the region holding the presidency that year. Main committee chairmanships are divided so that two go to Africans, one to an Asian, one to a Latin American, one to an

Eastern European, one to a Westerner and one alternating
annually between an Asian and a Latin American (Resolution
33/138). Since each of the Big Five is assured a vice presidency, it
is now the custom that they do not seek either the presidency or a
chairmanship. This formula specifies only the total number of
chairmanships to be allocated to each group. Some delegations
have proposed establishing a set rotation, but most resist the idea
(Kaufmann, 1980, pp. 29–30). The lack of set rotation means that
the regional groups must consult each year about which group
will hold which chairs.

The General Committee makes all decisions by a simple
majority. Since 20 of the 29 members come from Third World
states, the Third World majority controls it as well as the
Assembly. In such a situation, it might be expected to enjoy real
powers. Yet this has not been the case. The formal rules give the
General Committee powers that could allow it to develop into a
strong guiding hand for the Assembly, as was its League pre-
decessor (Burton, 1941, p. 110, describes League practice). The
rules give it five tasks: (1) recommending whether an item should
be included on the agenda, (2) suggesting where each item to be
included should be sent for consideration (to the plenary or to one
of the main committees), (3) assisting the President in setting the
agenda for each plenary meeting, (4) coordinating the work of
main committees and (5) revising resolutions adopted by the
Assembly to improve their form, subject to acceptance by the
plenary (Rules 40, 41, 42 and 44 of the Assembly Rules of
Procedure). Full use of these powers would make the General
Committee the center of Assembly work, as powerful a coord-
inator as are the bureaux of presiding officers and party leaders
that guide the work of many national legislatures.

The General Committee has never fully exploited any of these
powers to the full, and some are now exercised by other groups.
It has seldom used its power to screen the agenda to keep items
off. It also has few opportunities to make a difference in the
allocation of items because of the broad specialization among
main committees and the well-developed tradition that an item
which has been considered before (such items now comprise
some 80 percent of the total agenda each year) remain in the same
committee unless new developments justify a change of committee or a shift to the plenary. The work of coordinating main
committee schedules and prodding the laggard to work harder
has devolved to an informal group consisting of the President,
the chairman of the main committees and the Under Secretary-
General for Political and General Assembly Affairs, which has

met at a weekly lunch since 1947 to settle these questions in a more efficient manner that would be possible in the full General Committee (remarks of Under Secretary-General Stavropoulos in A/AC.149/SR.5, 30 Mar. 1971, para. 59). The full General Committee retains some vestiges of this role through recommending a closing date for each session and approving general suggestions for the speedier flow of work (Kaufmann, 1980, p. 30). The General Committee has never asserted its authority to propose editorial changes to resolutions, on the grounds that it is difficult to tell when a particular change is one of style or one of substance (as shown in A/C.3/17/SR.1164, 26 Oct. 1962 paras. 49–51). It also knows that a plenary reluctant to give it much authority on other questions would not easily accept any revisions it might propose. Further, many resolutions today are the product of extensive negotiations, the results of which could easily be destroyed by changes in any part of the draft.

All of this means that the General Committee is largely a decorative body, though, as will be seen below, its individual members do perform important functions. The General Committee's decorative nature is shown most clearly by the fact that it seldom meets. If it were to equal the activity of the corresponding bodies in the general conferences of the specialized agencies, which do have an active role, it would have to meet weekly (Joint Inspection Committee report, A/8319, 2 June 1971, para. 337). Only at the 1st, 3rd and 16th sessions did the General Committee equal that schedule; since 1975 it has never met more than four times a session (see records for each session in the A/BUR/SR. series).

Several things limit the General Committee. Even at its original size of fifteen, but even more so as it expanded, it is too large to function efficiently. Edvard Hambro, President of the 25th session, believes that any committee larger than 10 is too formal to be used as a coordinating committee (A/AC.149/SR.5, 30 Mar. 1971, paras. 58–9), while C. Northcote Parkinson says 5 or 9 is best though a group with as many as 20 can act efficiently (1957, ch. 3). Members' determination to ensure that significant decisions are made in meetings of the whole has not waivered since 1947, when Rule 41 was written to include a clause saying that the General Committee "shall not, however, decide any political question." This formal prohibition was reinforced in 1949, when Rule 40 was rewritten to provide that the General Committee "shall not discuss the substance of any item except insofar as this bears upon the question," of whether to put the item on the agenda and, if so, how to allocate it for preliminary discussion. Finally, the development of other mechanisms for performing a number of General Committee tasks has narrowed its role. The close correspondence between General Committee and plenary composition has not so far diluted weak state distrust of limited-membership bodies in this case, though it is possible that the persistence of the regionally based Third World majority might someday lead to greater willingness to rely on the General Committee.

The Credentials Committee has remained a nine-member body since 1945, in sharp contrast to all other limited-membership organs of the Assembly. This reflects the lack of competition to get on the committee (Kaufmann, 1980, p. 31), which in turn stems from the very limited nature of its activity. Rule 28 even specifies that it should be "appointed by the General Assembly on the proposal of the President." In practice this means that the Secretariat consults the members – now through the medium of the regional groups – to secure generally acceptable nominees. The membership is announced at the first plenary meeting of the session even before the President of that session is elected, and the committee sets to work at once. By custom, the Soviet Union, the United States and China are always members; the other six include one Latin American, one Western, two African and two Asians states.

The Credentials Committee's formal task consists of ensuring that delegates have received proper authorization to act from their governments. This usually means simply checking to see that the diplomatic credentials naming individuals are in proper form: written and signed by the head of state, head of government, or foreign minister of the state naming the delegate. Occasionally, however, the arrival of two rival delegations each sent by a government claiming to rule the same state, or a desire on the part of some members to cast doubt on the international legitimacy of some government not then facing serious domestic opposition, forces the Credentials Committee to make choices that amount to political decisions about the status of governments. These are examined in detail in Chapter 6.

Though the rules of procedure specify that the committee "shall report without delay," it was long in the habit of not reporting until very late in the session except when the appearance of two delegations from one state forced an early choice. This delay made challenges to the credential of delegates from governments not involved in civil wars almost meaningless because Rule 29 provides that delegates whose credentials are challenged can be seated on a provisional basis and participate fully in Assembly work until the Credentials Committee has reported and the plenary has made a decision on its recommendations. In recent years, however, challenges to the credentials of delegates whose governments were not involved in civil wars have become another method of embarrassing states in the Assembly. For these to have any effect, the Credentials Committee has to report, at least on that set of credentials, early in the session. In the 1950s and 1960s it often delayed its report until the last week of the session, but since 1973 it has reported by mid-October.

Substantive Phase

Once the plenary has decided the organizational details, the General Assembly is ready to begin its substantive work. All main committees except the First now begin work as soon as they receive the initial notification of items allocated to them, usually around 28 September. The First maintains its custom, dating from the time when it considered general political questions as well as disarmament, of not beginning work until after the plenary General Debate ends in early October. This was initially justified by the need to have heard the General Debate before tackling the political items on its agenda and by the fact that heads of delegation usually sat on the First Committee. Today the First Committee agenda deals mainly with disarmament items, but the old custom persists as a way to limit the number of simultaneous meetings for smaller delegations. The end of the General Debate also means that the plenary is free to begin work on the items allocated to it.

In October and November, therefore, most of the Assembly's work is done in committee. The plenary does begin adopting resolutions, some based on its own work and some based on early reports from main committees. Most committee reports submitted at this time deal with routine items such as selecting members for UN and General Assembly bodies or noting the reports of other UN organs, but a few resemble the work being done in plenary by covering political questions that have produced confrontation. Thus resolutions condemning South Africa and other governments maintaining extensive relations with it appear by mid-November regardless of whether apartheid has been discussed in the Special Political Committee or the plenary. The infamous "Zionism is a form of racism" resolution, based on a proposal from the Third Committee, was passed on 10 November 1975. The second condemnation of the Soviet invasion of Afghanistan, Resolution 35/39 (the first came in Resolution

ES–6/2 of 15 January 1980), was passed on 25 November 1980 after a plenary discussion of the issue.

The Assembly's main committees were created as committees of the whole for two reasons. First, there was no party system or other way to divide states into mutually exclusive groups and assign a few members of each group to committees. Second, the Assembly inherited a strong international tradition that the formal consideration of proposals in conferences or intergovernmental organizations should be undertaken by the full membership. This means that every member has the right to be present and participate, though smaller delegations find it impossible to cover every meeting of every main committee. Yet a committee of 51, much less one of 157, is not an efficient body for detailed negotiations. From the start, main committees have sought to overcome this problem by using formally constituted subcommittees, "contact groups", or "working groups" and other informal groups to work out the details of resolutions and decisions while the full committee continued hearing debates on issues before it.

Each main committee elects a chairman, two vice chairmen, and a *rapporteur*. The chairman presides over the committee and encourages the informal consultations on procedural and sustantive questions necessary to the smooth functioning of the committee. The vice chairmen replace the chairman as needed and in most committees are assigned the taks of organizing or promoting informal discussions on specified items before it. The *rapporteur* drafts, with assistance from the Secretariat, the summaries of committee debates and decisions that constitute its reports to the plenary. In early sessions the *rapporteur* occasionally presided over the committee when both chairman and vice chairman were absent, but the shift to having two vice chairmen has made this unnecessary. The four officers together also serve as a *bureau* for the main committee, recommending schedules, proposing deadlines for debate and the submission of draft resolutions and prodding the rest of the committee to remain within the deadlines for work set by the plenary's target date for ending the session.

Like any desirable position in the Assembly, committee offices are shared among the regional groups. The lack of a set rotation for chairmanships allows the same region to provide the chairman two or more years successively. This has happened five times: Latin America in the Sixth Committee for the 15th and 16th sessions, Asia in the Third Committee for the 16th and 17th sessions, Latin America for the Third Committee at the 18th and

20th sessions (main committees did not meet during the 19th session), the West for the Fifth Committee at the 15th through 18th sessions and Africa for the Fourth Committee at the 24th and 25th sessions. In general, however, members prefer that a different region provide the chairman in successive years. The other four committee offices are divided so that no two are filled by delegates from the same region.

The General Assembly has seven main committees, each specializing in a particular range of issues as shown in Table App. 1

Table App. 1 Main Committees of the General Assembly

First Committee	Disarmament
Special Political Committee	Political questions and particular crises
Second Committee	International financial and economic questions
Third Committee	International social, humanitarian and cultural questions
Fourth Committee	Decolonization and the Trusteeship system
Fifth Committee	UN administrative and budgetary questions
Sixth Committee	International legal questions

Together with the plenary, these main committees make the Assembly eight bodies in one. This is true not only in the formal sense of having eight places where negotiations can take place but also in the practical sense that the main committees specialize in certain types of issue, and delegates from the larger delegations specialize in the affairs of one committee. This double speciali-zation has created a situation in which each main committee has its own character.

The First Committee was once the scene of the liveliest debates in the General Assembly. In the early years it was the only main committee dealing with political matters and was the scene of many a Cold War confrontation between the superpowers. It was not long, however, before its agenda was so heavy that it had to be given assistance. In 1947 a special committee of the whole was created to deal with the Palestine question. In 1948 the usefulness of a supplementary committee was formally admitted, at least temporarily, with the creation of the *Ad Hoc* Political

Committee, which was a committee of the whole given the same status as the other main committees by having its chairman included in the General Committee. In 1956 the Assembly admitted that it would always need two committees for political questions, and transformed the *Ad Hoc* Political Committee into a seventh main committee under the name Special Political Committee.

For the next decade the two political committees had overlapping agendas, new items being allocated as often on the basis of which had the lighter agenda as on the basis of their relation to other items already being considered. In the early 1960s, however, some specialization did begin to emerge. The Special Political Committee continued to handle the Palestine question in its various forms, and took on the issue of apartheid in South Africa. Disarmament and outer space came to be discussed in the First Committee. In 1971 reformers of Assembly procedure proposed that the work-loads of the two committees be brought into greater balance by having the First Committee deal with disarmament and general problems of maintaining peace and security while the Special Political Committee considered the specific political crises brought to Assembly attention (see discussion in A/AC.149/SR.22, 7 June 1971, pp. 136–51). Though the Assembly endorsed the idea, it was not put into practice until 1978, when the First Committee was entrusted with monitoring the progress of the disarmament programs adopted at the 10th special session (First Special Session on Disarmament) (Resolution S–10/2, para. 117).

This specialization in disarmament, in questions relating to nuclear weapons (such as non proliferation, the effects of radiation, or efforts to create nuclear-free zones) and in activities in outer space has transformed the First Committee. Its work now proceeds in a relatively businesslike manner, with delegates competing in professions of their states' desire for peace. The occasional polemic seldom lasts very long. The Special Political Committee, having kept charge of most of the hot issues of the day, remains a place for strident accusation and heated exchanges.

The Second and Third Committees sometimes have trouble keeping their mandates separate when new issues arise, because the development questions now before the Assembly in such large numbers often have both economic and social implications. They quickly found a rough guide in the different chapters of the annual reports from the Economic and Social Council, and have built on them since. Both began as relatively quiet committees, marked by differences of opinion but by no great tendency toward grandstanding, having comfortable work-loads. In the late 1950s, but even more after the Third World majority became conscious of itself, the work-loads began to get heavier as questions of economic growth and industrialization were brought to the Second Committee, and questions of social development and eliminating discrimination were brought to the Third. Their agendas grew more through the 1960s as the Third World coalition expressed its distrust of the Economic and Social Council by insisting that any issue it deemed important be handled mainly in the General Assembly. This trend was unaffected by enlarging the Council to twenty-seven members in 1963 because the Third World coalition wanted the extra prominence Assembly consideration would give the issues. In the 1950s and 1960s the Third Committee also spent huge amounts of time working out the details of draft treaties for fear that limited-membership committees would not heed majority desires.

In 1970 it was proposed that the overlap between the two committees' mandates and the duplication of debates be overcome by allocating all aspects of development to the Second Committee while having the Third concentrate on human rights and/or concrete problems requiring immediate attention. This idea attracted little support then, but as the decade progressed some of this division of labor did develop. The Second Committee now deals with broad-scale issues of development, more specific questions being left to the United Nations Conference on Trade and Development or other bodies, while the Third Committee now devotes some three-fourths of its time to human rights questions (ending racism, the status of women, the status of minorities, enhancing respect for human rights conventions). Their work-loads have been eased by a greater willingness to rely on the now 54-member Economic and Social Council or other limited-membership bodies to do preliminary work. Starting with the 40th session in 1985, the Second Committee will further rationalize its work by considering agenda items on a biennial schedule synchronized with that of the Economic and Social Council (Resolution 39/217).

Both committees, but particularly the Second, are used by the Third World majority to advance its demands, claims and ideas on the questions of development, restructuring international economic relations and the proper definition of human rights. Debates usually avoid mention of specific quarrels, though feature sustained attacks on Western policies or, in the Third Committee, long diatribes against Israel and South Africa.

The evolution of the Fourth Committee has been linked to

changes in the one question falling within its competence: the treatment of non-self-governing territories. It deals with both UN Trust Territories administered by members under supervision from the Trusteeship Council and other colonies administered as regular parts of the colonial empires built before the First World War.

When the US-led coalition controlled the Assembly, debate and decisions took an anti-colonial turn but usually showed some understanding of administrators' point of view. Since the 1960 endorsement of the idea that independence is the only acceptable form of self-determination and since the creation of the Committee of 24 (formally the Special Committee on the Situation with regard to the Implementation of the Declaration on the Granting of Independence to Colonial Countries and Peoples) to oversee the process of attaining independence, debate has usually taken a stridently anticolonial tone even if the resulting decisions were more balanced.

Between 1955 and 1965 the Fourth Committee had the heaviest schedule of meetings, in large part because of the many hearings it granted to individuals from territories the future of which was under discussion. As most colonies attained independence in the 1960s and joined the United Nations as member states, the Fourth Committee had less work to do. Like all durable organizations, however, the Fourth Committee has found itself other tasks. The existence of a few colonies (the official list includes eighteen territories) gives the Fourth Committee a reason to exist, and it fills the rest of its time with explorations of such questions as the ways in which "foreign economic and other interests" impede the exercise of self-determination. Soviet bloc, other Marxist–Leninist and radical Third World states use the committee as a forum for attacks on Western imperialism, colonialism and "neocolonialism".

The Fifth Committee supervises the general operations of the Secretariat, provides guidelines for general policies on staff conditions and recruitment, works out the UN budget, works out the amount of money each member must pay toward the regular budget and examines the financial implications of any proposed decision that would involve spending money. It is assisted in these tasks by two committees of individual experts, the sixteen-member Advisory Committee on Administrative and Budgetary Questions and the eighteen-member Committee on Contributions. The ACABQ receives the Secretariat's proposed budget and makes recommendations about whether particular requests should be cut, increased, or kept the same. This makes Fifth Committee discussions of the budget estimates a three-sided dialogue, with the Secretariat presenting its requests, the ACABQ making comments and the committee after some questions and discussions deciding between them, generally favoring the ACABQ if the two differ. Like most budget scrutineers, the ACABQ usually recommends reductions when it differs with the original estimates. The Committee on Contributions takes the Assembly-mandated guidelines for assessments, works out detailed formulas and then estimates what each member should pay. This spares the Fifth Committee a lot of routine calculation.

By 1970 attempting to deal with both the budget and staff halves of its agenda was proving impossible. The Fifth Committee was rescued from its predicament by a decision that the UN budget should be established on a biennial basis, with the main budget for the next 24 months decided one year and only necessary adjustments (usually upward) for the second 12 months decided during the following year (Resolution 3043 [XXIV]). This means that the Fifth Committee can devote most of its time to staff questions in the years not marked by major budget debate. This change, part of a more general move toward greater forward planning of the UN budget, allows the committee to give closer attention to each half of its work than would otherwise be possible.

The Sixth Committee is composed of a distinguished group of international lawyers who feel their talents are greatly under-utilized. While other main committees, *ad hoc* bodies and other non specialist UN organs tackle such matters as drafting international conventions, drafting declarations of principles on which the members hope to build international law in the future, or interpreting the Charter and other existing international law, the Sixth Committee has been left with the lightest agenda of all. Successive recommendations that the Sixth Committee be used more often have only recently begun to be heeded. From 11 items in 1977 the Sixth Committee agenda increased to 18 in 1985. In general, though, states have preferred to negotiate the future of international law in bodies where political arguments are more likely to be given explicit attention.

Most Sixth Committee debates are measured comments on the legal issues that come before it. Criticism of other states' policies is usually indirect, focusing on weaknesses of the legal doctrines they sponsor or the lack of congruence before their conduct and their professions. However, even the Sixth Committee witnesses polemical exchanges between delegates. Its spirit can be seen by the fact that at least twice it took the unusual step of expressing collective disapproval of such behavior by adjourning the meeting as bilateral exchanges heated up (A/C.6/32/SR.50 and 59, 18 and 30 Nov. 1977). The most predictable opportunity for polemical debate is provided by the consideration of reports from the Committee on Relations with the Host Country (established in 1971 to replace an informal group existing since 1966), which deals with how United States and New York City authorities treat diplomats accredited to the UN. These provide annual excuses for Soviet bloc attacks on the United States for "tolerating terrorism", "encouraging fascist attacks" on diplomatic premises, and failing to take sufficiently vigorous (by Soviet standards) action against attacks on diplomats, or for various delegations' general disquisitions on the decadence of New York City.

By the beginning of December the plenary has finished considering all the items referred directly to it, and is working on reports coming in from the main committees. The main committees are working hard to meet their deadlines. Proposals with financial implications must be adopted by the end of the first week of December so that the Secretary-General can prepare and the Fifth Committee consider statements of how much they will cost and whether this will require new budget authorizations or can be accommodated within existing ones. Other proposals are supposed to be ready by the middle of the month. The last weeks of December see the Assembly meeting mainly in plenary, rushing to get all proposals adopted before the projected closing date of about the 20th. Much of the work now appears rather dull. In most cases, committee drafts are adopted without comment and without change. On a few occasions, however, one or more members continue efforts to secure changes or delays by offering amendments to the committee's draft, a whole draft to replace the committee draft, or procedural motions to defer a decision at least until the next session. Then there will be a brief debate and probably formal votes. On a few others, last-minute consultations produce agreement on a change, or last-minute developments render a committee draft obsolete. For instance, the more rapid than expected conclusion of the Lancaster House negotiations on Rhodesia/Zimbabwe in 1979 forced the Assembly to drop the Special Political Committee's draft in favor of a whole new one (A/34/PV.108, 18 Dec. 1979). These flurries of excitement apart, the session ends with the rapid adoption of all the proposals brought to the plenary by the main committees, often at a rate of 20 to 30 a meeting (e.g., A/34/PV.107–9, 18–19

Dec. 1979). The session thus ends, as do the sessions of most national legislatures, with a rush of work leaving delegates exhausted when the final gavel falls.

The Role of Presiding Officers

The President of the General Assembly and the chairmen of main committees occupy an important place in Assembly proceedings. They are also in an interesting position, being individuals given a certain amount of authority over the representatives of member states. Members realize that they need this authority to assure the efficient and fair working of the Assembly but hedge it so that it cannot be taken too far. The President of the General Assembly has three tasks: presiding impartially over formal meetings, encouraging informal negotiations among the members and representing the General Assembly on ceremonial occasions. Chairmen of main committees have little representational role, but actively perform the other two tasks for their committees.

The formal authority of the President and chairmen is laid out in detail in the written Rules of Procedure. Rule 35 defines the President's powers as follows:

> In addition to exercising the powers conferred upon him elsewhere by these rules, the President shall declare the opening and closing of each plenary meeting of the session, direct the discussions in plenary meeting, ensure observance of these rules, accord the right to speak, put questions and announce decisions. He shall rule on points of order and, subject to these rules, shall have complete control of the proceedings at any meeting and the maintenance of order thereat. The President may, in the course of the discussion of an item, propose to the General Assembly the limitation of the time to be allowed to speakers, the limitation of the number of times each representative may speak, the closure of the list of speakers or the closure of debate. He may also propose the suspension or the adjournment of the meeting or the adjournment of debate on the item under discussion.

Other powers are implied in Rule 68, which permits him to call speakers to order for irrelevant remarks; Rule 90, which implies that the President can determine which amendment is furthest removed from the original proposal and so should be voted upon first, or that some amendment is so far removed that it constitutes a separate proposal; Rules 74, 75, 76, 78, 88 and 91, which permit him to impose limits on the length of speeches in certain procedural debates and in explanation of vote on his own; and Rule 78, which allows him to bring amendments to a vote even if they have not been circulated in writing twenty-four hours previously.

At the same time, the Rules of Procedure limit presidential authority by providing that almost all rulings from the chair can be appealed. This is first noted generally in Rule 36, which states that "The President, in the exercise of his functions, remains under the authority of the General Assembly." The full implications are elaborated in other rules. Rule 67 reminds the President that a quorum – one-third of the members for debate and one-half plus one for taking procedural and substantive decisions by consensus or vote – must be present for the meeting to begin and continue. Rule 71 permits appeals to rulings on points of order, and specifies that a simple majority of those present and voting may decide whether to sustain or overturn the President's ruling. Rules 72 through 76 provide that all procedural motions, whether initiated by the President or by a member, are submitted to the meeting for decision by a simple majority. Rules 106, 107, 108, 109, 113, 114, 115, 116, 117, 118, 120, 129, 130 and 131 govern the activity of main committee chairmen in similar fashion. In sum, the rules permit the President or chairman to take a number of initiatives but subject them to acceptance by a majority of the members.

The rules have been interpreted in a continuous process of balancing presiding officer authority and members' rights. In general, presiding officers tread carefully. Gladwyn Jebb, who presided occasionally at the 5th through 9th sessions because the United Kingdom's head delegate is always elected as a vice president, wrote later:

> The great thing in chairing any difficult assembly or large meeting is to choose the right second for striking the "come on now, let's chuck it and get down to business" note. Nothing is more painful than a nervous or hesitant chairman; but equally a bullying type may provoke a riot. The collective animal in front of you has to be handled, in other words, like a horse which is inclined to bolt.
>
> (Jebb, 1972, p. 253)

Getting into trouble is fairly easy. Paul-Henri Spaak provoked a storm of criticism at a plenary meeting during the 1st session with what he thought was a joke. He had announced that delegates would have 15 minutes for statements. Several delegates then went beyond this limit, the Salvadorian taking a full 30. Before calling on the next speaker, Spaak said, "I should like to remind delegates that I have limited speakers to a quarter of an hour each, and by this I do not mean a Latin American quarter of an hour." This provoked general comment, during which the Chilean delegate in particular said that he would not allow his country to be insulted in that way. The tumult subsided only after Spaak apologized for the remark (Spaak, 1971, p. 109).

In general, presiding officers do not push their authority too far because they do not want to risk rebuff (Queneudec, 1966, p. 904; Buckley, 1974, p. 43), because they are delegates serving for a year as officers and therefore not anxious to push their power lest it create restrictive precedents (Cocke, 1959, p. 657), or because they find it wiser to keep a low profile in formal meetings to preserve their usefulness in informal consultations. Since they are so heavily involved in informal consultations, they usually have a good idea what the majority will tolerate or desire and avoid rulings they know would lead to a successful challenge from the floor. For example, Amintore Fanfani of Italy, President of the 20th session, refused to rule that representation of China was an important question requiring decision by a two-thirds majority. The United States and other supporters of keeping the Taipei government's delegates seated thereupon had to raise the idea in a procedural motion of their own, which they were able to get adopted (Queneudec, 1966, p. 904). Several Western delegates feel that Baron Rudiger von Wechmar of West Germany, President of the 35th session, used his powers abusively to aid a majority effort to prevent South African delegates from participating in the resumed session debates on Namibia (interviews; also the formal South African protest in Doc. A/ES–8/12, 12 Sept. 1981).

Sometimes, though, a presiding officer in touch with majority sentiment can help proceedings by suggesting a compromise most members can accept. A fairly typical example occurred during debate on West Irian during the 24th session. The Dahomean delegate requested a 10-day suspension of debate so that his government could study the report on the plebiscite held in West Irian. Under the terms of a 1961 Dutch–Indonesian agreement West Irian had been transferred to Indonesia on condition that a subsequent plebiscite let the local population decide whether to stay with Indonesia or become a separate state. Instead of acting as though the Dahomean request was a formal procedural motion to suspend debate, which would limit discussion of the idea, the President, Angie Brooks of Liberia, allowed a fairly general discussion of the idea. The Saudi delegate objected to any delay. The Ecuadorian, Ghanaian and Togolese delegates supported the request. The Dutch delegate suggested a compromise, a delay of one day. The Saudi delegate then spoke again to complain that discussion had been permitted to run too long and to insist that the Dahomean request be put to a vote. The President then explained that she had wanted to hear members' views before putting the question to a vote or making a ruling of any sort. She then proposed a three-day suspension, to which the Assembly agreed (A/24/PV.1810, 13 Nov. 1969, paras. 40–97).

Although most presiding officers lean toward the light-handed side, they have become more active over the years. As main committees have adopted more detailed programs of work, chairmen have become more active in exhorting members to abide by the schedule and more ready to question the need for some last-minute delay (though still granting most requests). Some presiding officers attempt to enforce the standards of courtesy in debate (e.g., the chairman of the Fourth Committee during the 14th session), though all agree that there is no stopping the vituperation in exchanges inspiring use of the right of reply. Most are careful to rule quickly on points of order and procedural motions; others sometimes delay their rulings and help create situations in which several motions are before the meeting at once and create great confusion (particularly notable examples of confusion in A/SPC/15SR. 198, 11 Nov. 1960, paras. 14–25, and SR. 199, 14 Nov. 1960, paras. 1–5; A/24/PV.1812, 19 Nov. 1969, paras. 42–102, and PV.1813, 19 Nov. 1969, paras. 1–182).

The role of presiding officers as coordinators and encouragers has increased as the Assembly has relied more on informal consultations for working out procedures and reaching substantive compromises. Many consultations are routinely centered upon the presiding officer. In elections, the regional groups usually name their candidates to the President, who then informs the meeting. The naming of *ad hoc* committees is usually entrusted to the President on the understanding that he will use the agreed distribution of seats among regional groups and consult the groups about their preferred candidates. Similarly, committee chairmen usually have a say in naming the working groups, contact groups and subcommittees appointed to resolve issues that come up in their committees. A good presiding officer keeps in close touch with the informal discussions, and occasionally offers suggestions for reaching compromises.

Though never entirely absent, this informal role has become broader and more important over the years. In the early sessions, presiding officers often did not know what motions would be made or what proposals advanced. By 1962 matters had advanced so far that Muhammad Zafrulla Khan of Pakistan, who was President of the 17th session, later recalled that he was never faced with an unanticipated request for a ruling from the chair (Khan, 1964, pp. 234–5). The progress in procedural and sub-stantive understandings became clear to the public at the 19th session when all Assembly decisions were made by having delegates inform the President privately of their preferences and then having him announce the results to the meeting (A/19/PV.1286–331, 1 Dec. 1964–1 Sept. 1965).

Greater use of decision-making by consensus has increased the informal role and the importance of the presiding officer (Cassan, 1977, pp. 459). Encouraging and keeping track of informal negotiations is now such an important part of the job that the vice chairmen of main committees actively assist their chairmen, each being assigned to coordinate talks on certain issues before the committee (e.g., organizational discussion in A/C.3/34/SR.3, 24 Sept. 1979, para. 7). As negotiations come to an end, the presiding officer consults the various groups to determine whether consensus had been reached or if a formal vote will be necessary, so that he knows how to proceed when the mater comes up for decision. If consensus has been achieved, he must also consult to determine whether the members want it adopted "by consensus", "by acclamation", "without objection", or "without a vote", because each of these formulas has a distinct meaning. When the draft resolution embodying the consensus is to be presented at the meeting, the President or chairman will announce that, unless he hears objection, he will consider the resolution adopted by whatever formula he has been advised to use, wait for any objection and then announce that the resolution is adopted if no delegate speaks up to object to the formula or insist on a vote. While this means that delegates can prevent a presiding officer from making a mistake, most presiding officers find it embarrassing to have last-second objections raised.

On certain ceremonial occasions, such as the expression of condolences to member states on the death of a political leader or other famous citizen, or on the occasion of a natural disaster, and the expression of congratulations on important anniversaries or achievements, the President speaks on behalf of the whole Assembly. This representational role remains fairly restricted, however. The President of the Assembly has never been viewed as representative of "the UN" as a whole. Particularly since Hammarskjöld's time, the Secretary-General has been seen as the main representative of the whole organization and the person most active in mediation efforts of all kinds. A British proposal to have the Assembly President take this role died for lack of interest (Liang, 1949, p. 711), and one observer (Queneudec, 1966, p. 903) argued that Presidents had a wider representational role in the early years than in the mid-1960s. This situation has not changed since. Chairmen of main committees speak ceremonially for their whole committee, and sometimes present its conclusions to the plenary (though this is usually the *rapporteur's* task), but have no representational role outside committee meetings.

Delegations and Permanent Missions

Unlike the Swiss *Landesgemeinde*, where the members are individuals acting on their own behalf, or the British House of Commons, where they are elected representatives having discretion to act on behalf of a particular constituency and controlled by the need for periodic reelection, the General Assembly consists of delegates sent by and acting on behalf of member governments. Again, unlike the members of the *Landesgemeinde*, delegates normally operate in teams. Article 9 (2) of the Charter states that "Each member shall have not more than five representatives in the General Assembly." while the rules of procedure permit the appointment of five alternate representatives and whatever number of experts and advisors a member state cares to send. Most members take full advantage of these provisions. This means that not only must a delegation remain in close contact with its own government, but it must also be sure its members are not working at cross-purposes.

The fact that delegates are diplomats acting under more or less comprehensive instructions from their governments about the goals they should seek, the opinions they should express and the general line of conduct they should follow means that they act somewhat differently from legislators, even legislators in disciplined political parties who are bound to follow party directions in most matters. Legislators form their own coalitions and settle positions among themselves. They will be approached by various interest and social groups, but ultimately decide for themselves checked only by their own beliefs about what is moral or expedient and by the need to win the next election. Delegates often initiate coalition building, but their efforts must be accepted or approved by their governments if the coalition is to persist. This puts them in a more complicated situation because they must worry about how important bureaucratic actors or private groups at home will regard their efforts. There is also the possibility that other governments will seek to influence their positions not only by direct contact between delegates but also by contacts with the foreign ministry. Many delegates regard this as an extraordinary step to be used sparingly, but foreign ministries are generally not reluctant to press their case in this way.

It is difficult to present a single picture of how delegates behave in the Assembly because the range of instruction is so great. Rigid instructions leave a delegate little room to carve out an independent role; vague ones allow a great deal of independent activity and permit the delegate to act almost as if a legislator. Edvard Hambro has aptly described the extreme differences:

> Rumor has it that a permanent representative from a country which shall remain unnamed cabled home for instructions during one important crisis and was told in no uncertain terms that he was sent to New York to take care of that part of his country's foreign policy and that his asking for instructions was quite uncalled for. Another delegate, it is said, not only gets detailed instructions about every vote, but has all of his speeches sent verbatim from his capital with instructions on when to speak with sincerity and when to inject an ironic inflection.
>
> (Hambro, 1972, p. 287)

Not only do some governments instruct their delegates more closely than others, but the same government may give different types of instruction on different issues. One United States delegate estimated that two-thirds of the delegations get no instructions on procedural matters like inscription of an item on the agenda. Another thinks that this kind of instruction is more common, or can be elicited through representations to the home government on particular occasions (interviews quoted in Franck, 1985, pp. 200–1). Sometimes a delegate is told how to vote without reference to other states' positions. At others, he is given a broad outline such as "vote more or less like ——— ," "you can abstain if ——— votes no," or "avoid being left in an isolated position" (Baehr, 1970, p. 13; Kaufmann, 1980, p. 110). Most governments allow more leeway when a decision will not involve the spending of any money than when it does (Hadwen and Kaufmann, 1962, p. 32).

Both the necessities of diplomacy and the facilities of modern communications make the relation between delegate and government a two-way one. Governments learn what is happening at the UN from their delegates. Delegates also provide a steady stream of advice about positions to take or tactics that should be adopted. Most write their own speeches, getting them approved by the foreign ministry before delivery (US practice described in Buckley, 1974, pp. 151, 157–8, 183, 196). Some have sufficient influence at home to have a hand in the writing of their own instructions or the formulation of proposals to be submitted to the Assembly. Finally, there are a whole range of tactical matters, usually raised by procedural motions, that must be settled on the spot. Though these arise less frequently today than in 1946 because of greater informal consultation, such situations require that delegates use their own judgement.

On important matters, modern communications permit delegates to seek or receive last-minute changes of instruction. Depending on their budgets, the distance from their capital, the closeness of home government supervision over their activity, or their own needs, delegates can communicate with their foreign offices by telex or telephone as needed (see Baehr, 1970, p. 14, on Dutch practice; Finger, 1980, pp. 28–9, on US practice). Kaufmann cites the case of one delegate who was first instructed to vote against a particular draft resolution, then told early on the day the vote was scheduled to vote against or abstain depending on whether a particular friendly country voted no or abstained, but also to call the foreign ministry for final instructions just before the vote (Kaufmann 1980, p. 111). General Assembly rules and practices make it easy to secure instructions. Committee plans of work and the *Journal of the United Nations* provide advance notice of what items will be discussed at particular meetings. The extensive informal consultations that now precede the formal submission of most draft resolutions allow delegates to learn their general terms, if not their exact language (Hadwen and Kaufmann, 1962, p. 34, say this was already the usual practice in 1960). Assembly Rules 78 and 120 provide that draft resolutions and amendments normally cannot be voted upon until twenty-four hours after their official circulation in writing, and the rule is seldom waived. Delegates still without instructions at decision-making time can always request the proceedings be suspended long enough to get them. Such requests are generally granted because all delegates know they may be in a similar position themselves on another day.

Because they work with each other so intensely, delegates

usually have good ideas about the extent to which others are instructed, both generally and in specific cases. All agree that Soviet and Soviet bloc delegates are the most closely instructed. A former Western European delegate says Soviet ambassador Troyanovsky often received cables 2½ to 3 feet long during Security Council meetings, and the meeting was suspended while he retired to a side room to read them (interview, 1982). Western delegates come second, Asian and Latin Americans next, with Africans generally the least instructed of all. In the Soviet bloc, this reflects the basic style of governance, which puts a premium on central direction. Westerners get detailed instructions largely because their governments must attend not only to the usual bureaucratic struggles that accompany decision-making but also to legislative and public opinion. Africans, and their colleagues from the new Pacific island states, report to governments having small bureaucracies and thin cadres of experts. These governments tend to send a very strong team to the Assembly and rely upon it to make policy. A lack of instructions does not mean that a delegation must act entirely on its own. Today the regional and other groups provide a structure that allows the small or the uninstructed delegation a way to get information and advice. Even the large and instructed delegations use groups to coordinate positions and approaches with like-minded others. The role of the groups will be explored at greater length below; here it is sufficient to note that delegates generally operate in a three-sided relation of selves, own governments and groups.

Even legislators with staffs have fewer problems of coordination than a delegation in the General Assembly. In 1982 delegations ranged in size from 1 for Belize and 2 for Samoa through 31 for India, 45 for Cuba, 53 for China and 78 for France to 85 for the United States and 127 for the Soviet Union (see delegation lists in A/INF/37/9, Sept. 1982). While speaking and voting in plenary meetings, Assembly offices and committee offices are reserved to representatives and alternate representatives, the advisors, technical advisors and experts may speak and vote for their states in main committees. In fact, it is not unusual for several people from the same delegation to address a committee in the same meeting. Though a large delegation has advantages in dividing up the work, analyzing events and gathering information, it has to devote serious attention to coordination lest members inadvertently contradict one another or leave misleading impressions of their country's position on some matter. Coordination is attained in two ways, by reliance on the facilities and staff of the permanent mission and by delegation meetings.

The creation of permanent missions was not anticipated in the Charter. Members of the League of Nations had been able to operate without them, and the San Francisco Conference did not anticipate the expansion of Assembly sessions or the increase in other UN meetings that would make them indispensable. The only hint that representatives would be posted permanently at Headquarters came in Article 28(1) of the Charter, which mandated that "The Security Council shall be so organized as to be able to function continuously. Each member of the Security Council shall for this purpose be represented at all times at the seat of the Organization." The Charter and the rules of procedure were both silent on how Assembly delegations should organize themselves. Article 2(2) of the Charter simply specified their size, while the rules of the principal organs assumed that delegations to each would be appointed and sent separately.

Perhaps the example of the eleven Security Council members encouraged the others, but they probably would have established permanent missions fairly quickly anyway. The increase in activity as compared to the League, when the Assembly met for three weeks a year and the Council held its regular meetings quarterly, and the greater distance between many members' capitals and Headquarters because it is in New York rather than Geneva, would have led to permanent establishments relatively quickly. Whatever the reasons, permanent missions were a regular feature of Assembly life by 1948 (see debate on the status of permanent missions in A/C.6/3/SR.124–7, 26–9 Nov. 1948), before either the creation of the Interim Committee or the establishment of procedures for Assembly meetings on very short notice in emergency session made inter-sessional work involving all members of the United Nations likely. By 1960 the practice was so well established that all new members, no matter how small or poor, believed having a permanent mission was a necessary part of membership (Kay, 1969, pp. 23–4). Today only the tiniest of members forgoes one (Belize, Solomon Islands and Vanuatu in 1982; ST/SG/Ser.A/251, Sept. 1982, p. 7; Comoros and Vanutu in 1984; ST/SG/Ser.A/255, Oct. 1984, p. 7). Many of the smaller members combine their mission in New York and their embassy in Washington to save on staff, a practice made possible by the proximity of and good transportation between the two cities.

The permanent mission's main significance lies in the fact that it provides the support on which the larger delegation depends.

Its staff receives and analyzes the reports and other materials issued before the session begins, and makes initial explorations of others' views. The head of the permanent mission, the permanent representative, serves as head of the Assembly delegation unless the head of state, head of government, or foreign minister is attending Assembly meetings. Other members of the mission, whether delegates or staff, devote a considerable amount of time to helping inexperienced colleagues in the delegation, who often include legislators or public figures untrained in diplomacy (Baehr, 1970, p. 21; Buckley, 1974, pp. 24, 63; interviews with staff members from several missions, 1981–2). Most diplomats agree that a delegate must serve a year before learning how to negotiate and push proposals effectively. Some diplomatic services have formally admitted this by establishing longer tours of duty in the UN mission than at other posts. The West German service, for instance, increases the normal three-year interval to four and a half years in New York (interview, 1983). The mission's offices also provide the physical facilities for those aspects of delegation work, such as communicating with the home government, keeping track of documents, or internal coordination, that cannot be undertaken very well at UN Headquarters.

The delegation meeting is the main vehicle for coordination. Though the frequency and formality of these meetings vary from delegation to delegation, most find that they need to meet as a group at least once a week to keep all members informed of current business. These meetings are usually held in the morning before the Assembly plenary or main committees convene at ten-thirty, and are essentially briefing sessions in which the delegates and staff responsible for particular issues tell their colleagues what has just happened and what is likely to happen in the immediate future (Baehr, 1970, pp. 11, 18–19, on the Netherlands; Hambro, 1972, p. 292, on Norway; Buckley, 1974, pp. 36, 76–7, on the USA; Kaufmann, 1980, p. 108). The larger the delegation, the less time there is for any exchange of views among the members and the more likely members are to be so specialized that they will not have clear views on issues other than those for which they are responsible. Of course individual members of delegations and missions consult constantly with colleagues as their work requires.

Regional and Other Groups

One of the greatest differences between the General Assembly and national legislatures is the Assembly's lack of any party system organizing the members into stable clusters of the like-minded. Though legislative parties differ greatly in cohesion (United States parties being so loosely organized that they don't seem to be parties to Europeans accustomed to tight party discipline) and in number (ranging from one to ten or more), they all provide the framework within which individual members build coalitions to gain control of the legislature, coordinate positions on the issues of the day and link themselves to the voters. Parties operate in a vertical system where the government usually has both the material dominance and the moral legitimacy to provide binding and effective allocations of values for the whole society, and are an important link between the individuals comprising the society and those who operate the political system. Depending on the character of the political system, parties may be a mechanism for holding legislators and other officials responsible to the people or one for increasing governmental control over the activities of individuals. Either way, parties exist partly in the government and partly in society, helping to link the two.

The General Assembly operates in a very different situation. It is not the legislature in a vertical system; it is a central debating place in a horizontal system where the constituent units reserve to themselves wide ranges of discretion and accept little central direction. The United Nations lacks both the material pre-dominance and the moral legitimacy that would permit the exercise of powers comparable to those of a legislature.

Despite League experience, which showed that a number of stable clusters of like-minded states – the Latin Americans, the United Kingdom and its Dominions, the "Little Entente" of Czechoslovakia, Romania and Yugoslavia, the more amorphous Balkan group and a loose grouping of Austria, Hungary, Italy and Germany – did emerge and persist in the League Assembly (Burton, 1941, pp. 100–1), neither the UN Charter nor the Assembly Rules of Procedure made any provision for groups in 1945. Though aware that majorities could not be formed without some amount of consultation and negotiation among members, the framers of the Charter assumed that no clustering would be sufficiently stable, deal with enough issues, or be inclusive enough to make it the basis for organizing Assembly work. At the same time, however, the Charter and the rules are general enough that groups could form and acquire important roles in Assembly proceedings.

The distinction between electoral groups, based on geography, and caucusing groups, based on political, economic and other affinities, which still marks Assembly work, was born of the 1946 "Gentlemen's (or London) Agreement." It reduced the problem of managing elections to the Security Council's six elective seats by allocating seats to geographical groups into which states were put somewhat arbitrarily. Using regional criteria and additional considerations left over from League experience, states were divided into five groups: The British Commonwealth (5), Asia and the Mideast (8), Latin America (20), Eastern Europe (5) and Western Europe (6) (Hovet, 1960, p. 5). The same groupings, with the addition of a separate category for permanent members of the Security Council to accommodate traditions that they were always elected to Assembly vice presidencies and the other principal organs, were also used in elections (Bailey, 1960, p. 50).

A number of factors kept these early electoral clusters from taking on greater significance. First, understandings about what states were in what groups were not always clear. Second, numbers were manageable, so large caucuses to do preliminary work did not seem necessary. Third, the customs of informal negotiation and consensus-seeking remained weak until the mid-1950s, and the negotiations that did occur were usually organized formally in committee working groups or subcommittees. Even if groups had acquired prominence before 1955, they would have lost it in the following half-decade. UN membership rose from 60 states in 1954 to 100 in 1960, and the Assembly shifted from being a predominantly European and Latin body to being a predominantly African and Asian one. These facts forced a thorough rearrangement of the groups.

The first influx of new members, the sixteen states admitted in 1955 after a compromise between East and West, affected the balance between existing clusters and led to the demise of the Commonwealth as a separate group. In 1954, there were 14 Asian and Middle Eastern members, 6 Commonwealth ones, 20 Latin American ones, 5 Eastern European ones and 10 Western European ones, as well as the Big Five (calculated from Hovet, 1960, pp. 31–3). With the 1955 admissions, these numbers increased to 22 for Asia and the Middle East, 7 for the Commonwealth, 10 for Eastern Europe and 14 for Western Europe, while the Latin Americans remained at 20. Soon afterward the Commonwealth began to split, with the African and Asian members wanting to

join their regional neighbors for electoral and caucusing pur-
poses. In 1957 this division was accepted in understandings
governing election to a General Committee enlarged to 21
members by adding 5 vice presidencies. The old Asian and
Middle Eastern group became the Afro-Asian group, while the
"Old Dominions" of Australia, Canada, New Zealand and South
Africa were lumped with Western Europe to form the Western
European and Other group familiar today (not without complaints from the Commonwealth; see A/SPC/12/SR.79–82, 6–10
Dec. 1952). This change was just being absorbed when the wave
of decolonization in 1959–60 led to the admission of 17 African
and 1 Asian states. As Table App. 2 shows, this greatly changed
the regional balance in the Assembly, bringing it to 46 Afro-
Asian (25 African and 21 Asian), 20 Latin American, 10 Eastern
European, 19 Western European and Other, and the Big Five.
This change in the regional balance and in the number of
members soon led to agreements enlarging the Security Council
from 11 to 15, the Economic and Social Council from 18 to 27
and the Assembly's General Committee from 21 to 25, and
changing the formulas by which seats were allocated among
regions.

UN membership continued to increase after 1960. New
members have been added almost every year as decolonization
has proceeded. In 1985 the Assembly had 159 members: 51
African, 41 Asian, 33 Latin American, 11 Eastern European, and
23 Western. This continued expansion, together with different
rates of increase among the five regional groups, has led to

Table App. 2   Regional Composition of the General Assembly

	Total	African	Asian	Latin American	Eastern European	Western
1945	51	3	9	20	6	13
1946	55	3	11	20	6	15
1947	57	3	13	20	6	15
1948	58	3	14	20	6	15
1949	59	3	14	20	6	16
1950	60	3	15	20	6	16
1951	60	3	15	20	6	16
1952	60	3	15	20	6	16
1953	60	3	15	20	6	16
1954	60	3	15	20	6	16

Table App. 2 *continued*

	Total	African	Asian	Latin American	Eastern European	Western
1955	76	4	20	20	10[a]	22
1956	80	7	21	20	10	22
1957	82	8	22	20	10	22
1958	82	9	21[b]	20	10	22
1959	82	9	21	20	10	22
1960	99	25	22	20	10	22
1961	104	28	24[c]	20	10	22
1962	110	32	24	22[d]	10	22
1963	113	34	25	22	10	22
1964	115	36[e]	25	22	10	22
1965	117	37	26[f]	22	10	22
1966	122	39	27[g]	24	10	22
1967	123	39	28	24	10	22
1968	126	42	28	24	10	22
1969	126	42	28	24	10	22
1970	127	42	29	24	10	22
1971	132	42	34	24	10	22
1972	132	42	34	24	10	22
1973	135	42	34	25	11	23
1974	138	43	35	26	11	23
1975	144	47	36	27	11	23
1976	147	49	37	27	11	23
1977	149	50	38	27	11	23
1978	151	50	39	28	11	23
1979	152	50	39	29	11	23
1980	154	51	39	30	11	23
1981	157	51	40	32	11	23
1982	157	51	40	32	11	23
1983	158	51	40	33	11	23
1984	159	51	41	33	11	23

[a] In 1955–1970 Yugoslavia was deemed Afro-Asian for most Assembly elections

[b] Egypt and Syria merged to form the United Arab Republic.

[c] Syria withdrew from the UAR and resumed separate UN membership.

[d] Cuba was excluded from group activities.

[e] Tanganyka (UN member since 1961) and Zanzibar (UN member since 1963) merged to form Tanzania.

[f] Indonesia withdrew from the UN.

[g] Indonesia returned to the UN.

further expansions of the Economic and Social Council, the General Committee and subsidiary organs of the General Assembly, and to several adjustments in the allocation of seats among regions. The most important change occurred in the mid-1970s when the Asians began to approach the Africans in number and successfully engineered a change so that seats would be allocated to Africa and Asia separately rather than have the two continents lumped together in one group with the number of seats to be held by each governed by intra-group rather than Assembly-wide understandings.

In the early 1960s the regional groups became the main framework for Assembly negotiations. First, their hold over seats allocated to them was strengthened partly by formal inclusion to annexes to Assembly resolutions and partly by mutual recognition of the advantages of security. Being in a minority position from the start, the Soviet bloc always saw, and urged on others, the advantages of secure tenure. As they realized the erosion of their relative positions, the Latin American and Western groups began to uphold the idea as well. Next, the 1960 influx of Africans made all members realize that the character of the Assembly had changed. Third, the great increase in numbers made larger-scale preliminary caucusing necessary. Finally, the many inexperienced delegates of new members found regional groups a congenial place to get advice, information and cues from the more experienced.

Public indication of the roles groups could play came during the 19th session in 1964–5. As the Assembly prepared to meet, the superpowers were locked in a conflict over finances that was also a conflict over the whole nature and direction of the UN. The United States was insisting that the Soviet Union and others, including France, should pay their share of expenses for peacekeeping operations in the Sinai (UNEF) and the Congo (ONUC) or lose their votes in the Assembly under Article 19 of the Charter, which provides that penalty for all members late in paying the equivalent of two years' assessments. The Soviets, who believed that both operations served US purposes and were not interested in expanding the UN's ability to run up large expenses and impose them on members, argued that peacekeeping was an extraordinary expense that should be financed apart from the regular budget. They also threatened to leave the UN if they lost their vote. So that the Assembly could meet while efforts to resolve the superpower argument continued, the members agreed that the Assembly would deal with only those matters that could be decided without a formal vote (see explanation in A/19/PV.1286, 1 Dec. 1964, paras. 7–8). In the course of the session, the Assembly was able to elect members of the Security Council and the Economic and Social Council by the expedient of private polling in the President's office, and to pass resolutions on fourteen matters by agreement. The regional groups were crucial to this success because they provided the framework within which all the informal consultations proceeded.

In succeeding years the regional groups became more prominent. Though other caucusing groups continued to exist, the regional groups became the prime channel for consultations on procedural matters and the foci of most substantive negotiations. In part, this happened because three of the regional groups – Africa, Eastern Europe and Latin America – had or developed strong traditions of group cooperation. It was also encouraged because the regional groups could also be divided into two clusters roughly corresponding to the major economic division of the world between industrial and developing states. This gave them a new basis of common interest. Their importance was recognized formally in 1971 when the *Journal of the United Nations* began listing their chairmen. This is a useful service to delegates because most groups change chairman more than once a year.

The regional groups have evolved a flexible method of operation that allows them to fit their operations to the needs of the moment. By 1968 most of them had developed the two-tier structure of internal caucusing used today. The permanent representatives (or other heads of delegations) meet to select candidates for election and consult on the most important issues. Delegates assigned to particular committees or particular issues have separate meetings to coordinate tactics and work out proposals on matters within their purview (Baehr, 1970, pp. 33–5). Internal caucusing is supplemented by a variety of inter-group meetings. The three Third World regional groups often meet together to pursue initiatives agreed upon in their various extra-Assembly meetings (particularly those of the Non-aligned Movement and the Group of 77). Occasionally two or more regional groups will meet as a whole to hear or work out proposals. More often, however, inter-group meetings are small-group encounters. Some are organized by members of a group with a proposal hoping to get influential members of another group to endorse it. Others are organized by mutual desire to have a "contact group" work out a compromise between the different proposals each is advancing. Either way, these smaller groups report back to the full region, and its approval or acquiescence is necessary for the proposal or compromise to advance further.

Yet the groups differ greatly. The Eastern European group (from which Albania remains aloof while Yugoslavia is a member only for electoral purposes), being small, relatively united ideologically and having a clear leader, is not divided into sub-regional or other caucuses. It has long been considered the closest to a disciplined party in the Assembly, though some members have begun to deviate from the Soviet position more in recent years. All three Third World regions are riven by many tensions. There are pervasive differences stemming from varying success in economic development and different positions in the world economy, ideological differences and different ethnic or cultural heritages. These standing tensions are supplemented or supplanted by differences on particular issues. On debt, the relatively wealthier or less heavily indebted prefer the current case-by-case approach to debt relief, while the poorer or more heavily indebted favor a general settlement. The least developed are almost as worried about trying to compete with the newly industrializing as with the West (Fromuth, 1984, p. 7), and both groups have different approaches to a number of issues (Weiss, 1983, pp. 668–9). The Law of the Sea Conference demonstrated the divisions that could appear on particular issues. The long-coast and broad-margin states in Africa and Latin America got their regions to endorse the 200-mile zone concept despite the fact the more numerous land-locked and short-coast states would get little (Ferreira, 1979; Galindo Pohl, 1979). An alliance of Western and Third World land-based mineral-producing states secured agreement to production ceilings on deep seabed mining that assured greatly reduced revenues and hence greatly reduced sums for distribution to Third World members of the proposed International Seabed Authority (Hollick, 1981, pp. 295–6). Of all the groups, the Western European and Other is probably the weakest. Its membership includes two cohesive clusters that take many distinctive positions, the five Scandinavian states and the European Community twelve. The United States does not enjoy the material preeminence it once did, and many of its recent policies have deepened the division between it and the EC twelve.

The Scandinavians and the European Community are only the most coherent of the many sub-regional and cross-regional clusters in the Assembly. Most of these are relatively weak. The 41 members of the Islamic Conference agree on little other than supporting the Palestinians and condemning the Soviet invasion of Afghanistan. The 21 Arab states are divided into moderate and radical groups and large and small oil producers. A few of the smaller clusters, like the ASEAN or the Caribbean states, are able to present common positions on issues involving their region and consult one another extensively (on regional and other groups see Riggs, 1958; Hovet, 1960; Hadwen and Kaufmann, 1962; Baehr, 1970; Kaufmann, 1980).

This range of difference makes it difficult to compare the groups to parties in a national legislature. If the comparison is to be pushed very far, it would involve a legislature in which some parties were disciplined and others were not, something that seldom happens in national politics because the general political culture, not just the desires of party members themselves, determines party behavior. Though one of the regional and several of the sub-regional groups appear party-like today, there are real limits to the similarity. These will become more apparent as differences among Third World states increase and make maintenance of their coalition more difficult. Groups, then, remain an element of diplomacy where states advance their own and their friends' interests rather than political parties in a wider community where members combine both to secure their own power and to serve a vision of the common good supported by many in the wider society.

Works Cited

Adelman, Kenneth, and Plattner, Marc (1983), "Western strategy in a Third World forum," *Atlantic Quarterly*, spring 1983.

Agena, Kathleen (1982), "Letter from the UN," *Partisan Review*, 49, pp. 598–604.

Alger, Chadwick F. (1961), "Non-resolution consequences of the United Nations and their effect on international conflict," *Journal of Conflict Resolution*, 5, pp. 128–45.

Alger, Chadwick F. (1966), "Negotiation, regional groups, interaction, and public debate in the development of a consensus in the United Nations General Assembly," *Transactions of the Sixth World Congress of Sociology* (Evian), pp. 321–46.

Alger, Chadwick F. (1968), "Interaction in a committee of the United Nations General Assembly," in J. David Singer (ed.), *Quantitative International Politics* (New York: Free Press), pp. 51–84.

Alker, Haywood R., Jr, and Russett, Bruce (1965), *World Politics in the General Assembly* (New Haven: Yale University Press).

Anonymous (a former ambassador to the UN from a Third World state) (1980), "Moynihanism at the United Nations," *Third World Quarterly*, 2, pp. 500–21.

Arrangio-Ruiz, Gaetano (1972), "The normative role of the General Assembly of the United Nations and the declaration of principles of friendly relations," Hague Academy *Recueil des cours*, 137, pp. 419–742.

Araujo Castro, Joao Augusto de (1972), "The United Nations and the freezing of the international power structure," *International Organization*, 26, pp. 158–66.

Archer, Angus (1984), "Methods of multilateral management: the interrelationships of international organizations and NGOs," in Toby Trister Gati (ed.), *The US, the UN, and the Management of Global Change* (New York: New York University Press), pp. 303–25.

Asher, Robert, E. (1957), "Summary and appraisal," in Robert E. Asher (ed.), *The UN and the Promotion of the General Welfare* (Washington: Brookings Institution). pp. 1021–82.

Aspaturian, Vernon V. (1957), "The metamorphosis of the United Nations," *Yale Review*, 46, pp. 551–65.

Baehr, Peter R. (1970), *The Role of a National Delegation in the General Assembly* (New York: Carnegie Endowment, Occasional Paper, No. 9).

Bailey, Sydney D. (1960), *The General Assembly of the United Nations* (New York: Praeger).

Bailey, Sydney D. (1964), *The Secretariat of the United Nations*, revised edn (New York: Praeger).

Barber, Hollis W. (1973), "The United States versus the United Nations," *International Organization*, 27, pp. 140–63.

Bardach, Eugene (1977), *The Implementation Game* (Berkeley, Calif.: University of California Press).

Bastid, Suzanne (1973), "Observations sur la pratique du consensus," in J. Tittel *et al.* (eds.), *Multitudo Legum – Jus Unum* (Berlin: Inter Recht), 1, pp. 11–25.

Bennett, A. LeRoy (1980), *International Organizations: Principles and Issues*, 2nd edn (Englewood Cliffs, NJ: Prentice-Hall).

Bielawski, Jan (1981), "The socialist countries and the New International Economic Order," in R. Jatte and A. Grosse-Jatte (eds.), *The Future of International Organizations* (New York: St Martin's Press), pp. 70–90.

Bleicher, Samuel A. (1969), "The legal significance of re-citation of General Assembly resolutions," *American Journal of International Law*, 63, pp. 444–78.

Bloomfield, Lincoln P. (1958), "American policy toward the UN – some bureaucratic reflections," *International Organization*, 12, pp. 1–16.

Boker-Szago, Hanna (1978), *The Role of the United Nations in International Legislation* (Budapest: Academiai Kaido).

Bos, Maarten (1977), "The Recognized Manifestations of International Law," *German Yearbook of International Law*, 20, pp. 9–76.

Brownlie, Ian (1979), *Principles of Public International Law*, 3rd edn (Oxford: The Clarendon Press).

Buckley, William F., Jr (1974), *United Nations Journal* (New York: Putnam's).

Burton, Margaret E. (1941), *The Assembly of the League of Nations* (Chicago: University of Chicago Press).

Buzan, Barry (1981), "Negotiation by consensus: developments of technique at the United Nations Conference on the Law of the Sea," *American Journal of International Law*, 75, pp. 324–48.

Carter, Gwendolen M. (1950), "The Commonwealth in the United Nations," *International Organization*, 4, pp. 247–60.

Cassan, Hervé (1977), "Le consensus dans la pratique des Nations Unis," *Annuaire française de droit international*, 1977, pp. 456–85.

Cassese, Antonio (1975), "Consensus and some of its pitfalls," *Revista de diretto internazionale*, 58, pp. 754–61.

Casteñeda, Jorge (1969), *The Legal Effects of United Nations Resolutions*, Alba Amoia, trans. (New York: Columbia University Press).

Chang, King-yuh (1972), "The United Nations and decolonization: the case of Southern Yemen," *International Organization*, 26, pp. 36–71.

Charpentier, Jean (1966), "La procedure de non-objection," *Revue générale de droit international public*, 70, pp. 862–77.

Chaudhri, Mohammed A. (1973), "Origin, composition, and functions of the Sixth Committee," *Revue égyptienne de droit international*, 29, pp. 211–32.

Cheng, Bin (1965), "United Nations resolutions on outer space: 'instant' customary international law?," *Indian Journal of International Law*, 5, pp. 23–48.

Claude, Inis L., Jr (1961), "The management of power in the changing United Nations," *International Organization*, 15, pp. 219–35.

Claude, Inis L., Jr (1963), "The political framework of the United Nations's financial problems," *International Organization*, 17, pp. 831–59.

Claude, Inis L., Jr (1971), *Swords into Plowshares*, 4th edn (New York: Random House).

Cocke, Erle, Jr (1959), "The United Nations General Assembly – a captive of its own procedures," *Vanderbilt Law Review*, 13, pp. 651–62.

Cohen, Benjamin V. (1951), "The impact of the United Nations on United States foreign policy," *International Organization*, 5, pp. 274–81.

Conforti, Benedetto (1969), "The legal effects of non-compliance with rules of procedure in the UN General Assembly and Security Council," *American Journal of International Law*, 63, pp. 479–89.

Corea, Ernest (1977), "Nonalignment: the dynamics of a movement,," *Behind the Headlines*, June 1977.

Crane, Barbara B. (1984), "Policy coordination by major Western powers in bargaining with the Third World," *International Organization*, 38, pp. 399–428.

Crovitz, Gordon (1984), "Boss M'Bow," *Conoisseur*, May 1984, pp. 118–21.

Cutler, Robert M. (1983), "East–South relations at UNCTAD," *International Organization*, 37, pp. 121–42.

D'Amato, Anthony (1971), *The concept of Custom in International Law* (Ithaca, NY: Cornell University Press).

Detter, Ingrid (1965), *Law Making by International Organizations* (Stockholm: Norstedt).

Djonovich, Dusan J. (compiler) (1973), *United Nations Resolutions. Series I: The General Assembly*, 14 vols. (Dobbs Ferry, NY: Oceana).

Doxey, Margaret (1975), "International organization in foreign policy perspective," *Yearbook of World Affairs*, 1975, pp. 173–95.

Duroselle, J.-B. (1965), "France and the United Nations," *International Organization*, 19, pp. 695–713.

Dutheil de la Rochère, Jacqueline (1967), "Etude de la composition de certains organs subsidiares recemment crées par l'Assemblée Générale des Nations Unis dans la domaine economique," *Annuaire française de droit international*, 1967, pp. 307–65.

Eagleton, Clyde (1954), "The yardstick of international law," *The Future of the United Nations* (Annals of the American Academy of Political and Social Science, No. 296), pp. 68–76.

Eckhard, Frederic (ed.) (1985), *Issues before the 40th General Assembly* (New York: United Nations Association of the USA).

Elias, Taslim O. (1972), *Africa and the Development of International Law* (Leiden: Sijthoff; and Dobbs Ferry, NY: Oceana).

Ernst, Manfred (1978), "Attitudes of diplomats at the United Nations," *International Organization*, 32, pp. 1037–44.

Evatt, Herbert V. (1949), *The Task of Nations* (New York: Duell, Sloan & Pearce).

Falk, Richard A. (1966), "On the quasi-legislative competence of the General Assembly," *American Journal of International Law*, 60, pp. 782–91.

Falk, Richard A. (1971), "The United Nations: various systems of operation," in Leon Gordenker (ed.), *The United Nations in International Politics* (Princeton: Princeton University Press), 184–230.

Ferreira, Penelope S. (1979), "The role of African states in the development of the Law of the Sea at the Third UN Conference," *Ocean Development and International Law*, 7 pp. 89–129.

Finger, Seymour Maxwell (1980), *Your Man at the UN* (New York: New York University Press).

Finger, Seymour Maxwell (1984), "The Reagan–Kirkpatrick policies and the United Nations," *Foreign Affairs*, 62, pp. 436–57.

Finlayson, Jock A., and Zacher, Mark W. (1983), "The United Nations and collective security: retrospect and prospect," in Toby Trister Gati (ed.), *The US, the UN, and the Management of Global Change* (New York: New York University Press), pp. 162–83.

Finley, Blanche (1977), *The Structure of the General Assembly: its Committees, Commissions, and other Organs, 1946–73*, 3 vols (Dobbs Ferry, NY: Oceana).

Fitzmaurice, Sir Gerald (1973), "The future of public international law," in the Institut de droit international's *Live du centenaire, 1873–1973* (Basle: Editions S. Karger), pp. 169–329.

Forsythe, David P. (1972), "The United Nations and the Arab–Israeli conflict," *International Organization*, 26, pp. 705–17.

Fox, Annette Baker (1950), "The United Nations and colonial development," *International Organization*, 4, pp. 199–218.

Franck, Thomas M. (1985), *Nation against Nation* (New York and London: Oxford University Press).

Fromont, Michael (1961), "L'abstention dans les votes au sein des organizations internationales," *Annuaire française de droit international*, 1961, pp. 492–523.

Fromuth, Peter (1984), "Remember the G-77?" *The InterDependent*, July–August 1984, pp. 1, 7.

Frye, William R. (1956), "Press coverage of the UN," *International Organization*, 10, pp. 276–81.

Fukai, Shigeko N. (1982), "Japan's North–South dialogue at the United Nations," *World Politics*, 35, pp. 73–105.

Galindo Pohl, Raynaldo (1979), "Latin America's influence and role in the Third Conference on the Law of the Sea," *Ocean Development and International Law*, 7, pp. 65–87.

Galloway, Eilene (1979), "Consensus decision-making by the United Nations Committee on the Peaceful Uses of Outer Space," *Journal of Space Law*, 7, pp. 3–13.

Gilpin, Robert M. (1975), *US Power and the Multinational Corporation: The Political Economy of Direct Foreign Investment* (New York: Basic Books).

Goodrich, Leland M. (1951), "Development of the General Assembly," *International Conciliation*, No. 471.

Goodrich, Leland M., Hambro, Edvard, and Simons, Anne (1969), *The Charter of the United Nations*, 3rd edn (New York: Columbia University Press).

Goodwin, Geoffrey L. (1962), "The political role of the United Nations: some British views," *International Organization*, 15, pp. 581–602.

Gordenker, Leon (1983), "Development of the UN system," in Toby Trister Gati (ed.), *The US, the UN and the Management of Global Change* (New York: New York University Press), pp. 11–47.

Gordon, Lincoln (1978), *International Stability and North–South Relations* (Muscatine, Iowa: Stanley Foundation).

Graham, John A. (1980), "The Non-aligned Movement after the Havana summit," *Journal of International Affairs* (Columbia University), 34, pp. 153–60.

Gregg, Robert W. (1981), "Negotiating a New International Economic Order: the issue of venue," in R. Jutte and A. Grosse-Jutte (eds.), *The*

Future of International Organization (New York: St Martin's Press), pp. 51–69.

Grindle, Marilee, S. (ed.) (1980), *Politics and Policy Implementation in the Third World* (Princeton: Princeton University Press).

Gross, Leo (1966), "The United Nations and the role of law," *International Organization*, 19, pp. 537–61.

Gross, Leo (1983), "On the degradation of the constitutional environment of the United Nations," *American Journal of International Law*, 77, pp. 569–83.

Grzybowski, Kazimierz (1983), "Soviet Theory of International Law for the Seventies," *American Journal of International Law*, 77, pp. 862–72.

Gunter, Michael M. (1979), "Recent proposals in the United Nations to amend the Charter," *Case Western Reserve International Law Journal*, 11, pp. 763–83.

Haas, Ernst B. (1956), "Regionalism, functionalism, and universal international organization," *World Politics*, 9, pp. 283–63.

Haas, Michael (1965), "A functional approach to international organization," *Journal of Politics*, 27, pp. 498–517.

Hadwen, John G., and Kaufmann, Johan (1962), *How United Nations Decisions are Made*, 2nd revised edn (Leyden: Sijthoff).

Haig, Alexander M., Jr (1984), *Caveat: Realism, Reagan and Foreign Policy* (New York: Macmillan).

Hambro, Edvard (1972), "Some notes on parliamentary diplomacy," in W. Friedmann *et al.* (eds.), *Transnational Law in a Changing Society* (New York: Columbia University Press), pp. 280–97.

Hambro, Edvard (1976), "Permanent representatives to international organizations," *Yearbook of World Affairs*, 1976, pp. 30–41.

Hardin, Russell (1982), *Collective Action* (Baltimore: Johns Hopkins University Press).

Hardy, Michael (1975), "Decision making at the Law of the Sea Conference," *Revue belge de droit international*, 11, pp. 442–74.

Haviland, H. Field, Jr (1951), *The Political Role of the General Assembly* (New York: Carnegie Endowment).

Hazard, John N. (1977), "Soviet tactics in international law making," *Denver Journal of International Law and Policy*, 7, pp. 9–32.

Higgins, Rosalyn (1963), *The Development of International Law through the Political Organs of the United Nations* (Oxford: Oxford University Press).

Higgins, Rosalyn (1968–70), *United Nations Peacekeeping, 1947–67: Documents and commentary*, 2 vols (London: Oxford University Press).

Higgins, Rosalyn (1971), "Compliance with United Nations decisions on peace and security and human rights questions," in Steven M. Schwebel (ed.), *The Effectiveness of International Decisions* (Leyden: Sijthoff), pp. 32–52.

Hirschman, Alfred O. (1970), *Exit, Voice and Loyalty* (Cambridge, Mass.: Harvard University Press).

Hoffmann, Stanley (1956), "The role of international organization: limits and possibilities," *International Organization*, 10, pp. 357–72.

Hoffmann, Stanley (1957), "Sisyphus and the avalanche," *International Organization*, 11, pp. 446–69.

Hoffmann, Stanley (1968), "A world divided and a World Court confused," in L. Scheinman and D. Wilkinson (eds.), *International Law and Political Crisis* (Boston, Mass.: Little, Brown), pp. 251–73.

Hoffmann, Stanley (1971), "An evaluation of the United Nations," in R. Wood (ed.), *The Process of International Organization* (New York: Random House), , pp. 71–91.

Hollick, Ann (1981), *US Foreign Policy and the Law of the Sea* (Princeton, NJ: Princeton University Press).

Hollick, Ann (1984), "Planning science and technology policy," *Journal of Policy Analysis and Management*, 3, pp. 516–31.

Hovet, Thomas, Jr (1960), *Bloc Politics in the United Nations* (Cambridge, Mass.: Harvard University Press).

Hovet, Thomas, Jr (1963), "United Nations diplomacy," *Journal of International Affairs* (Columbia University), 17, pp. 29–41.

Hovey, Allen, Jr (1950), "Voting procedure in the General Assembly," *International Organization*, 4, pp. 412–27.

Hovey, Allen, Jr (1951), "Obstructionism and the rules of the General Assembly," *International Organization*, 5, pp. 515–30.

Hudson, Manley O. (1950), "Article 24 of the Statute of the International Law Commission," *Yearbook of the International Law Commission*, 1950, vol. 2, pp. 24–32.

Hurewitz, Jacob C. (1950), *The Struggle for Palestine* (New York: W. W. Norton).

Jackson, Richard L. (1983), *The Nonaligned, the UN, and the Superpowers* (New York: Praeger).

Jacobsen, Harold K. (1957), "Labor, the UN, and the Cold War," *International Organization*, 11, pp. 55–67.

Jacobsen, Kurt (1970), "Sponsorship activities in the UN negotiating process," *Cooperation and Conflict*, 5, pp. 241–69.

James, Alan (1969), *The Politics of Peacekeeping* (New York: Praeger).

Jebb, Gladwyn (1952), "The role of the United Nations," *International Organization*, 6, pp. 509–20.

Jebb, Gladwyn (1972), *Memoirs* (New York: Weybright & Talley).

Jessup, Philip (1956), "Parliamentary diplomacy", Hague Academy *Recueil des cours*, 89, pp. 181–320.

Joyner, Christopher C. (1981), "UN General Assembly resolutions and international law," *California Western International Law Journal*, 11, pp. 445–78.

Kanet, Roger (ed.) (1974), *The Soviet Union and the Developing Nations* (Baltimore: Johns Hopkins University Press).

Kaufman, Johan (1980), *United Nations Decision Making* (Alphen aan den Rijn: Sijthoff & Noordhoff).

Kay, David A. (1969), "The impact of African states on the United Nations," *International Organization*, 23, pp. 20–47.

Kelsen, Hans (1950), *The Law of the United Nations* (New York: Praeger).

Keohane, Robert O. (1967), "The study of political influence in the General Assembly," *International Organization*, 21, pp. 221–37.

Keohane, Robert O. (1969), "Institutionalization in the United Nations General Assembly," *International Organization*, 23, pp. 859–96.

Khan, Muhammad Zafrulla (1964), "The President of the General Assembly of the United Nations," *International Organization*, 18, pp. 231–40.

Kim, Samuel C. (1979), *China, the United Nations, and World Order* (Princeton: Princeton University Press).

Kirkpatrick, Jeanne J. (1983), "Global Paternalism,," *Regulation*, 7, pp. 17–22.

Kolassa, Jan (1967), *Rules of Procedure of the United Nations General Assembly: A Legal Analysis* (Wroclaw, Poland: Academy of Sciences and Letters of Wroclaw).

Korey, William (1978), "The Kremlin's anti-Semites," *Mainstream*, October 1978, pp. 8–16.

Krasner, Stephen D. (1981), "Transforming international regimes: what the Third World wants and why," *International Studies Quarterly*, 25, pp. 119–48.

Krishnamurti, R. (1980), "Comment: restructuring the United Nations system," *International Organization*, 34, pp. 929–40.

Lacharrière, Guy de (1968), "Consensus et Nations Unis," *Annuaire française de droit international*, 1968, pp. 9–14.

Lande, Gabriella Rosner (1966), "The effect of the resolutions of the United Nations General Assembly," *World Politics*, 19, pp. 83–109.

Lauterpacht, Elihu (1976), "The development of the law of international organization by the decisions of international tribunals," Hague Academy *Recueil des cours*, 152, pp. 387–478.

Lauterpacht, Sir Hersh (1955), *Separate opinion in South West Africa – voting procedure, advisory opinion, ICJ Reports*, 1955, pp. 90–123.

Lerner, Daniel, and Kramer, Marguerite N. (1963), "French élite perspectives on the United Nations," *International Organization*, 17, pp. 54–75.

Liang, Yuen-li (1955), "Notes on legal questions concerning the United Nations," *American Journal of International Law*, 49, pp. 705–31.

Lipson, Charles (1983), "The transformation of trade: the sources and effects of regime change," *International Organization*, 36, pp. 417–56.

Luard, Evan (1983), "Functionalism Revisited: the UN family in the eighties," *International Affairs* (London), 59, pp. 677–92.

McWhinney, Edward (1967), "The changing United Nations constitutionalism," *Canadian Yearbook of International Law*, 1967, pp. 68–83.

Mandel, Ernest (1970), *Europe versus America: Contradictions of Imperialism* (New York: Monthly Review Press).

Manno, Catherine Senf (1965), "Problems and trends in the composition of nonplenary UN organs," *International Organization*, 19, pp. 37–55.

Maynes, Charles William (1977), "The United Nations: out of control or out of touch?," *The Yearbook of World Affairs*, 1977, pp. 98–111.

Mazrui, Ali A. (1964), "The United Nations and some African political attitudes," *International Organization*, 18, pp. 499–520.

Meagher, Robert F. (1983), "United States financing of the United Nations," in Toby Trister Gati (ed.), *The US, the UN, and the Management of Global Change* (New York: New York University Press), pp. 101–28.

Meltzer, Ronald I. (1978), "Restructuring the United Nations: institutional reform efforts in the context of North–South relations," *International Organization*, 32, pp. 993–1018.

Meltzer, Ronald I. (1983), "UN Structural Reform: Institutional Development in International Economic and Social Affairs," in Toby Trister Gati (ed.), *The US, the UN, and the Management of Global Change* (New York: New York University Press), pp. 238–62.

Misra, K. P. (1981), "Burma's farewell to the Nonaligned Movement," *Asian Affairs*, February 1981.

Mitchell, Barbara (1983), *Frozen Stakes: The Future of Antarctic Minerals* (London: International Institute for Environment and Development).

Morgenthau, Hans J. (1951), *The Politics of Nations* (New York: Knopf).

Morgenthau, Hans J. (1954), "The yardstick of national interest," in *The Future of the United Nations* (Annals of the American Academy of Political and Social Science, No. 296), pp. 77–84.

Mosely, Philip E. (1966), "The Soviet Union and the United Nations," *International Organization*, 19, pp. 666–77.

Moynihan, Daniel P. (1975), "The United States in Opposition," *Commentary*, March 1975, pp. 31–42.

Moynihan, Daniel P. (1980), *A Dangerous Place* (Boston, Mass.: Little, Brown).

Moynihan, Daniel P. (1981), "Joining the jackals," *Commentary*, February 1981, pp. 23–31.

Mudge, George Alfred (1967), "Domestic policies and UN activities," *International Organization*, 21, pp. 55–78.

Munro, Sir Leslie (1969), *United Nations: Hope for a Divided World* (New York: Holt & Co.).

Munves, James (1970), *A Day in the Life of the UN* (New York: Washington Square Press).

Nicaragua Ministry of Foreign Affairs (1983), *The Movement of Non-Aligned Countries – an Indispensable Force in the Anti-Imperialist Struggle.*

Note (1971), "The representation of China at the UN," *Harvard International Law Journal*, 12, pp. 478–94.

Note (1975), "The United Nations, 29th session," *Harvard International Law Journal*, 16, pp. 576–613.

Nye, Joseph S. Jr and Keohane, Robert O. (1977), *Power and Interdependence* (Boston, Mass.: Little, Brown).

Nyerere, Julius K., President of Tanzania (1979), "Third World negotiating strategy," *Third World Quarterly*, vol. 1, no. 2, pp. 20–3.

Onuf, Nicholas G. (1970), "Professor Falk on the quasi-legislative competence of the General Assembly," *American Journal of International Law*, 64, pp. 349–55.

Osieke, Ebere (1983), "The legal value of ultra vires decisions of international organizations," *American Journal of International Law*, 77, pp. 239–56.

Padelford, Norman J. (1959), *Elections in the UN's General Assembly* (Cambridge, Mass.: MIT Center for International Studies).

Parkinson, C. Northcote (1957), *Parkinson's Law* (Boston, Mass.: Houghton-Mifflin).

Pastor, Robert (1984), "The international debate on Puerto Rico: the costs of being an agenda-taker"), *International Organization*, 38, pp. 574–95.

Peck, Richard (1979), "Socialization of permanent representatives in the United Nations," *International Organization*, 33, pp. 365–90.

Pilon, Juliana G. (1982), "The United States and the United Nations: a balance sheet," *Backgrounder* (Washington: Heritage Foundation), January 1982.

Pressman, Jeffrey, and Wildavsky, Aaron (1973), *Implementation* (Berkeley, Calif.: University of California Press).

Puchala, Donald J. (1983), "US national interests and the United Nations," in Toby Trister Gati (ed.), *The US, the UN, and the Management of Global Change* (New York: New York University Press), pp. 343–65. Also in *Political Science Quarterly*, 97, pp. 571–88.

Puchala, Donald J. (ed.) (1981), *Issues before the 36th General Assembly* (New York: United Nations Association of the USA).

Puchala, Donald J. (ed.) (1982), *Issues before the 37th General Assembly* (New York: United Nations Association of the USA).

Puchala, Donald J. (ed.) (1983), *Issues before the 38th General Assembly* (New York: United Nations Association of the USA).

Puchala, Donald J. (ed). (1983), *Issues before the 38th General Assembly* (New York: United Nations Association of the USA).

Queneudec, Jean-Pierre (1965), "Le President de l'Assemblée Générale de l'Organisation des Nations Unis," *Revue générale de droit international public*, 70, pp. 878–915.

Quigg, Philip W. (1983), *A Pole Apart: The Emerging Issue of Antarctica* (New York: McGraw-Hill).

Ramphal, Shridath S. (1979), "Not by unity alone: the case for Third World organization", *Third World Quarterly*, vol. 1, no. 3, pp. 43–52.

Rana, Swadesh (1970), "The changing Indian diplomacy at the United Nations," *International Organization*, 24, pp. 48–73.

Riggs, Robert E. (1958), *Politics in the United Nations* (Urbana, Ill.: University of Illinois Press).

Riggs, Robert E. (1981), "Civil Service Attitudes towards the UN in Guatemala, Norway, and the United States," *International Organization*, 35, pp. 395–405.

Robinson, Jacob (1958), "The metamorphosis of the United Nations," Hague Academy *Recueil des cours*, 94, pp. 497–589.

Rodley, Nigel (1979), "Monitoring human rights violations in the 1980s," in Jorge Dominguez *et al.*, *Enhancing Global Human Rights* (New York: McGraw-Hill), pp. 117–51.

Roosevelt, Eleanor (1958), *On My Own* (New York: Harper).

Ross, Alf (1966), *The United Nations* (Totowa, NJ: Bedminster Press).

Rothstein, Robert L. (1980), "The North–South dialogue – the politics of immobility," *Journal of International Affairs* (Columbia University), 34, pp. 1–18.

Rothwell, Charles E. (1949), "International organization and world politics," *International Organization*, 3, pp. 605–19.

Rowe, Edward T. (1971), "The United States, the United Nations, and the Cold War," *International Organization*, 25, pp. 59–78.

Rubenstein, Alvin Z. (1964), "Soviet and American policies in international economic organizations," *International Organization*, 18, pp. 29–52.

Rubenstein, Alvin Z. (ed.) (1975), *Soviet and Chinese Influence in the Third World* (New York: Praeger).

Rubins, Monique (1984), "West gains, Soviets lose ground as new Security Council takes shape," *The InterDependent*, September–October 1984, p. 4.

Rudzinski, Alexander W. (1951), "The influence of the United Nations on Soviet policy," *International Organization*, 5, pp. 282–99.

Rudzinski, Alexander W. (1955), "Majority rule vs great power agreement in the United Nations," *International Organization*, 9, pp. 366–75.

Rudzinski, Alexander W. (1959), "Election procedure in the United Nations," *American Journal of International Law*, 53, pp. 81–111.

Russell, Ruth B. (1955), *A History of the United Nations Charter* (Washington: Brookings Institution).

Russell, Ruth B. (1966), "United Nations financing and 'the law of the Charter," *Columbia Journal of Transnational Law*, 5, pp. 68–95.

Russett, Bruce M., and Sullivan, John D. (1971), "Collective goods and international organization," *International Organization*, 25, pp. 845–65.

Schachter, Oscar (1963), "The relation of law, politics, and action in the United Nations", Hague Academy *Recueil des cours*, 109, pp. 171–256.

Schachter, Oscar (1964), "The quasi-judicial role of the Security Council and the General Assembly," *American Journal of International Law*, 58, pp. 960–3.

Schachter, Oscar (1971), "Towards a theory of international obligation," in Steven M. Schwebel (ed.), *The Effectiveness of International Decisions* (Leyden: Sijthoff), pp. 9–31.

Schachter, Oscar (1980), "Editorial Note: Richard R. Baxter," *American Journal of International Law*, 74, pp. 890–1.

Schreuer, Christoph (1977), "Recommendations and the traditional sources of international law," *German Yearbook of International Law*, 20, pp. 103–18.

Schreuer, Christoph (1978), "The relevance of UN decisions in domestic legislation," *International and Comparative Law Quarterly*, 27, pp. 1–17.

Schwebel, Steven M. (1979), "The effect of resolutions of the General Assembly on customary international law," *Proceedings of the American Society of International Law*, 73, pp. 301–9.

Schwelb, Egon (1972), "The 1971 amendment to Article 61 of the United Nations Charter and the arrangements accompanying it," *International and Comparative Law Quarterly*, 21, pp. 497–529.

Shaplen, Robert (1979), "A reporter at large: alignments among the Nonaligned," *The New Yorker*, 22 October 1979.

Siverson, Randolf M. (1973), "Role and perception in international crisis," *International Organization*, 27, pp. 329–45.

Skubiszewski, Krzystof (1972), "Recommendations of the United Nations and municipal courts," *British Yearbook of International Law*, 46, pp. 353–64.

Sohn, Louis B. (1973), "The development of the Charter of the United Nations," in Maarten Bos (ed.), *The Present State of International Law* (Deventer: Kluwer), pp. 39–60.

Sohn, Louis B. (1974), "United Nations decision-making: confront-ation or consensus," *Harvard International Law Journal*, 15, pp. 438–45.

Spaak, Paul-Henri (1948), "The role of the General Assembly," *International Conciliation*, No. 445, pp. 591–615.

Spaak, Paul-Henri (1971), *The Continuing Battle* (Boston, Mass: Little, Brown).

Spencer, John H. (1962), "Africa at the UN," *International Organization*, 16, pp. 375–86.

Stanley Foundation (1975)," *Decision-making Processes of the United Nations* (Muscatine, Iowa: Stanley Foundation).

Stoessinger, John G. (1961), "Financing of the United Nations," *International Conciliation*, No. 535 (November 1961).

Stoessinger, John G. (1977), *The United Nations and the Superpowers*, 3rd edn (New York: Random House).

Stokman, Frans N. (1977), *Roll Calls and Sponsorship* (Leyden: Sijthoff).

Suy, Erik (1978), "The Status of Observers in International Organizations," Hague Academy of International Law, *Recueil des cours*, 160, pp. 75–180.

Tanaka, Kotaro (1966), *Dissenting opinion in the South West Africa case (merits)*, ICJ Reports, 1966, pp. 248–324.

Tunkin, Grigori I. (1974), "International law in the international system," Hague Academy *Recueil des cours*, 147, pp. 1–218.

United Nations (1975), *The Seventh Special Session of the General Assembly, 1–16 September 1975: Round-up and Resolutions* (New York: United Nations Office of Public Information).

United Nations Secretariat (1955), *Repertory of Practice of United Nations Organs* (New York: United Nations).

Urquhart, Brian (1972), *Hammarskjöld* (New York: Knopf).

Vallet, Francis A. (1959), "The competence of the United Nations General Assembly," Hague Academy *Recueil des cours*, 97, pp. 203–92.

Van der Eijk, C. and Kok, W. J. P. (1975), "Nondecisions Reconsidered," *Acta Politica*, 10, pp. 277–301.

Vernon, Raymond (1983), "International trade policy in the 1980s," *International Studies Quarterly*, 26, pp. 483–510.

Volgy, Thomas (1973), "The role of the 'outsider' in quasi-legislative systems," *International Organization*, 27, pp. 86–97.

Volgy, Thomas (1974), "Reducing conflict in international politics," *International Studies Quarterly*, 18, pp. 179–210.

Volgy, Thomas, and Quistgard, Jon E. (1974), "Correlates of organizational rewards in the United Nations," *International Organization*, 28, pp. 179–205.

Wallace, Helen (1973), *National Governments and the European Communities* (London: Chatham House).

Wallerstein, Immanuel (1974), *The Modern World System: Capitalist Agriculture and the Origins of European World Economy in the Sixteenth Century* (New York: Academic Press).

Warren, Bill (1980), *Imperialism: Pioneer of Capitalism*, John Sender (ed.) (London: NLB).

Waltz, Kenneth (1979), *Theory of World Politics* (Reading, MA: Addison-Wesley).

Weiss, Thomas G. (1983), "The United Nations Conference on the Least Developed Countries: the relevance of conference diplomacy in Paris for international negotiations," *International Affairs* (London), 59, pp. 649–75.

Werners, Siegfried E. (1967), *The Presiding Officers in the United Nations* (Haarlem: De Erven F. Bohn).

Wessels, Wolfgang (1980), "New forms of foreign policy in Western Europe," in Werner J. Feld (ed.), *Western Europe's Global Reach* (New York: Pergamon), pp. 12–29.

Wilkinson, David (1968), "The Article 17 Crisis: the dispute over financing the United Nations," in L. Scheinman and D. Wilkinson (eds.), *International Law and Political Crisis* (Boston, Mass.: Little, Brown), pp. 211–50.

Wohlgemuth, Patricia (1963), "The Portuguese territories and the United Nations," *International Conciliation*, No. 545.

Wolfrum, Rüdiger (1981), "Restricting the Uses of the Seas to Peaceful Purposes: Demilitarization in Being?," *German Yearbook of International Law*, 24, pp. 200–41.

Yemin, Edward (1969), *Legislative Process in the United Nations and its Specialized Agencies* (Leyden: Sijthoff).

Yeselson, Abraham and Gaglione, Anthony (1974), *A Dangerous Place: the UN as a Weapon in World Politics* (New York: Viking Press).

Zamenek, Karl (1961), "Neutral Austria in the United Nations," *International Organization*, 15, pp. 408–22.

Index

DATE DUE
